I ONCE WAS YOUNG

History of the Alfred Street Baptist Church

1803–2003

Alton S. Wallace, Principal Author
Katherine E. Cain, Editor
Carolyn C. Rowe, Lead Researcher

November 2003

Tapestry Press, Ltd.
Littleton, MA 01460

Printed in the United States of America.

ISBN 1-56888-767-1

C

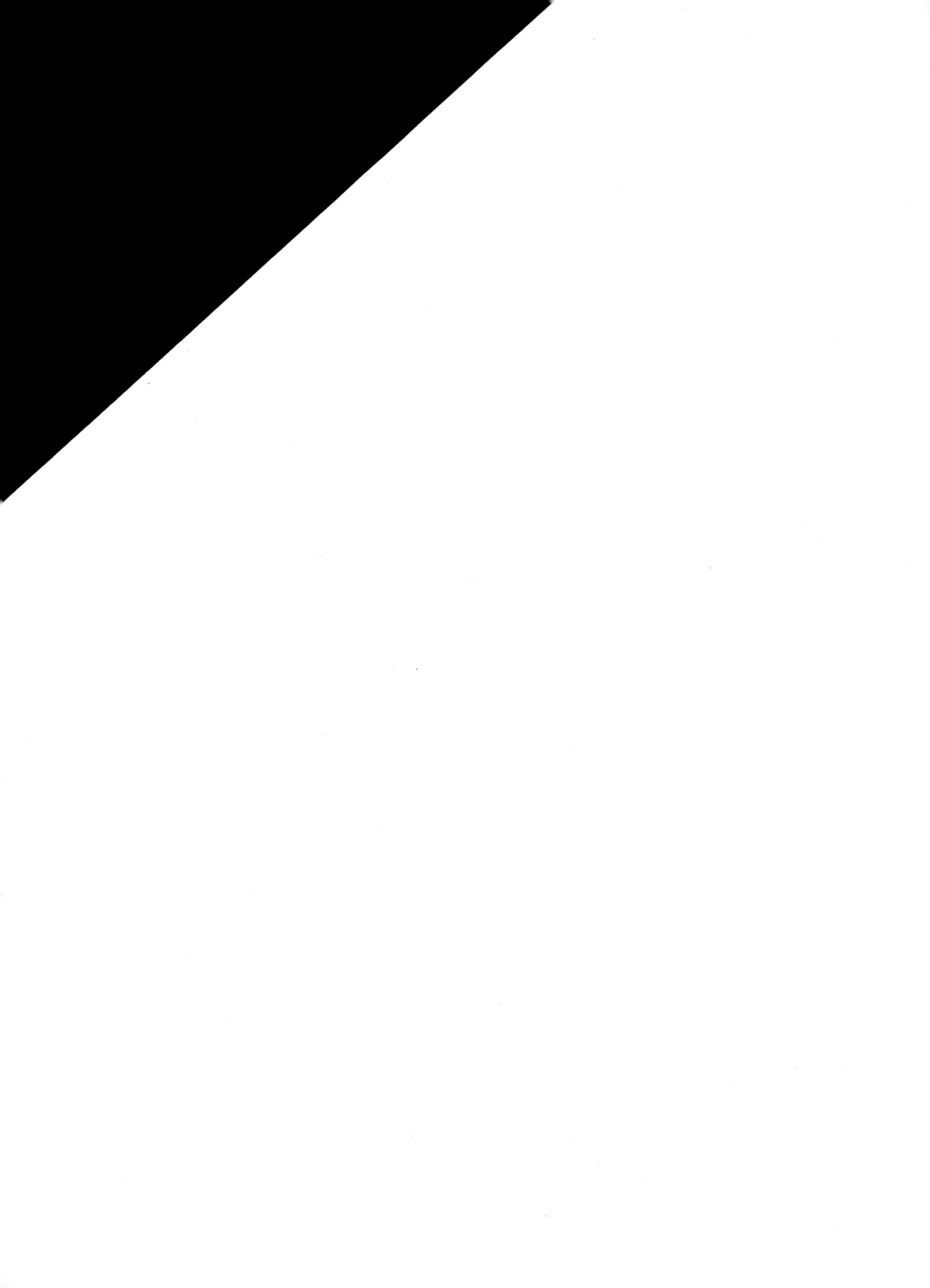

**I have been young,
and now I'm old;
yet have I not seen the righteous
forsaken, nor his seed begging bread.**

Psalm 37:25

Foreword

This is the first attempt at trying to assemble the entire history of the Alfred Street Baptist Church, a congregation that dates back to 1803. Some of the history was passed down orally from generation to generation. Other parts of the information were gathered from many other sources. We are delighted that Deacon Alton S. Wallace and his committee have been able to assemble this first attempt that covers so much of our history. If the reader detects any errors, omissions or other helpful information that should be added, please notify the church at 703-683-2222, 301 Alfred Street, Alexandria, VA 22314.

Certainly in covering over 200 years, there may be some pertinent parts of the story that have been omitted. We solicit your indulgence as you read this volume and beg your assistance to help us to improve.

John O. Peterson
Pastor

Preface

This volume documents the history of the Alfred Street Baptist Church from its beginning in 1803 until its bicentennial in 2003. As with most black churches of that era, from its very beginning challenges and conflicts defined the history of the church.

These conflicts and challenges led to the selection of a passage attributed to King David of the Old Testament as the theme for the church's bicentennial celebration. The theme taken from the 37th Psalm is:

200 Years: Yet Not Forsaken.

The Bicentennial Committee felt this an appropriate theme, as the life of the church has in many ways paralleled the life of King David.You will recall that King David of the Old Testament reigned from about 1055 BC to about 1015 BC and, during his life and reign, he saw just about all that life had to offer. As a lad, he had been a shepherd boy, tending his father's flocks near Bethlehem. Then came King Saul and the opportunity to play his harp for the King. Then came Goliath of Geth, whom David slew. Then there was David's marriage to Saul's daughter Michol, and his conquests of the Phillistines that led to his being anointed King of all Israel.

There were many wives and concubines who begat many sons and daughters. There was the arrival of the Ark of the Covenant and David's dancing for joy. There was a marriage to Bathsheba, incest with his daughter Amnon, and the fratricide of his son Absalom. Then David's death at age 70, and his burial on Mount Zion.

So King David really saw just about all that life had to offer. As he aged, he looked back over his life and in the 37th Psalm he spoke reflectively about being *young* and of God's faithfulness throughout this period. His reference to having been young is not a chronological reference, but is a metaphor for all that being young represents: young and foolish; young and sinful; young and deceitful; young and mischievous. David reminded us in this Psalm that through both his youth with its mischief, and through his agedness with its wisdom, he had never seen God forsake the righteous.

And so it is with the Alfred Street Baptist Church. As this volume will show, in the past 200 years this church has also experienced most of what life had to offer. On reflecting, the reader will likely reach the same conclusion as King David realized in his agedness. The church has seen wars, and it has seen famine; it has seen death, and it has seen divisiveness. But through it all, Alfred Street can testify, as did King David in the 37th Psalm:

I have been young,
and now I'm old;
yet have I not seen the righteous forsaken,
nor his seed begging bread.

So we have entitled this volume **"I ONCE WAS YOUNG"** as a reminder of all of the youthful indiscretions Alfred Street Baptist Church has experienced as a church body. The reader will be exposed to numerous mistakes, failures and triumphs by the young church. Therefore, as we reach our bicentennial, we too look back upon these years from a position of experience, having witnessed 200 years of God's faithfulness to us.

As Chair of the Bicentennial Committee, I would like to thank those persons who helped to tell Alfred Street's story over these 200 years. First, I would like to thank Deacon Alton S. Wallace, the Church Historian, for leading the research effort and writing the text of this volume. Special thanks also to Mrs. Katherine E. Cain for researching the church's musical organizations and editing the various drafts. A special acknowledgement also goes to Mrs. Carolyn C. Rowe for her research covering the early years when little in-house church records were available.

I would also like to acknowledge other persons on the Historical Research Committee who contributed to this volume including Mrs. Rebecca S. Briggs, Mrs. Wanda E. Gill, Deacon Thomas H. Howell, Mrs. Guinevere S. Jones, Mrs. Joyce K. Peterson, Mrs. Margarette Peterson, Rev. Beverly A. Moses, Rev. Samuel Nixon, Jr., and Mrs. Gladys Quander-Tancil (deceased). Many other members provided assistance, as did persons outside the church including Mr. Reginald Washington at the National Archives and Records Administration, Ms. Michelle Cadoree at the Library of Congress, and Ms. Ruby Saunders, George Washington/Mount Vernon Family researcher. To each, a special thank you.

There are few churches in America that have experienced 200 years filled with such challenges and triumphs. And as the Alfred Street family moves forward to a third century in HIS service, we go forward with the blessed assurance that God will never forsake us.

Patricia L. Wallace
Chair of the Bicentennial

Chapter One

The Setting

In the beginning was the WORD; and the WORD was with God.
And the WORD was God.

Alfred Street Baptist Church's beginnings in 1803 go back a century before its year of establishment and include the advent of European culture and religions on America's shores. Those beginnings include the arrival of Negroes* from Africa and their embrace of these European religions. Alfred Street Baptist Church's beginnings follow the founding of the city of Alexandria in 1748 and the spread of religious protest against the established State Church in the region during a period of dissent in Virginia. These events laid the foundation for the establishment of the first assembly of Negro Baptists in the Northern Virginia area.

Religion in Virginia

During most of the 1600s and 1700s in colonial Virginia, religious activity centered on Anglicanism (Episcopalianism) from the Church of England. The Episcopal Church was the official church of Virginia and the parish vestry (church officials who managed the temporal affairs of the church) served as the local government authority. Through the vestry system, the state taxed the citizens to take care of the church so there was little need for special appeals for tithes or offerings.

The General Assembly also protected the church from the influence of other denominations (e.g., Baptists, Methodists) that might attempt to establish competing religions. The Toleration Act of 1772 even reserved the word *church* for exclusive use by the Church of England.[1] Other denominations were limited to referring to their congregations as *societies* and their buildings as *meeting-houses*. The State controlled the affairs of the Episcopal Church and this established church rose or fell on State support.

The Episcopal Church in Virginia, established in 1607, started to fall from grace around 1765. The church almost disintegrated because of problems with the vestry system, and some vestry officials were crooked and others were just sinful. Slowly, anti-

*The terms Negro, colored, black, and African-American are used synonymously. For a given era, the authors use the terminology that was in common usage during that time frame.

England sentiment began to grow against the state-supported church, so the late 18th century was known as the Rise of Dissent in Virginia.

After a decade of dissent and protest, the Virginia State Assembly stopped taxation to support the Episcopal Church and repealed the laws against dissent against the established church in 1776. Then, in 1784, the State Assembly formally disestablished the Church of Virginia. This change placed the Episcopal Church on the same level as other religious denominations.

Around 1800, a near total collapse of the State Church occurred, primarily because of the petitions and lobbying from other denominations that called for confiscation of the property owned by the Episcopal Church. The State Assembly soon passed the Glebe Act that called for all church lands *(glebes)* purchased by vestry to be seized by each county and sold for public benefit. Groups called the Overseers of the Poor in each county saw to the repossession of the land from the vestry.[2] The Episcopalians were *out;* the Methodists, the Presbyterians, the Quakers, and the Baptists were *in.*

The dissent within the church was taking place against a backdrop of national dissent. In 1776, the U.S. colonies had adopted a Declaration of Independence from Great Britain, after the outbreak of hostilities between the colonies and Great Britain in the summer of 1775. Following that war (1775–1783) and the adoption of a U.S. Constitution, the newly formed country adopted a set of amendments in 1791 called the Bill of Rights, which addressed the religious issue. Specifically, the First Amendment stated: "Congress shall make no law respecting an establishment of religion, or prohibit the free exercise thereof . . ."

The Baptist and Presbyterian denominations, which represented a democratic form of church government, appeared well suited to the preferences of many of the people who had just formed a democratic form of national government. So, with the collapse of the established Anglican church, the door was opened for the Baptists to establish churches in Virginia. These Baptists were an outgrowth of the Baptist groups established in 1638 by Roger Williams in Providence, Rhode Island. From Rhode Island and the New England region, this religious denomination migrated to the southern region of the country, including the states of Virginia and the Carolinas.

Two types of Baptists were being established in Virginia, each representing a somewhat different doctrinal point of view. The General or Armenian Baptists came to America directly from England and established several churches in Virginia. The Regular Baptists in Virginia originally came from Philadelphia.[3] One group of Regular Baptists, dismissed from the Philadelphia Association, met at Ketocton in Loudon County, Virginia, and formed a new association of churches that would eventually unite the Baptists in Northern Virginia. Most of these churches were predominantly white, though some started taking Negro members from their outset.

Negro Religious Life in Virginia

In most of these early white churches, Negroes were allowed to worship within certain limits. Initially, enslaved Negroes and freedmen were found in congregations at the same hour, but in different sections. In some congregations with large numbers of Negro believers, services were held at different hours to accommodate the large numbers.

Though Negroes were first introduced to America in 1619 in Jamestown, Virginia, the first church primarily for Negroes did not open until 1773, more than 150 years later. The first recorded evidence of a Negro church was the Silver Bluff Baptist Church in Silver Bluff, South Carolina. The church, founded between 1773 and 1775, was located in Aiken County on the banks of the Savannah River about twelve miles from Augusta, Georgia.[4]

Another early church organization among Negro Baptists was the First African Baptist Church of Savannah, Georgia, instituted January 20, 1788, by Abraham Marshall (white) and Jesse Peter (colored).[5] It was located at Brampton's barn, three miles west of Savannah. In time, other Baptist churches for Negroes would open, including the First Baptist Church in Lexington, Kentucky (1790), and the Springfield Baptist Church in Augusta, Georgia (1793). In Virginia, two of the first Negro churches were the First African Baptist Church of Richmond, founded in 1780, and the First Baptist Church of Williamsburg, founded in 1785.

White ministers frequently served as pastors in these churches even though they had Negro congregations. Dr. Robert Ryland, the white president of Richmond College, for example, headed the First African Baptist Church of Richmond. While rare, black crossover ministers who preached to white congregations did exist during this time period. Josiah Bishop, a black man, was hired to preach to the white Portsmouth Church in Virginia in 1792. Similarly, William Lemon, a man of color, served as pastor for the white Gloucester Church of Pettsworth.[6]

While some Negro churches were initially established as independent churches, most of the early Negro churches grew out of white congregations. In the white churches, many white clergy allowed or even encouraged worship in ways that many Negroes found to be similar or adaptable to their prior African worship practices. Still, other white owners and clergy preached a message of strict obedience and insisted that enslaved persons attend white-controlled churches, fearful that if slaves were allowed to worship independently they would ultimately plot rebellion against their owners.[7]

In the slave quarters, however, the Negroes frequently organized their own invisible institutions. Through signals, passwords, and messages not discernible to whites, they called believers to *hush harbors* or *bush harbors* where they freely mixed African rhythms in their singing and their beliefs with evangelical Christianity. Only a few records of the locations or activities of many of these bush harbors still remain.[8] But it was here that the spirituals, with their double meaning of religious salvation and freedom from slavery, developed and flourished, and where black preachers polished their chanted sermons or intoned style of extemporaneous preaching.

Negroes in Early Alexandria, Virginia

The religious activities that were taking place throughout the country would eventually reach the city of Alexandria, Virginia, originally known as Bel(le) Haven. The city took its name from a Scotsman, John Alexander, who is credited as the original founder of the city. The original city, established as a separate entity by the Virginia General Assembly in 1748, consisted of sixty acres, bounded by Duke Street on the south, by Pendleton Street on the north, by the Potomac River on the east, and by an imaginary line on the west side in the vicinity of West Street. The rest of the local area that today we call Alexandria was out in the country, populated here and there by small farms. By 1791, Alexandria had grown to become the eleventh most important port in America. It was a major port in the Virginia colony for tobacco crops in the upper Potomac area.

Until the end of the 18th century, virtually all Negroes living within the current boundaries of the city of Alexandria were enslaved persons. In 1755, the town's population included about 372 Negroes, all slaves. The federal census, first taken in 1790, listed approximately 520 Negroes in Alexandria. About ten percent of the Negro population was then *free* and the other ninety percent was enslaved. Within the next twenty years, the number of free Negroes grew to 836, a sixteen hundred percent increase.[9]

Welcome Sign to Alexandria, Virginia

The term *free* is something of a misnomer to describe the condition of Negroes who were not enslaved. Though called free, there were still severe restrictions on their activities. By 1783, free Negroes were not allowed to move into the state of Virginia from other states, and by 1806, the state declared that free Negroes must leave Virginia within a year, or be re-enslaved. Those who wished to remain in Virginia were required to request permission from the state legislature or local officials. As Alexandria had become a part of the District of Columbia by this time, rules for free Negroes living in Alexandria were somewhat relaxed when compared with the rest of Virginia.

Generally, the slaves within the city of Alexandria were not field hands like the slaves who lived in rural areas. Individuals involved in commerce owned most of the enslaved Negroes within the city of Alexandria. In fact, the early census for Alexandria lists only five male and five female Negro slaves as being owned by farmers. Merchants (375), attorneys (42), bakers (46), physicians (40), tavern keepers (50), and individuals in other similar enterprises owned the remaining slaves. So, most of the enslaved persons in Alexandria spent their work lives in support of commercial enterprises, not farming.[10]

The small number of Negroes in Alexandria who were not enslaved began settling in two adjoining free black neighborhoods—*The Bottoms* and *Hayti*—around 1800. In both neighborhoods, free Negroes rented from select white families—usually Quakers—until they were able to buy homes of their own. The most densely populated blocks were in *The Bottoms,* which consisted of about twelve adjacent blocks near Duke Street and included Alfred, Wolfe, Columbus, and other nearby streets of the city. *Hayti,* the second free neighborhood, occupied a somewhat smaller area in the vicinity of Wolfe and Royal Streets.[11]

The streets in these neighborhoods were named for various historical figures. Alfred Street was named for King Alfred the Great (849–899) of England and Columbus Street was named for Christopher Columbus.[12]

The Negro community, both enslaved and free, provided the bulk of labor to manufacture Alexandria's major products: robes, bricks, ships, and sugar. Many free Negroes were self-employed as draymen, seamstresses, laundresses, coopers (barrel makers), and market gardeners. Several free Negro men also ran their own taverns.

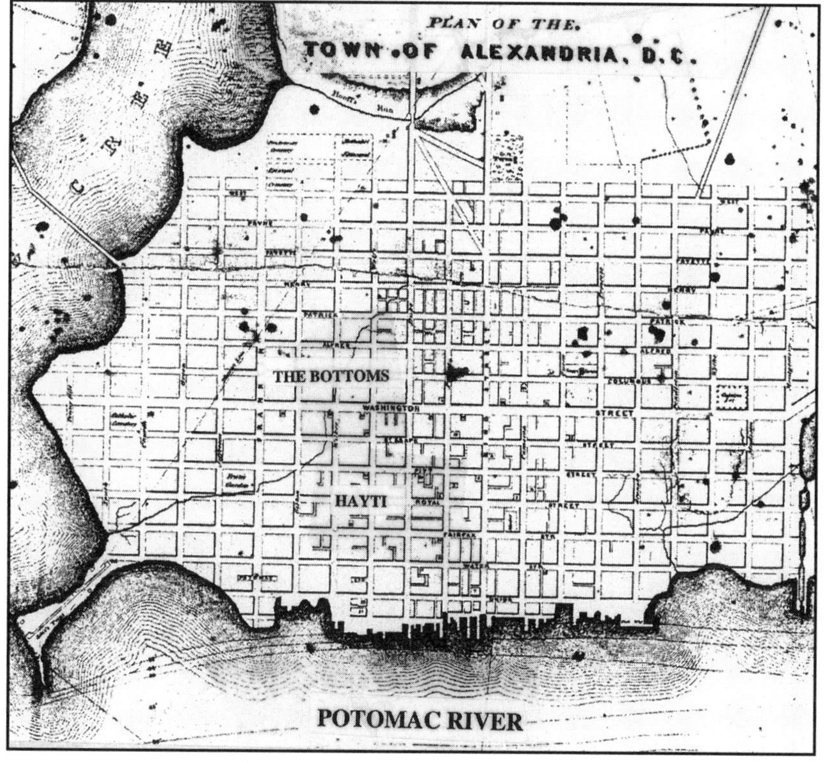

Free Negro Neighborhoods in Alexandria

As there were so few free Negroes in Alexandria at the turn of the century, their worship practices did not have a major impact on religious activities within the city. Worship among the numerous enslaved persons nearby, however, was widely practiced. They were Methodists, Episcopalians, or Presbyterians, or they took the faith of their owners.

Around the turn of the 19th century, Negroes were especially sought after by the Methodist and Baptist congregants. Perhaps this was because white persons of higher social position who attended the liturgical churches looked with contempt upon these evangelical denominations and excluded Negroes. But the less well-to-do whites who populated the Baptist and Methodist denominations embraced blacks to help add to their numbers. In time, however, when poor white persons who had joined the Baptist and Methodist churches accumulated wealth and became slaveholders themselves, they frequently assumed superior and often hateful attitudes and Negroes found it intolerable to worship in their presence. In such cases, independence from the white congregations became the only remedy for the repressed people.[13]

Chapter Two

1800–1825: The Founding of the Alfred Street Baptist Church

. . . *And upon this rock, I will build my church; and the gates of hell shall not prevail against it.*

The actual establishment of the Alfred Street Baptist Church followed dual paths—one well documented and consistent with established religious practices of the times, the other less official, more secretive, and not very well documented. One path followed customs of the day in which Negroes were constrained by their white overseers and were prohibited from assembling without the presence of a white person. The other path was similar to the Underground Railroad—illegal, but somewhat effective in meeting the goals of the people involved.

Baptists Arrive in Alexandria

As the vestry system ceased to exist in the state of Virginia, churches of other denominations arrived as replacements. The Episcopalians and the Presbyterians were the first of these denominations to establish churches in Alexandria in 1760. Next, the Methodists opened Trinity United Methodist Church and the Catholics established a Catholic church in the city in 1773. Most of these four churches used formal liturgies during their worship services.

By 1803, a number of Baptist associations had also begun operating within Northern Virginia. For example, the Ketocton Association of Baptist Churches listed member churches from Loudon, Fairfax, Prince William, Stafford, Fauquier, and other neighboring counties. That year, the Ketocton Association recorded thirty-one member churches and around 2,220 members.[1] The Ketoctons were Regular Baptists aligned with the Philadelphia Association as distinguished from the General Baptists discussed earlier.

One of the Ketocton Association's congregations, Back Lick Church, was located some distance from Alexandria in Fairfax County, along Little River Turnpike. The location was about two hundred yards north of the old Springfield Station on the Southern Railroad.[2] This congregation increased in size from around forty-five in 1780 to almost one hundred by the turn of the century. Reverend Jeremiah Moore, the fiery Baptist minister who assisted in getting freedom of religion included in the Constitution, served briefly as the minister of the Back Lick Church. Reverend Moore also assisted with the establishment of several other local congregations—including the First Baptist Church in Washington, D.C., in 1802.

Some of the members who attended the Back Lick Church, including those from Alexandria, had to travel great distances to attend services. On April 16, 1803, a group of twelve people from Alexandria (five men and seven women) requested a *dismission* from the Back Lick Church for the purpose of creating their own church. Dismission was a definitive religious term, describing a condition in which persons were permitted to leave a church without prejudice for the purpose of starting or uniting with a church of like believers. Their letter of petition to the Back Lick Church read:[3]

> The Baptist Church of Back Lick holding eternal and particular election, justification by the imputed righteousness of Christ; . . . Whereas several of our members have made application for dismission: Resolved, by voice of this meeting that brethren Alexander Smith, . . . Alice Lawrason, . . . be dismissed agreeably to their request in order to be constituted into a regular Baptist Church, . . . and when thus constituted, no more be under our care.
>
> 16th April 1803,
> William Halley, for Giles Cook, Clerk

Six days later, on April 22, 1803, the Back Lick Church granted permission to the group from Alexandria to leave and start their own church. The splinter group then drew up and signed a covenant that created the first Baptist church in Alexandria. The covenant subscribed to the common Baptist principles of adult baptism of believers, the authority of the scriptures in all matters, individual relationship with God, Jesus Christ as Lord and Savior, and the discipline of the church over all aspects of individual life. The covenant read:[4]

> We, the underwritten subscribers . . . humbly desiring to be constituted into a regular church, hoping it may be for the glory of God . . . do hereby, as in the presence of His Supreme Majesty, solemnly unite as a regular society to worship Him and promote His ordinances, maintain His truth, and endeavor to promote His Glory in the world. . . . No one shall be received as a member, except such as are willing to sign this covenant.
>
> Signed,
> Alexander Smith, William Simms, Thomas Beedle, David Henderson, William Fraser, Alice Lawrason, Joanna Craig, Nancy Davis, Mary McLean, Rachel Smith, Reness Williams, Catherine Cahale

The small group of five men and seven women that left Back Lick in April was called the Alexandria Baptist Society and initially began meeting in Alexandria City Hall.[5] Baptism of additional members began right away and by August 1803, when the newly constituted church requested admission into the Ketocton Association as an independent body, membership had grown to twenty-five persons.[6]

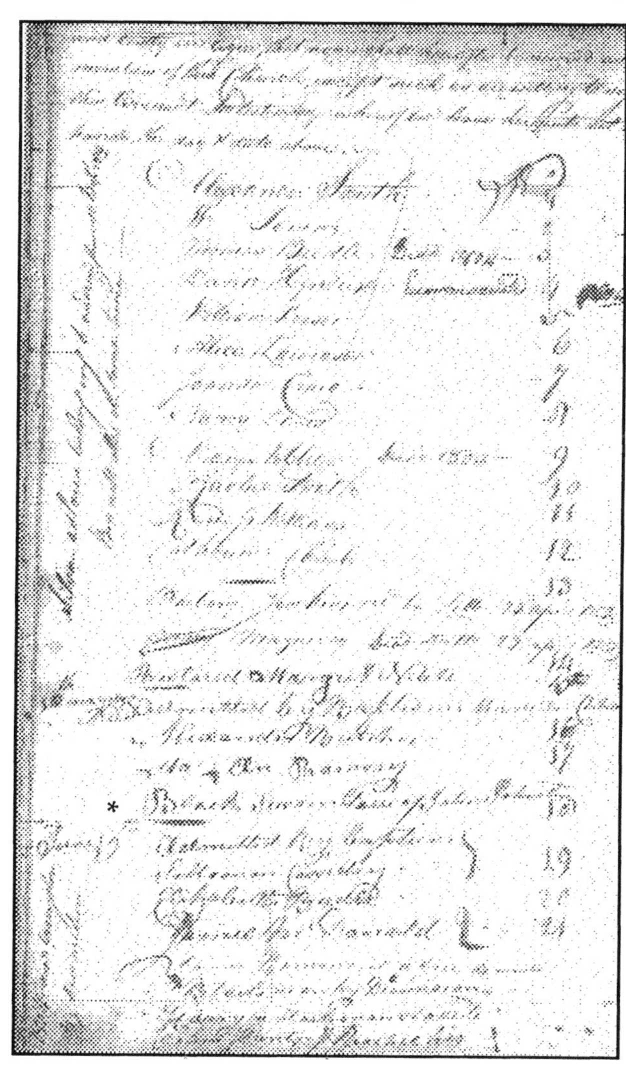

Black Susan Joins Baptists, May 1803

One of the early members baptized into the Alexandria congregation was a Negro slave named Susan Black, or Black Susan. She was baptized in May 1803, shortly after the covenant was signed. Susan is listed as the eighteenth member on the membership rolls and she became the first Negro to be baptized into the fellowship of the Alexandria Baptist Society. Susan Black or Black Susan was the slave of John Johnson, a hatter in Alexandria who owned five slaves.

After worshipping at City Hall for a brief period, the Alexandria Baptist Society chose a site at 212 South Washington Street in Alexandria to build a sanctuary. Within fifteen months, a humble meeting-house was erected at a cost of about $2,000, borrowed from Alexander Smith, one of the twelve charter members. For their first pastor, the group called Rev. Jeremiah Moore, who had been arrested in Alexandria three times for refusing to conform to the fiats of the established Anglican Church.[7]

During the early years, the church was lighted with candles. Within the decade, they would switch to whale oil. Gas lights would come in another fifty years, while electricity for lighting was almost one hundred years away.[8]

Within the first five years, the congregation of Alexandria Baptist grew from the original twelve members to forty-seven members, inspired by Rev. Jeremiah Moore's fiery sermons. Included in this number were Negro members who followed Black Susan to this congregation. Other Negro members baptized that first year included Betty, a slave of Thomas Swann; and Silvia (or Silver), owned by Andrew Jameson.[9] And so it went through the early years. Every month or so, another Negro was brought into the membership at Alexandria Baptist Society, some by baptism and some by dismission, some enslaved and some free.

Parallel Development of an Independent Negro Church

At the same time that the Negro people in Alexandria were officially joining the Alexandria Baptist Society, there were indications that activities may already have been underway among the Negro members to form their own church in order to worship in their own way.[10] In a sense, members may have led double lives, one as part of the official Alexandria Baptist Society, and another as part of a separate Negro fellowship that probably met in wooded areas or individual homes to worship in their own way.

During this era, bush harbor or hush harbor, or brush harbor churches operated in some communities. These were groups of persons who would assemble in secret places, perhaps at night, to worship. In some cases, these groups would meet in wooded areas and hang wet blankets on broken limbs from the trees to shield their outbursts.[11] In other cases, they may have met in the home of an individual or at a business location. Though never formally documented, oral traditions within Alexandria's Negro community suggest that some of the Negro Baptists may have worshipped in bush harbors, even as they were officially joining the Alexandria Baptist Society.[12]

There was at least one other documented local church, developed during this same era, which offers a possible development scenario for the independent Negro Baptists. In Alexandria, while a sizable number of Negro residents united with the Baptist church, even more of them united with the Methodist church. Between 1803 and 1806, membership rolls of Trinity United Methodist Church listed approximately 240 Negro members. This is seven to eight times the number of Negro persons who were attending the local Baptist church during this same period.

In the early days of Methodism in Alexandria, Negroes and whites also worshipped together, as did the Baptists. However, the Negro Methodists also had houses where they went in the afternoons and evenings to hold their own revivals and prayer meetings. These sessions were generally held under white leaders. One of the places where the Negro Methodists held their afternoon meetings was a house on Pitt Street, between Duke and Wolfe.[13] The seats in this meeting-house were made of rough boards, and the floor was dirt. Later on, the meetings were held in an old schoolhouse on North Columbus Street, referred to as Old Zion. They met in Old Zion until the whites and blacks separated as two independent institutions some twenty years later.

While the oral traditions and the above example offer the possibility of the Baptists holding separate worship services in homes or in a bush harbor or some other location separate from the whites, no definitive data has been found of their separate activities in those early years. However, by 1806, there is evidence that the Negro members had formed a separate assembly, the Colored Baptist Society of Alexandria. This society or church was to become the first Negro Baptist church in Virginia north of Richmond.

Records on the worship activities of the Colored Baptist Society have not been found. Most early records relate primarily to property transactions. Each person identified to date as having been a member or official of the Colored Baptist Society (Negro) was also a member of Alexandria Baptist Society (white). Thus, a duality continued into this period, and although there were now two different organizations, records indicate that persons were still baptized and disciplined primarily within the construct of the Alexandria Baptist Society. The Colored Baptist Society and the Alexandria Baptist Society coexisted as two conjoined bodies.

The Conjoined Church: The First Years

Although it is impossible to tell what the exact attendance was at a given meeting or worship service at Alexandria Baptist Society, church rolls indicate that Negro members soon totaled roughly one-third of the congregation. That number would eventually grow to over sixty percent and would remain so for many years, before the conjoined church separated into two distinct congregations.[14]

The colored members were generally restricted in what they could do, consistent with state law at the time (e.g., assembly required a white person to be present). And whenever there were Negro-white relations and power issues, the colored members generally lost because the Negro congregants were usually under close white supervision.

The early records of the church do not track sermons, songs, activities of auxiliaries, or very much at all about the spiritual side of the members' collective lives. There is no reference made to Women's Day or Christmas musicals. There are no references to Sunday School or choir rehearsals. Instead, the minutes of church activities primarily describe church finances and the behavior of people, especially those who deviated from prescribed behavior. The minutes also describe the individuals who were admitted, and those who were dismissed, either to join another congregation or for sins against the church.

Unlike the Anglican Church, Baptist congregations concerned themselves with details of personal responsibility and spirituality. The Baptist church was a self-selected group of baptized believers, not simply a congregation of people who lived within the region covered by the parish, as was the case in Catholic churches. For this reason, Baptists worried about whether or not members lived up to their covenant.

The church suspensions or exclusions for behavior fell into three main categories: breaking the Ten Commandments, worldliness, and sins against the church. The Ten Commandments were those laws passed down by God to Moses, and are documented in the Book of Exodus. For instance, Ten Commandment sins resulting in expulsion included one woman who was caught stealing from an employer. Another woman was suspended for adultery, or ". . . unlawful correspondence with a man to whom she was not married."

Worldly expulsions resulted from behavior the congregation saw as sinful, but which were not explicitly stated in the Ten Commandments. For example, a woman was suspended for attending the theater. A man was suspended for talking ill of his neighbor and another person was suspended for fighting. Sins against the church involved shortcomings specific to Baptist rules. For example, a woman was expelled for taking communion at the Methodist church. Another person was suspended for preaching without permission.

In the early years, the Alexandria Baptist Society held meetings on Saturday, prior to the first Lord's Day of every month. Communion was celebrated quarterly on the first

Lord's Day of November, February, May, and August. In early 1806, the church changed its meetings from monthly to quarterly on the Saturday before Communion, unless some urgent business arose.

Prayer meetings within the Alexandria Baptist Society were initially held on the Lord's Day in the evening, but were soon increased to twice weekly, to include service on Wednesday, over and above the Sunday evening prayer session. At a typical Sunday worship service, the church would collect four to six dollars, sometimes less in the general offering. Meeting dates, times or sites for prayer services within the Colored Baptist Society have not been documented in this early period.

The location of the seats of the colored members within the Alexandria Baptist Society meeting-house on Washington Street in the early years is not known. However, by October 1810, the Church agreed that ". . . the Colored shall be confined in the future to that part of the meeting-house below the north door of the meeting-house . . ." The north door faced Prince Street, which ran perpendicular to the front of the church facing Washington Street. The colored members may have sat in a side galley along the side of the church parallel to Prince Street until 1813, when they were assigned to the gallery.[15]

Activities of Colored Members During the Early Years

It was a rare occasion for Negro congregants to be given any real responsibility at the Alexandria Baptist Society in the early years. Harry Montacue was the exception in this case. Harry and his wife Rachel joined the congregation in 1804. They were slaves to John Hunter, a prominent shipwright in town. By the 1810 city census, Harry Montacue was recorded as a ship carpenter, so he may have been free by that time. On the 1810 census, he listed two free black persons and three slaves as living in his home. Though he did not own slaves, his household illustrates a practice of enslaved and free persons living together in the same quarters, which was not uncommon in urban settings such as Alexandria.

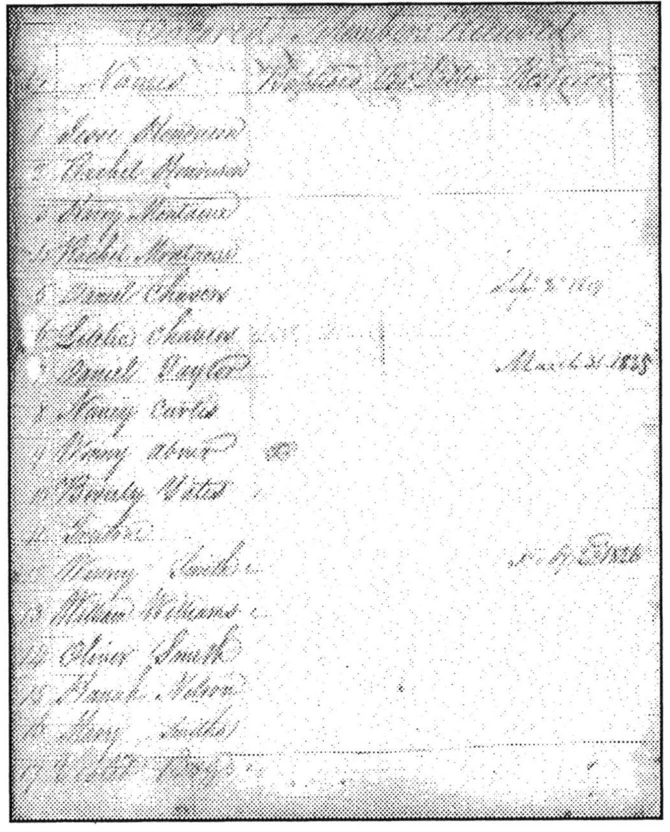

Roster of Early Negro Members

Harry Montacue was given a job at the church of caring for the meeting-house on Washington Street—a role similar to that of sexton. Twice in 1814, the congregation voted to pay him five dollars for lighting and sweeping the meeting-house. Additionally, he was chosen twice to assist in dealing with problems among the colored members—once to notify a Negro woman to attend meetings and once to help solve an argument between two Negro women. Later, the tables were turned. Harry Montacue and his wife were investigated by the church for poor behavior, but were found favorable.

Little or no data are available on activities of the other Negro members during worship services. Most of the information that is available on them only describes instances of baptism, punishment, or death. For example, James Hammons, a free Negro man, joined by dismission in 1805, indicating that he already belonged to another Baptist church. Records show that he was among the first free Negroes to join the church.[16] James Hammons owned an oyster house at the corner of Washington and King Streets in Alexandria, about two blocks from the Alexandria Baptist Society meeting-house. He obtained a license to operate a tavern in 1803 and placed an ad in the local newspaper encouraging citizens to patronize his establishment. But he admonished patrons not to ask for credit, as his resources were very limited. In 1820, he married Grace Hanson (colored).

Another fairly prominent Negro during this period was George Parke, who joined in 1804. He had been manumitted in 1803 and immediately began accumulating wealth through the purchase of several city lots in the vicinity of King and Henry Streets. He also purchased his wife Polly and their three children who, under the existing laws, were slaves since children assumed the status of the mother—even if the father was a free man.

The following table lists the other early colored Baptists, including those already described above, the mode of admission to membership, and their legal status, free or enslaved.

Negroes in Alexandria Baptist Society: 1803–1810

Name	Date Joined	Bapt/Dism	Free/Slave
Susan Black	May 1803	B	S
Betty (Swann's)	16 Aug 1804	D	S
Silvia (Jamieson's)	16 Aug 1804	-	S
Phillip (Patten's)			
Letty (Swan's)	2 Sept 1804	B	S
Harry Montacue	1804	-	S
Rachel Montacue	1804	-	S
James Hammons	1805	D	F
Harry (Hinter's)			
Rachel (Hinter's)	1804	D	S
Sarah Beane	Aug 1804		
Elizabeth Smoot	Aug 1804		
Elizabeth Sample	Aug 1804		
Harry Hanson	Aug 1804		F
Harry	Aug 1804		F
George Parke	Aug 1804		F
Renes			
Elija Shay			
Black Sukey (John's)			S

(continued)

Name	Date Joined	Bapt/Dism	Free/Slave
Letty (Marshall's)	4 June 1808		
Snelly (Scott's)	4 June 1808		S
Sarah Ransom	1 Oct 1808		
Winney Grant	1809		F
Catherine Moore	1809	D	S
Samuel Packer			S
Nansey Packer			
Will (Swan's)			S
Phissis (Critton)		D	S
Phillis		D	
Godfrey Fisher		D	
Sally Ranson		D	F
Nancy Smith	June 1810	-	S

Catherine Moore, a slave belonging to William Hodgson, a merchant in Alexandria, is among the listed members. She joined the church by a letter of dismission from Nomini Church in Westmoreland County, which boasted 875 members in 1809. Samuel Packer and his wife, Nansey, also of Westmoreland County, joined during this period. They were slaves of Nathaneal Washington, a judge in Alexandria. In 1811, Samuel was suspended from the fellowship at church after an ad appeared in the newspaper listing him as a *runaway*. Nansey's situation thereafter is not known.

As these and others joined, still others were being suspended or excluded. In February 1806, George Parke, a free Negro man who had joined in 1804, was suspended for selling spirited liquors on the Lord's Day. He did not deny the facts when charged, but, when questioned, did indicate that doing so was necessary due to his financial circumstance. And in October 1807, Black Sukey, a slave belonging to Mr. Johns, was excluded from Communion for adultery, or "unlawful correspondence with a man to whom she was not married."

During the summer of 1808 several more blacks joined the congregation. On June 4, 1808, Letty, a slave belonging to Polly Marshall, joined, as did Nelly, a slave of Richard M. Scott. Mr. Scott was a merchant and member of the Alexandria City Council who owned nine slaves. Others who joined were Will, belonging to Thomas Swann; Phissis, a servant of Mr. Critton's; and Phillis, who joined by dismission from the Williamsburg Church in James City County. The Williamsburg Church belonged to the Dover Association of Baptist Churches, and had over 500 members—mostly Negroes—in 1809.

Sally Ranson, a free black woman who had two other free persons living in her home, joined by dismission from the Kingston Church in Matthews County. This church had 430 members in 1809. Thus, though the Alexandria church remained small, many others were growing quite large by early 19th-century standards.

During the first seven years of its existence, the Alexandria Baptist Society membership grew from twelve in April 1803 to around fifty in 1810. Twenty-five black persons had joined and accounted for roughly half of the membership. Most of the colored members were slaves of the city's merchants, as was the general Negro population in the city.

Negro Members from Mount Vernon and Related Plantations

While most of the members who joined the Alexandria Baptist Society (the Society) were slaves who belonged to merchants within the city, several also came from the outlying plantations. The largest and best-known plantation—Mount Vernon—was among those that contributed Negro members to the Society. Several slaves from Mount Vernon are listed as members of the early group of colored individuals who joined the Society in the 1810–1820 time frame.

Sign to Mount Vernon

George Washington and George Mason, a prominent Virginia legislator, were two of the larger slave owners on the outlying plantations. Mount Vernon, owned by George Washington and located ten miles south of the city, had over three hundred slaves. Gunston Hall, owned by George Mason—who opposed slavery at the signing of the Constitution—was home to ninety slaves.[17] Gunston Hall was located just south of current day Fort Belvoir.

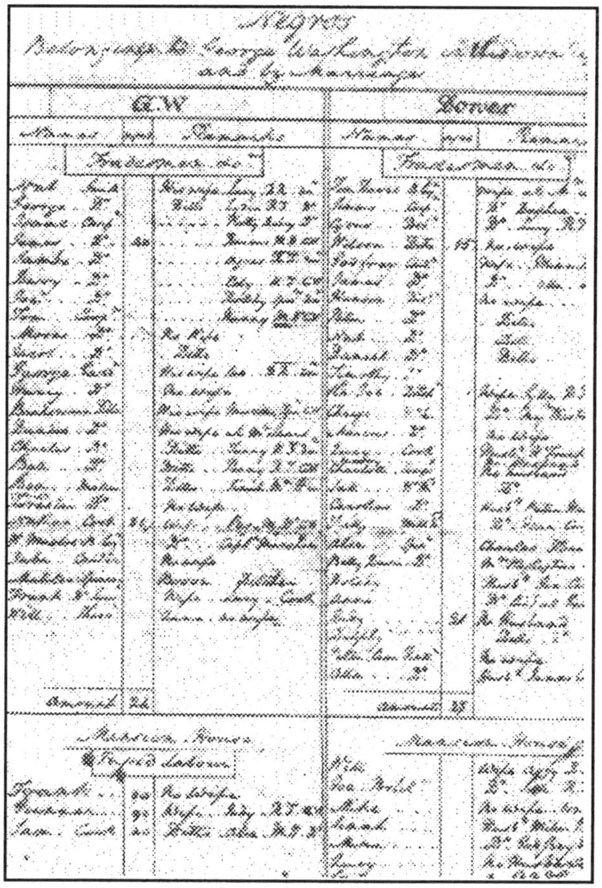

In addition to these two plantations, there were several other large plantations in the area. George Washington's adopted step-grandson, George Washington Parke Custis, owned the Custis Plantation that was located in the area occupied today by Arlington House, the Arlington Cemetery, and the Pentagon. Approximately 70 slaves served on that plantation. And in the vicinity of present-day Reagan National Airport, there was the Abbington Mansion, located in the general area of the rental car parking garages, that was owned by John Parke Custis, George Washington's adopted stepson. Most of the other local farms were small and contained only five to ten slaves. Indeed, fewer than five percent of the total farmers owned and controlled about ninety percent of the slaves on their various estates in the local area.

1799 Slave Inventory at Mount Vernon

Following George Washington's death in 1799, and his wife's death a couple of years later (1801), Bushrod Washington, a nephew, inherited the farms comprising George Washington's estate. Many of the enslaved persons were set free and continued working at Mount Vernon or at the other farms for hire. Other former enslaved persons went to work for the other heirs, including some who moved to Arlington House on the

Custis Plantation.

Bushrod Washington was a Justice of the United States Supreme Court and served as president of the American Colonization Society—a group exploring the possibility of relocating slaves to Africa. He was one of George Washington's executors and was responsible for the care of elderly former slaves from Mount Vernon. When he moved to Mount Vernon, he brought his own slaves with him, and some of the people who later joined the Alexandria Baptist Society may have been from this latter group.

There is little evidence that George and Martha Washington provided anything specific in the way of religious training or services for the enslaved workers on their estate beyond giving them Sunday off. In fact, one of Martha's maids' (Oney Judge, 1774–1848) major complaint about Mount Vernon, upon converting to Christianity after escaping to Philadelphia, was that she never received any moral instruction of any kind there.

The slaves at Mount Vernon were permitted to go into Alexandria on Sunday mornings to sell produce at the market near the current city hall. The market closed at 9:30 a.m., and some may have stayed over for church or other activities. The practice of closing the market early was in response to a slave outbreak in Haiti in 1790, and a desire by the government to keep groups of slaves small and to limit their interactions.

Three of the earliest slaves from Mount Vernon who joined the Baptists in Alexandria were Ham Clark and two women, Dinah Jordan and Hannah [no last name was given]. All three persons had letters from [Bushrod] Washington to join the church.[18] Ham was forty years old in 1815 and lived at Union Farm, one of the outlying farms of the Washington estate. His wife Pat, who was thirty-five years old, also lived at Union Farm but is not listed among the members of the Alexandria Baptist Society. The couple had at least four children, ages one to eight years old. Dinah Jordan also joined the Alexandria Baptist Society at twenty-eight years of age in 1815. She had four children, all of whom lived with her at Union Farm.[19]

There were two women at Mount Vernon named Hannah and it is not clear which of them joined the Baptists. Both women lived at the Home House or Mansion House Farm. The first Hannah was fifty years old and was married to a man named James, who was ten years her senior. The second Hannah was eighteen years old in 1815.

In addition to the three individuals who joined in 1815, there were several other slaves from Mount Vernon who later joined the Alexandria Baptist Society. According to the Minutes Book of the Alexandria Baptist Society, others among the Washington slaves who joined the Baptists included Penne and Sukey on April 25, 1818; Jenny on June 7, 1818; and James on June 7, 1818. Some years later Patty joined on October 1, 1821, and Nancy joined the Society on August 29, 1822.

Early Negro Members Connected to Mount Vernon

Name	From	Joined
Ham Clark	Union Farm	1810 (?)
Dinah Jordan	Union Farm	
Hannah	Mount Vernon	
Penne		1818
Sukey	Mount Vernon	1818

(continued)

Name	From	Joined
Jenny	Mount Vernon	1818
James	Mount Vernon	1818
Patty		1821
Nancy		1822
Nate	Arlington House	1824
William	Arlington House	1824
George	Arlington House	
Meshack	Arlington House	
Stilley	Arlington House	
Maria	Arlington House	
Aggey	Arlington House	
Bazey	Arlington House	

In total, seventeen persons associated with Mount Vernon or possibly belonging to the heirs of the Washington family have been identified as members of the Colored Baptists in the city of Alexandria. While they can be identified with early Alexandria Baptist worship, they weren't really among the founders of the Colored Baptist Society, as several years had passed before they joined. The table above lists the early Negro members who were connected to Mount Vernon and those who belonged to Bushrod Washington, or who belonged to George Washington Parke Custis and lived at Arlington House.[20]

According to information from an 1815 list of Bushrod's slaves at Mount Vernon, in some cases several persons had the same name, so it is not always possible to make clear distinctions about individuals. There was a woman named Suck on the 1815 list at Mount Vernon who is likely the Sukey who joined Alexandria Baptist. She was fifty-five years old that year and lived at the Mansion House. She appears to have been married to sixty-year-old Ben and was the mother of two sons named Ben and Emanuel, and a daughter named Caroline. Jenny was also a slave from Mount Vernon, purchased for three hundred dollars, who joined the Baptists at forty years old in 1815.

There were two men named James, either of whom may have been the James who joined Alexandria Baptist. The first man was sixty years old and lived at the Mansion House. The second James, purchased for four hundred dollars, was thirty-five years old in 1815.

Several more slaves joined Alexandria Baptist who belonged to "GWP Custis" or George Washington Parke Custis, who lived at Arlington House. Unfortunately, there are big gaps in information about slaves who lived at the Arlington plantation. Surviving documentation includes an 1802 and an 1858 list of slaves at the plantation. Some of the individuals on the earlier list may have died and been replaced by a person with similar or identical names. Thus, it is impossible to say with certainty whether they refer to the same people.

The Custis slaves from Arlington House who match names on the Alexandria Baptist list include eight individuals, as shown in the table. Persons from Arlington House who joined in the 1820s time frame included Nate and William in April 1824. Later, George, Meshack, Stilley, Maria, Aggey, and Bazey joined, all of whom belonged to GWP Custis. All of the above-named individuals were still alive and active in 1831, when the first

Minutes Book covering the early years of church history ended.

The people from Arlington who were joining the church in the 1820s might have either been at Mount Vernon during George Washington's lifetime, descendants of people who were at Mount Vernon during the Washingtons' lifetimes, or from the Fitzhugh family (GWP Custis's wife), or descendants of Fitzhugh family slaves.[21]

Expulsions of Colored Baptists

With time, more and more Negroes joined Alexandria Baptist from within the city and from neighboring plantations. Under Pastor Jeremiah Moore's leadership, the membership at Alexandria Baptist grew to fifty-four members by 1811, including the colored members. Though they sat apart from the white members, the colored members were permitted to share in the grace of the church, and were disciplined for wrongdoings along with their white brethren. Some were expelled, some were dismissed, and some died.

A review of minutes of several church meetings provides insights into the ebb and flow of Negro members into and out of the assembly, including those being excommunicated for various offenses of concern to the Baptists. For example, at a meeting in January 1810, Alse Butler was excommunicated for unlawful connection with a man who was not her husband. In August of that year, Charles Thomas, a colored man, was excluded for ". . . persisting in public speaking, contrary to orders on the subject." Charles had been attempting to preach in spite of the fact that the church had passed a rule stating that only persons displaying a certain level of giftedness would be permitted to speak. As he did not appear to possess the gift, he was suspended when he continued preaching.

Nancy Smith, who was a slave of Mr. Sumers, joined by dismission in June 1810. She was excluded for ". . . going to bed with a man and another woman." Nancy married Saham Curtis, another Negro member, in 1816, but was excluded again on April 4, 1818, for an unknown offense. Still later, Hannah, a colored woman belonging to Mrs. Wilson, was excluded from Communion for stealing from her mistress, a crime to which she confessed. The list of offenses is long and contains offenses of fighting, adultery, and running away.

Catherine Patons, on the other hand, left the church in 1814 because she was sold. Members also left to join other churches. Winney Grant, who had joined in 1809, left the fellowship by dismission to unite with another church. In 1817, two of the early members were excommunicated for unknown offenses—Winney Smith on January 3, and Daniel Chavers on February 28. At the December meeting, Miss Hannah Nelson was at first suspended from Communion for doubtful report against her character. Hannah was later excluded, an even more severe punishment, on May 30, 1817, for marrying a second husband while the first one was still alive.

Frequent marriages among the slaves were a constant problem as slaves were sold or ran away. Marriages were such a problem that churches often sought guidance on this issue from the larger associations to which they belonged. For example, the Ketocton Association to which the Alexandria Baptist Society belonged issued guidance on handling the marriage issue in 1809, specifying that special latitude to remarry should be allowed for slaves whose spouses had been sold.[22] In spite of this guidance, Hannah Nelson was excluded and in February 1816 she appeared before the church, provided evidence of her uprightness and conduct, and was released from suspension by a vote of the congregation.

In decisions such as these, the Negro members attended the meetings, but do not appear to have been able to vote. Generally, they were not even listed as attendees at the meetings. The minutes listed the white persons who attended and those who voted, but only stated that "a number of Colored brethren were present" when referring to the colored persons in attendance.

Even as members were being expelled monthly for various offenses against Baptist doctrine, new members continued to join in even greater numbers. Beginning around 1816, five to six new colored members were being fellowshipped each month. With a total of 55 white people and 135 Negroes, the Alexandria Baptist Society had become majority black, and decidedly female, though the church was still administered primarily by white males.

Ministers and Other Key Leaders of the Colored Baptist Society

During this period, several Negroes identified as members of the Alexandria Baptist Society were permitted to preach to the other Negro members. Charles Thomas was one of the first colored persons reported to have preached among the colored Baptists in 1810. After first hearing Charles Thomas, a free man of color, exercise his gifts more than once, the congregation of the Alexandria Baptist Society stated it was fully of the opinion that he was not qualified to preach. But he would be permitted to ". . . give a word of exhortation whenever the Black congregants invited him to do so." In 1810, Charles was reprimanded for persisting in speaking before the assembly. He was granted a dismission in 1814 to unite with another church.

Minutes from the Alexandria Baptist Society also indicate that Brother Jesse Henderson was a preacher. Jesse Henderson and his wife Rachel Henderson were received in the Baptist Society by dismission from the Buck Marsh Church on April 23, 1814, almost eleven years after the Alexandria Baptist Society was formed. Jesse became a trustee of the Colored Baptist Society and signed some of the early deeds of purchase of church property. In the 1820 census, he and his wife were listed as free, and both over forty-five years old. He was listed as ". . . engaged in agriculture." They lived at the corner of St. Asaph and Princess Streets on land they purchased in 1816.

In addition to being a trustee, Jesse was also a preacher and was permitted to continue speaking at the church of the Alexandria Baptist Society on Washington Street, with restrictions. Specifically, church minutes state that ". . . he who has long been permitted to speak publicly, shall have liberty to speak in the meeting-house when it is not occupied by some White preacher, but in the meantime, the people of color are to occupy the gallery as usual. . . ."

On September 28, 1820, the congregation withdrew Jesse Henderson's license to preach and suspended him for an unspecified offense. He was restored on November 20,

1820, after he expressed sorrow, and his license was reinstated on November 30, 1820.[23] Jesse Henderson died on April 14, 1823, and Rachel died in 1825, according to the church minutes.

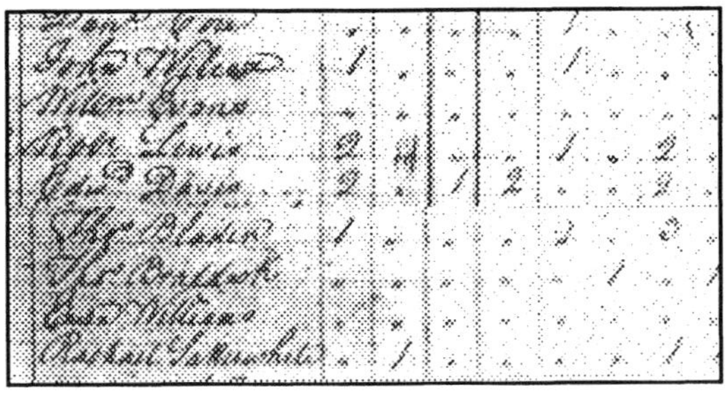

1820 Census Listing Evan Williams and William Evans

Several early references on the church also show Evan Williams and William Evans as early Negro leaders. In the references the two men are frequently discussed as if they were one individual who occasionally reversed his name, as many individuals did to mask their true identity. However, the 1820 census indicates they were two separate individuals with separate families. The same census taker recorded family information for the two individuals on page 186 (Evan Williams) and page 209 (William Evans), respectively. Evan Williams was a trustee within the black congregation. William Evans was a preacher within the same group.[24]

Evan Williams, born in 1784, was cited in the references for acquisitions he made on behalf of the church and for his personal holdings. The 1820 census lists four free colored persons (three males and one female) as members of his household. He and his wife were married in 1807. He may have died or left the area after 1820, as no further records of him have been found.

William Evans is listed as having been baptized into the Alexandria Baptist Society on December 5, 1819. He is listed as the 120th colored person to have joined this fellowship. Not much is known about William Evans's early life. His name appears in the 1820 census with a household of three persons that included two males and a female. However, in the Census of 1850, Alexandria Virginia City and County, William Evans is listed as a sixty-six-year-old brickmaker. Elizabeth, his wife, was sixty-seven at the time and he had a son, Simon, twenty-three years old. Several other relatives were also brick masons, including Edward Evans, thirty-seven, whose wife was named Letty. There was also a son, James Evans, forty, who lived in the home with his wife, Milly, and five children.

In the 1834 business directory for the city of Alexandria, William Evans's business address is listed as 313 South Alfred Street, and his occupation as *minister*. This fact may account for his being referred to as the pastor in some literature, though other sources, including a report by the U.S. Congress in 1870,[25] indicate there were no *real* Negro pastors among the Colored Baptist Society until much later.

Similarly, Daniel Taylor was an early leader within the Colored Baptist Society. He is not known to have preached but was a trustee of the Society. He was listed in the census as a ship carpenter. He was born on November 22, 1777, and later married a young lady named Eliza. The 1820 census shows that nine free persons lived in his home.

During this era, all free persons were required by law to register annually with the county as a means of tracking and controlling their movements. On September 3, 1821, Daniel Taylor registered as a free person as required. His free registration form states he was manumitted by Nancy Cole, who purchased him from William Weems. He was forty-three years old at the time of manumission and was described as being five feet, seven inches tall, and as having lost the first joint of his thumb on his right hand.

Colored Members Secure New Place of Worship

During the period 1806–1818, the colored members continued to join and worship with Alexandria Baptist, but also continued meeting and worshipping separately as part of the Colored Baptist Society. Finally in 1818, the trustees of the Colored Baptist Society rented property at 313 South Alfred Street to hold their meetings, the beginning of a long arduous process to obtain complete independence from the white Baptists.

Records in the Archives of the Clerk of the Court, City of Alexandria, volume H-2, pages 327–31, show that on November 1, 1818, James Lawrason and his wife, Alice Lawrason, rented property to the Colored Baptist Society of Alexandria, District of Columbia. The Lawrasons were members of the Alexandria Baptist Society and sold or rented property to several black families in the neighborhood. The ground rent for the church property was $32.50 a year, payable every first of November. The deed read:

> . . . Witnesseth that the said James Lawrason and Alice his wife, in consideration of the sum of one dollar . . . do give, grant bargain, and sell alien forever a parcel of ground lying . . . between Alfred Street and Duke bounded as follows: beginning at a distance of 101 feet from the northwest corner of Wolfe and Alfred Street, thence Northwardly toward Alfred Street and binding thereon 26 feet to an alley 13 ft. 5 in. wide, thence westwardly with the line of the alley parallel to Duke Street. 110 feet to another alley 13 ft. 5 in. wide, thence South with line of this alley and parallel to Alfred Street/26 feet Eastwardly parallel to Wolfe Street, 110 feet to the beginning. . . . In trust, however, for the use of the COLOURED BAPTIST SOCIETY of the Town of Alexandria, District of Columbia to be managed, governed, disposed of, or conveyed for such purposes . . . as the said Society . . . shall appoint.
>
> Signed, James Lawrason
Alice Lawrason
Jesse Henderson
Evan Williams
Daniel X Taylor (his mark)

This plot of land, secured by the three Negro trustees, was in the midst of the free black neighborhood known as *The Bottoms*. The figure below depicts the location of this plot relative to some of the homes of other free Negroes who had also leased property from the Lawrasons. In total, there were over a dozen lots in the block. The lot for the church was located at 313 South Alfred Street. The Colored Baptist Society began worshipping there in 1818, and in 1819 secured the lot adjacent to the original lot. They would continue at that site for the next 185 years.

At the time of the lease agreement, the Colored Baptist Society was moving into an area that was already essentially in the hands of other colored residents. The particular

Deed to Lot Secured in 1819

plot occupied by the Colored Baptist Society had been leased earlier by Pompey Poorer, a free colored man, as early as 1799. Pompey had been manumitted in 1798 and a year later he began leasing property from James and Alice Lawrason. When the Baptists leased his lot, Pompey and his wife, Lucy Clarke, purchased another property farther up on Alfred Street.

To the north of the plot occupied by the Colored Baptist Society was a plot rented by Henry Johnson (1804), and next to it was a lot leased to John Colbert (1805)—both free Negroes. William Goodard, a very prosperous free colored man, occupied the lot on the corner next to Duke and Alfred Streets. William owned several lots in the Bottoms neighborhood as well as at least ten enslaved Negroes whom he manumitted before his death. Other free persons—Margaret Johnston (1804), Sampson Sumby (1804), and Archilles Richardson (1802), who occupied the corner lot next to Wolfe Street—leased the remaining lots south of the church.[26] Thus, by the end of 1818, the colored Baptists were surrounded by neighboring colored residents who owned or leased property. Each lot was approximately twenty-five feet wide and about one hundred feet deep.

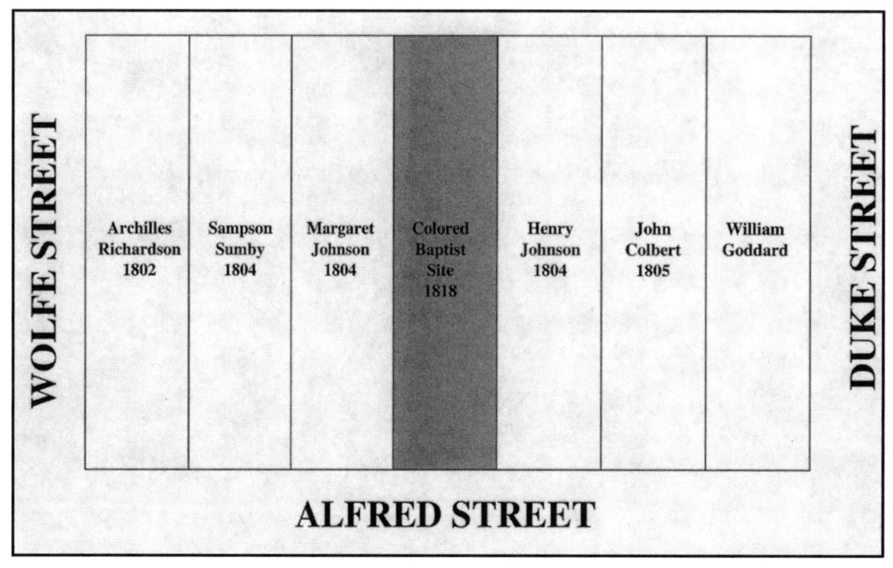

Lots Adjacent to Colored Baptist Society

Following the opening of a colored meeting-house, the Alexandria Baptist Church on Washington Street continued to exercise some involvement in affairs of the Negro congregation that now worshipped around the corner on Alfred Street, three short blocks away. It was during this period that it was first proposed and agreed to among the congregation at Alexandria Baptist Society that ". . . the collections taken weekly from the people of Colour be, so long as the Church shall deem it expedient, appropriated to the purpose of assisting in paying the debt incurred by the brethren in erecting a place of worship. . . ."

At a meeting of the Alexandria Baptist Church on January 1, 1819, a committee exploring a constitution and by-laws for the Alexandria Baptist Church sought to formalize a working relationship between the conjoined bodies—the Colored Baptist Society and the Alexandria Baptist Society. The committee reported the following preamble and articles to the congregation at the regular business meeting:[27]

> . . . The White and Colored Brethren of the Town of Alexandria, denominated Baptist, constituted but one Church. As our color'd Brethren have just erected a Brickhouse for public worship, the church deem it expedient at this juncture to adopt the following articles for the conduct of the color'd Brethren relative to the church conjointly and their distinct meetings, separately—
>
> 1st—The Colored Brethren are at liberty to hold meetings for divine worship on the afternoon of every Lord's day, and also on evenings; or any other evening that may not interfere with the order of the church.
>
> 2nd—On every Wednesday evening immediately preceding the regular Church meeting, they are authorized to meet for the purpose of having relations of experience from people of color, who wish to offer themselves as candidates to the church—and
>
> 3rd—All cases of complaint produced against disorderly colored members are to be brought forward, heard, and investigated in due order at the aforesaid meeting; and the results of their proceedings to be regularly reported to the church at its immediately ensuing meeting, that they may finally decide the business. . . .

These statements in the proposed constitution provide one of earliest references to the construction materials—brick—used in the building of the first colored Baptist worship center in Alexandria.

Independent Colored Worship Services

By 1820, membership within the conjoined Alexandria Baptist Society had increased to over 225 members. Worship services were held at the meeting-house on Washington Street every Sunday, and the Negro members continued to attend services there, and to be baptized, disciplined and expelled.

However, with their new place of worship on Alfred Street in place, the roots of total independence and separation from the Alexandria Baptist Society were now being established. In 1823, the parent church granted permission to the colored brethren to open their meeting-house for public worship on the afternoon of each Lord's Day, and on such evenings through the week as would not interfere with the public worship in the Alexandria Baptist Church. Thus, the Negro members met on some occasions with their white brethren, and then were permitted to worship separately in their own way at their new brick meeting-house at 313 South Alfred Street.

During much of this period, the conjoined church remained primarily a Negro congregation as the colored members outnumbered whites. This predominance of Negroes within the congregation began around 1815 and would remain so for the next thirty-five years. The predominance of minorities and women within the male-dominated church was a fairly common occurrence among local churches and it often led to conflicts. Such issues would be raised at the annual meeting of the Ketocton Association of Baptist Churches to which Alexandria Baptist Society belonged for most of this period.

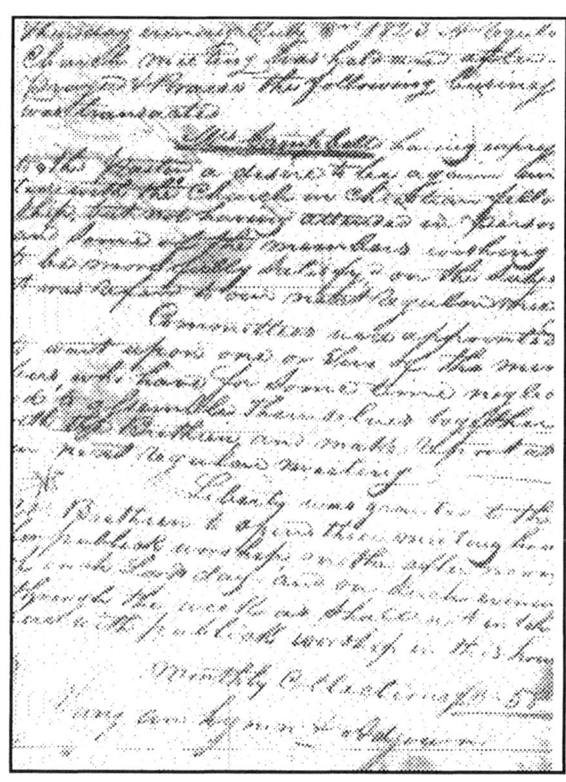

Permission for Negroes to Hold Public Worship

In addition to keeping track of membership, the Association also acted as a clearinghouse for issues that arose within the various congregations. While each church was sovereign, consistent with Baptist polity, each sought to remain true to generally accepted Baptist practices, and would bring before the Association difficult problems they were dealing with for resolution. For example, the congregation at Buck Marsh wanted to know what should be done with a slave whose wife had been taken from him such a distance as to make it improbable that he would ever see her again. The Association recommended that in situations such as this, the church should tolerate his remarrying.

A question arose from the Back Lick Church as to whether colored persons could vote or exercise any authority in governing, even when they were in the majority. The Association recommended that Negroes be prohibited from voting, though they should not be denied Communion. Another church group questioned whether Negroes could be members at all, if they lack the basic qualities necessary for church membership. The Association recommended tolerance and understanding.

Another issue brought before the Association was how to deal with colored people who wanted to preach. With time, more and more Negroes felt the call to preach and wanted permission to do so. Churches were concerned with the large numbers of such requests and brought the issue before the Association. The Association ruled that the Laws of the State of Virginia did not prohibit slaves or free persons from preaching the gospel. However, there was a strict prohibition on unlawful assembly in the State laws. The Association thus recommended permitting colored people—free and slave—to preach. Even so, as there were severe restrictions on assembly to hear the sermons, receiving a license to preach was in many cases a hollow victory.

Chapter Three

1825–1850: Growth and Independence

. . . And there shall come forth a rod out of the stem . . . and a Branch shall grow out of his roots. (Isaiah 11)

The period between 1825 and 1850 would see great changes in the life of the Colored Baptist Society. Shortly after obtaining a separate meeting place, the small assembly would experience severe restrictions on all forms of worship and assembly. In 1850 they would finally be granted complete independence from the parent church—establishing a separate branch of Baptists in Alexandria.

Activities Among the Colored Baptists: 1820s

During the decade of the 1820s, Negro members continued to be fellowshipped and baptized into the Alexandria Baptist Society. Though the Colored Baptist Society still held its own separate worship services, baptisms and other rites were still conducted at the meeting-house of the Alexandria Baptist Society on Washington Street.

Membership in this conjoined church on Washington Street had increased from twelve in April 1803 to approximately fifty by 1810, and 228 by the beginning of the 1820s. Twenty-eight additional persons would join during the mid-1820s. During the latter period of that decade, the majority of the new persons who joined the Alexandria Baptist Society were Negroes.[1]

Even as these new persons were joining, older colored members began to pass on to their final reward. Within the 1820–1830 time frame, about one-half of the early Negro members, among the first fifty who joined, had passed on. This list of deceased members includes two of the original trustees of the Colored Baptist Society, Jesse Henderson and William Taylor, who had signed the first property lease along with Trustee Evan Williams. Jesse Henderson had joined the church with his wife, Rachel, in 1814. He had been the second identified colored minister to be permitted to preach in the meeting-house of the Alexandria Baptist Society on Washington Street. He died in 1823 and was followed shortly by Rachel. In his will he left his property to his wife Rachel, and following her death, portions of his property were transferred to Mimy, who had cared for them when they were ill. Specifically, his will stated:[2]

June the 29th 1821 Alexandria

I Jesse Henderson take my pen in hand to write my last will and testimony in site of God and man. To My wife Rachel Henderson I gave this house and lot to her as long as she lives and the said Rachel Henderson shall pay to Mr. Hepburn estate fifteen dollars every year and when it please God to call Rachel Henderson to himself and she die, then I gave this house and lot to Mimy Wheellar and her ears forever and she must pay to Mr. Hepburn estate fifteen dollars every yeare the reason I give these houses to Mimy Wheelar is because when my wife Rachel wast sick and I myself wast sick both of us for three or four months Mimy Boles (Wheelar) wateed on us both nite and day and I never wast able to give her a sickpence therefore I leave these houses and lot to her at Rachel death.

My hand and seal	Witnesses
June the 29th, 1821	*Joseph Gale*
Jesse Henderson	*Mrs. Cool X Hopwood*

Daniel Taylor, who had also signed the original property deed on behalf of the Colored Baptist Society, died some years later in July 1829. After joining the church, he was excluded in May 1822 for an unknown offense, but was restored in March 1825. While exclusion was a common practice in the early years, restoration of excluded members was less common. About thirteen of the first fifty Negroes who joined the Colored Baptist Society had been excluded at some point for some offense. Of these, only six persons were ever restored.[3]

The first member among the Colored Baptists to die has not been identified. The earliest recorded dates of Negro members passing are in 1814 when Nelson Healey, Nelly (Mason's), Rose Grant, and Phebe Hall are listed as having passed. Others who passed later in the 1820 to 1830 time frame included those listed below.

Deceased "Early Members" of the Colored Baptist Society

Name	Date Passed
William Taylor	Feb 1819
Benja Thompson	25 April 1822
Charles (Smitty)	1822
Phillip (Paton's)	1823
Jesse Henderson	14 April 1823
Rachel Henderson	1825
Betty Moore	1826
Sam Jordon	1826
Nancy (Washington's)	1826
Henry Moxley	1827
Hannah Dutcher	Feb 1828
Nancy Thomas	1828
Peter Leftridge	1829
Ruber Harris	1829

(continued)

Name	Date Passed
H. Haines	1829
Harry Montacue	1829
Rachel Montacue	1829
Daniel Taylor	1 July 1829
James Evans	1829
Margaret Mitchell	1829
Clarissa Furrill	1830
Cleary Ferrill	1830

Mr. Harry Montacue and his wife Rachel were also listed as having passed. Harry had served as a sexton at the Alexandria Baptist Meeting-House on Washington Street. He had gone from slavery, to freeman, to entrepreneurship within his lifetime. He had become a ship carpenter after obtaining freedom for himself and his wife, Rachel. They both passed in 1829.

Death also continued to visit among some of the lesser-known colored members, including Nancy (one of George Washington's slaves) who passed in 1826. Nancy had joined in August 1822 and had been a member for only four years. In 1828, Nancy Thomas also passed, and in 1829 eight additional early members went to that final reward.

During this early period, many of the larger churches in Alexandria maintained cemeteries to bury their members in the vicinity of the present-day Lee Center near the beltway and U.S. Route #1. Churches had opened new sites in this area after the city banned burial inside the city limits in 1809 over concerns of sanitation and the possibility of polluting drinking wells. Churches with cemeteries for the burial of their members included Christ Church, the Methodist Church, and the Presbyterian Church. Neither the colored nor white Baptist congregations had such a cemetery.

Burial Site of Early Negro Members (Penny Hill Cemetery)

Persons who did not belong to churches with cemeteries were generally assigned burial plots in Penny Hill Cemetery. Penny Hill was a cemetery set aside for indigents, and was located in the general vicinity of the large cemetery complexes near South Payne Street.[4] Early members of the Colored Baptist Society were likely buried at Penny Hill, but their final resting place within this cemetery is known but to God.

Nat Turner's Rebellion: 1830s

While worship at the two meeting houses provided a spiritual outlet for the Negro members, slavery itself was the factor that had the greatest impact on their daily lives. There were laws forbidding just about anything they would have wanted to do, including assembly for worship, and Negroes could be severely punished for doing so.

Slavery, the status of most of the early members of the Colored Baptist Society, was on the rise in America in the 1830s. The need for slaves was fueled in part by King Cotton in the South, which helped fuel the booming U.S. economy created by the Industrial Revolution. So, by 1830 Alexandria had become home of the largest slave trading company in the United States for buying and selling slaves.

Slave trading firms, like Alexandria's Franklin and Armfield Slave Market just up the street from the Colored Baptist Meeting-House on Duke Street, were making a tidy profit selling surplus Virginia slaves to new owners in the Mississippi Valley.[5]

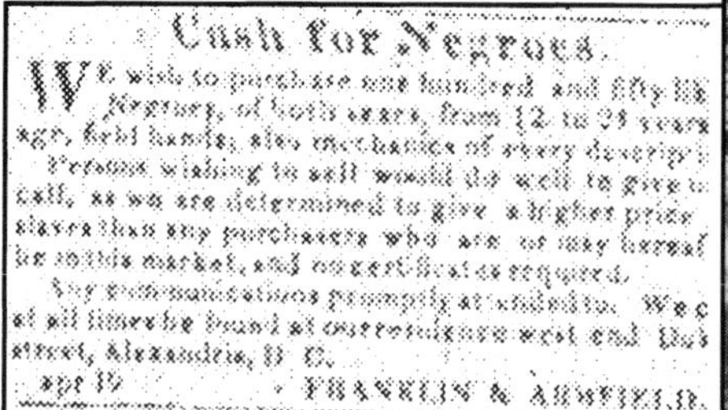

Cash for Negroes.

WE wish to purchase one hundred and fifty likely Negroes, of both sexes, from 12 to 25 years of age, field hands, also mechanics of every description. Persons wishing to sell would do well to give us a call, as we are determined to give a higher price [illegible] than any purchasers who are or may hereafter be in this market, and [illegible]

[illegible] at all times be found at our residence west end Duke street, Alexandria, D. C.

[illegible] FRANKLIN & ARMFIELD.

Slave Market on Duke Street Near Colored Baptist Meeting House

To keep this large slave population in check, laws and ordinances were passed that the city of Alexandria deemed appropriate for the regulation of morals within the city. Accordingly, in May 1826, the Common Council of Alexandria enacted the following law:

> . . . shall have power to restrain and prohibit the nightly and other disorderly meeting of slaves, free Negroes, and mulattoes, and to punish such slaves by whipping, not exceeding 40 stripes, or, . . . a fine of confinement to labor not to exceed three months for every one offense; and to punish such free negroes or mulattoes for such offences . . . $20 for one offence . . . and if unable to pay, such free Negro or mulatto to be confined to labor for any time not exceeding six months. . . .

As indicated by this law, discrimination against Negroes continued even after they were manumitted. Thus life for Negroes in Alexandria, whether free or enslaved, was very restrictive regarding assembly and the opportunity to interact with other Negroes.

An incident occurred in Virginia in 1831 that made these restrictions even more repressive. Early in the morning of August 22, 1831, a band of eight Negro slaves, led by a lay preacher named Nat Turner, entered a house in Southampton County, Virginia, and killed five members of a white family. This was the beginning of a slave uprising that was to become known as Nat Turner's Rebellion. Turner believed that God had chosen him to lead the Negroes to freedom, and began the revolt after seeing a halo around the sun that he believed to be a sign from God. Over a thirty-six-hour period, this band of slaves grew to sixty or seventy in number and they killed fifty-eight white persons in and around Jerusalem, Virginia (seventy miles east of Richmond), before members of the local community could act to stop them.[6] This rebellion raised southern fears of a general slave uprising and had a profound influence on the attitude of southerners toward slavery. There had been other rebellions dating back to the 1790s when slaves under

Toussaint L'Ouverture rebelled in Santo Domingo and slaughtered thousands of people. But none frightened Southerners as much as Nat Turner's Rebellion.

Nat Turner's Rebellion in Southampton electrified the white population of Virginia, including the Alexandria region. The fear of additional slave revolts was pervasive and spread throughout the city. At the same time, Alexandria's colored population feared white reaction against Negroes. To allay these fears, Reverend William Evans of the Colored Baptist Society and forty-four other colored freemen forwarded a petition to the mayor of Alexandria, which was published in the city newspaper in September 1831. The petition stated their willingness to defend the authorities of the city against any insurrections, and read as follows:[7]

September 21, 1831

> Honored Sir—the undersigned, free colored inhabitants of the town of Alexandria most respectfully beg leave to represent to your honor that they have heard with deep concern the various reports relating to the colored people of the South, and pray your permission to express their abhorrence of the recent outrage; and to accept and credit their solemn asseveration that they would unite heart and hand in defending the authorities of the town and community against whatsoever enemy should rise up against them. And further do most devoutly assert, that they would promptly give public information of any plot, design, or conspiracy that might come to their knowledge to disturb the peace and jeopardy the safety of the community.

—signed by Reverend William Evans and forty-five colored men

In addition to Reverend William Evans, the persons who signed the letter included David Jarbour, Lewis Campbell, Joshua Taylor, Luke Lee, William Bennett, Alfred Perry, Philip Hamilton, and many others whose relationship to each other is not known. As indicated in the petition, all signers were free men in the city of Alexandria.

Following Nat Turner's Rebellion, the state and local government took several steps to minimize the reoccurrence of a slave rebellion. Within Alexandria, the whites petitioned the Common Council to take some actions within churches to ensure that meetings among Negroes were not used as a guise to plan another insurrection. This concern was fueled in part because Nat Turner, a preacher, formulated parts of his plan ostensibly during meetings set aside as worship gatherings.

The Common Council of Alexandria sent an inquiry to local churches that asked questions of each church about the size of the colored membership and accommodations that were available for Negroes. At least seven Alexandria churches responded, representing a cross-section of the denominations in the city of Alexandria at that time.

The response from the Episcopal Methodist Church indicated that there were about 223 people of color attached to their church, but there were seats assigned for them, which would accommodate from 300 to 350 persons. The Methodists had always exerted a large presence among Negroes within the city, having over 220 colored members at a time when the size of membership of colored Baptists was half of this number. At the other end of the spectrum were the Quakers, who though strong supporters of the anti-slave movement, did not have a large Negro membership. At that time they reported having no Negro members, though any sober person, colored or white, was invited to join them.

The response from the Baptist Church was not published, but at that time Negroes numbered around 100 in the conjoined assembly of the Colored Baptist Society and the Alexandria Baptist Society. Nat Turner's Rebellion, however, would cause further restrictions on the Colored Baptist Society for the next three to four years as a rash of violent outbreaks and rioting followed throughout the United States.

The crackdown in Negro assembly at the Colored Baptist Meeting-House and among the Negro Methodists, the only two major Negro assemblies in the city, was codified in a series of city ordinances passed in 1831. Specifically, in October 1831, the city passed an ordinance stating:

> . . . that all meetings or assemblages of free Negroes and mulattoes, or of slaves, . . . at any meeting or other house, either in the day or night, under the pretence or pretext of attending a religious meeting, or for any amusement, shall be . . . hereby prohibited, and any such meeting or assembly shall be considered an unlawful assembly.

This crackdown on assembly impacted not only religious activity, but the education program at several local churches and schools as well. Public schools, such as the Washington Free School located in the 400 block of South Washington Street, were shut down. In addition to public schools, education for Negroes was sometimes conducted in church Sunday Schools, or Sabbath Schools, including one in the Colored Baptist Meeting-House. These church schools were crucial in the development of Negro literacy in the first half of the 19th century.

A school more formal than a typical Sunday School was set up in the Colored Meeting-House during this period by Mr. Nuthall, a teacher from the city of Washington. However, he abandoned this school after three years because of opposition by whites fueled by the fears of continued Negro uprisings after Nat Turner's Rebellion. Even though the state legislature reinforced legislation passed in 1830 to prevent Negroes from receiving any type of formal education, it appears that the Sunday School at the Colored Meeting-House remained open anyway. The Sunday School at the only other predominantly colored congregation at that time in Alexandria, Davis Chapel (later known as Roberts Memorial), was forced to close.[8]

As additional fallout from Nat Turner's Rebellion, beginning in 1832 the state of Virginia passed a statute that prohibited Negroes from preaching in the State.[9] Prior to this, several churches had licensed and ordained numerous colored ministers. Thus, while Rev. Evans continued as leader within the Colored Baptist Society, legally he may have been prohibited from preaching in Virginia. In some instances Alexandria, which was then still part of the District of Columbia, followed customs in the District, and in some cases, the city adhered to practices in other parts of Virginia until retrocession.

The issue of slavery and its restrictions on education, religion and assembly continued to haunt the nation with petition after petition and group after group approaching the Congress about some final resolution. In 1840, Congress passed the so-called *Gag Resolution* that stated it would no longer even consider any resolution related to the slavery issue. Thus, slavery and its restrictions upon Negroes in Alexandria and the nation were to remain in place for another twenty-five years.

Purchase of the Colored Meeting Site: 1840s

While suffering under the severe restrictions placed upon them by the fallout of Nat Turner's Rebellion, the Colored Baptist Society continued to hold its worship services under the mandated restrictions. State law prohibited Negro assembly without a white man present, and as evident by the continuing operation of the Sunday School, it is likely that the Colored Baptist Society functioned under these provisions.

But not only did they function, they continued to grow and prosper. In 1842, the Colored Baptist Society had finally saved sufficient funds to purchase the site at 313 South Alfred Street on which their meeting house stood. They had been leasing the building for twenty-four years, and had been saving since at least the late 1820s when the Alexandria Baptist Society permitted funds collected from the colored members to be used for their own purposes.

By the time of purchase, James and Alice Lawrason from whom they had rented the property, had died, and ownership of the land had passed from the Lawrasons to their daughter who lived in Baltimore. So, in 1842 the Lawrason heirs sold the site first to William Evans on behalf of the Colored Baptists for $650, for ground rent at $32.50 a year. Then, in 1846, four years later, William Evans transferred the property to the other trustees for $5.

The 1846 deed transferred the property from William Evans to William Evans, Beverly Yeates, William Weaver, and James Webster as trustees. According to the census records, all of the new trustees were free. Beverly Yeates was 71 and no longer working. Included in his household were his wife, Cassey (64), plus seven others. William Weaver was a 47-year-old laborer. His household included his wife Letty (51) and three others. There were three persons named James Webster listed in the census, and it is not possible to identify the profession of the one who was the trustee from available records.

By the time of the transfer, the name of the Colored Baptist Society had been changed to the African Baptist Church, one of three or four name changes over the next one hundred years. An abstract of the deed of purchase reads as follows:[10]

17 March 1846

> Indenture bet William Evans of the first part and Beverly Yeates and William Weaver and James Webster of the second part. William Evans for $5 sells and transfers to the above parties a certain lot and tenement situated in the town of Alexandria wherein—is located the African Baptist Church of Alexandria and bounded as follows: . . . which ground rent was transferred to Wm Evans by Romulus Riggs and Mercy Ann, his wife by deed, dated 1 Sept 1842, to hold as trustees for the African

Baptist Church of Alexandria which constitutes a member of the Columbia Baptist Association.

William Evans
Beverly X Yeates
William Weaver
James Webster

The site at 313 South Alfred Street has been owned by the church ever since, though possession was interrupted briefly by the Civil War. This property is among the oldest in the city of Alexandria to have remained continually under Negro ownership.

Independence for the Colored Baptists: 1850s

With the purchase of the South Alfred Street site, the African Baptist Church could worship in their own facility. But technically, they remained under the jurisdiction of the Alexandria Baptist Society as they had for over forty years. Though physically separate, they would remain a conjoined church for four more years until they were officially dismissed and accorded complete independence to govern their own affairs.

Complete independence would finally come in 1850 during the pastorate of Reverend O.W. Briggs of the Alexandria Baptist Society. At this time it was finally resolved that a committee consisting of the pastor, Brother Cawood Rogers, and the deacons be appointed to confer with the colored members of the church on the proposition of a separate organization, and report as soon as practical. Finally, in the summer of 1850, independence became a reality.

On Friday morning, June 28, 1850, the Alexandria Baptist Church convened and, after prayer by the pastor, the church proceeded with business. The four items on the agenda that morning follow:[11]

1. The church unanimously agreed to accept Sister Legg (white) as a member of the church, having provided a letter from the Church of Antioch in Prince William County.
2. Bro Rog joined the committee on delinquents.
3. On motion resolved that Brethren Cawood P. Rogers and the Pastor of the church be a committee with discretionary powers, fully to organize the coloured members of this body into a separate church, in the town of Alexandria, and report at the regular meeting of the church. The Clerk was directed to grant the col'd members of this church a Letter of Dismission to unite in a separate body in this Town under the name of—The Coloured Baptist Church of Alexandria . . .
4. The next meeting of the church was fixed at . . . etc.

Wm. H. Rogers, Clerk — O.W. Briggs, Chairman

On June 24, 1850, Letters of Dismission were finally granted to the colored members to unite in a separate body under the name of the Colored Baptist Church of Alexandria. The exact contents of these letters are not known. However, the common format of such letters from the Alexandria Baptist Society is documented in the front of the Minutes Book (Vol. 5). A dismission letter looked much like a handmade certificate. It was one page in length, and gave the bearer's name, identified the church from which one was being dismissed, and provided some general information on the beliefs of the Baptists.

A letter of dismission was also like a passport. It established the bearer as a bonafide member of the Baptist church and declared the recipient a "baptized, born again believer." The bearer was therefore authorized to unite with any Baptist fellowship upon mutual consent. Membership was taken very seriously at this time and was very controlled. Joining a church required vowing to live by the covenant of that church and when there were infractions against the church, the member was expelled promptly.

At the next church meeting of the Alexandria Baptist Church, one month later, on Friday, July 26, 1850, after prayer by Brother Cawood, the following business was transacted:[12]

1. Brother Briggs will remain the chair of Delinquent subscribers, etc.
2. The committee appointed to organize the Coloured Baptist Church reported through the Chairman of that Committee, Brother Briggs, that it had discharged its duties assigned them, in fully organizing this into a separate and independent church in this town, to be known by the name: The Colored Baptist Church of Alexandria: that they had adopted our Constitution and pretty much the same rules of Discipline and Church Government, with the exception of one Rule, which gives this Church authority in the final adjustment and settlement of difficulties, where they cannot agree among themselves.
3. Miscellaneous items . . .

Several other small items were discussed before the close of the meeting. And, finally, in July 1850, the conjoined congregations of the Alexandria Baptist Society and the Colored Baptist Society separated peacefully.

The Colored Baptist Church had finally reached a new day. After forty-seven years of duality, subjected to oversight of the Alexandria Baptist Society, and after almost twenty-five years of renting a site from the Lawrasons and their heirs, the Colored Baptist Church was free and independent. Now, there were two fully independent Baptist churches in the city of Alexandria.

The formation of this independent Negro Baptist church was reported widely in the media. The fall edition of the *Religious Herald*, published in September 1850, reported the dismission of the colored members from Alexandria Baptist Society in the following article:[13]

26 September 1850

. . . The Alexandria church dismissed 83 colored members, and gave them a separate

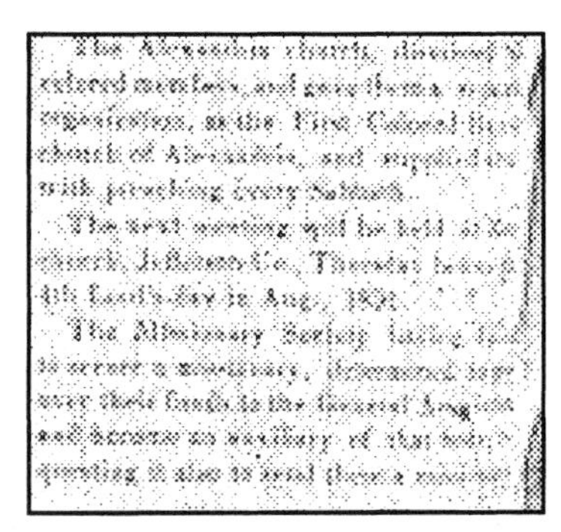

Negroes Now Separate, the *Baptist Herald*

organization, as the First Colored Baptist Church and supplied them with preaching every Sunday . . .

By the time of final dismission in 1850 under Reverend O.W. Briggs, there had been seven different pastors at Alexandria Baptist Church, each serving seven to eight years. Reverend Samuel Cornelius (1824–1841) had served the longest time. The Alexandria Baptist Church had grown from 12 at its inception in 1803 to 146 (83 Negroes and 63 whites) by 1850, the time of the final separation.

Pastors of the Colored Baptist Society during this era were not documented. However, Reverend William Evans was listed as minister of the Colored Baptist Society in the U.S. Census, with the church as his business address. Other documentation suggests his position was as a trustee and leader, but not truly a pastor in the true sense. Under Baptist polity at that time, those functions were retained with the parent church. Even after independence, the parent church provided preachers to occupy the pulpit every Sunday, as reported in the *Baptist Herald.*

As part of forming the independent body, the Colored Baptist Church adopted a constitution and rules for operation. The adopted constitution has not been found. However, if the Colored Baptist Church adopted rules that paralleled the constitution of Alexandria Baptist Church, as shown in the Minutes (Book 5) of the Alexandria Baptist Church, then it would have contained about ten articles that included the following provisions:

Articles of the Constitution

Article 1: Name
Article 2: Election of Officers
Article 3: Meetings of the Church
Article 4: Admission of Members
Article 5: Discipline
Etc.

The constitution for the Colored Baptist Church would also have included a provision ". . . which gives this Church (Alexandria Baptist) authority in the final adjustment and settlement of difficulties, where they cannot agree among themselves."

Additionally, the Alexandria Baptist constitution also contained several by-laws governing officers and delegates to convention that were likely included in the constitution for the colored assembly. Among the rules in the constitution and by-laws, the ones with the most impact on the life of the average member concerned discipline. For example, there was a by-law stipulating that any member absent for two months was automatically brought on charges, and likely excluded from Communion. At the church's beginning, at the time of its independence, and for the next 150 years, discipline would remain the hallmark of the First Colored Baptist Church of Alexandria.

Activities of Other Local Negro Churches

At the same time that the Colored Baptist Church of Alexandria was obtaining its complete independence from Alexandria Baptist, other local churches were following suit. The Negro Methodists, which numbered as many as 250 persons in 1830, were now also independent. Their church, Davis Chapel, later called Roberts Memorial, was located a couple of streets over from the Colored Baptist Church, at 606 South Washington Street. Their church also began as part of the predominantly white First Methodist Episcopal Church, today referred to as Trinity Methodist. In 1830, five Negroes and four white members purchased a lot and began the foundation for a separate church. Work stopped in 1831 because of the reaction to Nat Turner's Rebellion, but the church finally moved to the present site in 1834, and remains the oldest Negro church edifice in Alexandria.[14] Just these two Negro churches, the Baptist and the Methodist, existed in Alexandria for the colored people until the Civil War.

Roberts Memorial Church

The phenomenon of independence for colored churches was also taking place across the river in Washington, D.C. Nineteenth Street Baptist Church in downtown Washington, D.C., was now an independent Negro Baptist Church that had been granted independence in 1839, as the first colored Baptist church in the District of Columbia. It had split from the First Baptist Church of Washington (white), also started by Reverend Jeremiah Moore, who had started a Baptist church in Alexandria, Virginia. The development of the Baptist churches in the District of Columbia, white and colored, very closely paralleled the situation with the Alexandria Baptist churches. For a while they too had existed conjointly as part of First Baptist Church of the District of Columbia, and later as separate entities.

Like the church members in Alexandria, the Negro members in the District of Columbia had been a part of First Baptist Church of D.C. (white) when it was first organized in 1802.[15] Negro members worshipped on an equal basis with their white counterparts at first, but were soon assigned to the gallery, just as other churches were doing. When the white church first built its new building on Tenth Street in a facility later to be known as Ford's Theater, Negroes were again given the balcony. Soon, the discontented Negroes bought the old church on the corner of Nineteenth and I Streets Northwest from them and organized the first church of the Baptist denomination among Negroes in D.C. Here, too, the colored members had requested permission to form their own church much earlier, but had been refused.

Each new independent church of this era in Alexandria, Washington, D.C., and other parts of the South had basically the same story, initially a white and colored conjoined body that was predominantly white, then an increasing Negro presence, then Negroes requesting and being permitted to form their own independent church organizations. The independent churches were formed sometimes with the assistance of their white counterparts; in other cases it was done independently. But independence became the new watchword and, in years to come, the Negro independent Baptist church would proliferate and flourish.

Chapter Four

1850–1875: The Civil War and Reconstruction

Go down Moses, way down in Egypt land; tell old Pharaoh, let my people go.

After spending forty-seven years in some form of subjugation to the white Alexandria Baptist Society, the independence that the Colored Baptist Church secured in 1850 was soon threatened by the Civil War. In the history of the Colored Baptist Church, and even the nation, few events have left as permanent a scar on the psyche of its people as the Civil War. But the church was to survive the war that led to the freeing of its remaining enslaved members, and would prosper and grow during Reconstruction, a period that offered such great promise.

Activities in Alexandria in the Early 1850s

The 1850s were a period of commercial and industrial expansion in the city of Alexandria as it emerged from the economic doldrums. The town's population increased from around 8,700 in 1850 to 12,600 by 1860. There were 1,301 free Negroes and 1,061 slaves within the latter population count. At the beginning of the century, free Negroes constituted approximately ten percent of the city's colored population; by 1850, they accounted for a little more than half of that population.[1]

The large free population had been made possible in part by the practice of slaves *renting* themselves to local merchants. In this practice, the slave and owner would share the rental wages according to a prior agreement. The slaves would then save part of their wages until they could buy freedom for themselves and their families. Though the free population increased through this technique, life in Alexandria for its colored citizens continued to be dominated by strict controls that limited their mobility.

When the city of Alexandria was retroceded to Virginia in 1846 after almost fifty years as part of Washington, D.C., Negroes became subject to local Virginia laws, including a law whereby no group of more than five Negroes could meet without a white man being present. Moreover, no colored person could be in public after the ten o'clock curfew. In February of 1858, the Alexandria City Council, then called the Common Council, passed yet another act that permitted the city to hire free Negroes out if they could not pay their taxes. The act, as published in the February 12, 1858, *Gazette Newspaper*, read as follows:[2]

> Section 1. That any free Negro failing to pay his or her Corporation taxes, and not having . . . property out of which they may be made by distress, shall by order of the Mayor, be hired out by the Collector of the Corporation . . . for such a time as will suffice, at not less than ten cents a day to raise the said taxes. . . .
>
> Thomas Smith, president pro tem
> W. D. Massey, Mayor

Thus, for Negroes, whether free or slave, there were few opportunities for upward mobility as severe restrictions existed for all activities, including worship.

By 1850, there were still just two major Negro church assemblies, the Baptists and the Methodists. The church continued to be about the only place where Negroes, slave or free, exerted any real influence, and churches became a training ground for colored leaders.

During this period, two additional Negro neighborhoods came into existence on the north end of Alexandria, the *Berg* and *Uptown*, to join the Negro neighborhoods of the Bottoms and Hayti. The Berg or Fishtown, so named because of its location near the waterfront, was in the northeast section of the city, and Uptown was located at the western edge of the city. From these neighborhoods came the people who fueled the growth of Alexandria's early Negro churches in the 1850s.

Colored Baptists Build New Brick Church

As membership at the Colored Baptist Church continued to grow to more than 130 members, a need arose for a larger worship facility. To accommodate the growing membership, the Colored Baptists purchased some additional property adjacent to the lot on which the existing small brick church stood. According to the deed, dated 1853, between Ann B. Levering (daughter of James Lawrason) of Baltimore and James Webster, William Weaver, and William Evans, trustees of the First Colored Baptist Church of Alexandria, an additional lot was purchased for $150. The plot of ground was 25 feet across the front and 110 feet deep and adjoined the existing African Baptist Church lot on the south. The church now owned two adjacent lots, providing over 50 feet of frontage along Alfred Street.

The trustees listed on the deed (Webster, Weaver, and Evans) had replaced some of the previous trustees who purchased land on behalf of the Colored Baptist Church in 1846. Listed among the old trustees was Brother James Webster, born in 1813, and who had been a member since 1840. He was one of the patriarchs of the Burke family that was to remain an influential family within the church congregation for the next 150 years.

The purchase of new land was the starting point of an expansion program fueled by the new growth within the congregation. In 1855, the Colored Baptist Church erected a new building on this site where it had been worshipping since 1818, almost thirty-seven

Deed of Purchase of Lot (1853)

years. The cornerstone, still visible today on the old church building, was dated June 28, 1855. An article was published in the August 23, 1855, edition of the *Alexandria Gazette* describing the new building the church had constructed. The article includes the following description:

> . . . The Colored people belonging to the Baptist Church of this city have erected a handsome, and commodious brick church on the site of the old church on Alfred Street, and it is expected that religious services will be held in it on Sunday next. The congregation deserves great credit as they have by their own exertion, succeeded in this work.

Trustee James Webster of the Colored Baptist Church

A detailed description of the old, smaller church has not been found, though early minutes of the Alexandria Baptist Church during the 1820s indicate the old church was brick. In this case, the old brick church was replaced by a larger ". . . handsome and commodious brick church."

Colored Baptists Join Associations

Among early Baptist churches such as the First Colored Baptist Church in Alexandria, membership, belonging, or recognition appeared to have been a large part of a church's focus and activities. Thus, shortly after gaining its complete independence from the Alexandria Baptist Church in 1850, the Colored Baptist Church of Alexandria sought recognition as an independent church in one of the Baptist associations that had formed in Maryland.

On October 20, 1853, the Clerk of the First Baptist Church (white) of Alexandria was requested to write a letter of introduction to the Maryland Baptist Union Association on behalf of the Colored Baptist Church of Alexandria so they might unite with that association.[3] The Maryland Baptist Union had been formed about twenty-five years earlier by six churches in Maryland and one church from the District of Columbia to ". . . advocate the cause of true religion in Maryland and that part of the District of Columbia north of the Potomac. . . ."

The reasons that the Colored Baptist Church first sought to unite with an association in Maryland instead of Virginia are not clear. The Colored Baptists may have sought membership in this particular association because it had been denied membership in some Virginia associations. Or, they may have sought membership in Maryland because this particular association had been very proactive with Negro churches, and had a long history of activity with Colored Baptists. Indeed, its founder, William Crane of Richmond, had assisted the missionary Lott Carey with his early missionary activities.[4]

> New Church.—The colored people
> longing to the Baptist Church in this c
> have had erected a handsome, and c
> modious Brick Church on the site of the
> Church on Alfred street, and it is expec
> that religious services will be held in it
> Sunday next. The congregation dese
> great credit as they have, by their own ex
> tions succeeded in this work.

Article Describing New Colored Baptist Church

Whether or not the Alexandria Colored Baptist Church was ever admitted to the Maryland Baptist Union Association is not clear. Though they applied, the church is not listed in Association records among the colored churches that were admitted, and so the application here may have been rejected also.

However, by 1856, the Colored Baptist Church, now known as the First African Baptist Church, applied for and was accepted for membership in the Potomac Baptist Association in Northern Virginia that included churches from Loudon, Prince William, Fauquier, and Fairfax Counties.[5] This organization was an outgrowth of the Salem and Columbia Associations, which the Alexandria Baptist Church (white) had joined in earlier years. So, in 1856, the African Baptist Church of Alexandria and the Alexandria Baptist Church (white) both belonged to the same association as two independent bodies.

At the time of joining this new association, the Colored Baptists reported a membership of 136 members. Thirteen of these new members joined that year by baptism. Its sister church, the Alexandria Baptist Church, reported a membership of only 80 members, having lost 12 members to dismissions during the past year.

Prior to the period when the African Baptist Church joined the Potomac Association, very little is recorded concerning the activities of colored members who may have still attended the Alexandria Baptist Church. Hannah Bruce, a distant relative of the Quander family, was the only colored member listed as having joined the Alexandria Baptist Church during the early 1850s. She was admitted by baptism; however, by 1853, she had left and minutes show no colored members.[6] All of the colored members had received letters of dismission and had become members of the African Baptist Church of Alexandria or some other local Negro congregation.

Activities of the Colored Baptists: 1855–1860

With a new sanctuary, the church was poised for a period of even greater expansion. Minutes of the Potomac Baptist Association indicate that in 1856 seventeen new persons joined the African Baptist Church by baptism and two by letter. Additionally, two were excluded, and five had died since the last report. At the end of 1856, the church had almost doubled in size from eighty-three members in 1850 to a total of 150 members. The church was "seeking aid to support a new pastor . . . ," according to Association minutes.[7]

In 1857, the Association minutes show that the Church was still continuing to prosper, and had finished paying off the mortgage on its beautiful brick house of worship after two years. The total amount paid for the structure had been $10,000. The church added seventeen new members that year by baptism, and would add forty more members the next year. The church reported it had paid $250 during the year to various ministers who had acted as pastors.

Records are also not specific as to the founding date of the first choir—later called the Senior Choir—that sang at the church during this period. Records of its earliest existence have not been found. Nevertheless, the choir was likely in existence by 1855 when they reportedly performed several concerts to raise money to pay off the mortgage on the first building.

A pastor for the congregation had been an issue for several years. Although members such as Reverend William Evans served in a leadership role as a trustee, and a ministerial leader within the religious life, Association minutes indicate that he was not really the pastor in a conventional sense. The church reported to the Association that year through its delegates, S.M. Shute and William Miller, that it had no pastor. The ministers who were listed as having served the church during this period included T.B. Shepherd, S.M. Shute, and T. Triplett.[8] Each minister was associated with the Alexandria Baptist Church (white) and Reverend Samuel Shute served as their pastor during this time. Elder T.B. Shepherd preached twice each Sabbath in services at the African Baptist Church during portions of this period. The African Baptist Church still met each Sunday, in contrast to many other churches that met only once monthly.

By 1858, the membership had grown to 187, and to 204 members at the close of 1859. The Association minutes indicate that the church still had no regular pastor. Other ministers who served short terms and preached for the colored Baptists included J. Latouche and J. Porter. While the names of all the various ministers who served have not been identified, McPhail (1971) notes that ". . . Only white ministers served the present African Baptist Church from its beginning through the year 1859."

An entry in the *Religious Herald* in March 1860 provides additional insights into worship practices during this era. One of the writers from the paper spent a period in Alexandria visiting the Alexandria Baptist Church (white) and the African Baptist Church. He noted that the white Baptist church had a large Sabbath School in which, among the several classes, ". . . a converted Catholic was diligently engaged in teaching a class of Jews. . . ." The writer found this new and unusual.[9]

During his visit to the African Baptist Church, the writer noted that contrary to the customs in other parts of the state, the Colored Baptists held meetings at night, very much to the annoyance of the white Baptists. Members of the colored congregation suggested that it seemed strange that nobody in town but the white Baptists opposed their meetings at night. The colored Methodists at Roberts Memorial Methodist Church, just around the corner from the African Baptist Church, also met at night during this period.

Colored Baptist Convention Meets

The African Baptist Church of Alexandria initially joined the predominantly white Potomac Association (which soon merged to become the Columbia Baptist Association) as few all-Negro Associations existed at that time. National conventions were slower to form among Negroes than whites due to the numerous impediments. It was not until around the end of the century that the first national colored association, the National Baptist Convention, would be organized. However, in the 1850s there were several regional colored associations, including those in which the colored Baptists of Alexandria soon began participating.

One such regional Negro convention with which the African Baptist Church soon developed a relationship was the American Baptist Missionary Convention. This convention was first organized in 1840, and held its 19th anniversary at the Baptist Church of Newburgh, New York, beginning on Friday, August 19, 1859.[10] Ordained ministers at this convention included Reverend William Evans of the African Baptist Church in Alexandria, Virginia; Reverend Sampson White, of Brooklyn, New York; and several other ordained ministers listed in their program. Licentiates at this convention also included Brother Samuel W. Madden, then a resident of Baltimore, Maryland. Each of these men would at some point occupy leadership roles at the African Baptist Church in Alexandria.

Article Describing Activities of the African Baptist Church

During a convention business session on the morning of August 19, Reverend Sampson White resigned as president of the convention and was replaced by Reverend Chauncey Leonard. Brother Samuel Madden, along with Brothers Dixon and Miller were appointed to the Auditing Committee during the morning session. In the afternoon session, Reverend William Evans of the African Baptist Church of Alexandria spoke from John 4:29—*Come, see a man, which told me all things that I have done*. After a collection of $1.04, the convention adjourned at 7:30 p.m. until the night session.

At the night service, Reverend Sampson White preached from Romans 15:20—*Yes, I strive to preach the gospel, not where Christ was named.* On the next day, Reverend William Evans was appointed to a committee to nominate new preachers for their introductory sermon.

This convention, like the Columbia Association to which the African Baptist Church also belonged, provided the church with opportunities for fellowship, collective missionary activities, and opportunities to train and identify new pastors. Evolving from this convention meeting in New York in 1859 would be the next two pastors of the African Baptist Church, Reverend Sampson White and Reverend Samuel Madden.

Reverend Sampson White Arrives As Pastor

While Reverend William Evans's leadership role was recognized within the African Baptist Church, sources are contradictory as to whether he was a pastor in the conventional sense. However, all records found are in harmony on the arrival of Reverend Sampson White as pastor in 1859.

Reverend Sampson White came to Alexandria upon resigning from the presidency of the American Baptist Missionary Convention. He had already experienced an illustrious career as the minister of several churches and as convention president before he came to the First African Baptist Church in Alexandria. However, the circumstances of his calling to the church are not well known. It is known that the church had been looking for a regular pastor for several years and perhaps the growing congregation, now with over two hundred members, proved attractive to the dynamic leader.

Reverend White was born in 1804, shortly after the first Baptists arrived in Alexandria. Not much is known about his place of birth or early education. But, based on histories of other churches where he served, it appears he was a dynamic leader who played a role in establishing multiple Negro churches, much like Reverend Jeremiah Moore had done in establishing numerous early white Baptist churches.

Records indicate that Sampson White may have first pastored at the Gillfield Baptist Church in Petersburg, Virginia, in the mid-1830s. Gillfield Baptist is listed as one of the oldest Negro Baptist churches in America, with a history beginning as early as 1797. After a period as the pastor, Reverend White left Gillfield Baptist in 1839 to help organize the 19th Street Baptist Church in Washington, D.C., which had separated from its white counterpart in much the same way as the Negro Baptists in Alexandria had done.[11] One of Reverend White's first acts at 19th Street Baptist, then known as the First Colored Baptist Church of Washington, D.C., was to get the church admitted into the Philadelphia Baptist Association at its meeting in Philadelphia in October 1839. Also, while at 19th Street Baptist, he established the Sunday School and was its first superintendent. After a little over two years of service, he left 19th Street Baptist on January 31, 1841, where the text of his final sermon was ". . . Peace I leave with you . . ." from John 14:27.

Reverend Sampson White, Pastor of the African Baptist Church

Reverend White's whereabouts during the next several years are unknown, but did include a stint as pastor of the Abyssinian Baptist Church in Harlem, New York. However, he returned to 19th Street as pastor a second time twelve years later, in 1853, and served until 1856. After pastoring at 19th Street this second time, and serving as president of the American

Baptist Missionary Convention, his travels eventually brought him to Alexandria in 1859. In Alexandria, he would serve the congregation of the African Baptist Church for four years, from 1859 to 1863, and would later pastor at other churches. During his pastorate in Alexandria, little is known of his accomplishments or of activities of the church. But looming in the background during his pastorate was a conflict that would disrupt the church and divide the nation—the Civil War.

The Civil War Begins

Even as the African Baptist Church was prospering in Alexandria, slavery was an issue still creating conflicts within the national conscience. In Alexandria, there was an occasional racial disturbance during this period. There had been a riot between whites and ". . . persons of color" in December 1853 during which stones were thrown, pistols were fired, and services at the African Methodist Church on Washington Street were disrupted. But while the slavery issue continued to fuel political debate within the city and the country, in the mid-1850s few racial incidents were reported in Alexandria.

The decade of the 1850s was violent elsewhere, however, and gradually the polarization over slavery reached a crisis. The Compromise of 1850 struck at the institution of slavery by first outlawing slave trade in Washington, D.C., and then by admitting California as a free state. Around the same time, a small civil war broke out in Kansas over whether it should be admitted as a slave or free state, leading to a conflict commonly referred to as Bleeding Kansas.

At the Republican Political Convention in Chicago in 1860, the Republicans nominated Abraham Lincoln of Springfield, Illinois, as their candidate for president. The Democratic Party was split over two candidates, with the Northern democrats nominating Stephen Douglas, and the Southern democrats nominating John Breckinridge. Helped by the division within the Democratic Party, Abraham Lincoln won the election and became the nation's first Republican president.

Lincoln's election spread alarm throughout the Southern states, as they feared that a Republican president would not respect their rights or their properties. Secession activities began as early as December 1860 when South Carolina, the first of eleven states to withdraw, seceded from the Union even before Lincoln's inauguration in March 1861. Only six weeks after his inauguration, the Civil War began on April 12, 1861, with the famous shelling of Fort Sumter in the harbor at Charleston, South Carolina.

At the beginning of the war, the city of Alexandria was a vibrant typical southern city boasting a population of 12,652, with ninety-six commercial firms that produced everything from bark to tin ware. During the presidential campaign in the fall of 1860, the business-minded Alexandrians were decidedly pro-Union. However, when South Carolina seceded from the Union, Virginia soon followed suit with the people in Alexandria voting eight to one in favor of secession.[12] Within months, the Confederate capitol would move to Richmond, and Virginia would become one of the key states to form the Confederate States of America (CSA).

Because of Alexandria's strategic importance as both a port and railroad center, and its proximity to the U.S. Capitol, federal troops under the command of General Charles

Sanford of the New York State militia occupied the city on the morning of May 24, 1861, the day after the local vote to secede. The ease with which the Northern soldiers had occupied Alexandria pointed out the vulnerability of Washington itself, as both Alexandria and Washington were set in low marshy land bordered by high ground. Additionally, each was cursed with excellent accessibility from all directions, including the river. In response to these fears, the Union soon built a network of forts (e.g., Ft. Ward, Ft. Stevens, Ft. Dupont) totaling 162 forts and batteries that surrounded Washington, D.C. and Alexandria (in much the same way that the Beltway encircles it today) in an effort to protect it from a Confederate invasion. Alexandria was to remain in Union hands for the entire war.

The occupation of Alexandria forever changed the social and economic fabric of the old seaport town. For four years, the city experienced the longest continued military occupation by Union forces of any town within the Confederacy. Although there was little fighting near Alexandria, the influx of so many soldiers meant that residents could no longer continue the life of the old antebellum South. Upon taking office as the Military Governor of Virginia in 1862, General Slough instituted a curfew and a ban on the sale of alcohol and many other activities. Many of the white citizens, most of whom were Southern sympathizers, left town and fled south. The city became primarily a large depot or logistical center for moving supplies to the Union armies fighting in Virginia.

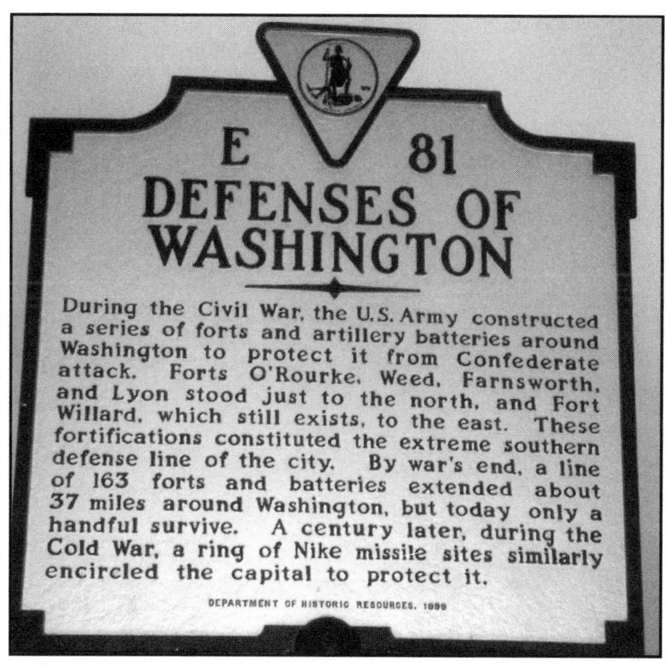

Defense of the Federal City During the Civil War

By 1863, only slightly more than one-third of the city's prewar population still lived in Alexandria. The majority of those who stayed behind were white women of largely secessionist disposition and their children, plus a large Negro population. And although a majority of the native population (white) left town as the war unfolded, a massive influx of colored refugees, carpetbagging profiteers, and Union soldiers swelled the city's population by more than ten thousand people, bringing the population up to 18,000 people.[13] But these were to be difficult times for the population that remained as the Army took over most public facilities, including churches.

Use of Churches During the War

During the Civil War, most churches in Alexandria were taken over and used as hospitals. The First Baptist Church (white) on Washington Street continued to hold services and continued functions for several months. But it was ultimately shut down and used as a Union hospital. The African Baptist Church was also ultimately closed to worship and used as a Union hospital and recruiting station. Christ Church, which had been the home church of George Washington and Robert E. Lee, before he left the city to lead the Confederate forces, was one of the few churches to have continued worship services during the war. The church was taken over by Union forces that conducted services using Union chaplains. It is not known whether regular parishioners were permitted to attend or not.

Most of the other churches went underground. The parishioners met in homes, in business establishments, or wherever it was convenient. Handling the influx of contrabands (slaves escaping from the South and being declared property of the Union) and providing them with food, shelter, and burial services became major activities of some churches. This was particularly true for the two colored churches, Baptists and Methodists, that existed at the start of the war.

During the Civil War, several other Negro churches emerged as the city was flooded with more and more colored contrabands. Beulah Baptist (or Second Baptist) was started in 1863. The church was initially built at 320 South Asaph Street shortly before the Emancipation Proclamation and at a time when African Americans were legally unable to buy property. Reverend Clem Robinson, the founding pastor of the church and a schoolteacher, used the church as a school for contraband during the war. Later in the Civil War the church property was confiscated and returned to the former owners. Following the Emancipation Proclamation, the trustees, exercising their legal rights, repurchased the property.

Third Baptist Church opened its doors in 1863 near the Potomac River in the Petersburg section of the city. The name Petersburg ostensibly came from the large number of contrabands who had come up from Petersburg, Virginia, to places within Union Army lines. The church later purchased a vacant church formerly owned by whites and moved to their current site at Prince and North Patrick Streets.

Similarly, Zion Baptist Church was organized in 1864. The church originally assembled in an old brick building east of the Wilkes Street Tunnel. The congregation later occupied a frame building, which was moved to the 700 block of South Lee Street. The current brick building was constructed around it. Reverend Robert Woodson was their first pastor.

Shiloh Baptist was organized in 1865 in the Toussaint L'Ouverture Military Hospital near Duke Street, just up the street from the African Baptist Church. The congregation later built a frame church on West and Duke Streets. They would build yet another brick structure at that site around the end of the century, and they occupy it today.[14]

Each church served a different role. The African Baptist Church in Alexandria was used as a recruiting station for colored soldiers during portions of the war. Recruitment of Negro soldiers, which was illegal at the beginning of the war, increased significantly after the release of the Emancipation Proclamation. The final proclamation, issued on January 1, 1863, was about three pages long. However, the essence of the document was contained in the second paragraph and said:

Beulah Baptist Church—1863

Third Baptist Church—1863

Zion Baptist Church—1864

Shiloh Baptist Church—1865

Other Colored Churches Started During the Civil War

> . . . That on the first day of January, in the year of our Lord one thousand eight hundred and sixty-three, all persons held as slaves within any state or designated part of a state, the persons whereof shall then be in rebellion against the United States, shall be then, thenceforward, and forever **free**; and the Executive government of the United States . . . will recognize and maintain the freedom of such persons, and will do no act . . . to suppress such persons, in any efforts they may make for their actual freedom. . . . And I further declare and make known, that such persons of suitable condition, will be received into the armed services of the United States. . . .

The Emancipation Proclamation served as a catalyst for the introduction of Negro soldiers into the conflict. Colored regiments originally commanded by white officers and designated the United States Colored Troops (USCT) were quickly raised by the War Department following the announcement. The 54th Massachusetts Regiment was the first colored unit organized in the North, and became perhaps the most famous Negro unit of the war. Their exploits in attacking Fort Wagner in South Carolina on July 18, 1863, were immortalized in the movie, *Glory*.

Approximately 180,000 Negro soldiers would eventually enter the war, comprising more than ten percent of all Union forces. Later in the war, Negroes became officers, but there were fewer than one hundred colored officers by the war's end.

Although the Proclamation technically only freed the slaves in the rebellious Confederate States such as Virginia (it did not apply to slaves in Union states, e.g., Maryland, or those of Union-held areas of the South), it made it apparent to everyone that slavery in the United States was on its last leg. With the Proclamation in 1863 came a massive exodus of slaves who moved into Alexandria and other Union camps. It is estimated that nationwide over 500,000 slaves would eventually leave the plantations and move into Union camps or Union-held territory for the remainder of the war.[15]

In addition to the refugees, Negro soldiers poured into Alexandria. Many of the colored troops arriving in Alexandria were injured and spent their last days at the L'Ouverture Hospital on Duke Street near the site of the current Shiloh Baptist Church. And while the L'Ouverture Hospital and the African Baptist Church served as hospitals for soldiers, Beulah Baptist Church on Washington Street served the newly liberated contraband civilian population that arrived behind Union lines in other ways. Beulah Baptist was the home church to Reverend Albert Gladwin, who was assigned as Superintendent of Contrabands in the city, responsible for their education, welfare, and burials.

A separate cemetery was opened for the contrabands on Washington Street where today the George Washington Parkway crosses over the Beltway at the foot of the Wilson Bridge. The site, referred to as the Freedmen or Contraband Cemetery, would eventually hold almost 2,500 persons who died during the period April 1862 to December 1865. In fact, 836 colored persons were buried there during its first year, 1862. It is reported that there was a severe epidemic of smallpox in Alexandria that year, which may have accounted for this large number. Slaves, freemen, contraband, and local Negro residents were buried there, including some members of the African Baptist Church.[16] The cemetery eventually fell into disrepair, and is today the location of a gas station.

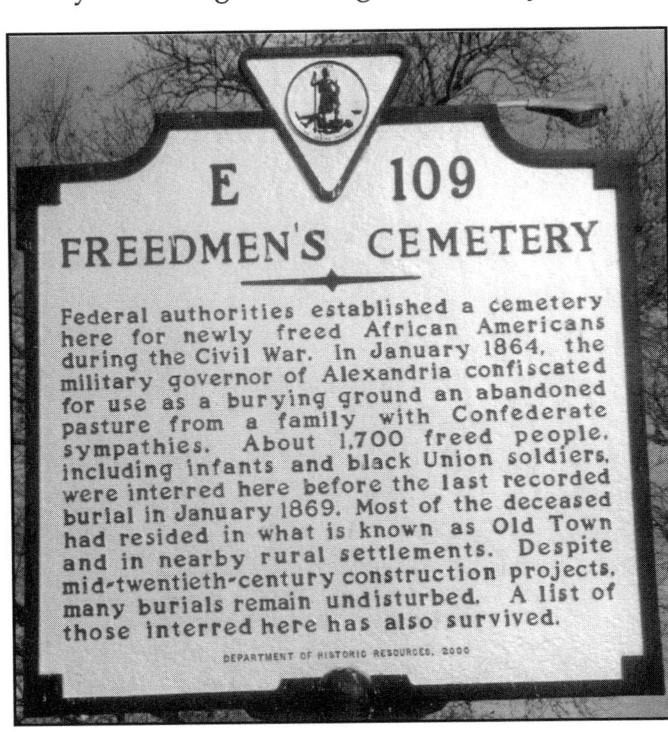

Freedmen's Cemetery

A New Pastor Arrives at the African Baptist Church

Shortly after the issuance of the Emancipation Proclamation and the massive influx of Negroes into Alexandria, a major change also took place at the African Baptist Church.

Reverend Sampson White, who was pastor of the church at the start of the Civil War, would soon leave for other duties and would be replaced by Reverend Samuel Madden who arrived in 1863 and would serve until 1896.

The new pastor, Reverend Madden, had been born to free parents, Mr. and Mrs. Willis Madden, in August 1829 in Culpepper County, Virginia. His home was near Brandy Station, a small town situated on current U.S. Route 29 about five miles south of Warrenton. He was the great-grandson of an 18th-century Irish immigrant, Mary Madden, and a Negro man. His parents, Willis and Kitty Madden, owned an eighty-seven-acre farm near Culpepper. Willis Madden was also the owner and operator of the famous Madden Tavern on the old Fredericksburg Road. The Maddens were a relatively prosperous family that had always been free and included ancestors who had fought in the American Revolutionary War.[17]

Reverend Madden lived in Virginia from the time of his birth until 1847 when, at the age of eighteen years old, he moved to Baltimore where he lived until 1852. In Baltimore, he earned a living as a school teacher. He also joined the now defunct Saratoga Street Baptist Church and served as clerk under the pastorate of the Reverend Noah Davis, a former Virginia slave, autobiographer, and noted preacher of the day.

Samuel Madden then went to school in Allegheny City, Pennsylvania, a suburb of Pittsburgh, where he remained until 1855. In Pennsylvania, he attended Western Theological Seminary, which had opened about thirty years prior to his entrance to educate individuals for the Christian ministry. From Western Theological Seminary, he graduated as both a minister and a teacher at the age of twenty-six.[18] After graduating from Western Theological Seminary, he returned to Baltimore and, while there, he was married briefly to a young lady identified only as Mrs. Madden. She passed away on February 15, 1859, in Baltimore, and was buried in Laurel Cemetery.

Reverend Samuel Madden

In 1863, in the midst of the Civil War, he arrived in Alexandria from Baltimore to pastor the African Baptist Church. Activities during his first year as pastor are not known. At that time the church was still in use as a hospital and recruiting station for Negro soldiers. By then, considerable damage had been inflicted on the edifice. According to a sworn testimony by Emily Lickett, one of the members who testified after the war:

> . . . they did a great deal of damage to the church; the floor was torn to pieces, the benches were burnt up and it was a perfect wreck when they left it. The windows were shattered out.

According to her testimony and that of others, the Union soldiers did not occupy the church for the duration of the war, but the dates of their departure and the resumption of services there is not known.[19]

Shortly after Reverend Madden arrived in Alexandria from Baltimore, he was commissioned as a chaplain in the Union Army. To obtain his commission, Reverend Madden wrote directly to President Abraham Lincoln in August 1864. On November 19, 1864, he received a letter from the Executive Mansion (White House) addressed to the Secretary of War requesting that Reverend Madden be assigned the position of Chaplain of the Freedmen's Hospital in Washington, D.C. His oath of office was taken December 1, 1864.[20]

Even as he was preaching at his new church in Alexandria and caring for the wounded in Washington, D.C., his boyhood home near Brandy Station was being ravaged by the war. Several battles were fought near his home, including the famous Battle of Brandy Station. This battle was the largest cavalry battle ever fought on the North American continent, with over 17,000 of the 22,000 soldiers involved belonging to the mounted horse cavalry branch.

During several of the battles fought near Brandy Station, the Union Army took horses, cattle, bacon, corn and other produce from his father's farm. His father, Willis Madden, reportedly begged them not to take his horses and food, but the soldiers pushed him aside and remarked: ". . . No colored person has ever owned a farm like this; you are just keeping it for someone else. . . ."[21] They then proceeded to take everything they wanted.

The National Archives in Washington, D.C., retains records that show that the U.S. Government repaid the Madden family after the war for damages done to the farm during these battles. After the war, persons who had not borne arms against the United

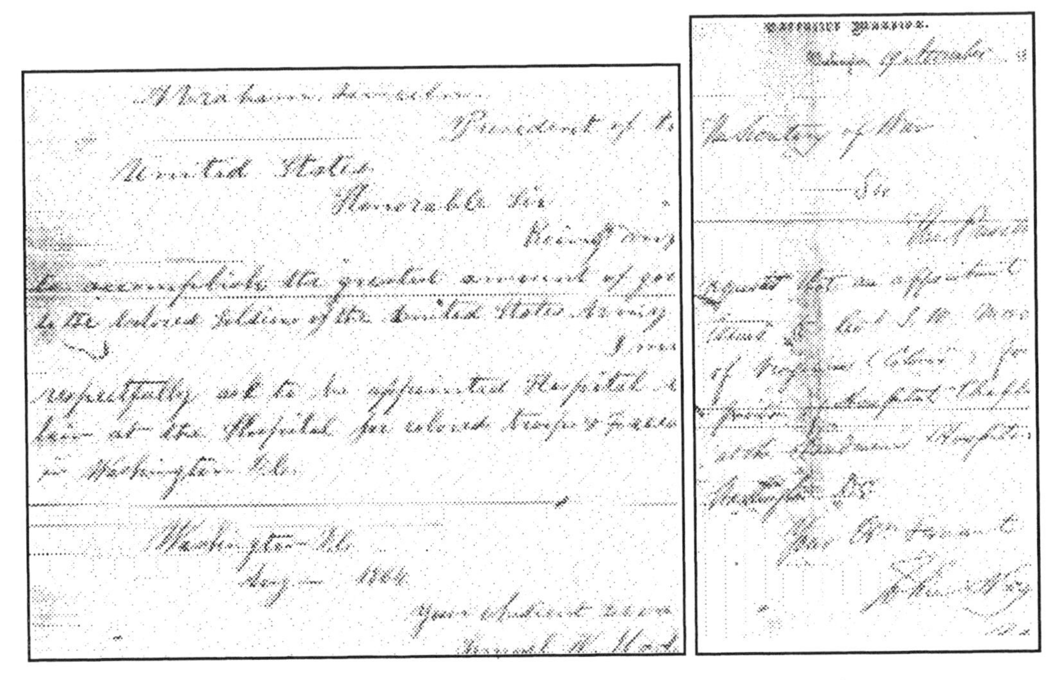

Abraham Lincoln
President of the
United States
Honorable Sir
Being ...
to accomplish the greatest amount of good
to the colored soldiers of the United States Army
I ...
respectfully ask to be appointed Hospital ...
at the Hospital for colored troops & freedmen
in Washington D.C.

Washington D.C.
Aug — 1864
Your obedient servant

Reverend Madden's Commissioning Records As Chaplain

States were entitled to an indemnity for damages or the loss of property. The Maddens claimed $2,440 in materials lost in the war that included a horse, a cart, bacon, farm produce and wood. The claim was settled later for a lesser amount.[22]

During the remainder of the war, Rev. Madden's activities and the activities at the African Baptist Church are not known. Records do show that the church sustained considerable damage to pews, broken windows, and damage to the walls.

Most other churches were still operating underground, meeting at homes or other secret locations. Reverend Madden may have held similar secret services for the colored Baptists, but records are nonexistent. During the war, even the conventions ceased meeting. The last entry (1861) for the African Baptist Church of Alexandria in the Potomac Baptist Convention minutes only notes that the church had 198 members at the beginning of the war. Thereafter, there were no reports on the African Baptist Church.[23]

Just as with Reverend Sampson White before him, Reverend Madden came to Alexandria from the 19th Street Baptist Church in Washington, D.C. Nineteenth Street Baptist had been formed in 1839 and remained the dominant Negro Baptist congregation in the District of Columbia for several years. Eventually, members of 19th Street broke away to form Fourth Baptist Church of Washington, D.C., later called Metropolitan Baptist, in 1863. In 1865, some members of Metropolitan Baptist split off to form Vermont Avenue Baptist Church. Thus, 19th Street, Metropolitan, and Vermont Avenue Baptist Churches are all related congregations.[24]

The End of the War and the Return to Normalcy

Most of the immediate area around Alexandria was spared heavy fighting, though there were major battles at Brandy Station near Culpepper, two Battles of Bull Run near Manassas, and a series of battles south of Alexandria near Fredericksburg. Additionally, there was a major battle at Fort Stevens in Washington, D.C., in 1864 where President Lincoln observed Union soldiers defeat Confederate General Jubal Early.

Finally, on April 9, 1865, General Ulysses S. Grant defeated General Robert E. Lee at Appomattox Courthouse, and the war soon ended!

When news of the war's end reached Alexandria, Union soldiers and sympathizers celebrated wildly in the streets. A victory parade formed at the end of North Washington Street and wound its way through the city. The celebration among Negroes, however, was short-lived. For just five days after the surrender, President Abraham Lincoln was assassinated at Ford's Theater in Washington, D.C., by John Wilkes Booth. The news of the assassination of this beloved friend of the Negro, the Great Emancipator, was the source of great outpouring of grief throughout most of the country and the world. His body was borne back via train to Springfield, Illinois, for burial. The funeral coach that carried his body had been constructed in Alexandria at the United States Military Railroad Yard at the corner of Duke and Alfred Streets adjacent to the African Baptist Church. Today, the new sanctuary of the colored Baptist sits on that spot.

At war's end, the city of Alexandria found itself in a state of physical, mental and economic depression. With the withdrawal of most of the troops, little commerce remained.

Hundreds of Confederate troops, many missing limbs, faced the daunting prospect of beginning life anew. The town was filled with refugees, white and colored, and the city was forced to set up charity soup kitchens each winter to prevent starvation. The surrounding landscape was totally denuded of trees. The Alexandria harbor lay in ruins.

Beginning in the summer of 1865, the outlying forts, blockhouses, and army camps were dismantled and surplus materials were sold at public auction. Gradually, the wounded Confederate soldiers and the Southern sympathizers who had fled the city returned. They later constructed a monument to the soldiers who fought the "Lost Cause." The monument, named *Appomattox,* was placed near the front of Alexandria Baptist Church, the site where the early Baptists—white and Negro—had begun worship in 1803.

**Appomattox:
Monument to the "Lost Cause"**

The war had settled two issues: (1) that the nation would remain whole, and (2) that slavery was dead. The end of slavery was codified in the 13th Amendment, which was not ratified until December 1865 by the required number of states. It read:

Neither slavery nor involuntary servitude, except as a punishment for crime whereof the party shall have been duly convicted, shall exist within the United States, or any place subject to their jurisdiction.

At war's end, the population of Alexandria was nearly fifty percent Negro due to the massive influx of colored freedmen. With the return of pro-Confederate whites, the situation introduced racial tensions. A riot between Negroes and former Confederate soldiers broke out on Christmas day in 1865, resulting in a call by many of the citizens for more Union troops to maintain order. Union troops arrived to keep order and continued to occupy Alexandria for several years. The city and the state of Virginia would finally be admitted back into the Union in 1870, five years after the end of the war.

Slowly, things returned to normal in Alexandria. Worship services resumed at the colored churches and conventions began to hold meetings again. At the African Baptist Church, services were held, and trustees and deacons met. Although the earliest date that deacons served at the African Baptist Church is not known, at least one deacon has been identified who served during this period. Deacon Pompey Jackson (born in 1836) served as a deacon shortly after the war.

The choir also rehearsed and sang. Records are also not specific as to the founding date of the first choir—later called the Senior Choir—that sang during this period. Most records of its earliest existence were destroyed in a fire that swept through the church office shortly after the Civil War. Nevertheless, records do suggest that the choir was likely formed around 1855, but was clearly in existence late in 1865 when they performed at the Baptist convention held at the church.[25] The choir's first recorded director was Reverend Jacklyn Strange (1837–1923), a Methodist minister and prominent member of Roberts Memorial Methodist Church on Washington Street.

Though most conventions had ceased meeting during the war, one of the first actions of the First African Baptist Church of Alexandria after the war's end was to host the annual convention of the American Baptist Missionary Convention, one of the regional conventions to which it belonged. The 25th anniversary of the convention was held in Alexandria on August 19–30, 1865.[26]

Reverend Jacklyn Strange

Elder Edmond Kelly (church affiliation unknown) attended the convention and wrote several letters home that give some insights into the activities. According to the letters of Elder Kelly, the convention met first on August 19 at First Colored Baptist Meeting-House in Alexandria, with Reverend L.A. Grimes of Boston as Moderator, and Rev. William T. Dixon of Brooklyn, New York, as Recording Secretary. Delegates who attended were from Virginia, Tennessee, and Georgia, representing churches that had previously joined. Also, several new churches attended from Richmond, Petersburg, Savannah, and Nashville, and each was granted membership.

Elder Kelly noted in his letters that things were already beginning to improve in Alexandria, just two months after the war ended. The Negro family with whom he was staying (unnamed) owned two houses in the city valued at $500 each. Four years earlier they had both been slaves living near Warrenton, Virginia. They were not members of the Colored Baptist Church, but belonged to Beulah Baptist (1863) that was pastored by Reverend Robinson. Elder Kelly spoke of the change in laws and practices he observed when traveling since the last meeting of the convention and commented on the improvements in space and access for Negroes on public transportation.

Following the close of the convention, a delegation of fourteen persons, including Elder Kelly, went to meet with President Andrew Johnson at the White House. President Johnson had replaced the recently assassinated Abraham Lincoln and met with the group to discuss race relations. Reverend Madden, as pastor of the African Baptist Church and host of the convention, also attended the meeting with Elder Kelly and the convention delegates.

During the meeting, President Johnson indicated that equality would eventually come to Negroes, but he was not specific on a time table or method. The period of Reconstruction that was to follow, it was thought, would offer great promise for colored equality. However, it would eventually fail and full equality would have to wait another one hundred years.

Activities at the African Baptist Church During Reconstruction

The period following the war was called Reconstruction and officially covered the period 1865–1876. The Reconstruction period was marked by a variety of events that affected Negroes in Virginia and elsewhere. This era was the first period in U.S. history in which Negroes were allowed to vote, and those in Alexandria voted for the referendum to readmit Virginia into the Union in 1870—ten years after initial secession.

While voting was a newfound liberty, other liberties were slow to come. Throughout the Reconstruction period, the political state of affairs remained unstable with respect to the Negro issue and, given little guidance from Washington, southern whites turned to the traditional political leaders for reorganizing their governments. The regimes that evolved looked suspiciously like those of the antebellum period. Slavery was abolished, but each reconstructed southern state government adopted a set of Black Codes to regulate the rights and privileges of the freedmen. Varying from state to state, these codes treated Negroes as inferior, with restrictions on whether they could own land, or bear arms. Negroes could still be bound out in servitude for vagrancy or other small infractions or offenses.

Negro gains in social equality during Reconstruction were very slow and gradual. Colored persons could now legally marry, and the "jump-the-broom" variety of weddings gave way to official weddings before ministers and magistrates. Negroes quietly seceded from white churches and formed their own places of worship. But, without land or money, most freedmen had to continue working for white masters. Sharecropping gradually became the accepted labor arrangement in most southern states. Planters, short of cash, preferred it because it did not require them to pay cash wages. Many Negroes accepted sharecropping because they could live in cabins on tracts of land they rented, and they had independence in choosing what to plant and how to cultivate that which they planted.

By 1867, the return to normalcy made possible by Reconstruction was beginning to affect the life of Reverend Madden. At this time, he had been at African Baptist Church for four years, and in addition to pastoring at the church, he was now prepared to take on additional responsibilities. So, on February 21, 1867, Reverend Madden, at thirty-eight years old, was united in holy matrimony (his second marriage) to Miss Matilda A. Jones of Washington, D.C. Matilda was the daughter of Mr. and Mrs. Alfred Jones who were free at the time of her birth. Her father, an educated man, was a prosperous merchant in Washington, D.C., and was the first colored trustee of public schools in the District. Matilda's father fathered 22 children, by two marriages. Matilda was a graduate of Oberlin College in Ohio. After marrying and moving to Alexandria with her new husband, she became a teacher in Alexandria and later became a principal of the Hallowell School for Negro girls.

The new Mrs. Matilda Madden, the church's first lady, was described as a comforter and helpmate to her husband with the numerous tasks that he had to perform. Though quiet, humble, and sympathetic, she was positive, sincere, and courageous. Reverend and Mrs. Madden became parents of nine children—five boys and four girls. In order, they were Willis, Alfred, Samuel, Osceola, Jesse and Jeanie (twins), Ellicott, Eddith, and Anna Gertrude. The son Jesse, who was born in 1877, would later marry Lelia Truatt, the daughter of Reverend Alexander Truatt, the minister who would succeed Reverend Madden as pastor near the end of the century.

Church records of some of the activities of the African Baptist Church during the early years of Reverend Madden's ministry, such as baptisms, building projects, etc., have not been found. A fire in the church office is reported to have burned official office materials. Edgar Johnson, then a member, testified under oath at a subsequent investigation by the U.S. government that:

> . . . the records of the church were destroyed by a fire after the close of the war when the office of the secretary of the church was burned. . . .[27]

However, it is believed that by then the church had begun to take on the form of a contemporary church with trustees, deacons and choirs.

Music had always been an integral part of worship among Negro congregations. The type of music that was performed is not documented. By 1860, spirituals had become an integral part of colored singing on the plantations. Additionally, within the white churches where Negroes worshipped, they were exposed to the hymns and anthems sung in those congregations. Many such songs were then "made over" by Negroes or improvised to meet the desires of the colored churches. The improvisations included molding the rhythms and harmonies to reflect Negro styles and the use of "call and response" techniques borrowed from African singing. Gospel and some other religious music forms were still another seventy-five years away.

While church minutes of the 1865–1870 time frame are missing, minutes of 1872–1875 are available and provide an indication of life in the church during this era. The church's early preoccupation with membership and discipline so common in the church's beginning in 1803 remained in effect during the Reconstruction period.

At every meeting, most of the business conducted concerned members who were brought up on charges and dismissed or excluded for behavior against the church. For example, at the regular meeting in January 1872, Brother Douglas and Sister Rector were notified to settle a dispute between them by the next church meeting or the church would have to settle their differences for them. But, at the February meeting Sister Rector and Brother Douglas still had not settled their dispute so they were given another month to settle their differences. The church continued to serve as a clearinghouse for settling private disputes just as it had done in the previous seventy years.

Also, joining the church was still a fairly formal process that required an individual to come before the congregation, describe what the Lord had done in their lives, and their reasons for wanting to join this particular church. At a January 1872 meeting, Miss Sallie Seals, Mrs. Ann Nelson and Mrs. Martha Hampshire came forward and related their hopes in the Lord and were received as candidates for baptism. Sister Annie Strawther also spoke and was received by Christian experience.

Discipline remained a big issue in the African Baptist Church as it had from the church's inception. The right hand of fellowship was withdrawn from one brother for selling whiskey and permitting gambling in his home. Sister Mary Atley who had earlier been excluded was restored to the church. In early 1873, Brother James Webster, one of the trustees who had signed the deed of purchase back in 1853, offered a resolution that any member of the church caught in adultery be excluded for six months. The resolution was discussed, back and forth, until it was referred back to the individual making the motion for reconsideration.

At a meeting in 1873, Brother Douglas, who had been brought before the church for a disagreement with one of the ladies of the church, was silenced for not coming to order when directed so by the Moderator. However, within the next several months, he would be called upon to become the church clerk, after several clerks resigned and he became the next most acceptable candidate.

Activities During Church Business Meetings: 1870s

Occasionally, non–discipline related business was discussed during the church meetings. In 1872, the Deacon Board, which is believed to have come into existence just after the war, proposed that the church adopt the regular church manual for its rules of government. This manual, which described procedures and rules of conduct for church members much like a constitution, was the basis of many of the expulsions. It also contained detailed instructions for the conduct of church business. For example, one of its provisions was that any person desiring to speak or make a motion must come forward to a position above the stove, before he could be heard. During that summer of 1872, the Deacons also announced that they planned to take an offering for the poor every Communion Sunday. This was the first reference to collection of a "Poor Saints" offering on Communion Sunday, a practice that has continued now for over 125 years.

The church also agreed to take a collection on the third Sabbath of each month for repairing the church. A committee of seven was appointed to devise plans for these repairs, and to bring the plans before the church for approval. The committee appointed by the Pastor included James Webster, George Seaton, George Simms, James Tancil, John Taylor, and John Scroggans. Beginning in March 1872, money was collected on the first Sunday of each month for building repairs. Additionally, fifteen dollars from the central treasury was given to the Sunday School, and fifty dollars was deposited in an account for the missionaries.

Though Reverend Madden's tenure as pastor appears to have been rather successful and relatively free of conflict, after nine years he offered his resignation to the church on April 19, 1872. The cause of the proposed resignation is not known. However, the church did not accept the resignation, and instead offered Reverend Madden an increase in salary to $600 per year. In June, a special call meeting was held to consider ways of paying the $600 as the church's small budget was not structured to accommodate such a large expense.

The church soon passed a resolution that did away with preaching in the afternoon. The church had been holding two services each Sunday, one at 11:00 a.m. and a second service in the afternoon. Over the years, afternoon services would be held for several years, discontinued, then resurrected. The third Sunday in March 1873 was set aside for fasting and prayer. The church minutes reported a prosperous Sunday school, and church membership grew to over 400 persons by 1873. The next year, there was an unexplained boom in the membership with over 100 persons joining. In fact, over ninety new members were added to the rolls during the three-month period of May through July.

The number of people joining is shown in the following table:

Members Fellowshipped During May–July 1874

	Baptism	Letter	Experience	Restored
May	17	2	1	-
June	54	-	-	-
July	14	-	-	3
Total	85	2	1	3

As the membership grew, so did the need to assist various members with personal problems. A loan of seven dollars was granted to Brother Wells with which to go on a missionary tour. And Brother Addison Blackburn asked for aid in bringing his son home for burial. The sum of $5.78 was taken up to assist him.

In the fall of 1874, the business activities of the church were published and distributed, causing a bit of consternation within the congregation. A committee composed of George W. Simms, Philip Turner, and James Webster was appointed to investigate the activities of the editor and ascertain who was responsible for the unauthorized release of the church's business activities. At the next meeting, the committee reported that Brother Lumpkin and Brother Lee were the guilty parties. Actions taken against them were not reported.

Other Key Leaders from the Reconstruction Era

Most contemporary churches today have an assortment of assistant or associate ministers to assist the Pastor, but churches during Reconstruction did not have that luxury. Churches would occasionally ordain another minister within their ranks, but usually, and within a short time, that individual would leave to pastor another church with an open pulpit. There were generally more pulpits than ministers. In 1873, the African Baptist Church of Alexandria granted licenses to preach to Brother Wilson Gordon and later to Brother Lawrence Laws, both of whom appear to have left shortly thereafter.

Perhaps the most prominent person ordained during this era had come in 1872 when the congregation ordained Brother Harvey Johnson. A special council was convened late in that year to consider the ordination of Brother Johnson as a minister, and the council found him favorable. He had been born on August 4, 1843, in Fauquier County, to Tom and Harriet Johnson, who were both slaves on a local plantation. His family moved to Alexandria at the end of the Civil War, and he later joined the African Baptist Church. He received a call to preach and was ordained on November 14, 1872.[28]

Reverend Johnson attended Wayland Theological Seminary in Washington, D.C., entering in 1868 and graduating with honors in 1872. While in school, he spent a brief time working at rural churches in Maryland and Virginia, and with the Home Mission Society.

In Baltimore, the Reverend William P. Thomas, then pastor of Union Baptist Church, died unexpectedly at the age of thirty-two. The church issued a call to the Reverend Harvey Johnson, recently ordained by the African Baptist Church, in November 1872, which he accepted. He served as pastor at Union Baptist for fifty years, helping the church to grow into one of the larger Baptist churches in Baltimore with over 3,000 members. Perhaps his greatest legacy was his role in Civil Rights, where he initiated several lawsuits that changed the lives of Negroes in Maryland and the surrounding area.

Reverend Harvey Johnson, Ordained by the African Baptist Church

In addition to ministers, the African Baptist Church was home to other prominent Negro families during Reconstruction. George L. Seaton, a member of the Deacon Board, was one of the more prominent Negroes in Alexandria during the last half of the 19th century. George Seaton was born in 1826 to free Negro parents. His mother, Lucinda, had been a slave to George and Martha Washington, and was freed by Martha when Lucinda was an infant. The 1860 Census listed George Seaton as a free man. He was then 34 and his wife Maria was 35. Six children lived with them ranging from one to 13 years, and he owned real estate that totaled $4,000.[29]

By 1868, George Seaton had become a prominent free master carpenter and had founded the Colored Building Association. He lived at 404 South Royal Street in an area of the city called Hayti, located about six blocks from the church. He built several classical Greek revival–style homes including one at 323 South St. Asaph Street, on the northwest corner of Wolfe and St. Asaph Streets.

Residence by George L. Seaton, a Deacon at African Baptist Church

Two of Mr. Seaton's legacies as a builder were the colored schools he designed to educate Alexandria's Negro population during Reconstruction and well into the 20th century.[30] By 1871, there were two public schools for the Negro community, which had been started by the Freedmen's Bureau around the end of the Civil War. The Snowden School for Negro boys, built in 1867, was located on Pitt Street between Gibbon and Franklin Streets. The school was a two-story, well-built frame building with six classrooms, designed to accommodate fifty pupils in each room. The school had an assembly hall and was appropriately furnished. The average attendance was approximately 130 pupils. A board of trustees consisting of Negro citizens owned the building. William F. Powell was the school's first principal, and still served in 1871, with Misses Sarah A. Gray and Carrie Claggett listed as assistant teachers. Originally, the school was called the Seaton School, named after its builder. The building continued to be called the Seaton Building occasionally even after it was renamed, giving rise to some confusion.

The Hallowell School for Negro girls, also built by George Seaton in 1867, was located on North Alfred Street between Princess and Oronoco Streets. This building looked very much like the Seaton building for boys. It was frequently called the Lee Building giving rise to even more confusion through the years, as there was also a Lee School for white girls located elsewhere in the city. The title to the Hallowell School or the Lee Building was also held by a board of trustees consisting of Negro citizens. In the early years, Mrs. Matilda A. Madden, the wife of the pastor at African Baptist Church, was principal, while Mrs. Jane A. Crouch and Miss Harriett Douglas were listed as assistant teachers. Enrollment at the Hallowell School was about 135 students.

While the construction of the first two public schools for Negroes were George Seaton's most visible legacies, he also founded the local Negro Young Men's Christian Association (YMCA) and was a member of the Virginia State Legislature in 1877–78. He is remembered also for serving as a juror during the trial of Confederate President Jefferson Davis while a member of the Virginia State Legislature.[31]

George L. Seaton died on July 5, 1881, and his funeral was held the following Thursday at the African Baptist Church. According to the *Washington Post,* one of the fiercest thunderstorms ever experienced in Alexandria prevailed that afternoon. The paper is quoted as saying ". . . The horses attached to the hearse and carriages became frightened at the heavy peals of thunder and it was said at the time that lightning ran into the grave while the body was being lowered into it." Mr. Seaton, a Republican who had been worth over $100,000 during his years in the Virginia legislature, was buried in a local cemetery.

Chapter Five

1875–1900: The Jim Crow Years

Keep me as the apple of the eye, hide me . . . from the wicked that oppress me. . . .

Psalm 17

The period following Reconstruction was characterized by tremendous growth at the African Baptist Church in membership and in the physical facility. Two dynamic leaders would serve as pastors, as the old pastor would be replaced late in the century by a newer one. However, the overarching issue that affected the activities of all Negroes within the church and within the community was the arrival of "Jim Crow Laws." The growth and progress experienced by the church may have been even greater, except for the constraints these policies imposed.

The Arrival of Jim Crow

The Reconstruction era following the Civil War officially spanned the years 1865 to 1876, and with its end came a withdrawal of all Union troops from the South. Troops had already been withdrawn from Alexandria, with the readmission of Virginia into the Union a couple of years earlier. And with the withdrawal of troops, white oppression descended like a blanket on the entire South.

For many colored persons, fleeing to a better place in the North or the Midwest was the only option. As a result, in the late 1870s, Negroes began the first massive migration in the nation's history, with over 50,000 Negroes leaving the South in a few short months—many headed for Kansas. Others sought to form a separate state. Oklahoma was still a United States Territory at that time, and many sought to establish all-Negro towns in that area, with Langston and Boley being two of the more famous towns started in this way.[1]

Negro voting privileges were continually diluted by a series of practices that effectively disenfranchised them. There was widespread intimidation of black people that, in its most horrid form, was lynching. During this era, there were up to 150 lynchings throughout the South during some years.[2] In Virginia, more lynchings occurred in southwest Virginia than in any other section, even though the number of blacks there was much lower. In total, over one hundred lynchings were held in the state of Virginia before the practice ended. The era of Jim Crow had arrived!

Lynching in Charleston, SC, January 1881

During this era, Frederick Douglass continued to serve as the unofficial spokesperson for the Negro. He had been one of the foremost leaders of the abolitionist movement, which fought to end slavery within the United States in the decades prior to the Civil War. In the 1870s and 1880s, he continued the battle against the daily humiliations that Negroes were forced to endure throughout the country. Whenever he encountered discriminatory practices in a restaurant, hotel, or railway car, he would write a letter of protest to the local newspapers. In such ways, he kept the issue of the mistreatment of Negroes before the American public.

As had been the case during slavery, the church remained the major source for stability within the Negro community and was the source of most of its leaders. Associations of Negro churches of various denominations took the lead in educating Negroes—particularly at the college level. The Baptists in Virginia founded Virginia Union in 1865, the same year the Baptists in North Carolina had opened Shaw University.

Prior to 1870, there were only eight to ten Negro colleges in the entire country (e.g., Lincoln University founded in 1837 by Quakers); but, in the late 1870s and 1880s a rash of new colleges were opened, created through religious affiliations. Church-related schools, located primarily in the southern states, included Bennett (1873), Knoxville College (1875), Stillman (1876), Livingstone College (1879), Florida Memorial (1879), Morris Brown (1881), and Lane (1882). For the next several decades, these and similar church-supported colleges would remain primary sources of college education for a large portion of the Negroes in America. Without them and the church, it is not clear what would have happened to a still-oppressed people suffering under a new form of bondage called Jim Crow.

During the post-Reconstruction era, there were also some new educational opportunities for Negroes locally in the city of Alexandria. For example, in 1884 the city of Alexandria purchased the old Alexandria Academy, which had opened originally in 1785 as one of the first free schools in Virginia. The building was located at the corner of Washington and Wolfe Streets, about four blocks from the First African Baptist Church. The free schools continued to function until the end of the century.

In addition to their education, another pressing local need for Negroes during post-Reconstruction was where to bury their dead. During the Civil War and several years thereafter, most of the colored persons who had flooded the city were buried at the Contraband Cemetery on Washington Street near the current Beltway. But, by 1870, the Contraband Cemetery had been abandoned and Negroes were looking for new sites.

In the early 1880s, several Negroes in Alexandria formed an association called the "Silver Leaf Society of Alexandria" for colored persons. They petitioned Fairfax County Court for a charter for a Colored Cemetery Association in order to open a cemetery.[3] The president of the new society was Mr. Henry C. Boyd, then a deacon at the African Baptist Church. The Baptist Cemetery that was opened in the vicinity of Duke Street and Reichers Lane was operational for many years, though records of all who are interred there have not been found. This cemetery was also eventually abandoned and continued a downward spiral until an African American Heritage Park was dedicated on the site late in the 20th century.

African American Heritage Park

Growth Under Reverend Madden: 1870–1880

As the Jim Crow era began, the African Baptist Church was continuing to participate in international missionary efforts through its membership in the Virginia Baptist State Convention. The Virginia Baptist State Convention had been organized on May 4, 1867, at Zion Baptist Church in Portsmouth, Virginia. From its earliest inception the Virginia Baptist State Convention has had the work of foreign missions as one of its primary objectives.

Membership within the First African Baptist Church, which was also called the First Colored Baptist Church, grew from 500 in 1874 to 661 by 1878. Members were coming from all of the existing Negro neighborhoods within the city, and also from "out in the country." Alfred Street was a fast-growing church and Reverend Madden was a busy preacher splitting his time between Alfred Street and Bethlehem Baptist, a sister church that he assisted in getting started.

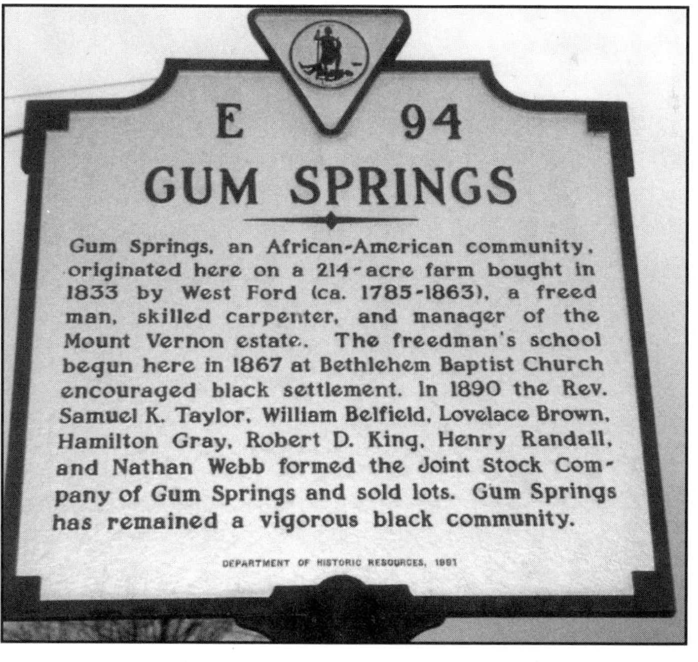

Bethlehem Baptist at Gum Springs

Bethlehem Baptist Church in the Gum Springs area of Fairfax County was formed in 1863 in the midst of the Civil War. The church was started by Negro churchgoers and included many who were descendants of those who had been freed from Mount Vernon. Samuel K. Taylor, a former slave from Caroline

County, Virginia, not yet ordained, was their spiritual leader. After escaping from slavery in Caroline County, Samuel Taylor arrived in Gum Springs where he continued his ministry—meeting in various homes to hold worship services. It was not until the end of the war that a building for worship was constructed.

Many of the first members of Bethlehem Baptist were also former members of First African Baptist Church who had been dismissed to unite with this new fellowship. As Brother Taylor was not an ordained minister, Reverend Madden served as an itinerant minister and looked upon Gum Springs with fatherly love, performing Holy Communion and baptisms there until Samuel Taylor's ordination in 1882. The relationship between the two ministers was that of a close-knit family and Bethlehem Baptist Church was to continue a close relationship with First African Baptist Church for the next one hundred years. During portions of that period, Bethlehem Baptist used the baptismal pool at African Baptist Church until they obtained one of their own.

The Remodeled First African Baptist Church

In addition to preaching at First African Baptist Church and sometimes at Gum Springs, Reverend Madden was busy with conventions and occupied with a major building project. In addition to belonging to the Virginia Baptist State Convention, the First African Baptist Church still belonged to the American Baptist Missionary Society that met at the African Baptist Church in 1865 at the end of the war. Almost thirty years later, desiring to invite the national convention to meet there again for its 1883–84 convention, the First African Baptist Church undertook an expansion program in the early 1880s. The additional building projects left the facility looking very close to how it appeared when many of the current, older members joined the church in the mid-20th century.

Prior to the remodeling, the then existing structure, built in 1855, was a brick structure, measuring approximately forty-one feet wide by sixty-two feet long. It sat on two adjoining lots, eighteen and twenty-five feet wide. The lots were obtained in 1818 and 1842, respectively. For the convention meeting, a larger edifice was constructed by members, probably without foundation or basement, between 1881 and 1884. This building was constructed surrounding the 1855 building and apparently the old building was torn down as the new building neared completion. In testimony given later during a damage claim against the U.S. government, persons reported that the newer building was a little wider and closer to the street than the old church.[4]

In the early 1880s, the name of the church changed again from First African Baptist Church to Alfred Street Baptist Church to avoid confusion with the First Baptist Church (white) that was located only four blocks away. Over time, the church had been known by several names: the Colored Baptist Society, the African Baptist Church, the Colored Baptist Church, and the First Colored Baptist Church. The new name reflected that of the street on which the church was located. Alfred Street had been named for King Alfred the Great, the Anglo-Saxon King of England (849–899) who fought the Vikings.

Around the early 1880s, the church members decided to excavate a basement under the new church. The Number One Willing Workers' Club was organized in June of 1880 to aid the minister and church in raising funds to excavate the basement, and add a vestibule and a new church front.[5] In addition to raising funds, the Willing Workers also assisted with the actual construction. The exact dates for each of these additions are not clear and estimates range from the 1880 time frame to 1887, according to varying sources. At some time between 1878 and 1890, the organ chamber, which remains today, was added.

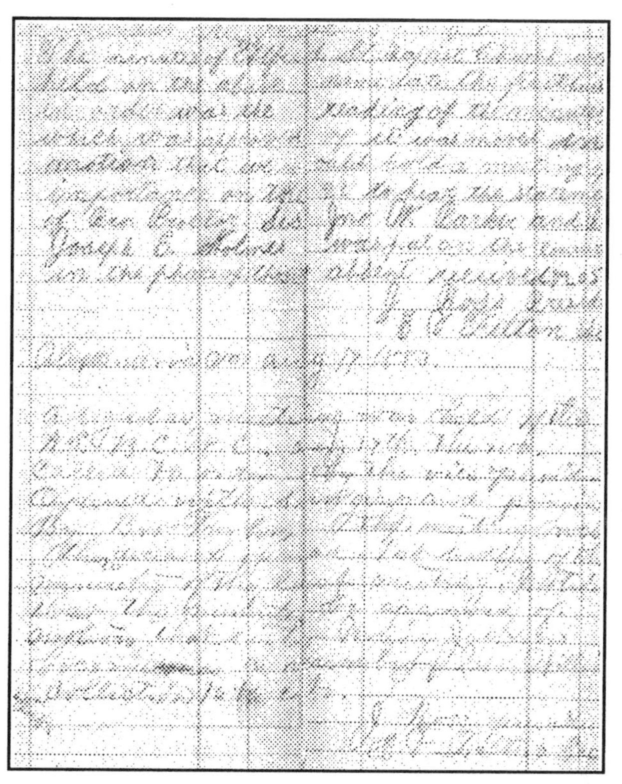

Minutes from the Willing Workers' Club

Based on historical maps, the configuration of the building at 313 South Alfred Street experienced several changes during this period. Until 1877, the front of the church was set back several feet from the street. By 1891, the front abutted the property line along the street as seen today. Thus, it was likely that there was the addition of a vestibule, making the newer building approximately forty feet wide and seventy feet long. The church remained in this configuration for most of the next fifty to sixty years.

Minutes of the Number One Willing Workers' Club, which raised the money to build the basement under the church, provide a detailed account of contributions. The Club met regularly, sometimes weekly, to elect officers and plan fund-raisers. From their minutes, it appears that "dues" were required, and a listing of all who contributed is provided in the minutes.

At its peak, about seventy-five members belonged to the Willing Workers' Club, with James Morris serving as president in 1883 and E.V. Felton serving as secretary. Dues appeared to have been ten cents, and at a typical meeting the club might collect $1.25. In May 1883, the club decided to have a festival as a fund-raiser and selected Sister M.L. Davis as chair for that event. Her committee consisted of eight other persons, including J. Homes who was elected Doorkeeper and P. Taylor who was Assistant Doorkeeper.

Thomas Day became the new president of the Willing Workers in 1884, with J. S. Pratt as secretary. In February of that year the club held a dinner as a fund-raiser in which members contributed food items. Sister Milly Barker baked a cake, while Sister Betty Tyler provided three pounds of croakers (fish). Sister L. Davis prepared two chickens, while Sister Alice Garrad provided four dozen of her best rolls. At the July Rally, $27 was raised, which contributed to a total of about $45 for the first half of the year.

Reverend Madden's Residence on South St. Asaph Street

The Willing Workers would remain a church auxiliary for many years after the original basement construction was completed. In subsequent years, they would continue to assist with financial projects whenever called upon by the church.

Church Practices During the Late 1880s

Financial records for the newly named church indicated that in the 1880s finances remained strained, as was the case during the early years. No central treasury was maintained; instead, a series of collections were taken for specific purposes. For example, there was a special collection and a special account for the pastor. From this collection the pastor's salary was paid, as was the purchase of Communion elements. There was a special offering and account for the poor, and another offering or special account for the missionaries. The Sunday School would maintain a separate account, and yet another account would be maintained for miscellaneous expenses. When one account was depleted, the church body would make a motion to have one account (e.g., organist fund) loan money to another (e.g., the account for the poor), or vice versa.

In 1887, Reverend Madden, now in his twenty-fourth year, was paid $25 dollars twice each month, plus a few additional dollars for miscellaneous services. From his annual salary of $650, he was charged for Communion expenses that amounted to approximately $10–15 a year. The pastor now lived on South St. Asaph Street, about five blocks from the church.

The Poor Saints Offering was now collected each Sunday and amounted to about one to two dollars. At that time, these funds were used for a variety of purposes that included providing assistance to the needy to have a loved one returned home for burial. Assistance with funeral expenses was common during this era. Also, house fires were still frequent, and money would be given to persons who had been "burned out." During this time, too, persons designated as "poor saints" received a monthly stipend of one or two dollars for living expenses. Sister Ball, Sister Mitchell, and Brother Williams were

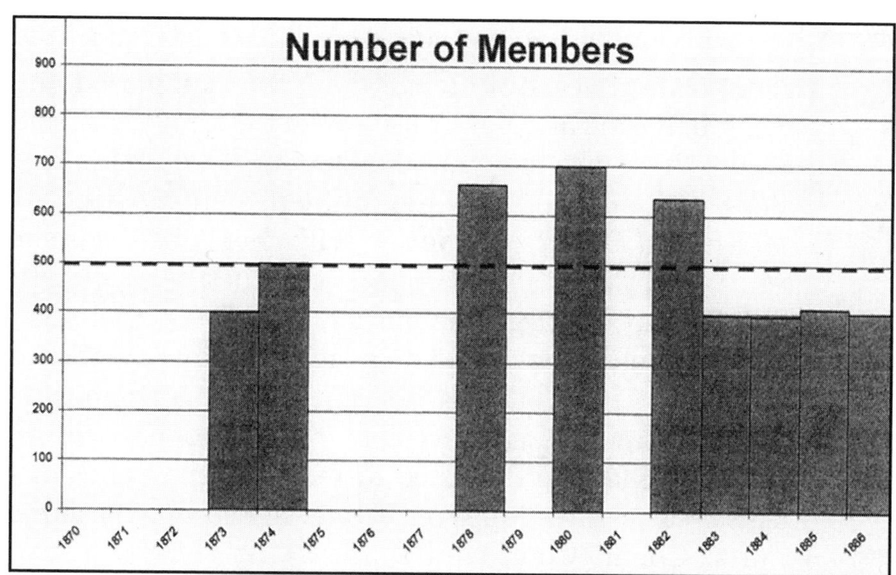

Membership During the 1870s–1880s

some of the persons identified in this category. Annual expenses in the Poor Saints Offering account averaged $65 to $70 a year.

The organist fund was, of course, to pay the musician. This account generally totaled about $35 for the entire year. The organist would be paid eight to ten dollars per quarter, based on the number of services held, to include special services. Another miscellaneous expense for the church was the Old Folks Home. The church maintained a special collection for the home and donated about $40–50 per year to this cause. The Missionary Fund totaled about $15 to $25 per year and most of these funds were expended for attendance at conventions such as the Northern Virginia Baptist Association.

According to church minutes, the church continued to withdraw the right hand of fellowship from members who committed acts unbecoming to Christians. Other misdemeanors that might result in dismission were non-church attendance, using abusive language, or swearing on the streets. One could also be brought before the church for civil offenses, or for taking someone to court without first trying to have the issue resolved in church. For example, the church reprimanded Brother Blackwell for beating his wife in the mayor's office. Sister Blackwell was then reprimanded by the church for taking her husband to court without first having consulted the church.

The strict adherence to the principles of church discipline began to wear on the congregation. Many members refused to come before the Deacon Board as required by church policy. The records show that members began to leave the church rather than humble themselves before the deacons and beg for forgiveness in order to be restored. Membership growth and drop-off during this era are illustrated above.[6]

By 1886, membership had dropped from a high of almost 700 around 1880 to approximately 400 persons. This represented a reduction in the membership of almost one-half, yet the church continued with the expulsions in spite of the large numbers of departures.

During his tenure as pastor of Alfred Street, Reverend Madden performed numerous weddings. Perhaps one of the more elaborate weddings was the one he performed at Mount Vernon, George Washington's estate home. On October 25, 1888, Reverend Madden conducted the wedding of Sarah Johnson, a member of Alfred Street Baptist Church, to Mr. William Robinson in an elaborate ceremony at Mount Vernon.[7]

Sarah had been born a slave at Mount Vernon in 1844, after the estate had been

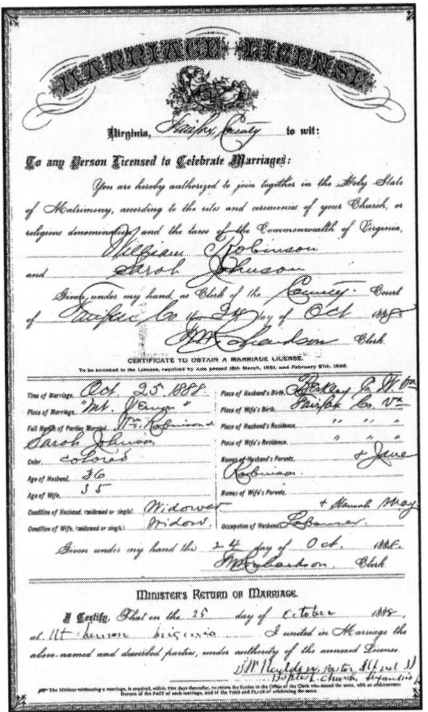

MARRIAGE LICENSE

Virginia, Fairfax County to wit:

To any Person Licensed to Celebrate Marriages:

You are hereby authorized to join together in the Holy State of Matrimony, according to the rites and ceremonies of your Church, or religious denomination, and the laws of the Commonwealth of Virginia, William Robinson and Sarah Johnson

Given under my hand, as Clerk of the County Court of Fairfax Co the 24 day of Oct 1888

Clerk

CERTIFICATE TO OBTAIN A MARRIAGE LICENSE.

Time of Marriage. Oct. 25 1888

Place of Marriage. "Mt. Vernon"

Full Names of Parties Married. Wm. Robinson & Sarah Johnson

Color. colored

Age of Husband. 36

Age of Wife. 35

Condition of Husband. (widowed or single) Widower

Condition of Wife. (widowed or single) Widow.

Place of Husband's Birth.

Place of Wife's Birth. Fairfax Co. Va

Place of Husband's Residence. " " "

Place of Wife's Residence. " " "

Names of Husband's Parents. & Jane Robinson.

Names of Wife's Parents. & Hannah May

Occupation of Husband. Laborer.

Given under my hand this 24 day of Oct. 1888

Clerk

MINISTER'S RETURN OF MARRIAGE.

I Certify, That on the 25 day of October 1888, at Mt Vernon Virginia I united in Marriage the above-named and described parties, under authority of the annexed License.

Sarah Johnson's
Wedding Certificate

turned over to George Washington's heirs. She was about sixteen years old when the Civil War started and went to live in Fauquier County with the family that sold Mount Vernon as they fled the District of Columbia area along with many other white southern sympathizers.

After the war, and now with her freedom, she returned to Mount Vernon and continued to work, but now for pay. In 1888, she had an elaborate wedding at Mount Vernon, her second marriage, this time to William Robinson. This elaborate wedding included embossed wedding invitations that were mailed to her guests. Reverend Madden officiated at their wedding and later registered their wedding certificate, signed by him, at the Fairfax County Court House.

Around the end of the century as interest in Mount Vernon increased and numerous authors began writing about the home, Sarah Johnson Robinson was interviewed frequently for insights into Mount Vernon history.

Activities During 1890–1895

As the church entered the decade of the 1890s, Reverend Madden marked his twenty-seventh year as a minister at Alfred Street Baptist Church. Each year the church sent representatives and a report to the Virginia Baptist State Convention that was usually held in August. Often Reverend Madden would attend the convention, sometimes as the church's only delegate, and sometimes he would be accompanied by Deacon J. Webster. In its 1890 report to the convention, the church indicated that it had a viable Sunday School, headed by G.W. Simms.

In the 1890s, many ancestors of the families who have been members of Alfred Street Baptist Church for one hundred years or more were joining and establishing leadership positions. From the Brooks family, Richard, Mary F. and Henry C. Brooks were active. Henry F. Burke joined Alfred Street and so did other members of the Burke family to include Ida, Benjie, Julia, Robert T. and Hollie. John and Louise Harris of the Harris family were still active and family members have maintained membership since around the 1870s. And, of course, the Quanders, who had been members since the early 1830s, were well represented. Members from this family who were active at this time included Robert H. Quander and Amanda Quander, born in the 1840s.

In June 1893, Reverend Madden conducted a funeral at the church for one of the early members of the Quander family. Mariah Quander passed away on June 17 of that year. She was eighty years old and had been born in 1813—just ten years after the Baptists first arrived in Alexandria. During this era, funeral practices at the church were not well documented, but burial practices within the city are well known.

In the city of Alexandria, a large public cemetery complex known as Bethel Cemetery

Bethel Cemetery

had opened in 1883 in the vicinity of the current Lee Center to accommodate burials. This site was near several *private* church cemeteries (e.g., Episcopal, Presbyterian) that started in 1809 when burials within the city limits were first outlawed. The new public cemetery had over 10,000 gravesites with about 3,500 set aside for Negroes in sections H, K and M near the rear. Mariah Quander was buried in Section M-50, and was one of the earliest documented members of Alfred Street Baptist Church to be buried there.[8]

Other aspects of the present-day worship practices were also emerging. By now worship services included the use of choirs, with the Senior Choir being the first official choir at Alfred Street. It performed several concerts for the Willing Workers' Club, while raising funds to enlarge the church in the late 1880s. Reverend Madden also instituted the use of deaconesses, in addition to the deacons. Reportedly, there were two deaconesses who served during his tenure, including Deaconess Catherine McQuay Butler. She was the mother of Lelia Butler Thomas, and the grandmother of former Trustee Marion Butler. Deaconess Butler was matriarch of the Butler-Thomas family whose members have worshipped at Alfred Street Baptist Church for more than one hundred years.

Deaconess Catherine McQuay Butler

During Reverend Madden's pastorate, other clubs and auxiliaries were formed in addition to the Willing Workers. The Mite Society, the predecessor to our current day Missionary Society, was formed during this time. There had been missionary activities (and offerings collected for them) at the church as far back as the early 1870s, but they were not formally recognized as an auxiliary until the 1880s. Taking their name from Jesus' parable of the "widow's mite," the Mite Society was founded by the following individuals:

Mrs. Mary Clisby   Mrs. Emma Price
Mrs. Hattie Parker   Mrs. Lelia Thomas
Mrs. Etta Robinson   Mrs. Mary Ware
Mrs. Emma Osborne

These dedicated workers realized that God had a mission for each of them. Thus, they busied themselves in the service of others, giving of their time, talents, and energies to aid the ill and less fortunate individuals. They visited the sick and shut-ins, and rendered whatever service needed. Some made aprons to sell; some took old garments and made new ones when new materials were not available. Mrs. Lelia Thomas, daughter of Deaconess Catherine Butler, spent many hours making garments for children. Monetary contributions to the Mite Society and fund-raisers made their efforts possible. As the Mite Society grew in numbers and in strength, they expanded their services in the United States and overseas.

In addition to spiritual outreach, the church was also involved in educational outreach. According to minutes taken by the Church Clerk, Brother H.B. Diggs, an offering was taken on the fourth Sunday in October 1895 for the benefit of the Manassas School in Manassas, Virginia. Jennie Dean, a former slave and early member of 19th Street Baptist Church in Washington, D.C., founded the school in 1893. Though Jennie Dean had been born a slave in 1852, she felt strongly about education for Negro students and founded the Manassas School primarily as a vocational or industrial school along the lines of the schools proposed later by Booker T. Washington to uplift the race. Over time, the school would educate many of Alexandria's Negro students, and would be one of only two high schools in Northern Virginia until the 1920s, when persons at Alfred Street Baptist Church were instrumental in opening a local high school within the city of Alexandria.

On April 6, 1896, the church held a meeting, which would be the last with Reverend Madden as moderator. It was a busy night. At that time, the church regularly had two Sunday services, and sometimes a night service for special occasions. Brother Webster, a trustee, had been appointed by the Sunday School to come before the church and investigate the possibility of having an Easter celebration on the second Sunday night in April. However, most of the brethren were unwilling for reasons of finance. They felt the church was behind in paying the pastor, and argued that night services of all kinds were to be set aside for that purpose. They argued that they needed all the money they could get to pay the pastor. The pastor replied: "Bring all the money that you have for the church to the morning and afternoon services, and let the Sunday School have the night for their program."[9] Brother Henry Boyd, the superintendent, remarked: "Amen! Amen!"

Reverend Madden loved the Sunday School and had worked untiringly to organize it and build it up to appreciable strength. The church finally granted the Sunday School use of the church for their program on the second Sunday in April.

At the next meeting in May 1896, Reverend Madden was absent and Brother Corbin acted as moderator in his stead. At this meeting, the church voted to take an offering on the fourth Sunday in May for the chorister. The account for the chorister was depleted, so the church took up a specific offering for this function, as no central budget existed.

The Pastor Departs

Before the July 1896 meeting, sadness visited the Alfred Street congregation. Their beloved pastor passed away. After thirty-three years of sweat and toil, Reverend Samuel W. Madden, Pastor of Alfred Street Baptist Church, heard the call ". . . Come unto me all ye that labour, and are heavy laden, and I will give you rest. . . ." He departed life on Sunday morning, June 28, 1896, at his home on South St. Asaph Street, about four blocks from the church. The cause of death was listed as "apoplexy," although he complained of

DEATH OF A COLORED MINISTER
ev. Samuel W. Madden, pastor of
lfred street Baptist Church, died
is home, on south St. Asaph st
esterday morning. The deceased
orn near Brandy Station, Culpe
ounty, sixty-seven years ago, and
he past thirty years has been in ch
f the church in this city. Before
e was pastor of the Nineteenth St
aptist Church, Washington. Du
he war he was a commissioned c
ain in the United States army, b
tationed at Freedman's Hospital
his city. He leaves a widow and e
hildren, most of whom are grown.
eceased, during his residence in
ity, had ever enjoyed the respec
he entire community.

Sunday morning, June 28th, 1896
o'clock, Rev S. W. MADDEN, pastor
street Baptist Church of this city, i
[illegible] year of his age. Funeral at
o'clock Tuesday afternoon from the ch
The remains may be viewed at the c
from 10 a.m. to 2 p.m. Tuesday.

Obituary of Reverend Samuel Madden

"diseases of the lung and rheumatism" in a pension claim he filed in May 1895 for disability as a Civil War veteran. His pension claim had been denied. He was sixty-seven years old at the time of his death.

As he was well liked and highly respected, his obituary was prominently displayed in the local Alexandria newspaper. At this time, the local papers generally did not print obituaries for Negroes, and would not do so routinely until after the civil rights struggles of the 1960s. But, Reverend Madden was special and was given front-page treatment in the *Alexandria Gazette.* The articles mentioned his birthplace, his service in the Civil War, and the arrangements for his funeral. The funeral was held on the following Tuesday at 2:30 p.m. at the church, with the wake being held earlier that morning from 10 a.m. until 2 p.m.

The size of his funeral is a testament to the influence he exerted around the city and the nation. The *Alexandria Gazette* carried details of his funeral and noted that over 2,000 people attended his funeral service. At that time, the old church in which the funeral was held would seat only about 400 to 500 persons. Thus, more than 1,500 persons were left to wait and watch from outside. Even so, they came and they stayed. The attendance was all the more remarkable given that, in 1896, there were no automobiles, buses, subways, or airplanes. The people who attended his funeral came by train, by riverboat, by horseback, by buggy, and by foot. Many of these people had been touched by his life and took whatever means necessary to get to the church.

Headstone of Reverend Samuel Madden

Following the funeral, Reverend Madden was buried in Bethel Cemetery, one of two or three local cemeteries that accepted Negroes at that time. Reverend Madden was buried in Section L within the area set aside for colored burials. A picture of his headstone is shown above. The epitaph on the headstone includes a quote from the poem *Resignation* by Henry Wadsworth Longfellow and reads:

Erected by Alfred St. Baptist Church
to the memory of SAMUEL W. MADDEN,
for thirty three years, pastor of the Alfred Street Baptist Church.
Born Aug. 31, 1829. Died June 28, 1896.
I have fought a good fight, I have finished my course, I have kept the faith.
This life of mortal breath is but a suburb of the life Elysian,
Whose portal we call death.

The church members purchased the headstone through the establishment of a special memorial fund. James Ross was elected president of the Memorial committee, with W. A. Price serving as secretary. After placing the headstone some months later, the committee reported that there was a $4.75 balance left in the memorial fund and indicated that they were considering adding a marble sofa or chair at the gravesite. When their work was completed, the church dismissed the committee with a vote of thanks.

Mrs. Madden applied for and received the Civil War pension that Reverend Madden had been denied after a protracted fight with the federal government. Several years later, she, too, would be buried in Bethel Cemetery next to him. Eventually, twelve other Madden offspring were buried in Section L of Bethel Cemetery with Reverend and Mrs. Madden.

Reverend Alexander Truatt

Reverend Alexander Truatt Arrives

Following Reverend Madden's death, Alfred Street Baptist Church members called Reverend Alexander Truatt to be their next pastor in the fall of 1896 after about a two-month search. He would continue as pastor until 1913.

Reverend Truatt was born in 1850 in LaGrange, Georgia, a town in the western part of the state near the Alabama border. The town is about fifty miles west of Atlanta. LaGrange had survived the Civil War essentially unscathed because of the reluctance of Union forces to attack a town defended by an all-female militia.

Reverend Truatt probably left LaGrange and the deep South after the Civil War and moved to Virginia as an adult. At some time prior to 1874 he met and married Rachael Payne, a Virginia nurse-midwife and, upon marrying, he inherited two young stepsons, James and Charles. Sarah, the first child of the Truatt union, was born during the second year of the marriage. Over the next fourteen years, Sarah was followed by siblings Bertha, Leonora, Lelia, Nathan, Lena, Manning, and Beatrice. The Truatt household consisted of ten children, one of whom (Lelia) would later marry Jesse Madden, the son of the previous pastor, Reverend Samuel Madden.[10]

The time and location of Reverend Truatt's ordination is not known. However, before coming to Alfred Street Baptist Church, it appears he had at least three pastorates, one of which was near Lynchburg in Goochland County, Virginia, in the late 1870s and early 1880s. From there he moved to the First Baptist Church of Charlottesville, Virginia, where he served as pastor from 1882 to 1889.[11] His next pastorate was at Ebenezer Baptist Church, also in Charlottesville. Ebenezer Baptist was a young church, and one of his first accomplishments there was to lead the congregation in building a new sanctuary, which opened in 1894.

When Reverend Truatt finally arrived at Alfred Street in the fall of 1896, the congregation was approximately 400 members in size. The membership had stabilized following the steep drop-off in numbers following the glory days of growth in the early 1880s. One of his first initiatives at Alfred Street was the adoption of a standard Baptist Hymnal for use by the choir and the purchase of new Bibles for the church. He nurtured an active Young Men's Bible Class, which he sometimes taught. The primary focus of the Young Men's Bible Class was studying the Word of God, but the group also became known within the community for its musical quartet and its sponsoring of other special programs, some of which had an emphasis on social justice (e.g., Lincoln-Douglas Memorial Services).

Among other special activities of the church during that time were all-day rallies, sponsored by the Sunday School, and the annual church-wide Autumn Rally. Rallies of various types became one of the principal vehicles for fund-raising, and would remain so for the next fifty years. For these occasions, other pastors and congregations throughout the Washington, D.C. area, were invited to participate.

A strong proponent of education, Reverend Truatt supported and assisted in establishing the old Colored School Improvement League in Alexandria. It was not uncommon for the League to meet at the church, and on at least one occasion, the church hosted a mass meeting of this group in support of the Manassas Industrial School. Alfred Street had supported the school since its founding in 1893.

Black Convention Activities

The church, through Reverend Truatt, also participated in several state and national conventions. Reverend Truatt served on many committees and otherwise took an active part in the deliberations of these bodies. He enjoyed ministerial fellowship with his contemporaries, both within and outside the denomination, including the late Dr. Walter H. Brooks of 19th Street Baptist Church, Reverend Anthony Binga of Richmond, Reverend Henry Williams, Jr., of Richmond, Reverend S.H. Brown of Roberts Memorial Chapel in Alexandria, and Dr. Harvey Johnson of Baltimore, who had been ordained at Alfred Street in 1872.

In August 1898, the Church first took steps to join the Northern Virginia Baptist Association. This was a local Negro association of churches that had been organized in 1877 in Warrenton, Virginia. It was one of about twelve associations of Negro Baptists of various types in the state of Virginia. At that time the state of Virginia had about 575 Negro churches, with about 130,000 members and about 375 ordained ministers. Most churches averaged 100 to 300 members, and there were still not enough ordained ministers to serve as pastors at all the churches. In fact, there were almost two churches for every ordained minister. Many churches met only once or twice per month, and many shared pastors.

The conventions provided a source of new ministers for these churches and provided opportunities for collaborative mission activities. Alfred Street had considered joining the Northern Virginia Baptist Association for some time, but never had the funds to do so. At the August 1898 meeting, the church agreed to collect a special offering on the fourth Sunday of August to send the pastor as a delegate. Many objected as they felt too many financial obligations were being heaped on them at one time. But the pastor did attend the convention held that year in Leesburg, Virginia, and reported being well received by the host church and the delegates at the convention. Alfred Street also continued its participation in regional conventions. Additional associations to which Alfred Street belonged included the American Baptist Missionary Society, since 1865, which reportedly met at Alfred Street in 1883 or 1884. Most of the numerous Negro Baptist conventions in existence at that time were focused on education, publications, and missions, both local and foreign.

It would be several years before the church could afford to join the Lott Carey Foreign Mission Convention in Richmond. The Lott Carey Foreign Mission Convention, which traces its origins to 1897, was somewhat different from the other conventions in that its singular purpose was conducting foreign missions. Lott Carey's beginnings, like that of many other church conventions, grew out of the midst of a conflict.

In 1895, various local and regional Baptist church societies around the country met in Atlanta, Georgia, and merged to form the National Baptist Convention. By 1897, the group decided to move the Foreign Mission Board component of the National Baptist Convention from Richmond, Virginia, to a new headquarters in Louisville, Kentucky. The members along the East Coast, particularly those from Virginia, had a rather high stake in foreign missions, and did not want to see the seat of power moved so far away. Fearing a loss of influence, they broke away from the National Baptist Convention in 1897 and incorporated the Lott Carey Foreign Mission Convention in Richmond. Alfred Street would later join both the Lott Carey and National Baptist Conventions.

Alfred Street was also active in the Virginia Baptist State Convention, where a similar rift related to education was occurring. At issue was the amount and nature of support that the Negro Baptists received from the white Baptist association for their schools. Reverend Truatt and Alfred Street supported interracial cooperation among Baptists in the United States. They recognized the very important role that the American Baptist Home Mission Society had played and was continuing to play in establishing institutions for Negroes such as Virginia Union University (1865) and Shaw University (1865) in North Carolina for the general and ministerial education of young students. Other churches were concerned about the amount of white support and felt that Negroes should only accept support from Negro organizations.[12]

A key element of the dispute was the issue of the creation of the Virginia Baptist Theological Seminary in Lynchburg, Virginia. In May 1899, the issue of funding for the school created a controversy that resulted in a majority of the 700 delegates at the convention of Virginia's Negro Baptists voting to sever all relations with the white Baptists and their missionary work. They supported the formation of the Lynchburg Seminary and wanted only Negro teachers and Negro funds. In fact, they adopted a new motto: "Faith in Self; Self Help; Negro Control of Negro Institutions; Negroes Only Safe and Efficient Teachers of Negroes."[13]

Members of the minority faction at the convention who favored maintaining a relationship with the whites met separately in June 1899 and formed the "Baptist General Association of Virginia, Colored" at a meeting at a church in Richmond. This association supported Virginia Union and continued cooperation with the white Baptists. Alfred

Street was the first black church in Alexandria to affiliate with the newly formed Baptist General Association of Virginia, and was one of the few churches in Northern Virginia to do so.

Reverend Truatt and Alfred Street were to continue to be active in these and other conventions over the years. And, every twenty to twenty-five years, there would be another rift, typically over an administrative issue (e.g., funding, tenure of officials) within one of the conventions and another one would be formed. In time, Alfred Street would shift its alliances several times as politics shifted within convention leadership.

The Congregation of the 1890s

The congregation of the 1890s consisted of approximately 400 persons, most of whom lived in the four major black neighborhoods that comprised the city's Negro population. Congregants were received by letter and baptism, and expelled for a myriad of sins. Some of the members joining during this period included the following persons:

NAME	DATE JOINED	METHOD
Ella Parsley	6 April 1891	Christian Experience
Annie Boiseau	9 November	Baptism
Amanda Grander	9 November	Baptism
Martha Thomas	9 November	Baptism
Mr. E. M. Williams	7 December	Christian Experience
Thomas Arrington	8 March 1899	Baptism
Mattie Burr	8 March	Letter
Samuel Keith	5 July 1899	Reinstated
Annie Jackson	5 July 1899	Reinstated

Most of these new members were "city-folk" who lived close to the church and walked to services. One of the more unusual member families was the Quanders, who lived out in the country. The Quanders were farmers who had purchased property about two miles south of the city shortly after the Civil War. As this was too far to walk, they traveled to church via horse and buggy. Members of the Quander family who attended Alfred Street during this era included Robert H. and Amanda Quander. The family made a living primarily by selling vegetables at the market in the city in the vicinity of the present-day City Hall.

The church now had both deacons and deaconesses, though the exact number is not known. Two deaconesses had been consecrated under Reverend Madden and the number of deacons, though unknown, was small, perhaps four or five at a time. An occasional minister would be ordained to assist the pastor with religious affairs. For example, before closing for the summer in 1899, the church met on June 27 to consider the examination of Brother George Dixon for the ministry. For the examination (location not stated), the church appropriated twelve dollars for the pastor to participate. Brother Dixon was ordained and would assist the minister with pulpit duties for several years. He would later serve as interim pastor for a brief period when Reverend Truatt's term expired.

The Senior Choir was actively performing at the church as well as in support of local fund-raising efforts. In 1897 the choir held a special concert at the church at which $11.61 was raised. In 1898, the choir held a special concert to assist Roberts Memorial Methodist Church, and the following year a similar concert was held to assist Meade Memorial AME Church.[14]

As this was in the midst of a period of limited economic growth for Negroes, members also frequently called on the church to assist with their financial affairs. At the September 7, 1898, church meeting, Sister Harriett Williams reported that she had been "burned out" and requested assistance. House fires were frequent during this period and persons who had been burned out frequently came to their church for support. In this case, Brother Henry Boyd, one of the deacons, made a motion to take a collection for her after Bible study the next week. He then started the offering himself by giving ten cents to the clerk.

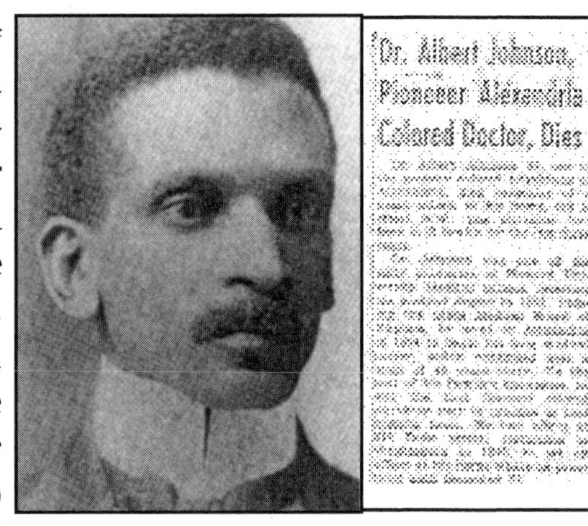
Dr. Albert Johnson,
Pioneer Alexandria
Colored Doctor, Dies

Dr. Albert Johnson

In addition to the poor who were in need of help, during this period Alfred Street had also begun to attract members of Alexandria's professional Negro community. Perhaps one of its better-known members at that time was Albert Johnson, a physician. He joined the church around 1894 and became a deacon of the church. At that time and for many years thereafter, he remained the only Negro physician in Alexandria. He lived just four or five houses from the church at 814 Duke Street. The home, a two-story red brick building with full basement, is currently a stop on the Black History Tour of the city, and has been nominated for inclusion in the National Register of Historic Places.

Dr. Johnson was born in Lynchburg, Virginia, on November 16, 1866, the son of former slaves, William and Harriet Johnson. Upon graduation from high school in Lynchburg in 1886, he was immediately employed in the public schools as a teacher for three years. He then entered Howard University's Medical School, the first medical school for Negroes, in the fall of 1889. After three years of study, he was awarded the Doctor of Medicine degree in April 1892 in a graduation ceremony held at the First Congregational Church of Washington, D.C.

He initially returned home to Lynchburg where he opened a practice, but returned to the Washington, D.C., area to live in Alexandria in 1894. After two years of practicing in Alexandria, he met and married in a storybook ceremony the first of two wives. At first, he had met and began courting Miss Maude Chinn, a native of the city, shortly after returning to Alexandria. While making plans to wed her, Miss Chinn became mortally ill. Yet the couple was married at her bedside as she lay dying. She survived the marriage ceremony by only a few hours.[15]

Dr. Johnson married a second time and spent several prosperous years in medical practice in Alexandria as its only Negro doctor. In addition to being a physician and a deacon at Alfred Street Baptist Church, Dr. Johnson was active in the Alexandria community. When the Alexandria Hospital was constructed on Washington Street just around the block from Alfred Street Baptist Church, Dr. Johnson was selected as chairman of the committee to raise funds to equip the men's ward. The new hospital also had a separate wing on the first floor to serve Negro patients.

He practiced in Alexandria for forty-six years before moving his practice to Washington, D.C. He passed in July 1949, and was buried in Union Cemetery.

This mixture of poor persons and professionals was to define the congregation of Alfred Street for the next one hundred years. In the early days the poor outnumbered the professionals but, in time, Jim Crow laws would give way to economic opportunities and the church would become known for its heavily weighted professional congregation.

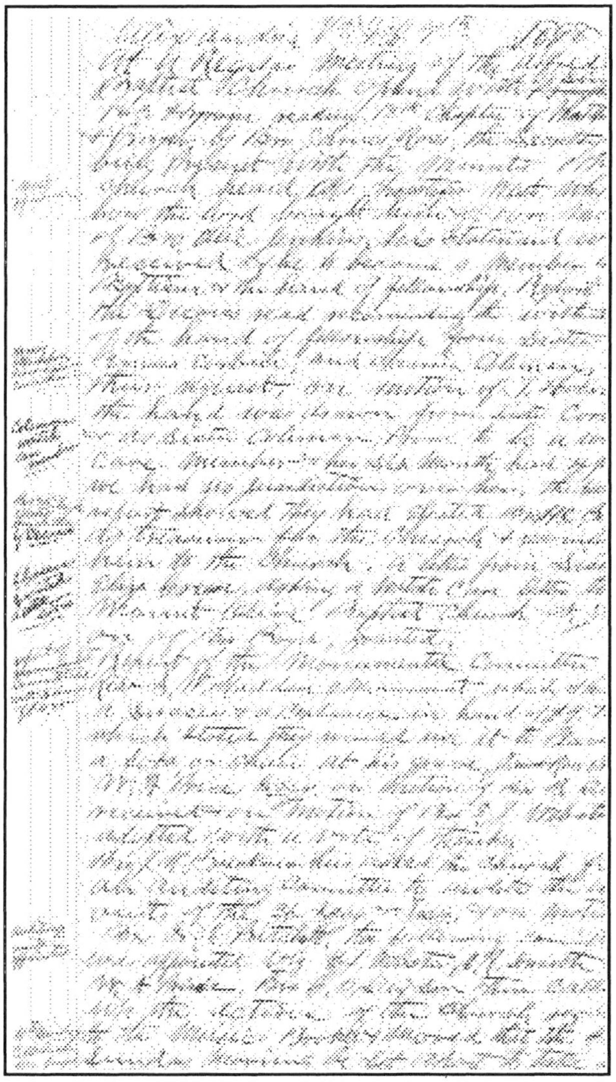

Minutes of Church Meeting, February 1898

Discipline and Dollars: The End of the Century

As the century came to an end, the church functioned much as it had one hundred years earlier, at its beginning. Brother James M. Buchner now served as church clerk and kept track of the flow of members in and out of the church. Sister Martha Parker served as sexton. Church meetings were generally held at night beginning around 8:00 p.m. and lasting two to two-and-a-half hours. At these meetings, individuals were received by letter and baptism, expelled for a myriad of sins, then restored, and the cycle repeated. During this era and for several years to come, joining church was done at the church business meeting. Individuals might present themselves as candidates to join during church services; however, actual acceptance into membership was done during the church meeting by voice vote.

Deportment and Christian conduct still dominated the activities carried on at church meetings. The church officials agreed at one meeting that no notices would be read of theatrical releases, or any form of entertainment that would not be permitted in the church. Given that persons were also prohibited from attending most of these functions, announcing such secular performances was an empty gesture, anyway. This close attention to discipline and deportment at church meetings sometimes created some rather amusing situations. For example, one lady requested a letter of dismission to join another church. However, Alfred Street did not recognize her as a member as she had participated so little in the ongoing affairs of the church. It, therefore, could not dismiss her. The church required her to rejoin on Christian experience and, after being active for a while, she was granted a letter of dismission in good standing.

At a meeting on February 9, 1898, the deacons recommended withdrawing the hand of fellowship from Sister Emma Corbin and Sister Mamie Coleman. Sister Coleman's offense was that she had been a "watch-care" member and her six-month term of membership had expired. During this period, watch-care status carried a limited term, unlike today when watch-care status can continue indefinitely. As her six-month term had expired, the deacons felt that the church no longer had jurisdiction over her.

The church concerned itself not only with the affairs of members of the church, but with neighborhood activity as well. At a meeting in early 1898, there was quite a bit of discussion about Kelly's Bar Room at the corner of Alfred and Wolfe Streets. The bar, just three or four doors from the church, was considered a nuisance because it was so close to the church and disturbed parishioners on their way to church. The church considered several legal avenues to close the bar or remedy the situation, but Kelly's Bar would remain a thorn in the side of the church for the next fifty years.

In addition to discipline, the other factors most discussed at the church meetings were finances. The minister's salary was a major item of discussion in many meetings, and the church always seemed to be behind in paying him. Most years the church collected a total of around $600 to $800 from all sources, of which $500 to $600 was used to pay the pastor. At the March 1898 meeting, the Auditing Committee reported that they were two years behind in paying Reverend Truatt as they owed him about $25 for 1896, and about $75 for the year 1897. The church agreed to a special collection by the trustees on the third Sunday in April to meet these financial obligations.

Because of financial concerns, at the July 1898 meeting the church voted to hold only one service per Sunday (except for two on Communion Sunday) during the months of July and August to save gas that was still used for heat and lights. Reverend Truatt also agreed to accept July and August as vacation months, but agreed that he would accept responsibility for having someone occupy the pulpit on Sunday, either himself or a visiting minister.

The church, last remodeled in 1890, was also in need of repair and upkeep that added yet another financial burden. Reverend Truatt introduced a plan at the June 1899 meeting for raising funds for the needed repairs. The plan involved printing of pledge cards and the clerk was requested to obtain 250 at a cost of $2.50. A banking committee consisting of J.R. Smith (deacon), James Ross (trustee), and James M. Buchner (clerk) was established to keep track of monies raised during the campaign.

Again, the church closed for that summer, saving money for gas and granting the pastor a much-needed vacation. And even as Alfred Street was trying to save money and was having problems raising money for its upkeep, other churches were in similar straits and were also asking for help. Mt. Zion Church in Arlington requested use of the Alfred Street sanctuary for some of its services. The fourth Sunday in October 1899 was granted to them all day for their use.

The last meeting of the century was held on December 6, 1899. The meeting was opened with the singing of Hymn 226 and the reading of Galatians, chapter 6. Another plan to raise money to repair the church (paint, tinting, etc.) was presented, this time by the trustees. Also at this meeting, Sister Viola Shanklins asked for a letter of dismission to join another church. Again the church refused to grant it. They argued that they knew nothing of her because she had been absent so frequently. Again, she was required to rejoin in order to be dismissed.

End of Century Recap

In summary, the century ended with a dismission just as it had begun with one. Approximately one hundred years earlier, in 1803, church members had been dismissed from the Back Lick Church to establish the first assembly of Baptists in Alexandria. In that congregation, they baptized the first Negro member, Susan Black or Black Susan, into their fellowship in May of that year. During the century that followed, there were hundreds of others who had come and gone.

For almost one-half of the time, the colored members had been conjoined with First Baptist Church, a white sister congregation. The sister church had assisted in securing the first place of worship for the colored Baptists in 1818 and in finally purchasing the site in 1842. By 1850, the colored members, now larger in number than the white members, would fully separate from the sister church to worship in their own, more spirited way.

Now independent, the colored Baptists built a beautiful new brick sanctuary only to see it taken for use as a hospital in the Civil War. The war would bring freedom from slavery for all members of the church. Though damaged during the war, the church would survive and would grow rapidly during Reconstruction to over seven hundred members. It would lose one of its most beloved pastors and witness a drop in membership occasioned by a strict set of rules that caused members to go elsewhere.

As the century ended, the church began to look much like a contemporary church with deacons and deaconesses, with choirs, and with new ministries involved in missionary efforts. New affiliations would be formed as the church joined an ever-increasing number of new Baptist associations.

After almost one hundred years, Alfred Street Baptist Church was now stable and was poised to enter the new 20th century with great prospects and great promise.

Chapter Six

1900–1925: A New Century and World War I

. . . and ye shall hear of wars and rumours of wars . . .

During the early decades of the new century, a national agenda for Negroes was evolving that would affect their lives for the next fifty years. At the Alfred Street Baptist Church membership remained relatively stable, but would experience a gradual decline as a repressive set of "rules" continued to aggravate the congregation. The church would have three different pastors within a ten-year period as new opportunities for advancement led to their early departures. The first war that engulfed the entire globe began near the end of this period and briefly interrupted life within the church. But the church would emerge from the war years stronger, more stable, and under new leadership.

The Setting

The new century began with William McKinley, a Republican, as the nation's twenty-fifth president. He was re-elected to a second term on a platform of "four years more of the full dinner-pail" following a period of national prosperity. His second term would be short-lived, however, as he was assassinated in September 1901, just one year into the second term. The vice president, Theodore Roosevelt, replaced McKinley and, at 43 years old, became the nation's youngest president. He served two terms until 1909. But, even before Presidents McKinley and Roosevelt took office, the foundations of the nation's agenda for Negroes had already been set. Two key events in the late 1890s, a new law and later a new black leadership, would serve to establish this agenda.

First, Negroes were suffering under a set of repressive laws that had been in force since the Reconstruction era. The Black Codes, as these laws were called, gave Negroes "equal" rights in some areas, but they were generally segregated in their daily life. This segregation was codified in the infamous *Plessy v. Ferguson* case just before the turn of the century. Homer Plessy, a 30-year-old shoemaker, had been jailed for sitting in the "white" car of the East Louisiana Railroad line in violation of Louisiana law. His case, originally argued in Louisiana before Judge John Howard Ferguson, eventually went all the way to the United States Supreme Court on appeal. In 1892, the Supreme Court justices ruled 8–1 in favor of the Louisiana law.[1] Based on that decision, "Separate but Equal" became the legitimized defining principle for Negro life in America at work, at play, and at worship for the next half century.

A second factor that affected life for Negroes in America was the change in Negro leadership styles from that of "protest" to "accommodation." Through much of the late 19th century, Frederick Douglass served as the "... voice of the Negro people." Following his death in February 1895, Booker T. Washington became the new national "Negro Leader." Booker T. Washington was a former slave who had been educated at Hampton Institute in Virginia. He founded and served as president of Tuskegee Institute in Tuskegee, Alabama. On September 18, 1895, he delivered a speech in Atlanta that helped to set the agenda for the Negro community for the next several years.

Booker T. Washington was invited to Atlanta to address the opening day audience at the Cotton States and International Exposition. In his speech at this affair, he recommended that Negroes "... cast down your buckets where you are ..." and begin to learn and master trades, industrial skills, and to focus later on social equality and educational pursuits. Perhaps the most remembered phrases from the speech came at the end when he said:[2]

> ... In all things that are purely social, we can be as separate as the fingers, yet one as the hand in all things essential to mutual progress.

The speech immediately became known as "The Atlanta Compromise." It represented a course of conservatism and patience that would perhaps not antagonize Southern whites and, at the same time, would prepare Negro youngsters for the type of work that would be offered to them in the South. The speech made Booker T. Washington famous, and set the tone for Negro leadership for the next quarter century.

The new laws and new leaders, coupled with few job opportunities beyond sharecropping, led to a mass migration of Negroes from the South to the North in an attempt to escape repression. The population of New York alone increased by 91,000 Negroes, and Chicago by 71,000 Negroes within the first couple of decades of the new century.[3] This exodus, known as "The Great Northern Drive," was the second mass migration of Negroes following an earlier migration during Reconstruction. This latter migration would provide the foundation for the growth of northern cities as well as produce increases in the sizes and numbers of Negro churches in the northern regions of the nation.

Activities at Alfred Street Baptist Church: 1900–1905

The new century began at Alfred Street Baptist Church much as the old one had ended. Reverend Truatt was still serving as pastor. He had been at Alfred Street for four years, and at the age of fifty was a seasoned "soldier of the cross." The first church meeting of the new century took place at the church at 8:00 p.m. on January 9, 1900. The meeting was opened with the singing of Hymn 425 and the reading of Romans 12.

At this first meeting of the new century, Reverend Truatt led the church in electing new church officers. Brother H.B. Diggs moved to retain current officers (viz., clerk, treasurer, and sexton) for the coming year. All of the current officers consented to serve for another year, including Brother W.A. Price, who served as sexton, and James Buchner, who continued as clerk. Whenever Brother Buchner was absent, Reverend A.A. Lott would serve as acting clerk. The renewing and withdrawing of hands, long-held customs among the Baptists, consumed much of the discussion for the meeting. At this first meeting, the hand of fellowship was withdrawn from Sister Elizabeth Jackson, for "unbecoming conduct."

Since the last meeting in 1899, the church had collected $292.29 from all sources and expended nearly all of that, leaving a balance in the treasury of approximately five dollars. Throughout most of the year, the church would retain a balance of between five and twenty-five dollars in all of its accounts. To save expenses, the church continued having only one service during the summer months and granted the pastor a vacation.

At this time, the church was functioning much as it does today with the meeting of auxiliaries, Communion, and baptisms. During church services on Sundays, two deacons sat in chairs in front of the pulpit. Generally, Brother H.C. Boyd and Brother J.R. Smith were assigned to occupy these chairs. When they were absent, other deacons were permitted to sit there.

Baptisms had been held along the banks of the Potomac River since the earliest days, but their exact locations have not been identified. However, beginning in the summer of 1900, the church agreed to a new baptism site along the riverfront near Battery Rodgers, one of the numerous Civil War batteries surrounding the Capitol area to protect against Confederate attacks. The new baptism site was located in the general vicinity of the present-day Zion Baptist Church near the corner of Lee and Jefferson Streets. At the turn of the century, that area near the foot of the Woodrow Wilson Bridge was still under water. Baptism pools that are common today in Baptist churches were another twenty years away.

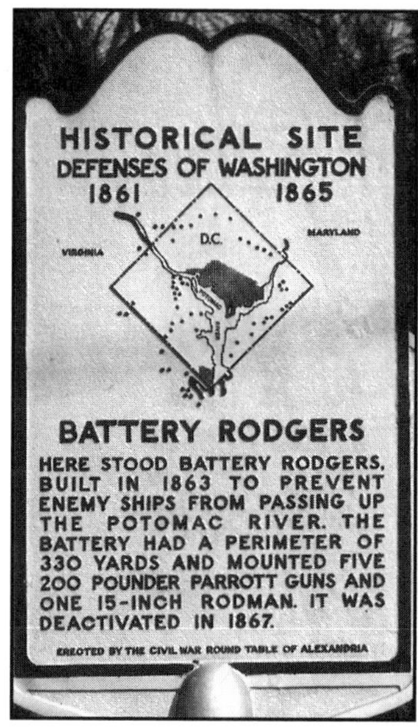

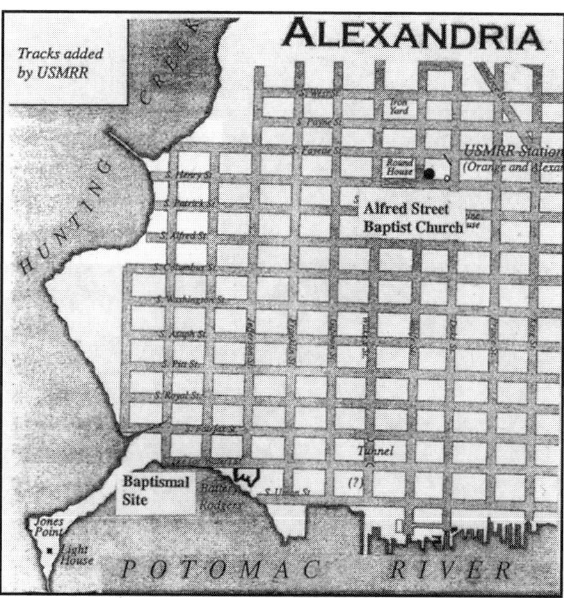

Map of Baptism Site at Battery Rodgers

During the May meeting of 1900, Sister Edithington requested and was granted permission to place a memorial window in the pulpit area of the church. The window honored Reverend S. Madden who had passed away four years earlier. She began soliciting funds in June 1900, and procured a stained-glass memorial window that is currently located in the "choir room" of the old church. The window was initially situated to the right rear of the church, to the right of the organ and pulpit. Many years later, the window was moved to its present location in the center of the rear wall.

Stained Glass Window of Reverend Madden

At the monthly meeting in August 1900, a bit of unpleasantness was dealt with regarding fighting among leaders of the church. Reverend A.A. Lott, who had been the acting clerk over most of the summer, was brought before the deacons for fighting. During the fight, he claimed that he was struck twice before he fought back, and that he had only struck the other individual in self-defense. After much debate among the members of the congregation over withdrawing the hands for the "good of the church," the issue was tabled. But this would not be the last situation involving Reverend Lott, who apparently had several run-ins with other members. At a later meeting during the summer of 1900, Reverend Lott came before the church to retract a statement he had made to Brother Diggs, which had offended him. Brother Diggs and the church hierarchy accepted Reverend Lott's retraction and apology.

By September, when Reverend Truatt returned to the pulpit, the church reported owing him ninety-two dollars and fourteen cents. This debt was in part due to poor attendance and failing offerings over the summer and, in fact, throughout the year. Many members were failing to live up to their obligations to the church, and so the church decided to begin enforcing the rules that it had previously agreed on. Specifically, the following two rules were enforced:

Rule 1: That any member failing to commune for 3 successive times without a lawful excuse, they shall be dealt with by the church.

Rule 2: Non-attendance and failing to communicate and contribute for 6 and 12 months, they shall be dropped.

While the intent of the rules was to improve attendance and contributions, strict enforcement of these rules only aggravated the situation, causing even more departures. During the year 1900, the church raised only $562.37 from all sources, and expended $550.92.

Another bit of unpleasantness was also raised at the first meeting of the New Year in 1901. Brother James Webster, one of the more outstanding members of the church, was refusing to take Communion. Brother Webster, a trustee who had signed the deed for the purchase of the original site in 1846, apparently had a run-in with Brother William Scroggings and Brother J.R. Smith, whom he felt were not worthy to be deacons. Therefore, he refused to take Communion from them. The matter was carried over to the meeting in February 1901, where it was finally settled and prayer was held for each of them.

At the July 1901 meeting, the pastor spoke of the wonderful work and his overall favorable impression of the Lott Carey Foreign Missionary Convention. The convention had been started in 1897 for the exclusive purpose of supporting foreign missions. Reverend Truatt first raised the issue and asked if the church would consider joining Lott Carey at its August meeting. The church members voted to join, and they voted to send the pastor as a delegate to the convention to be held in Philadelphia on September 4, 1901. The church also voted to pay the admission fee of five dollars. That summer, the pastor was also elected to be a delegate to the Northern Virginia Baptist Association, which was scheduled to meet in August at Lincolnia, Virginia.

At the October 1901 meeting, a need was identified for two new deacons, as two of them had become unable to serve. The church nominated and elected Brother Phillip Johnson as a new deacon and the next month Brother Range was nominated and elected. Also, at the October meeting, a need was identified to set aside a Sunday to raise money for the trustees for maintenance of the church. The church agreed that the third Sunday in October would be used for this purpose.

Revival was generally held in March and the church usually held two annual rallies. The dates for these rallies varied because there was no approved church calendar. Instead, the church hierarchy decided on revival, rally, and special days with perhaps a one- or two-month lead time, at which time committee chairs and other responsible positions would be assigned.

Another matter of concern at the church involved the appointment of a committee to check on the status of Kelly's Saloon, just down the street from the church. Kelly's had been a source of irritation at the church since the late 1800s. A committee was formed to petition the local judge for its closure. The committee consisted of Brother J.M. Buchner, Brother E. J. Webster and Reverend Truatt, who served as chair. The committee met with the judge, without resolution, and made plans to meet with him a second time. Ultimately, the church simply "went on record" as being opposed to the bar, as there was little they could do to force it to close. Even so, the bar closed for a while, but was back in business by the August meeting when a new committee was appointed to petition the judge again.

The Pastor and Congregation of the Early 1900s

At that time of his pastorate, Reverend Truatt lived at 710 Princess Street. The house, since destroyed, was opposite the parking lot behind the Alexandria Library that currently faces Queen Street. The pastor lived there with his wife and some of their children.

At this time, most of the Truatts' ten children were grown and had left home. The pastor continued to be granted a "leave of absence" from the church during August of each year to spend additional time with his family.

While the pastor held the most important leadership position in the church, other preachers assisted him with a myriad of duties. And there was no shortage of persons wanting to exercise their "gifts" and become ministers. Brother J.A. Hickerson asked the congregation for a license to preach in 1901, but the request was denied. He was instructed to exercise his gifts when and wherever he had a chance, but no license was granted at his first request.

Later, Brother Henry Tyler requested permission to preach a trial sermon. The church granted the second Thursday night of November 1901 for that purpose, and he was granted a license. Still later, Brother Albert Price was given a letter granting him the privilege to preach in September 1903. Brother Hickerson, who had been denied several years earlier, still wanted a license. After deliberations, the church decided he still needed more time so they could judge him. At a special call meeting in October 1903, permission was finally granted to him to preach.

In November 1903, the church agreed to grant a license to Brother John T. Diamond to preach. The request to grant the license to Brother Diamond had come from the Shiloh Baptist Church of Fredericksburg, Virginia, which was then without a pastor. A Committee on Arrangements of 22 persons was then appointed to examine his suitability for the ministry. The Council to consider his license was held on Wednesday, November 30, 1903, at 11 a.m., and a license was granted. In January 1904, the church granted to Reverend Diamond a Letter of Dismission, as he had been called as pastor of Shiloh Baptist Church in Fredericksburg, the church that had originally requested his ordination. His ordination brought to eight the number of new preachers ordained by Alfred Street since Reconstruction.

In addition to ordaining ministers, between five and ten new persons sought fellowship within the congregation each year. Persons still joined primarily by confession of faith and Baptism, but "Christian experience" began replacing dismission as the secondary method of joining. As society became more mobile with the introduction of the automobile in 1904, the practice of physically preparing and carrying Letters of Dismission waned. Instead, individuals who moved about and desired membership at a different church (and had already been baptized) simply confessed to having had a "Christian experience" at the new church. If found acceptable, they were admitted as new members without the requirement for another baptism.

Persons joining Alfred Street by Christian experience or Baptism during this period included:

NAME	DATE	METHOD
Mary E. Caster	April 10, 1901	Christian experience
Josephine Grason	April 10, 1901	Christian experience
Mary E. Murphy	April 10, 1901	Christian experience

(continued)

NAME	DATE	METHOD
Cora Butler	May 8, 1901	Baptism
Mary Baniker	May 8, 1901	Baptism
Ms. Oysker Williams	June 5, 1910	
Ms. Lizzie Taylor	June 5, 1901	Watchcare
Henry Quander	Dec 1901	Baptism
Mairing Broadus	Dec 1901	Baptism
J.H. Smith	Jan 1902	Restoration
Lu Belle	Jan 1902	Restoration
Carrie Belle	July 1903	Baptism
James Woody	Aug 1903	Baptism
Lelia M. Butler	Oct 1903	Baptism
Isaac Carter	Feb 1904	Baptism
William F. Evans	April 1904	Baptism
Miss Bertha Williams	April 1904	Baptism
Miss Theresa Williams	April 1904	Baptism
Wilbert Brown	—	Baptism

The church congregation still consisted primarily of "city folk," but more people from the country were also arriving. The Quanders, one of the oldest documented black families in America (1684),[6] were increasing in numbers. They had lived along the U.S. Route 1 corridor of Fairfax County since just after the Civil War, farming and raising produce. They initially settled in Maryland, but soon began migrating and subsequently settled in various areas of Northern Virginia, including the area just south of Alexandria. Nancy Carter Quander, a relative of the Quanders, worked for Martha Washington and was freed at George Washington's death when she was thirteen years old. Her offspring and other Quanders had been members of Alfred Street since around 1830, when Mariah Quander first became a member.

James Henry Quander, the father of Gladys Quander-Tancil and Deacon Welton Quander was one of the family members who joined the church around the turn of the century. James Henry Quander was born in 1882, the son of Charles Henry Quander, a slave born in 1840. James Henry and his wife attended the evening church services at Alfred Street near the turn of the century, coming to church by wagon. Sometimes when the "branch" or "run" that crosses U.S. Route 1 near Quander Road would flood following a heavy rain, the family would wait on the river banks and then catch a rather primitive ferry across the waters.[7]

Even as these new persons were arriving, older members were going to their final reward. During the early years of the new century, Reverend Truatt officiated at the funerals of four or five persons each year. Some of the persons funeralized in 1905 included:

NAME	DATE
Alexander Conway	14 Feb 1905
Addison Blackburn	17 Feb 1905
Sister Hannah Baker	17 March 1905
Brother William Gaines	17 March 1905
Sister Eliza Williams	6 April 1905

Families that buried their loved ones now had additional options for a final resting place. By this time, the Douglass Cemetery, named to honor Frederick Douglass who died in 1895, had been opened in the vicinity of the large cemetery complexes near the Lee Center and the Beltway. So, options for burial now included Douglass Cemetery; the Baptist Cemetery (Colored), founded earlier by a group that included deacons from Alfred Street; and Bethel Cemetery, the large public cemetery that offered space for Negroes in the rear.

Activities During 1905–1910

Fifteen to twenty-five people attended most church meetings during this period. At these meetings, even the most mundane issue was subjected to parliamentary discussion and debate. At one meeting, an issue arose as to how to best ventilate the church. The trustees submitted a proposal to ventilate the church through the windows. Others wanted added ventilation through the chimney and a third group wanted ventilation through the doors. There was considerable debate with a series of motions and counter motions, indicating the congregation's complete mastery of parliamentary procedures. Ventilation through the windows finally won by a vote of thirteen yeas, with twelve nays.

Every issue—the purchase of a safe for the trustees, purchase of a record book for the clerk—was aired and the rule of the majority prevailed in even the most mundane activities. For example, Sister Rachel Truatt, wife of the pastor, made a motion to put locks on the doors to the toilets, and that they remained locked when the church was not open. This, too, was debated and passed with a majority vote. And, at one meeting, the sole item on the agenda was whether or not to admit Sister Legrand by watch-care. The church members met and she was approved.

At the April 4, 1906, meeting, it was announced that the claim before the U.S. Court of Claims regarding the use of Alfred Street during the Civil War was settled. The church had filed a claim in 1905 against the U.S. government over damages to the church during the Civil War.[8] Mr. G.W.Z. Black, the attorney for the church, prepared the claim on behalf of Reverend Truatt and the trustees in late 1904. By January 1905, a formal claim had been filed under the provisions of the "Tucker Act," enacted by Congress in 1887 to make amends for damages sustained during the Civil War.

During the litigations, several people from Alfred Street Baptist Church who were members during the war and witnessed the destruction gave depositions on the church's behalf. These individuals included John H. Brent, Emily Luckett, Joseph H. Chilcott, Anthony Brenner, Edgar Johnson, and Deacon Pompey Jackson. Generally, their testi-

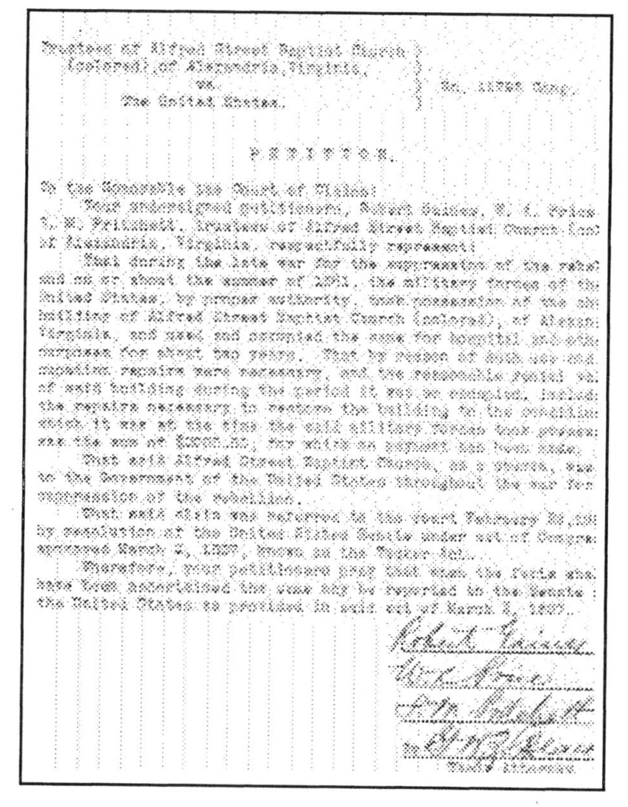

PETITION.

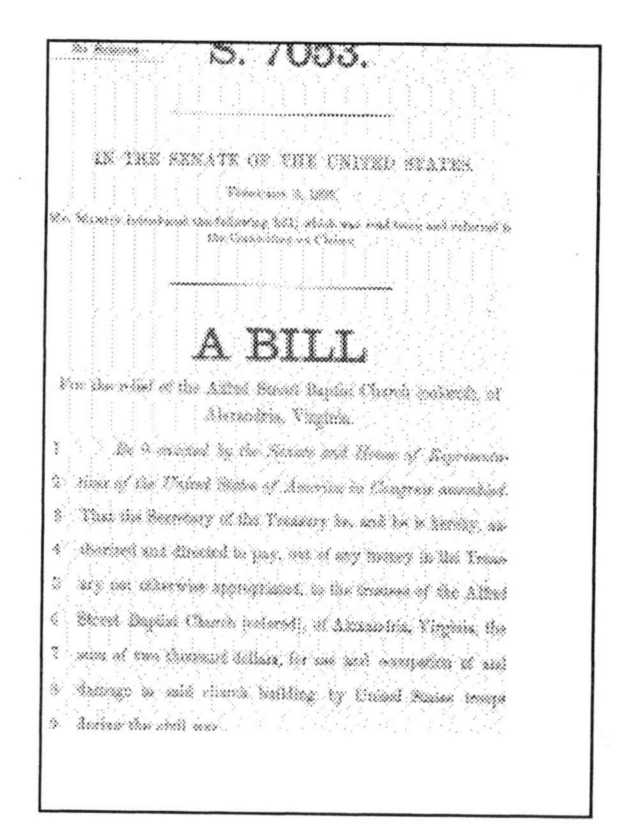

S. 7053.

IN THE SENATE OF THE UNITED STATES.

A BILL

Claims Against the U.S. Government

monies related that the church had been taken over for use by Union soldiers; that severe damage had been inflicted; and that the church had not rendered any aid to the Confederate cause during the war.

In March 1906, the U.S. Congress authorized the U.S. Treasury to pay up to $2,000 for the damages sustained by the church. Later, this amount was reduced to $900 when it was finally paid several years later.

The church already had a plan for how to use the claim money to remodel the church, even before the funds arrived. However, as it was another eight to nine years before the church actually received the money, the ongoing plans to refurbish the church had to be financed some other way.

Reverend George O. Dixon served as chair of the Building Committee and presented a plan for approval, which consisted primarily of painting plus some other renovations. Mr. Pitman was selected as the architect. In May 1906, the church received an estimate from Mr. Henry Wilson to complete work on the church at a cost of $1,165, which some members considered too high. Church members requested a second estimate from a decorator in D.C. who bid $700. Members agreed to let the D.C. firm do the work and, at the completion of his work, Mr. Striby, the decorator, donated a small gas stove to the church.

During this period, other renovations were made also at the church. At the December 1907 meeting, the trustees were authorized to put electricity in the basement of the church and they also installed a water pipe sufficient enough to run the pipe organ.

The No. 1 Willing Workers' Club, formed to raise funds for the basement in the late

1880s, continued to function and raise funds. At their February 21, 1908, meeting they agreed to have a social and assigned a committee consisting of Jennie Howard, Mildred Thompson, W.A. Price, Alice Colbert, Martha Felton, Mattie P. Price, and H.C. Boyd to plan the affair. At that time, Sister Lucy Boyd served as president of the No. 1 Willing Workers' Club, and Brother Henry Burke was secretary. There were now two such clubs—Nos. 1 and 2 Working Clubs.

The Building Committee reported at the June 8 meeting that it had collected a total of $2,925.53 and that they had spent $2,927.80 for all the upgrades. The Committee was to be disbanded when the debt was paid. To do so, the Committee borrowed $32.48 from the Poor Saints fund to pay off the debt in August 1908. By year's end, the church renovations were completed and at the December meeting the annual report was given as follows:

SOURCE OF FUNDS	AMOUNT
General Offering	$2,355.50
Window Club	109.00
No. 1 Club	228.00
No. 2 Club	202.00
Total for Year	$2,924.50

The church remained active in conventions and in the local associations. The Baptist General Association was usually held in May, with the pastor as the sole delegate. The church had cancelled its membership in the Virginia Baptist State Convention over the issue of Negroes receiving funds from white conventions and now belonged to the Virginia Baptist General Association. Occasionally, the church would agree to host a convention or association, providing that other local churches agreed to share in caring for delegates. For example, in January 1910, the church agreed to invite the Northern Virginia Baptist Association to meet at Alfred Street. In preparation, they identified a committee to prepare 200 badges for delegates. They also selected four young ladies to sell souvenir cards, with a photo of the church, outside the door during the convention. Since there was a "rule" against selling items on the church premises, at the meeting the church members voted to suspend the rule during the convention. The motion carried, and later that summer of 1910 the church hosted the association.

At the June meeting, a report from the committee on Homes and Delegates reported that the church had found boarding and lodging for 124 delegates, for which they collected ninety dollars and twenty-five cents to defray costs. Additionally, six dollars and eighty cents was collected for badges, and four dollars and forty-two cents for souvenir cards. After the convention, surplus money from the total of $121 collected, but not used, was divided among the church's many accounts to cover the pastor's salary and to pay the clerk for services rendered.

Deacons during this period included Edward Dixon, Major Johnson, Luke Raines, and Henry Boyd. Brother James Johnson, an ordained deacon from another church, was selected as a member of the Deacon Board to fill the vacancy left by Deacon Corbin. Deacon Henry Boyd was elected the chair of deacons at a regular church meeting. During that era, the entire congregation elected the chair, in contrast to contemporary practices where the officers of the Deacon Board are selected internally. Brother William K. Lee was elected as a new trustee.

Perhaps the church had ushers earlier, but the first reference to this position found in church minutes was at the meeting in August 1907. At that meeting, Reverend G.O. Dixon recommended that four young men be permanently appointed as ushers. The appointees were William Goins, Henry Harris, Alexander Jenkins, and William Evans. They served functions comparable to today's users including manning the door during services. Also, the ushers passed the plate for the penny collection for the poor at every regular service.

During this period, people continued to join at a rate of five to ten persons per year. Persons joining during the 1905–1910 period included the following ones:

NAME	DATE	METHOD
J.S. Settle	Mar 1905	Baptism
Minerva Scroggins	Mar 1905	Baptism
Lillian Lott	April 1906	Baptism
Fanny McKenney	May 1906	Baptism
Alexandria Brown	May 1906	Letter
Virginia D. Brown	May 1906	Letter
Andrew Smith	May 1906	Christian experience
Annie Hollinger	June 1906	Baptism
Mary Cave	June 1906	Christian experience
James Sparrow	July 1906	Christian experience
Charles Legrand	July 1906	Christian experience
Mrs. B.C. Legrand		Watch-care
Virginia Shelton	March 1907	Baptism
Hattie Young	March 1907	Baptism
Letitia Diggs		
Cora Bland		
Raymond Boysseau	March 1907	Baptism
James Brown		Baptism
Susie Wilson	April 1907	Baptism
Eliza Belle	April 1907	Baptism
Charles Belle	April 1907	Baptism
Andrew Smith	May 1907	Baptism
Sister Sally Caldwell		Christian experience
Dollie Johnson	July 1907	Letter
James Johnson	Nov 1907	Letter
Mary Johnson	Nov 1907	Letter
Willie Anne Greenfield	Dec 1907	Baptism
Alice Wooton	Feb 1908	Christian experience
Effie Tancil	April 1908	Baptism
Jamie Carter	April 1908	Baptism
Mary Robinson	April 1908	Baptism
Elizabeth Quander	April 1908	Baptism
Anne Quander	April 1908	Baptism

(continued)

NAME	DATE	METHOD
Jane Reynolds	April 1908	Baptism
Agnes Webb	April 1908	Restoration
Sadie Chinn	July 1908	Baptism
Ida Keith	April 1909	Baptism
James Earl	May 1909	Christian experience
Mary Earl	May 1909	Christian experience
Carrie Belle	July 1910	Baptism
Virginia Lane	October 1910	Letter
John Diamond	Feb 1910	—
Laura Benson	April 1910	Christian experience
Hattie Blackman	July 1910	Baptism
Luvenia Wallace	October 1910	Letter

In April 1909, Sister Ida Keith joined the church by baptism, while Brother James Earl and Sister Mary Earl joined in May by Christian experience. This increase in membership was offset by the dismissal of twelve persons in May for a myriad of offenses ranging from indecent conduct, to non-attendance, to uniting with another church.

The Scarlet Letter and Other Sins

. . . And the Pharisees brought the woman before Him, she who had been caught in the very act of adultery. . . . And they said . . . that the law required that she be stoned. . . .

Just as the early members who signed the original covenant in 1803 were expected to abide by Baptist principles and the authority of the Scriptures and the church over all aspects of personal behavior, so were the members in the early 1900s. Persons could be brought before the church for a variety of sins—the most egregious of the sins being adultery. In the New Testament times stoning was a common punishment for this sin and when Christianity first came to America, adultery was frequently rewarded by public flogging, or by forcing the offender to wear some emblem of shame (e.g., the Scarlet Letter) as a badge of dishonor for their sin. As late as the early years of the 20th century, Alfred Street Baptist Church continued the practice of publicly calling violators before the congregation to be censored and expelled for adultery. Each case was aired and debated before a vote to release the individual was taken.

In October 1906, hands were withdrawn from Sister S.W. for the sin of adultery. She was restored after confessing to the church and asking forgiveness in January 1907. In March 1908, hands were withdrawn from Sister Nellie Whiting for non-attendance and for selling intoxicating liquors.

In April 1909, twelve persons were dismissed for a myriad of offenses that included indecent conduct, non-attendance, and uniting with another church. Each case was aired and debated before a vote to dismiss the individual. In July 1909, hands were withdrawn from Sister J.C. for adultery, and later Brother J.W.R. was removed. In December 1909, Brother J.E. and Sister M.E., husband and wife, were both excluded for adultery. At a meeting in June 1910, the church members withdrew hands from Brother J.S. for adulterous living. The list of expulsions was quite long.

While adultery was one of the more publicized sins, other sins also resulted in expulsion. The "withdrawing of hands" spared no one—deacons, trustees, and even the pastor's son. The deacons recommended withdrawing the hands from Alvin Truatt for non-attendance. Brother Truatt appeared before the church, acknowledged his wrong, and asked for forgiveness. Even though several members spoke on his behalf, hands were withdrawn from him, but would be restored after an apology the next month.

At one meeting, hands were withdrawn from six persons, and the next month hands were withdrawn from three more individuals. Then, eleven persons were expelled at the next meeting—most for non-attendance, but Sister Effie Williams was expelled for fighting. Brother John Scroggins, Jr., the son of Deacon Scroggins, was dismissed once for non-attendance. Brother Isaac Thornton, Sister Georgina Johnson and Sister Harvey Johnson were expelled for uniting with a church of a different faith.

Members could be brought before the church for actions that may seem insignificant by contemporary standards. At a meeting in early 1910, Deacon George Dixon came forward and confessed and repented for sinning. He had attended a banquet—strictly forbidden by the colored Baptists of Alexandria. He came before the congregation and asked for forgiveness. In April 1910, Sister Beatrice Berry was excluded for dancing. A committee consisting of Martha Felton, Jane Randle, and Mildred Thompson was formed to counsel the offender on her ways. At the next church meeting, Sister Berry came before the church to ask to be pardoned for dancing, and to apologize to the deacons for saying harsh things about them. She was pardoned and restored by a narrow vote of eleven yeas and ten nays.

So it went through most of the 1900–1910 time frame. Discipline and the enforcement of rules took up much of the congregation's time and effort. With each new rule and with the enforcement of each rule, more people left the church. By the close of 1910, church membership stood at three hundred fifteen, down from three hundred twenty-one the year before. Four new members were added, seven individuals had died, and eight had been excluded.

The Rules

The church's obsession with "rules," evident at its founding, continued well into the 20th century. There was a rule to cover every conceivable situation. And the remedy for any new situation was to create a new rule. There was even a rule against communing with another church. Mrs. Delilah Price sent a letter to the church criticizing the church for this rule prohibiting persons from attending or communing with other congregations. Specifically, she thought it was wrong to punish members for attending Ebenezer Baptist Church, a sister Baptist church in the city. Brother Buchner, the clerk, pointed out that since all the members occasionally visited other churches, and since both former pastors and other people had broken the rule, he recommended that the church reconsider the rule. The vote was carried by seventeen to four in favor of rescinding this rule, with several abstentions.

The church's obsession with rules and regulations affected all areas of church life. On one occasion, Sister Emma Price asked the sexton to open the church for a wedding rehearsal. Brother Webster, one of the trustees, questioned the sexton as to what authority he had to let her use the church. After much debate, the church passed a resolution requiring that a couple pay fifty cents toward the cost of opening the church for wedding rehearsals.

Sister Emma Price

At the time, there existed a "rule" prohibiting the use of any musical instrument in the church except the organ and the piano. At one church meeting, Brother Buchner, the organist, made an impassioned plea to allow other musical instruments into the church. After much debate a resolution passed, sixteen yeas and four nays, to permit other instruments into the church, but an amendment restricted the music being played to sacred music. The church also voted to permit the cornet as a new instrument into church so long as only sacred music was played. The violin and mandolin were initially defeated as instruments to be played in church. However, the issue was resurrected later and it passed, twelve for to five against the motion.

There was even a rule concerning who could speak during worship services. The deacons proposed and the church adopted the following rule:

> In our public services, and worship on the Sabbath day, no member shall be allowed to address the church unless they have first presented the matter to the pastor of the church that he may judge whether it ought to come before the church at that time. Except Officers of the church whose right it is to address the church. It shall be the duty of the Deacons of the church to see that these rules are carried out.

Of course, there were rules against drinking or other secular activities. The church passed an "Act" stipulating that no person should frequent Kelly's Saloon, a business establishment on the corner near the church with which the church had several conflicts over the years. Moreover, the same Act stipulated that any person belonging to a local club called the "Bohemians" would automatically be subject to withdrawal of hands.

After several years of instituting individual rules to handle specific situations, in August 1910, Sister Emma Price requested that the deacons draw up a comprehensive set of rules for discipline within the entire Church. The deacons did so, and the set of "Rules" were read at the regular meeting in September 1910. A special call meeting was held on September 21 for their adoption. The rules, in six sections, were as follows:[9]

SECTION I: Any member knowing of the disorderly walk or violation of the Constitution and By-Laws of this church shall regard it as a solemn duty to report the same to the Deacons.

SECTION II: In case of disaffection between members, it shall be the duty . . . to comply with instructions in Matt 18:15–17. If this fails to reconcile, the matter shall be brought before the church through the Deacons.

SECTION III. It is the deliberate judgment of the Church, that duty and sobriety require that Christians abstain from . . . intoxicating liquors and beverages, and from making, buying or selling such liquors.

SECTION IV. As a Church, . . . we emphatically condemn the practice of Church members gambling, dancing, attending balls, circuses and the theater . . . and all other signs prohibited by the word of God . . . therefore each member of this Church is earnestly exhorted to abstain from same. That such persons shall be brought before the Church and disciplined if found guilty.

SECTION V. Charges against a member shall be in writing, and the offender notified by the clerk of the nature of the charge.

SECTION VI. No member against whom charges are pending shall be allowed to vote on any question, or partake of the Lord's Supper.

The rules were adopted one by one, but at the end of the meeting a motion was made to lay the set of rules on the table, and there they lay for the next two months. When the rules were reconsidered, the church agreed to form a committee that included lay persons as well as deacons to adopt a more suitable set of rules. Members of the committee were Sister Mary Johnson, Deacon E.P. Dixon, and Brother Frederick H. Rich, the church clerk.

That committee reported a set of revised rules that were approved by a vote of fifteen yeas and one opposed. In March 1911, 500 copies were printed. The exact wording of the revised rules is not known, as a copy has not been found. However, while they were perhaps more cordial in tone than the original set, the effect was the same as with the original list as members continued to be excluded for the types of offenses noted in the original set of rules.

Activities During 1910–1915

While discipline consumed an inordinate amount of the church's time, other church functions continued. The church still had two yearly rallies, the primary fund-raising efforts. Revivals were held sometimes twice a year. Money was raised at special functions to pay the pastor who now obtained a salary of around $650 a year. A special Sunday in October was set aside for the trustees who still maintained a separate treasury, as did the deacons. The church held Communion once every three months, at night. The members elected to hold Communion on the second month of each quarter, i.e., February, May, August, and November.

Beginning around 1910, additional special dates were added to the church calendar. Those dates included the first identified reference to a church anniversary. Over time, as reflected in anniversary bulletins, Alfred Street Baptist Church has acknowledged dif-

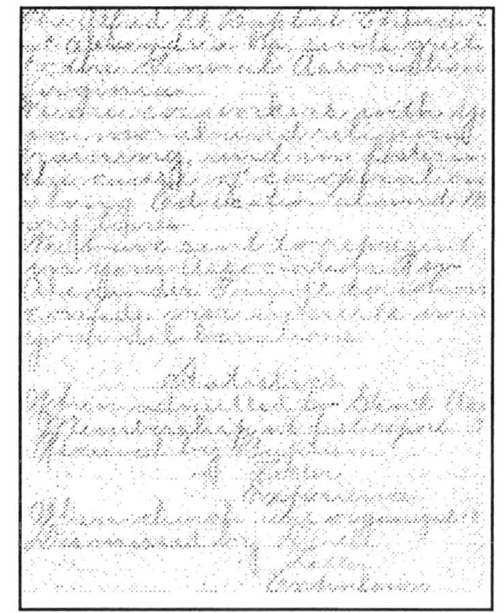

Letter to the General Association

ferent start dates at different times. The different dates are the result of varying definitions among the congregation as to what it means to "start" a church. Some considered the church as starting when an "assembly" first started meeting in homes. Others considered the start when a building was constructed to house the assembly.

To date, the earliest records of the church identifying a "start date" or "anniversary date" occur in church minutes of May 8, 1910.[10] The minutes include a draft of the letter that the pastor carried to the Baptist General Association. The church routinely sent letters of this type with the pastor, authorizing him to speak on the behalf of the members. The letter shows the date that the church joined the association (1899), the membership for that year (358), and the number that joined (14) or left (15) during the previous year. Also recorded is the entry: "When the church was organized 1852." The specific event in 1852 on which the church based this founding date is not recorded. Nevertheless, this was the first of several "start dates" that would unfold in the church's literature over the next one hundred years.

This Certifies That

were united by me in

HOLY MATRIMONY

on the 23rd day of Feby. in the Year of Our Lord One Thousand Nine Hundred and Eleven

at Alexandria, Virginia.

Witnesses

Minister

Marriage Certificate of Robert and Sadie Quander

At the August meeting in 1910, the church membership decided to have its first celebration of an anniversary. The dates selected were during the week of October 8–15, 1911. The money to be raised during the anniversary celebration would be used to buy fuel for the winter. The pastor appointed an eleven-person Anniversary Committee that consisted of the pastor, Reverend Truatt, as chair. Others on the committee included Deacon Dixon, George Lane, Frederick H. Rich, E.P. Dixon, Reverend W.A. Price, Wilbur Burke, Lottie Buchner, Lottie Burke, Hannah Strange, and Mary Brooks. The amount raised at this anniversary celebration is not known. Although the tradition may have continued, no references to anniversaries are found in subsequent minutes for another twenty years.

As some members were joining and leaving, others were engaging in a long-held tradition at Alfred Street—a wedding. In February of 1911, Reverend Truatt united in holy matrimony Robert H. Quander and Sadie V. Chinn. From this wedding would come several children who would later become members of Alfred Street including Roberta Quander, Grayce Quander, and Emmett Quander. The Quanders, who lived south of Alexandria, were growing into one of the larger families in the church.

At the February 1911 meeting, the deacons recommended an extensive list of over seventy new persons for membership—many by baptism. The list also included fifty-one persons who joined the church by confession of Christian experience, and included some persons who had been long-term members who were being restored. Seven members came by restoration, and three additional ones by watch-care. Then, on Tuesday night of that week, even more people joined, four by baptism and one by experience. On Thursday night after prayer service, four more people came by experience and four people requested baptism. So it continued through the rest of February and March 1911. At the annual submission to the Baptist General Association, the church indicated that membership had grown from 311 in May 1910 to 362 by May 1911, with forty-three baptisms, fourteen by experience, and four by letter. Six members had been lost to death, as reported in church minutes.

By now more church auxiliaries began to form. A Flower Committee was formed in June 1911 with Mary Brooks, Lottie Buchner, Lula Edmonds, and Jannie Willis as members. A Music Committee was formed with Henry Buchner, Lottie Buchner, F.H. Rich, Amanda Buchner, and Joseph Wooten as members. An Entertainment Committee that consisted of Sister E.V. Price, Mattie Taylor, and William K. Lee was also formed. Similarly, an Auditing Committee was established with Reverend G.O. Dixon, J.W. Rich, and William Goins as members.

The Auditing Committee reviewed the accounts of the various auxiliaries that still maintained individual accounts and they kept track of contributions from the membership. Church members who did not contribute regularly were disciplined. At a meeting in April 1912, the "delinquent" list was read, indicating there were thirty persons who had not met their financial obligations to the church.The deacons proposed that the right hand of fellowship be withdrawn from all delinquents, but the delinquent members' status remained in limbo until December when the church decided to notify them by letter. The church constitution contained a provision for expelling delinquents, and most members wanted it enforced.

At a July 5, 1912, meeting, the church voted to let Brother John Chase exercise his gifts in preparation for the ministry. He preached his trial sermon that following Thursday night. As Brother Chase was assuming a ministerial position, one of the other ministers was being assigned to the Deacon Board. Reverend W.A. Price was elected as deacon in January 1913 and was ordained in April of that year. About this same time, Brother E.P. Dixon resigned as Secretary of Deacons, but remained active with them.

In the summer of 1912, Reverend Truatt held a revival in the southern part of Virginia. The *Black Bee*, a local Washington, D.C., newspaper, reported in its fall 1912 edition that ". . . Reverend Truatt is one of the most successful pastors of the city, and last year conducted a great revival down in the southeastern section of Virginia. . . . Last fall, Reverend Truatt was given an elaborate celebration for his 15th anniversary as pastor of the church. . . ."[11]

In the early summer of 1913, Reverend Truatt was absent from a church meeting and Reverend Dixon acted as moderator. At that meeting, the church first withdrew hands from Brother J. H. for adultery and then from Sisters Mary Johnson, Hannah Strange and Letitia Diggs for creating a commotion in church. The church received their testimony and proceeded to grant pardons to each offender individually. Next, E.J. Johnson gave a report from the Music Committee that follows:

> 1st, That it would require $500 to make desired changes in choir stand.
> 2nd, that the committee be empowered to ask all members whose voices are not suited for choir work to resign.
> 3rd, that the choir be disbanded, and a new choir organized.
>
> Respectfully, E.J. Johnson

A great deal of debate followed this report, with a threat to remove the choir director if he did not immediately identify those persons who were not suited for singing. Brother Buchner, the choir director, continued to lead the choir and refused to ask for resignations from choir members, and he refused to resign. Ultimately, the congregation deferred, and the meeting closed with the Senior Choir still intact.

The Pastor Resigns

By 1913, conditions at the church were worsening. Finances were insufficient, membership was declining, and people were beginning to rebel against the rules. Tension had been building for some time, going back several years when Reverend George Dixon took over the chair from the pastor at the pastor's request during a business meeting in December 1908. The deacons then presented a list of charges against the pastor through the clerk, Deacon E.P. Dixon. A special report listed several complaints against the pastor that had occurred over a period of time. As a response to these complaints, the deacons proposed the following charge or decree as the remedy:

DECREE: That the Pastor's usefulness is at an end.

Signed:
Deacon H.C. Boyd
Deacon Robert Burke
Deacon E.P. Dixon
Deacon Luke Raines
Deacon James Johnson

Apparently, not all the Deacons signed the decree, including Deacon George Carroll and Deacon Philip Johnson. At the meeting the decree led to much discussion and a series of motions and counter-motions. Ultimately, the decree was "laid on the table" for later consideration and the meeting ended.

The cause of the disagreement is not known. It does appear that there had been concern over some of the pastor's actions, and the deacons had been asking individuals to sign a petition against the pastor. In fact, a large portion of the very next meeting was consumed with a debate about a disagreement between Deacon James Johnson and Deacon Legrand over the petition.

The records indicate that Deacon Johnson had asked Deacon Legrand to sign the petition, but Deacon Legrand refused to do so. Deacon Legrand then brought the request for signature to the attention of the church and Deacon Johnson denied asking him to sign the petition. During the church meeting both deacons came forward and took an oath kissing the Bible and swearing before God and the church that each was telling the truth. Some members of the church wanted both men to be silenced. After much debate, the church tabled any action, a common way of handling disagreements during this era. No action was taken against either of the deacons, nor was the pastor dismissed at that time. However, by 1913, conditions worsened. The deacons arranged a special call meeting on June 9, 1913, and Deacon Dixon read the following communication:

> We the Deacon Board of the Alfred Street Baptist Church after having prayer, fully studied the condition of all departments, feel that there should be improvements made in order to keep up and maintain our own.
>
> 1st, we notice the attendance is small.
> 2nd, the finances are not sufficient.
> 3rd, the social relations as members of Christ.
>
> We appeal to you to know if there is an hindrance known by you, that impedes the progress, and by God's help assisted by you, we want to bring about that harmony that should exist in our church home.
>
> H.C. Boyd, Chair
> E.P. Dixon, Clerk

A great deal of debate followed, but, ultimately, they deferred any action until the next meeting.

Another call meeting was convened on June 19 to consider the state of the church, with Reverend George Dixon again acting as moderator. Reverend Truatt did not attend this meeting; instead, a letter of resignation from the pastor was read. After debating the issue, it was decided to defer accepting the resignation until Reverend Truatt could present his letter in person.

At the July meeting Reverend Truatt was absent again and Reverend Dixon acted as moderator. The church members discussed routine matters that included the withdrawing of hands and receiving reports from the Music Committee. The resignation letter discussed at the special call meeting on June 19, 1913, was again discussed. The record does not indicate when or whether an actual vote was taken; however, Reverend Truatt never acted as moderator again.

The letter of resignation has not been found, so the cause of Reverend Truatt's resignation cannot be stipulated with certainty. One source postulates that it may have been due to poor health. Or, perhaps the situation at the church had gotten to be too difficult. At any rate, Reverend Truatt stepped down as pastor of Alfred Street Baptist Church in the summer of 1913, though he remained a member of the church until his death, some three years later.

ALFRED STREET BAPTIST
CHURCH
ALEXANDRIA, VA.

Minutes of Church Meeting Under Reverend Dixon

After Reverend Truatt's resignation, Reverend George Dixon remained as supply pastor for sixteen months in 1913 and 1914. During this period, the church continued to function and hold meetings, annual rallies, revivals and meet monthly, with Reverend Dixon acting as moderator. The church continued to support the General Association and attend its meetings.

In April 1914, a committee appointed to nominate a new pastor brought the name of Reverend J.C. Alston of Staunton, Virginia, before the congregation for consideration. However, after considering his qualifications, he was notified on July 8 that he had not passed the "Council" that was convened to consider his suitability. But by the fall, a new pastor would be selected, and Reverend Dixon could turn over the reins of the church to another pastor.

New Pastor Is Called, the Old One Dies

A new pastor was called to Alfred Street Baptist Church in October 1914. Reverend William Henry Rowland (W.H.R.) Powell was serving as pastor at the Ebenezer Baptist

Church in Blake, Virginia, a small town on the Virginia side of the Chesapeake Bay in Matthews County. Reverend Powell had been born in 1886 in nearby Middlesex County, Virginia, where the Rappahannock River meets the Chesapeake Bay. He was the sixth child born to William Joseph and Laura Ann Fleet Powell, both slaves in Middlesex County who ultimately parented twelve children.

Reverend W.R.H. Powell

Reverend Powell's early years are not well documented, though it is believed that the family lived through "lean years" and so his educational assistance from his parents was likely meager. At the age of twelve he professed his faith in Jesus Christ and was baptized into the First Baptist Church of Middlesex County in Amburg. When he was nineteen years old he was called to the ministry and attended the Virginia Seminary in Lynchburg, Virginia. Through the assistance of his uncle, Dr. Holland Powell, various church associations, interested friends and ministers, and the president of Virginia Seminary at Lynchburg, he never had to withdraw from school.

Reverend Powell later received Bachelor of Arts and Bachelor of Sacred Theology degrees from Lincoln University in Pennsylvania. He was ordained on August 21, 1913, at the request of Ebenezer Baptist Church in Blake, just a short distance south of Middlesex, Virginia, where he was born. He served as pastor at Ebenezer Baptist Church from May 1913 until he resigned to become pastor at Alfred Street, beginning the third Sunday in October 1914 at the age of twenty-eight years old.

When he first arrived at Alfred Street, Reverend Powell, a bachelor, lived just a short block away at 814 Duke Street, in the home of a deacon and prominent member of the community, Dr. Albert Johnson. He assumed the pastorate on the third Sunday in October 1914, at a time when membership was approximately 350 members. Upon being installed as pastor, Reverend Powell was paid sixty dollars a month. He never set a price for his ministerial services, but accepted whatever the church felt it was able and willing to pay him. At the time the church was a member of the Northern Virginia Baptist Association, the General Association of Virginia, and the Lott Carey Foreign Mission Convention. In May of 1915, the church also joined the Virginia State Convention.

In June 1915, Reverend Powell's status as a bachelor would change. On June 23, 1915, at the age of twenty-nine years, Reverend Powell married the lovely Miss Oscelletta Davies of Lynchburg, Virginia. After marrying, he and his new bride moved to 610 St. Asaph Street, midway on the block between Gibbon and Franklin Streets near the Lyles-Crouch School. He and his wife, a schoolteacher, became parents to six children.

During the first three years of his ministry at Alfred Street, Reverend Powell's predecessor, Reverend Truatt, continued to support the church. Even though he had resigned in 1913 and his name was no longer mentioned in church minutes, he continued to support Reverend Powell until his death on September 1916. Reverend Truatt passed away at his home at 403 Wolfe Street, just three blocks from the church. His obituary was published in the local paper, and it is shown below.

Reverend Truatt's funeral was held on the following Monday at the church. He was interred in Bethel Cemetery, about fifty yards from where his predecessor, Reverend Samuel Madden, was buried. Records do not indicate that any of his family members were buried there with him. His granddaughter, Mrs. Marie Madden Ford of Jamaica Estates, New York, and Sister Ulysses Jackson, a former Alfred Street member, were children during his pastorate. They remember his love for children, and the nickname "Foxy Grandpa" that some of the children gave him. Mrs. Ford remembers that Reverend Truatt dressed in a frocked coat, which he wore all the time. One never saw him without it. She also remembers that his favorite hymns were *Shall We Gather at the River, O Happy Day,* and *When Peace Like a River (It Is Well with My Soul).*

Reverend Truatt's Headstone

Death Notice.

Rev. Alexander Truatt died t
morning at 10:40 at his late r
dence, 403 Wolfe street. The fune
will be held Monday at 2 o'clock p.
at the Alfred street church. His
main will lie in state from 9 o'cl
until 1 p. m., on Monday.

Reverend Truatt's Obituary from *Gazette*

Mrs. Ford is the granddaughter of both Reverend Truatt and his predecessor, Reverend Madden. Reverend Madden's son, Jesse, married Reverend Truatt's daughter, Lelia. Mrs. Ford is one of the children of that marriage.

Reverend Powell's Early Years

Early in his career as pastor, Reverend Powell acknowledged that he was quite inexperienced. He said, "I was not well trained or equipped to be the overseer of God's flock. . . . Although I had graduated with honors from two theological seminaries, I did not know the Scriptures. I did not understand the meaning and character of the Christian life in a practical and personal sense."[13]

When Reverend Powell first came to Alfred Street in 1914, he still had a childhood fear of death. Being an inexperienced minister and having this morbid fear, he reportedly felt incapable of shepherding the flock in all areas required of ministers. Reverend Powell drew strength from the words God spoke to Joshua in Joshua 1:5:

> . . . There shall not any man be able to stand before thee, all the days of thy life; As I was with Moses, so will I be with thee: I will not fail thee, nor forsake thee.

Through these words, Reverend Powell drew strength to lead his new congregation and it helped him to overcome his fear of death.

According to Sister Laura McPhail, former church historian, Reverend Powell's fear of death was reportedly conquered early in his ministry at Alfred Street through two incidents that involved the deaths of Sister Hannah Strange and Sister Lucy Boyd.[14] Sister Hannah Strange, the wife of Reverend Jacklyn Strange, a Methodist minister, noted for his involvement in the community, lived at 807 Duke Street, just a block from Alfred Street toward Columbus Street. Reverend Powell visited her when she was gravely ill and also just a couple of hours before her death. Sister Strange, who was propped up in bed, rejoiced at his coming and outlined the program for her funeral services as he sat with her. The funeral was carried out by Reverend Powell just as she planned it, with the text being taken from the 23rd Psalm: ". . . Yea, though I walk through the valley of the shadow of death, I will fear no evil. . . ." His satisfaction with the service built confidence in his capabilities.

Later, on the Saturday before Easter in 1918, Reverend Powell made his last visit with Sister Lucy Boyd, wife of Brother Henry C. Boyd, Chair of the Board of Deacons. Reportedly, when asked how she was doing, Mrs. Boyd replied, "I hardly know how I am, Brother Pastor. But I have asked my Lord to let me spend Easter in heaven with Him tomorrow." After prayer and a few comforting words, Reverend Powell departed. When he was preparing for church Easter Sunday, he received word that she had passed.

From these two illnesses and deaths, Reverend Powell deepened his faith, cast out his fear of death, and continued doing whatever was asked in God's name. He is remembered as saying these two incidents led him to accept the biblical quote ". . . And deliver them who through fear of death were all their lifetimes subject to bondage."

During Reverend Powell's pastorate, the church experienced growth in most areas. The membership grew from approximately 350 when he arrived in 1914 to 400 members by June 1920. Of the clubs in the church, the Number One Willing Workers' Club, which had originated in 1880 to raise money to excavate a basement under the church, continued as the most noteworthy and most outstanding of the church's auxiliaries. Through it, Mrs. Emma Price and her daughter Mattie were the most outstanding fund-raisers and they usually brought in the largest sum of money of any group. Rallies were held twice yearly and remained the most common form of fund-raising to generate operating capital.

On May 4, 1915, the federal government finally paid Alfred Street $900 for use of the church building as a hospital to care for the ill and wounded solders during the Civil War. After lawyer's fees, Alfred Street received a total of $767. The war had been over for exactly fifty years and the U.S. government finally compensated Alfred Street and the First Baptist Church of Alexandria, the sister church from 1803. First Baptist received $3,900 from the government the same year for use of their facility during the war.

In 1916, shortly after receiving the Civil War funds, the church purchased two lots, 814 and 816 Queen Street, for $600 in order to erect a parsonage. With the remaining funds Reverend Powell bought materials to build the two-story, five-bedroom brick parsonage at 816 Queen Street. The parsonage was constructed during 1917–1918 with Reverend Powell as architect and builder. He did not accept any pay or any type of remuneration from the church, as all work was done gratis.

In October 1917, Reverend Powell and his wife, Oscelletta, moved into the new residence at 816 Queen Street. There, a second child, Oscelletta, named after her mother, was born on August 2, 1918. An earlier daughter, Mary Lauretta, had been born on April 17, 1916, at their previous residence on St. Asaph Street. Eventually, the Powells would have a total of six children. The remaining four children, W.H.R. Powell, Jr., Bertha Lenora Powell (Snead), Henry Ward Powell, and Geraldine Anita Powell (Adams), were born after Rev. Powell left Alfred Street. His son, W.H.R. Powell, Jr., followed his father's footsteps into the Baptist ministry.

The Alfred Street Baptist Church Parsonage

In 1917, the church had a most successful rally, raising $2,200. It was the largest amount raised during the Powell administration, or during any previous year, as far as church records show.

The First World War

In general, these were good times at Alfred Street. The church had a young, dynamic preacher in Reverend Powell; there were sufficient funds to purchase a parsonage; and large amounts of money were being raised at the yearly rallies. Times were good. Then, in 1917, the country entered World War I.

The war had been brewing in the background for several years before the United States entered it. World War I actually started in August 1914, but the United States tried desperately to avoid foreign entanglements and remained neutral for two years. Then, in February 1915, the German admiralty announced that all allied vessels operating in a broad area of the Atlantic Ocean would be torpedoed without warning. On May 7, 1915, the Germans sank the British liner *Lusitania*, killing 128 Americans, among others. Later, they began to sink U.S. ships indiscriminately. Finally, on April 6, 1917, President Woodrow Wilson signed a war resolution that was immediately approved by Congress. The United States was at war.

With the war came rationing. Food, shoes and fuel were strictly rationed and a war labor board used coercive measures to prevent labor strikes. Blue laws had already gone into effect on June 18, 1916, in the state of Virginia, so merchants were prohibited from opening stores to sell merchandise on Sunday.

The U.S. Army grew rapidly to 4,000,000 men, raised mainly by conscription under the Selective Service Act of 1917. Over 1,200,000 of these would serve in Europe. Within a short time, the Allied and American assaults resulted in the German government appealing to President Wilson for an armistice in October 1918. By January 1919, peace negations were underway in Versailles, France.

While the war was fought on European soil, its effects were felt worldwide, Alexandria included. According to his own account, the war and its side effects created one of the more moving experiences that Reverend Powell had while at Alfred Street Baptist Church. In the fall of 1918, there was a dreadful influenza or "Spanish flu" epidemic that spread throughout the world, transported by soldiers traveling as part of the war effort. The epidemic affected the entire globe with thousands of fatalities. The flu killed over 550,000 persons nationwide—over ten times the deaths from combat and other causes (e.g., illness) related directly to the fighting. For 17 weeks, starting in August 1918, there was a national shortage of coffins and gravediggers to bury the dead.

Locally, the flu hit its peak in Alexandria in October 1918 with nineteen influenza deaths on October 14, according to the *Alexandria Gazette.*[15] There were fourteen burials in the city the following Sunday alone. Church services and other public gatherings were canceled, and some churches (e.g., Christ Church, Westminster Presbyterian) were turned into emergency hospitals. Drivers traveled the streets, pulling wagons calling out, "Any sick or dead?" So many people were dying that undertakers could not provide enough coffins. Gravediggers worked through the night to keep up with the demand.

During the epidemic, Reverend Powell, his wife, and two daughters (thirteen months and two years old, respectively) became seriously ill. Reverend Powell waited on the family until he became too ill to be of any service. At that time, there was no one living at the parsonage but the four of them, all of whom were dreadfully ill and bedridden.

A committee of Alfred Street members, headed by Sister Emma Price, formed a chain service, taking turns, and stayed with the family day and night until they were all out of danger. This is all the more remarkable because most people were frightened of those sick and dying of flu and generally stayed away.

From Camp Humphrey (currently Fort Belvoir), about twelve miles south of Alexandria, Reverend Powell remembers a daily stream of dead soldiers as a constant sight. They were brought to the undertakers in Alexandria on army trucks stacked like cords of wood, according to his recollection. However, not one of the persons serving the Powell family became ill with this disease that was killing so many. Their perseverance in caring for Reverend Powell is remembered by his family as one of the most blessed experiences they encountered during their stay at Alfred Street Baptist Church.

Old Pastor Departs; A New Pastor Is Named

Even in the midst of the war, activities continued as usual at Alfred Street. Revivals and the annual rallies were held. In January of 1916, the church raised Reverend Powell's salary from sixty to seventy dollars a month. Then, it was raised again to seventy-five dollars a month in 1918, and to ninety dollars a month in 1919. In 1919, an additional lot, next to the church, was purchased from Mr. Chauncy for $800. But, even with the raises and other growth activities, Alfred Street was unable to keep the dynamic leader, who was just thirty-four years old. In June 1920, after five years and eight months at Alfred Street, Reverend Powell left to serve as pastor at a church in Pittsburgh, Pennsylvania. He was later called to the Shiloh Baptist Church in Philadelphia, Pennsylvania, from which he retired.

During Reverend Powell's tenure at Alfred Street, the membership had grown, the church had joined the new Virginia State Baptist Convention, and he left the church free of all debt and mortgage obligations.

Reverend Powell later became president of his alma mater, Virginia Seminary, in Lynchburg, Virginia. While there he purchased a 500-acre farm in western Virginia near Lynchburg and named it Hol-Reba (for his uncle and his aunt). The farm was converted into a church retreat that was operational for several years before falling into disrepair. After leaving Alfred Street, Reverend Powell continued serving as a pastor for fifty-seven years at four different churches. He returned to Alfred Street several times including visits in 1950 and again in 1968 to preach the sermon for the Church anniversary on November 17, 1968.

Reverend Andrew Warren Adkins

Four months after the close of Reverend W.H.R. Powell's ministry at Alfred Street, and on his recommendation, Alfred Street members called Reverend Andrew Warren Adkins as their next pastor. Reverend Adkins was born in Charles City County, Virginia on February 26, 1884. His home was located near the towns of Lynchburg and Farmville, and is situated about twenty miles from each town. He attended Virginia Union University from which he earned Bachelor of Arts and Bachelor of Divinity degrees. He began his pastorate at Alfred Street on the first Sunday in October 1920, and served as pastor for the next forty-three years.

Before coming to Alfred Street, Reverend Adkins was pastor at the Grafton Baptist Church in Middlesex, Virginia, a small community on the eastern shore of Virginia, just off U.S. Highway 13 near Chincoteague. While serving as pastor there for three years, he also taught at the Middlesex Training School and was united in holy matrimony to Miss Mattie Hamlette of Newport News, Virginia, a teacher in that city. They were married on June 15, 1918, when he was 34 years old. His wife had taught in Gloucester and Keysville, Virginia. Mrs. Adkins also taught school in Middlesex while living there as a young bride. She was a graduate of Thyne Institute in Chase City, Virginia and would later pursue advanced studies at Virginia Union and Virginia State College.

By the time of their arrival in Alexandria, the Adkins were the proud parents of a young daughter, Theresa. Mrs. Adkins taught for a while at the Spring-Bank School, a small school in Fairfax County south of Alexandria near Quander Road. Many of the members of Alfred Street who lived along the U.S. Route 1 corridor attended school there and were taught by Mrs. Adkins.[16] Mrs. Adkins was later appointed a teacher in Parker-Gray Elementary School, but she soon resigned to continue raising her family. Reverend Adkins also began teaching at Parker-Gray.

At that time, Parker-Gray was still a new school for Negroes. Beginning during Reconstruction and continuing up until the 1920s, the city of Alexandria maintained two separate schools for Negroes, the Hallowell School for Girls and the Snowden School for Boys. These schools were built by George L. Seaton, a noted builder and Alfred Street deacon, under the auspices of the Freedmen's Bureau. In 1920, the schools were merged to create a new school that was renamed Parker-Gray Elementary, named for John Parker and Sarah Gray, the respected principals of Hallowell and Snowden Schools. The newly created school provided education for Negro children from first through eighth grades.

Initially, Parker-Gray was to have been an elementary school with Mr. White as the teacher-principal and with eleven other teachers, some of whom had come from the two former schools. However, at some time during the year, Reverend Adkins, along with other teachers, cited the need and petitioned the Alexandria School Superintendent for a high school for colored children.

Prior to the opening of Parker-Gray, colored students in the city of Alexandria had attended high schools in the District of Columbia or elsewhere. Those high school students who lived in the counties of Northern Virginia (e.g., Fairfax, Fauquier) attended a single high school in Manassas, Virginia. These students traveled a lengthy bus route from their respective communities and those who attended Alfred Street Baptist Church traveled from Gum Springs through Franconia, through Fairfax, and on to Manassas.

Reverend Adkins, certified to teach Greek, Latin, math and science, asked if he might start a high school class. He was given permission to use one classroom in the new Parker-Gray building with the idea that additional grades would be added in succeeding years. The year 1921 marks the beginning of a major shift in Negro education. On November 21, 1921, the formation of a high school for Negroes was begun with one teacher, Reverend Adkins, and eighteen students. Although the high school did not grow as quickly as Reverend Adkins and others had hoped, Parker-Gray continued to offer some high school courses. It would be another five years before Parker-Gray Elementary became Alexandria's first full course Negro high school and another ten years before it would be recognized by the Virginia State Department of Education as an accredited, four-year secondary school.

Alfred Street Baptist Church has had a long history of involvement in the education of Negroes in Alexandria that goes as far back as the 1820s, and Reverend Adkins continued that tradition of educational involvement when he came to Alfred Street. Alfred Street's involvement in education was often with the public school system and with other education-related efforts such as public libraries. For instance, in 1917, Alfred Street opened a 1,600-volume library in the basement of the church because the city of Alexandria was without library facilities for Negroes. A Lending Book, showing the name, date, and number of the book borrowed by each individual, still exists among church records.

The record book of loans from the lending library covers book loans from 1920 to 1935 and is arranged alphabetically by the borrower's name. The church devised and used its own cataloguing system, similar to the Dewey Decimal System. The borrower's address, the catalogue number of the book borrowed, the date the book was borrowed, and the due date for return are also listed. In some cases, in addition to the catalogue number, the name of the book that was borrowed is listed. Some of the books loaned included *Black Beauty, Aesop's Fables, Little Miss Mouse, The Young Salem, Pilgrim's Progress,* and *Young Salesman*. The record book of ninety-five pages covers loans until

1935.[17] It provides a detailed look at reading habits within Negro families in Alexandria during this period.

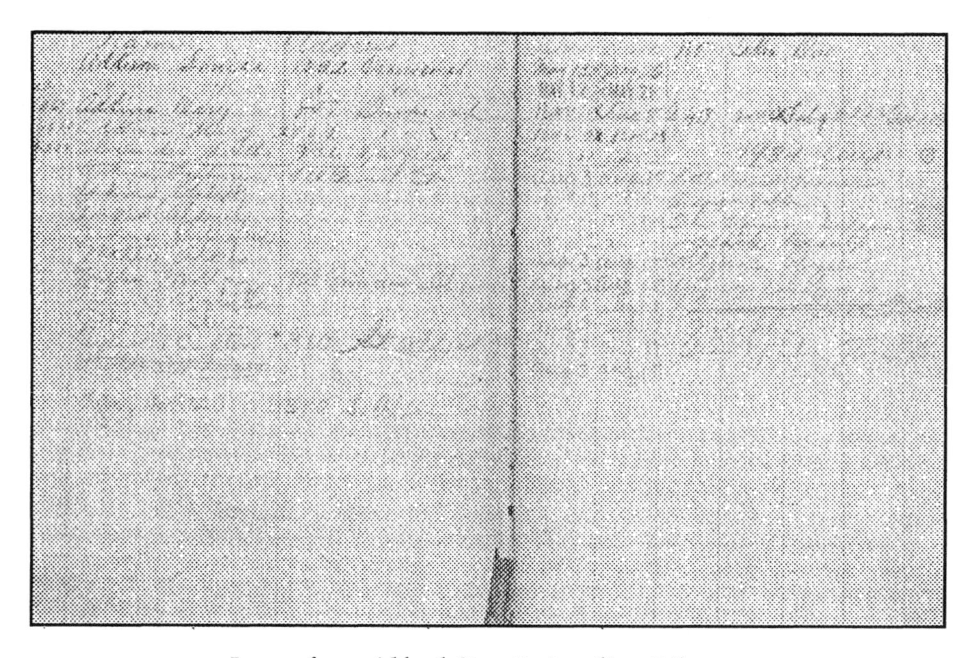

Loans from Alfred Street's Lending Library

Chapter Seven

1925–1950: The Depression and World War II

To everything there is a season . . . a time for war and a time for peace . . . (Eccles. 3)

The depression and the war that followed dominated the national agenda during this era and had its effects on Alfred Street as well. The economic situation created by the depression changed the focus of activity at the church from *rules and discipline* to *issues of funding*. The war that followed ended the depression and the economic problems for the church, but also created emotional hardships as the young men from Alfred Street marched off to war. The war's end would usher in a return to normalcy and more prosperity at the church and in the nation.

The Setting

The *Roaring Twenties*, as the beginning of this period is often called, was characterized by a period of prosperity and good times. President William G. Harding died suddenly in the summer of 1923 from a cerebral embolism and was replaced by the more sober-minded Calvin Coolidge, his vice president. President Coolidge seemed an odd choice as the nation's leader during the *Jazz Age* with speakeasies and *Flapper Girls* who had begun to assert the rights of women. Many young women, who had been forced to work outside of the home because of labor shortages during World War I, were unwilling to give up their social independence after the war ended. Having won the right to vote with the 19th Amendment, the new "emancipated" woman demanded to be recognized as a man's equal in all areas. She adopted a masculine look, bobbing her hair and abandoning her corsets; and she drank and smoked in public.

People were working fewer hours and earning more than ever before. New consumer goods—radios, telephones, refrigerators, motorcars—made life better. These were indeed good times! On the darker side, anti-foreign sentiment led to the revival of racist, anti-Semitic, and anti-Catholic sentiments and the resurrection of the Ku Klux Klan, especially in rural areas. During the decade of the 1920s, the Ku Klux Klan achieved a membership of approximately 500,000 members, gained control over many city and state governments, and increased their intimidation of Negroes.[1]

Locally, Negroes who attended Alfred Street also began to prosper. Many who lived out in the country, south of town, operated small but prosperous farms. In fact, during this period, most of what is known today as Northern Virginia was still all farmland. The Quander families who belonged to Alfred Street maintained a set of farms just south of the city. Most residents of that region attended school either at Spring Bank School in the vicinity of Quander Road and U.S. Route 1 where Mrs. Lorraine Funn Atkins taught in the mid-1920s. She was a graduate of the Manassas Normal School for Teachers and a member of Alfred Street. Some of her students who later became members of Alfred Street included Juanita Stanton, Gladys Quander–Tancil, Henry Quander, Edith Quander-Reeves, and Lecount Quander. Other students in that area went to a small school near Gum Springs, Virginia. The Gum Springs and Spring Bank schools went only to seventh grade. After seventh grade, the family was responsible for the education of its children at higher levels that might include individual tutors or sending the children off to boarding school to complete high school.[2]

Around this time, Fairfax, Prince William, and Fauquier Counties began supporting the Manassas Industrial School (founded by Mrs. Jennie Dean), as a public Negro high school for all of Northern Virginia. For students from Alfred Street such as Roberta Quander, Welton Quander, Evangeline Robinson and Russell Stokes, who lived in the Spring Bank area of the county, this meant a 33-mile commute to school in the morning and a comparable commute in the afternoon.[3]

Inside the city of Alexandria, Negro children of this era still attended Parker-Gray School. It was still an elementary school for boys and girls, with some classes taught at the high school level. In these early years of the school's founding, the school had a faculty of nine teachers. When Reverend Adkins arrived, he initially taught eighth grade and was soon appointed the first high school teacher. Though he taught some high school courses, it would be another ten years before Parker-Gray would become a full-fledged four-year high school and graduate its first high school class.

Mrs. Hattie Gaskins, a current member of Alfred Street, was a little girl in Alexandria during this period, and recalls that not all of the streets were paved. A couple of streets were cobblestone, but many were just dirt streets. She remembers when the northern end of Washington Street was paved beyond Montgomery Street, and how convicts in striped suits did the paving. Later, when tracks for trolleys were laid down King Street, she recalls that Negro men laid the tracks. They sang and pounded with their hammers similar to those pictured in the famous song about John Henry, the steel driving man. She recalls that they never missed a spike as they swung, always keeping a constant rhythm.[4]

During this time, Blacks from other parts of the state began moving into Alexandria. As an example, Mr. Ellis Eubanks, who currently lives adjacent to the church, moved to Alexandria from Lynchburg at the age of eighteen. He remembers a juke-joint named Kelly's being located down the street from Alfred Street at the corner of Wolfe and Alfred Streets.[5] Kelly's had been a thorn in the side of the church since before the turn of the century. Loud music and brawls that occurred there could sometimes be heard inside the sanctuary during worship services. After church, however, the children from Alfred

Street would stop by Kelly's to buy candy, sodas, and other sundries. For a time, it was the only commercial establishment in the immediate area surrounding the church. Residents living near the church had to walk uptown for food, wood, clothes, and kerosene.

Mr. Eubanks remembers that the area around Alfred Street, still called the *Bottoms,* consisted of some freestanding frame houses when he first moved here. The area to the rear of the church was low-lying like a swamp and when it rained one needed to wear thigh-high boots to traverse the area if they wanted to keep dry. During those years, he lived uptown and remembers that many streets were still not paved—not even King Street in its entirety.

And even as Negroes were moving into the city, some of the more progressive families were moving out into what was then becoming one of the area's first Negro suburbs. A Negro attorney had divided parts of a large farm into sizable lots just south of Crystal City in the area on Glebe Road and Four Mile Run, and started a new subdivision called *Sunnyside.* One could reach this new area by riding a trolley that ran out from the city along Commonwealth Avenue. By the late 1920s there were five Negro families living there, including the Theodore Lee and Warren Wair families of Alfred Street Baptist Church, and the Brooks family that, at the time, attended Zion Baptist Church. Some fifty years later, three of the little boys who played stickball in the streets, Leo Brooks and the twins Richard and Ralph Wair, would grow up and serve as deacons together at Alfred Street. A fourth boy, Lovell Lee, would become an usher and a member of one of the choirs.

Some persons owned cars, but others still used horses and buggies. Gladys Quander-Tancil recalls that her father had a car, but would winterize his car at the first freeze in November and return to using the horse and buggy. She remembers that each family had a parking space at the church for horses, just as for cars. The space where her father would park his mule, Maude, was in the 800 block of Wolfe Street.[6]

Life at Alfred Street: 1925–1930

By 1925, Reverend Adkins had served as pastor at Alfred Street for five years and had begun to leave his imprint on the activities of the church. He and Mrs. Adkins were now parents of six children. She had stopped work to rear the children but would soon return to teaching. Though the church had been renamed Alfred Street Baptist now for over twenty-five years, most members and persons on the street still referred to it as First Baptist. To the south of the church was a tombstone company, and to the north was an alley, and then an auto glass company called G&S Glass occupied the remainder of the block leading to Duke Street.

In 1925, Richard Hollinger was elected as Church Clerk. The church had just initiated plans to raise $3,200 for the purchase of a new organ. Sister Celia Blair was selected as president of the Organ Fund, with Sister Emma Price as secretary, and Sister Kate Franklin as treasurer. During this period, the church's total annual budget was only about $3,500, so raising an additional $3,200 would be comparable to raising an additional year's offerings in less than a two-year period. The pastor appointed a music committee to select an organist and to plan a dedication service when the organ arrived. Mr. Edward Walden was recommended as organist at sixteen dollars a month, and carfare twice a week. Brother Walter Butler accepted the position as choirmaster.

During 1925, rallies were held on the first Sundays in June and November. That year, each member was requested to contribute ten dollars each in the June rally, and was asked to give five dollars for the November rally. For each rally, captains were assigned who were expected to collect at least $100. Clubs and various auxiliaries (e.g., Parsonage Club) were also expected to contribute $100. The total collected in the two annual rallies that year was $1,371. For missions that year, a total of forty-four dollars was collected, and for the Poor Saints twenty-eight dollars. For all of 1925, a total of $3,331 was collected from all sources, including the general offering.

While the amount collected was a respectable sum, some members were still not contributing as expected. So the church agreed to post a roll listing the names of all members who were delinquent in their giving in the vestibule. A committee consisting of eleven young ladies was appointed and authorized to notify each member on the list personally about their indebtedness to the church.

Among the other occurrences during this period, Reverend A.A. Lott requested and was granted a Letter of Dismission to unite with another church. Reverend Lott had been a very active member of the congregation, and the source of several conflicts in the early 1900s. His request for a Letter of Dismission was one of only a few such requests during this time.

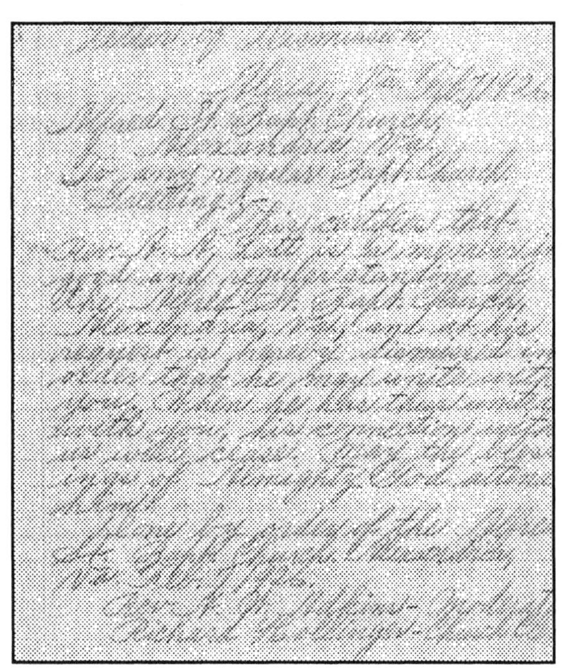

Letter of Dismission for Reverend A.A. Lott

In 1926, in order to strengthen the spiritual life of the church, Reverend Adkins asked all deacons to meet him in the study for prayer before the Sunday morning service. This practice of the deacons meeting with the pastor for prayer continued for the next seventy-five years occurring throughout Reverend Adkins' administration and into the administration of his successor. The meetings ceased when changes in the physical layout of the building made movements back and forth to the pastor's study more difficult.

In March 1926, the church finally received word that the organ that had been ordered in the previous year would arrive in three weeks. A committee that consisted of Sister Martha Miller (Chair Lady), Brother Rich, Sister Blair, Sister M.V. Ware, Brother Butler, Sister Annie Dixon, and Sister Mattie Coleman planned a dedication ceremony in April 1926. The new organ was dedicated at this special ceremony and Mr. Edward Walden became the first organist, while Brother Walter Butler continued as choirmaster.

Interior of Sanctuary with New Organ

Most meetings during this era were poorly attended. Reference is made in the minutes to the fact that nine persons constituted a quorum. Even though the church elected officers each New Year, no one at church kept records of all the officers' names. As an example, at a July 1926 meeting, the church decided to drop Brother Walter Stanard's name from the Trustee Board. Yet most people did not know who the trustees were, as deeds and other official documents had several different names affixed. In fact, most of the names of trustees had not been registered at the courthouse, as is required by law. To rectify this situation, the pastor was made a committee of one to assess the status of trustees, and he discovered that only two were registered—Brother Walter Stanard and Brother George Hurbert Turner. At the October 1926 meeting, the church selected a full slate of new trustees to include J.H. Rich, Walter Butler, Jerry Barrett, and Reverend W.A. Price. Brother Barrett was also still serving as a deacon, and was elected Chair of Deacons at that meeting. The pastor pointed out that any meeting of trustees or deacons without him present was illegal.

At the October 1926 church meeting, minutes refer to a discussion about ". . . the success of the Homecoming. . . ."[7] This is the first reference found to such an event, and may well have been the first one that was ever held. Homecomings, to welcome home former members who had moved north as part of the great migration, were just becoming a tradition in many churches. Generally, in the late summer or fall of the year, churches would host a homecoming when former members returned for a visit. The homecoming events became great fund-raisers though the amount raised in the 1926 homecoming is not recorded. However, the total amount raised from all sources in 1926 was $3,830. That amount included $1,174 from the rallies and $1,639 in a special collection for the pastor. At this time, the church still maintained separate accounts for various collections and expenses. The end-of-year balance in the bank for all accounts was $345.31.

Over the years, Communion had been celebrated at different times and with different frequency. In the earliest years, Communion was celebrated once monthly, then once quarterly. It had been celebrated on Saturday afternoons, Sunday mornings and at other times. In February 1927, the church decided that Communion would be changed from Sunday morning to Sunday afternoon and that on Communion Sunday no night service would be held.

In like manner, evening and night services were initiated and ceased over time. They were reinstituted in the late 1920s to serve a special need. Many of the women of the church worked as domestic help in the homes of neighboring white families. And in the tradition of that period, on Sunday mornings they prepared breakfast and lunch, and then put on a simple boiled dinner that could be handled by the lady of the house. They were then given the rest of the day off. Members of many of the white families of this era remembered the boiled dinners served on Sunday afternoons after the help got the day off. For these maids, the evening and night services were frequently the only services they could attend on Sundays.

Members continued to join during the late 1920s at a fairly good rate. Persons who joined Alfred Street during this era included:

NAME	DATE	METHOD
Louise Tyler	February 1927	Letter
George Hurbert Turner	March 1927	Baptism
Ernest Eugene Pollard	March 1927	
Arville Howard Pollard	March 1927	Baptism
Willie Mae Williams	March 1927	
Nannie M. Williams	March 1927	
Sarah Davis	March 1927	
Maude V. Lewis	March 1927	Baptism
Alice Tyler	April 1927	Baptism
Theresa Adkins	April 1927	Baptism
Elnora Tyler	April 1927	
Maude Lewis	April 1927	
Mattie Martin	April 1927	
Mattie Middleton	April 1927	
Florence Mack	April 1927	Baptism
Wilbur Brown	July 1927	Baptism
Ester Neal	August 1927	Baptism
Netti Harris	November 1927	Baptism

Reverend Adkin's oldest daughter, Theresa, was among those listed as joining the church on the first Sunday in April, Palm Sunday, and was baptized by her father. Also shown as joining was George Hurbert Turner who would later become a deacon of the church. Mattie Middleton also joined during this period. She would later become an organist for the Sunday School.

And, even as new members were arriving, old ones were retiring to that all sufficient rest. Reverend George O. Dixon passed on March 6, 1928. He had served as a supply pastor for sixteen months during 1913–1914 following Reverend Truatt's resignation. He served until the church selected Reverend Powell as the new pastor.

The fall of 1928 was a busy season with numerous major events. Homecoming that year was a weeklong celebration that began on the second Sunday in November and ended with a rally on the third Sunday. There was preaching and singing all through the week. To increase the level of spirituality, the deacons also asked for a revival in the fall. Deacon Price remarked: "If we set the trap, we never know what we might catch." However, Reverend Adkins resisted and would not hold a revival for several more years.

On the fourth Sunday in December 1928, the choir director requested use of the church for the Christmas Cantata. Collectively, the cantata, the homecoming, the annual rally, and the general offering produced $3,967 from those sources that year. Still, money continued to be an issue within the church even though it was being raised in fairly significant amounts.

To increase giving some years earlier, the church had posted the names of delinquents in the vestibule. By 1929, it was suggested that the financial roll be called at each of the church's quarterly meetings in January, April, July, and October. There was much discussion as some members felt that only an overall financial report was necessary. Still, in 1929, the financial rolls were being called at each meeting, as were the financial collections of various clubs. Overall, 1929 was a good year and Reverend Adkins thanked all clubs for doing commendable work.

The Depression Begins

Even as Alfred Street Baptist Church was beginning to express concern about financial matters, things were about to get worse as the Great Depression loomed on the horizon. Prohibition and religion had been the major issues of the 1928 presidential election between Democrat Herbert Hoover and Republican Alfred E. Smith, governor of New York. Then, in October 1929, only seven months after Herbert Hoover took office, the stock market crashed. The average value of the fifty leading stocks fell by almost one-half in two months. The market crash, in addition to other factors, led to the Great Depression that would engulf the entire nation for the next twelve years.

When the stock market crashed in October, whites were caught by surprise, but Negroes had been feeling the pinch for some time. Very few Negroes were involved in the stock market, so their loss was not in investments. Instead, as factory after factory failed or cut production, Negro men joined the ranks of the unemployed. In Detroit, sixty percent of black workers were unemployed by 1931, while in Houston, Texas, thirty-five percent of black workers were out of work. And for the next five or six years, approximately forty percent of Negro men were unemployed nationwide.[8]

As the depression continued, Negro families turned to relief or welfare in vast numbers. In the North where there was less discrimination, fifty-two percent of all black families were drawing some form of government aid. In the South twenty-five to thirty percent of black families received government aid. These rough conditions led blacks to look for anything to give them some promise of relief. Many turned to numbers, an illegal game similar to today's legal state lotteries in which, for a small bet, a player could possibly win a large amount of money. Others sought relief in entertainment from the big bands (jazz bands) of Louis Armstrong, Louis Jordan, Cab Calloway, and Count Basie. In Alexandria, Mr. Julian Dove, who would later become a trustee at Alfred Street, made arrangements to have many of these big bands play at the Elks Home in Alexandria.

Still others seeking relief from the depression sought solace in churches, many of them storefronts that sprung up overnight. For example, in Chicago some fifty-five storefront churches were spaced along South State Street in a ten-block stretch. In the early 1930s, these new churches of the north developed a new form of religious music called "gospel hymns." This music emerged out of the northern part of the country and represented a northern counterpart to Negro spirituals that emerged from the South. These songs that evolved from Philadelphia, Detroit, and Chicago expressed a joy of living and a deep religious faith. However, it would be many years before many mainline churches would embrace them, partly because of their pedigree and their emotionalism.[9]

In Alexandria, as elsewhere, the depression created a class system of the haves and have-nots. The haves included many of the members of Alfred Street Baptist Church who were teachers or government workers. Even in the midst of the depression, the schools were required to function as was the federal government. For example, Warren Wair, who had moved his family out of the city to *Sunnyside*, continued working as a postman, and Reverend Adkins continued as a teacher. Additionally, many of the women members of Alfred Street worked as domestic workers in the large homes in the Belle Haven section of Alexandria. During the depression, some employers cut back on domestic help, so the persons who provided maid services were impacted. Therefore, some families of the congregation of Alfred Street were hit hard while others were not. Yet, as most of the congregation was comprised of teachers and government workers, the church was not impacted as much as some other local congregations.

During the depression, Negro men in Alexandria mowed lawns and worked on day jobs to make ends meet. Several worked at Robinson Sand and Gravel in the vicinity of the present-day Robinson Terminal near the waterfront. The company would hire men to assist in dredging the Potomac River channel, and would then sell the sand that had been collected. Walter Butler, Roberta Quander's uncle and the choirmaster at Alfred Street Baptist Church, worked there and was mortally wounded in the 1930s when a cable snapped on the sand dredge.[10]

Among the members of Alfred Street Baptist Church who lived in the county, money was also scarce for buying cars and clothes, but most farmers had plenty to eat, particularly the Quanders. They were vegetable farmers and during the depression continued to grow produce to sell at either the large market in Washington, D.C., on Maine Avenue, or the smaller one in Alexandria near City Hall. At the market, they would sell vegetables for cash, but would also barter vegetables for fish, pork, and occasionally beef. Moreover, each family farm had two or three hogs and cows that provided milk and meats. The families also had an earthen cellar under the house in which potatoes and other ground crops were kept during the winter. Thus, although times were tough, there was never a shortage of food around the Quander farms.[11]

Nationally, many veterans from World War I were destitute and camped out on the national mall to demonstrate and demand help from the federal government. Some three years into the depression, Franklin Delano Roosevelt would be elected as the thirty-second president of the United States and would initiate a series of civil work projects that would improve conditions somewhat. But the economic damage was already done and the depression would continue for about eight more years until the next war ended the economic downturn.

Activities at Alfred Street During the Depression

During the early years of the depression, life at Alfred Street took a sudden turn for the worse as conditions did nationally. The church was still holding quarterly business meetings in January, April, July, and October. The church celebrated its anniversary—a six-night affair—in late 1929, and at the January 1930 meeting the pastor reported that the Anniversary Rally had been a great success, raising $1,159. These anniversaries were initiated primarily as fund-raisers and the first in 1910 had been to raise money for winter fuel. By the time of the depression, the needs were different, but anniversaries continued to be held in the late fall to stock the treasury before the onset of winter.

However, even though the rally of 1929 was a success, overall collections were down by one-third for 1929, and amounted to $2,903 for the year as the depression set in. The church ended the year 1929 with only sixteen dollars and sixty-two cents on hand.

For 1930, the previous officers were retained. Revival was again discussed but Reverend Adkins still thought the time was not yet right. He wanted to have a spiritual awakening within the congregation before holding a revival. The June rally was held as usual, as were the other special days. Expenses and finances were beginning to consume a large part of the church's attention by the April quarterly meeting. At that meeting the church agreed to cut expenses to $145 a month, and another special meeting was held just three weeks later to discuss finances. Because of the worsening situation, the church asked each club to be responsible for $200 a year, up from $100 just two years earlier. The pastor indicated that the church needed all the help it could get with its dwindling income. By July, the total indebtedness of the church had reached nearly $400.

The worsening financial condition at the church resulted in a special deacons' meeting on September 1, 1930. After the meeting, the deacons forwarded the following recommendation to the church body:

(1) That the Committee on Delinquent Members be made a little more active.
(2) That a new registration be made of all members.
(3) That we have a week of prayer.

Brother Jerry Barrett, Chair
Brother Walter Butler, Act. Secretary

As a result of the recommendation, new persons were appointed to the registration and finance committees. These committees were responsible for ensuring that the church roll was accurate and that all members lived up to their financial obligations.

While finances took up most of the church's energies, other activities also continued. The pastor and choir took their usual vacations in August. The church held another church anniversary in the fall, and Brother Wilbur Brown, who had joined in 1927, was ordained a deacon during anniversary week. The pastor's anniversary celebration began on the third Sunday in October and ended the next Friday night. At the October quarterly meeting, the pastor set a goal of fifty new members for the next year. Some of the new persons who joined the church included Mrs. Helen Carroll, who was baptized, and

Misses Edith and Eunice Quander, who joined in October 1930.

At a special call meeting in December 1930, the hand of fellowship was withdrawn from Sister Mattie Melton. Sister Melton had joined back in 1927, on the same Sunday as Reverend Adkins' daughter (Theresa). The withdrawal of hands after three years marked the first reference to a withdrawal since about 1915 when the practice was so rampant. However, after making a verbal statement acknowledging her wrongdoing, Sister Melton was restored to membership. Sister Melton had been given music lessons at the expense of the church and Sunday School so that a trained musician would be available when needed. She was one of a small number of persons granted permission to practice on the organ. She played the piano for the Sunday School and was a productive member of the music department; but there were occasional incidents that brought her conduct into question before the church that prompted yet another withdrawal six years later. These two incidents are the only withdrawals of hands recorded during this period.

The New Year, 1931, began much as the old year had ended. Lots of routine business was conducted at the first quarterly meeting in January. Financial reports were presented and dates for the next rallies were set. A new trustee, Brother Wilbur Brown, was selected. Brother Brown, who joined in 1927, had been ordained a deacon just three months prior to his election to the Board of Trustees. The previous year's church officers were retained. Reverend Adkins thanked everybody and remarked that though financially strapped, 1930 had been one of the happiest years he had spent at Alfred Street Baptist Church.

In 1931, the sexton was paid fifteen dollars a month and Brother John Jackson, who had accepted the proposed terms, was now the new organist. He replaced Brother Walter Butler who had been killed in a work-related accident at the Robinson Terminal sand company. Brother Jackson would serve as organist for the next twenty-five years. Brother Benjamin Burke assisted him and became the assistant organist in November 1931. The church still exercised close control over the use of its new organ, and restricted its use primarily to church services. Not only was the use of the musical instruments in the church still restricted, the types of instruments that could be played at Alfred Street were also restricted. The Sunday School was still strictly forbidden from using the organ during morning devotions.

At one of the church meetings, a question was raised as to whether ". . . sinners could sing in the choir." Reverend Adkins indicated that he felt the organist and choir members should be Christians who can walk in harmony with others. The choir, musical instruments and the music departments were frequent sources of conflict during this period. One of Reverend Adkins' early controversies, and possibly the most serious that he experienced during his tenure, involved the choir. The issue involved the music department in general and the organist, Mr. John Jackson, in particular.

It is not clear whether the issue was over the organist's pay, the types of music he selected, or his tenure as organist. However, the issue caused a great deal of concern with the trustees and with some of the members. Many members left the church due to this rift. Those members who left included the Whitmore adults and their daughters Liza, Helen, Corrine, and Joyce, who were long-term members and whose association with

Alfred Street went back into the latter part of the 19th century. Many of the records dealing with this misunderstanding are missing, but many of those leaving the church did return later and assumed leadership positions in the church.

Overall, donations for 1931 were down as the effects of the depression worsened. The church opened the year with a balance of sixty-seven dollars and sixteen cents in the church's treasury. By mid-year, the church had raised only $1,092, which included $692 raised at the June rally. By way of illustration, the amounts raised for the month of June 1931 were as follows:

SOURCE	AMOUNT
Envelopes	$ 76.82
Baskets	8.36
Missions	.87
Poor	1.28
Rally	692.49
Total	**$ 779.82**

Just three years earlier, total collections for mid-year were approaching almost $2,000. During the midst of the depression, most yearly collections were only one-half of the old collections. Money was received from several sources: envelopes, baskets, missions, collections for the poor, and rallies. Without the rally totals, a typical month's income for the entire church was $100 to $150. Expenses generally equaled or exceeded contributions, so there was generally little money saved. The largest expense was for the pastor's salary. Reverend Adkins was generally paid twice a month, but the amount varied depending upon what was being raised. He was *salaried*, but the church was frequently delinquent in paying him.

At the beginning of 1932, new officers were elected: Brother Samuel Turner was Treasurer; Sister Katie Franklin was Financial Secretary; Sister Hattie F. Parker was retained as Clerk/Recording Secretary; Sister Louise Tyler was Sexton; and Mr. John Jackson was retained as organist. The trustees accepted Brother Jerry Barrett's resignation. Brother Samuel Turner replaced him on the Board of Trustees.

Because of weakening finances, Brother John Jackson, the organist, was asked to accept a five-dollar cut in his salary. At the same time, Sister Tyler, the sexton, was given an increase to fifteen dollars per month, due to the increased workload of having to start a fire each Sunday to heat the sanctuary.[12]

During this period, the position of sexton was an elected position within the church. Later, this role would be taken over by janitors or custodians who may not have even belonged to the church. But in the 1920s and 1930s, the sexton held a key position within the church hierarchy.

At the April 1932 meeting, Sister Mattie Adkins, the pastor's wife, asked permission to organize a Junior Church among the youth. The church agreed and a Junior Church was formed that held services on Sunday night. This gave young people a chance to conduct services and make themselves useful. Within the next several months, she would also open a library for the young people. Eventually, the Junior Church or various youth departments would be started and discontinued several times. But the foundation for these programs was laid in the summer of 1932.

The June rally, normally the largest fund-raising event, raised only $420 in 1932. Over the summer, the Number One Willing Workers' Club put on several fund-raisers to raise money to repair the church. They were given a vote of thanks for remodeling the windows of the church at a cost of seventy-eight dollars to repair the front windows, and two hundred sixteen dollars to repair the side windows. However, there was still a need for additional work on the church as both the roof and the baptismal pool were in need of repairs. The exact date that the church installed a pool and moved baptisms indoors, as opposed to conducting them in the Potomac River at Battery Rodgers, is not known. But by the early 1930s the baptismal pool had already been installed and damaged.

During this era, the church was frequently loaned out to other organizations for their functions with proceeds going to the church treasury. In June 1933, the church was loaned to Sister Martha Miller for the school closing exercises. Sister Katie Franklin asked to use the church for the Eastern Star service. Sister Mattie Adkins asked to use the church on May 29 for school closing for her school. Brother Henry asked for use of the church on June 4 for use by the Masons of St. John's Day. And Sister Parker requsted use of the church on the first Wednesday in August for a two-day convention of the Princesses of Abyssinia.

In August, the pastor and the choir members were given their usual vacations. Sister Martha Miller was granted permission to elect her officers for the newly formed Pastor's Aide Club. She had formed the club at a meeting on May 10, 1933, to take care of special needs of the pastor such as handling visiting ministers or other functions for which there was no one to help. Also, the church agreed to have only a morning service during the summer, doing away with the afternoon service.

On August 27, a special call meeting was convened to explore the financial condition of the church. It was agreed to have a special collection, with each member giving a dollar on the third Sunday in September. The trustees had set aside a separate table for those who could contribute a dollar and the collection on Dollar Sunday was very successful. But the idea of exposing members who gave and those who could not give a dollar did not go over well with some members of the congregation even though most did contribute. The church decided to do away with the extra table on future Dollar Sundays which remained part of the church calendar through the remainder of the depression.

The Depression Deepens

During the entire year 1933, only three people were baptized and four joined as watch-care. This was a reduction in new members from previous years when more than fifteen to twenty-five people had joined. Thus, even though many churches experienced an increase in membership during the depression, this was not so at Alfred Street Baptist Church. Even though only a few new members were joining, those who remained at the church continued to want to be preachers and deacons. On November 9, 1933, Brother W.T. Henry, the father of Jacqueline Henry-Green, requested a license to preach. Permission was finally granted at the January 1934 meeting, and the ordination occasion was a special one. A year earlier, Deacon Barrett nominated Warren Wair, the father of Richard and Ralph Wair, as a new deacon. Deacon Warren Wair was one of the younger deacons, having been ordained in 1933. He had recently moved his family to *Sunnyside*, the new suburban enclave near Four Mile Run just south of present-day Crystal City. He would soon become Chair of the Board of Deacons, and would remain so for most of the remainder of Reverend Adkins' tenure.

In February 1934, finances still dominated the church's agenda and the deacons' report to the church contained the following recommendations:

(1) That we have a Woman's Day and $1 Rally on the 3rd Sunday in March 1934.
(2) A special collection be taken for payment of Gas and Water.
(3) A Revival be started 2nd Mon in April.
(4) Pastor will be paid on Monday after the 2nd and 4th Sunday of each month.

This is the first known reference to a Woman's Day that would ultimately become one of the biggest events on the annual church calendar at Alfred Street Baptist Church.[13] During the early years, these occasions were primarily fund-raisers, though in later years they would focus more on spiritual development and music.

Reverend Henry and Deacon Wair

During the depression years of the 1930s, every "special" day was basically a fund-raiser, and the focus was on which auxiliary could raise the most money on their special day. In these early years Woman's Day was a fairly simple event with a newly assembled women's choir, and the selection of a prominent woman speaker. Generally, these speakers were lay persons as the idea of women preachers had not fully developed. There may or may not have been refreshments after service, depending upon the wishes of the chairlady for the event. Women's Day would continue in this manner for most of the next forty years, before becoming one of the most anticipated events in the church calendar year at Alfred Street.

At the February 1934 church meeting, the church agreed to celebrate its 113th anniversary in the fall of the year. Alfred Street had begun celebrating anniversaries in 1910, when it celebrated its 58th anniversary that assumed a church start date of 1852. The celebration now planned for 1934 was the first time that the assumed start date had changed from 1852 to an assumed start date of 1821.[14] The specific events on which these possible start dates were based are not known. Over time, the start date for planning church anniversaries would change several times before it was agreed that the church's origins were in 1803. Although the year on which anniversaries were based would change, anniversaries were always held in the late fall—initially to raise funds for fuel, and later by tradition.

For most of the early 20th century, the church continued to have but a single choir. In the middle of the 1930s, however, the Junior Choir was formed. The exact date of its formation is not known. Perhaps it began as part of the Junior Church started by Sister Mattie Adkins in 1932. At any rate, by August 1934, a Junior Choir existed and they sang for the 11 a.m. services during August when the regular choir and pastor were given their usual vacations. Also, in October 1934, use of the church was granted to Mrs. Franklin for a Halloween party for the youth as more and more opportunities for youth were being created.

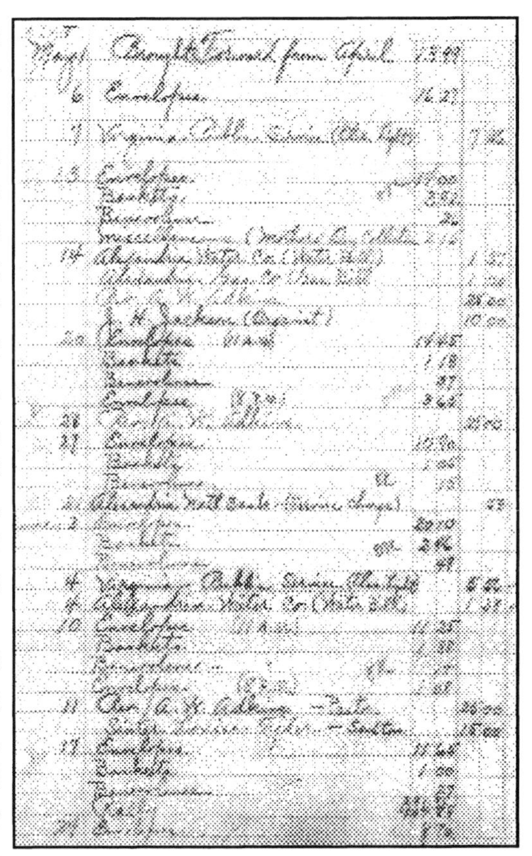

Financial Records of Church, 1934

As of May 1934, the church was still paying the pastor in a sporadic manner. His salary had been increased now to ninety dollars per month. However, the church paid whatever they could monthly and then caught up after a rally or major fund-raiser. For example, in May of 1934 the pastor was paid twenty-five dollars after the first and third Sundays. Then, in June, the Spring Rally was held at which $391.96 was raised. The pastor was paid $290 that month as the church sought to catch up on delinquent payments.

Finally, Reverend Adkins relented in his resistance to a revival and, upon the recommendation of the deacons, one was held in 1934. Revivals had been held earlier at the church under Reverend Madden in the 1890s, but had been dropped from the church calendar in the intervening years. The spring revivalist in 1934 was Reverend A. Mackley, who was paid five dollars for the week-long revival. In July, Reverend B.F. Gant was paid four dollars for preaching during the morning service as the pastor took his usual vacation. During August, while the pastor and choir were on vacation, Sister Benjie Burke played the organ and the Junior Choir again served.

In August, Reverend W.T. Henry, recently ordained, attended the Northern Virginia Baptist Association on behalf of the church. Expenses and a contribution to the convention by the church totaled fifteen dollars. Alfred Street Baptist Church, which had joined the Northern Virginia Baptist Association in 1898, remained active during this period, and reported annual church membership to the Association as shown on the following page.

YEAR	CHURCH MEMBERSHIP
1926	300
1927	350
1928	310
1929	—
1930	350
1931	—
1932	185
1933	—
1934	327

Membership dropped from over 300 at the beginning of the depression to as low as 183 by 1937. This was the smallest membership recorded in over eighty years, since just before the Civil War.

While the church continued its membership in the Lott Carey Baptist Convention and other national associations, there is little data to suggest any real involvement such as attendance at conventions or major contribution of funds. The church did continue to support the two Negro Baptist religious colleges of that era—Virginia Union and the Virginia Seminary. Although Alfred Street had supported Virginia Seminary in previous years, the church did not send money there in 1937. Instead the members collected three dollars and fifty-four cents in a special offering to support Virginia Union in Richmond.

Life at Alfred Street During 1935–1940

At the January 1935 meeting, the church agreed to keep all installed officers. Brothers John Cole and William Russell were nominated as deacons, and Brother Walter Butler was selected as Chair of the Deacon Board. Also, Brother Milton Franklin was elected as a trustee to replace Brother Wilbur Brown upon his death. Brother George Hurbert Turner was selected as Chair of Trustees. Also, Sister Martha Miller suggested that the church have female deaconesses. Deaconesses had been assigned during Reverend Truatt's pastorate in the late 1880s, but there had been none now for over forty years. The motion was set aside, and deaconesses at Alfred Street Baptist Church would have to wait another thirty years.

The number of deacons during this period was generally seven to eight. Those who served during this period included Deacons George Hurbert Turner, who had joined in 1927, and Deacons Cole, Price, Gossner, and Jerry Barrett. Deacon Cole was a short, heavy-set man who, along with Deacon Gossner, is remembered for praying *hard*. In fact, the most remembered characteristic of this group of deacons by persons from that era is their ability to pray. Each prayer was an occasion for intense utterances and each deacon prayed hard.

Deacon Jerry Barrett lived on Duke Street between Alfred Street Baptist Church and Shiloh Baptist Church. He was light-skinned and small in stature. Deacon Jerry Barrett passed in October 1934, and the church donated a funeral wreath. He had previously been Chair of the Board of Deacons prior to Deacon Butler's tenure.

Deacon George Turner, who had joined in 1926, lived on Prince Street and later on

Payne Street. He was nicknamed *Daddy Bad* by those close to him and he had two children, Herbert and Francis, who also attended Alfred Street. Deacon Turner was a fireman on the Southern Railroad and was killed during a horrible train wreck at Madison, Virginia, in the region near Culpepper. Scalding water from the train's boiler exploded and severely burned him. As his was a horrible and unexpected death, a large number of persons from the community attended his funeral at the church.

As the depression deepened, the church began the year 1935 with only two dollars and twenty cents in the treasury. Lack of funds led to a series of fund-raisers as contributions in the Sunday collections were sparse. In March 1935, the church held a Talent Rally that raised eighty-three dollars. Women's Day in April raised twelve dollars and seventy-five cents, while the June rally raised $300.51. The June rally remained the largest fund-raiser of the year.

During this period, rallies of every conceivable type were used to raise funds. There were Fashion Rallies, Oyster Rallies, Tea Rallies, and Pig Feet-and-Chitterling Rallies. The church held Pew Rallies, Shoe Rallies, and Bag Rallies. Sometimes the rally was held as part of the worship service (e.g., June rally), and sometimes the rally would be held on Saturday. For those rallies involving the selling of foods, persons could either eat in the church basement, or have the plates delivered to their homes by a cadre of young men who were just learning to drive the few cars owned by members of Alfred Street. Other auxiliaries of the church attempted to assist with the financial problems where possible. The Missionary Circle donated twenty-five dollars that year, while the Pastor's Aide contributed ninety-six dollars and sixty-two cents that they raised at a Novelty Wedding. Mrs. Martha Miller continued as president of the Pastor's Aide during this era.

Whenever additional funds were needed for church expenses, another special fund was set up to raise money to resolve that particular issue. For example, in October and November of 1935, the church started a Paint Fund to raise money to paint the sanctuary and the vestibule. A total of $636 was collected that included a bank loan of $450 that was repaid over several years. The upgrade to the sanctuary included installing lights on the organ and the rostrum in the sanctuary. The church building was closed during the period of repairs, and the church had a joint re-opening ceremony in concert with the pastor's 15th anniversary during the two-week period of December 1–13, 1935. Special programs for the celebration were printed at a cost of six dollars and thirty-five cents. Collections were taken each night of the celebration, and forty-eight dollars and ninety cents were raised.

During November of 1936, there was a major problem with the baptismal pool. The bottom of the pool contained welded joints that would expand when heavy persons stood in the pool to be baptized. Water would then seep from the pool into the kitchen area in the basement. In November the sexton, Sister Louise Tyler, was given an additional fifty cents for bailing water from the basement. To correct the problem, the church then held a Pool Rally to raise money to repair the pool, with each person being asked to donate one dollar. By May 1937, the church made the first payment of thirty-five dollars to the contractor for the repairs. Then, after the pool was repaired, problems with the organ led to the formation of an Organ Repair Fund. Each member was asked to donate fifty cents and nine dollars and fifty cents was raised by the close of the year.

Paying the pastor remained the major expense of the church, and the church always seemed to be delinquent. The church attempted to pay him in equal payments twice per month, but frequently they were delinquent due to limited income. To assist with the problem, on Easter Sunday 1938, the Pastor's Aide Society began a Pastor's Salary Table for funds specifically designated to pay the pastor. During the first three months of operations, they raised $183. In May 1938, they held a chicken dinner for the Pastor's Table, raising an additional four dollars and fifty cents.

The church received income from several sources during these difficult financial times by frequently loaning out the facility to other churches for their activities and charging them a nominal fee. Zion Baptist once paid five dollars to use the auditorium, while Bethlehem Baptist paid six dollars and forty-five cents for use of the baptismal pool. Their baptisms generally were held at Alfred Street on Tuesdays during the mid-1930s. However, later, as the depression worsened, Alfred Street reduced its charge and only charged them five dollars for use of the pool. Zion Baptist across town on Lee Street also used Alfred Street Baptist Church's pool and was charged a comparable fee.

In 1939, a problem arose with the church's roof. The usual practice of starting a Roof Fund was the solution. To supplement the Roof Fund, the No. 1 Willing Workers' Club, which had been formed in the 1880s to raise funds for a church basement, continued with its fund-raising efforts and held an Oyster Supper in February and a Shoe Rally in March 1939, raising thirty-seven dollars. By now, money was really scarce and was becoming harder and harder to obtain. A Spring Revival was held the first week of May that year and on successive nights the church raised fifty-two cents, sixty-four cents, fifty-five cents, and one dollar on the final night. To pay the revivalist, Reverend A.J. Edwards, the church later took up a special collection specifically for that purpose.

In July 1939, a major upgrade to the basement of the church, which was now over fifty years old, was started. The church borrowed $230 from First Citizens National Bank and began pouring 190 yards of concrete on July 7. Mr. George Penic did the concrete work to repair the basement and completed the work in August. Mr. Henry White charged thirty-six dollars for doing the necessary painting. Then, in November, he also painted the church kitchen after all repairs were completed on the basement.

During the 1935–1940 time frame, two additional events took place outside of the church that affected the lives of members of Alfred Street and other Negro residents of Alexandria. First, after over fifteen years of operations, Parker-Gray School was now a *real* high school. Reverend Adkins had been instrumental in starting its first high school classes in 1921. In 1936, the school finally received its accreditation from the state of Virginia and graduated its first class of seniors. A typical graduating class might only consist of four or five students. For example, only four graduated from Parker-Gray in 1939—Carlton Tyler, Louise Ewell Hernandez, Gladys Wair, and Aldrich Adkins.[15] Though about thirty to forty students might start together in elementary school, by high school graduation only a few would remain. Reverend Adkins continued teaching at the high school full-time and preaching at Alfred Street Baptist Church for another twenty years. Sometimes, he also served as the assistant principal. Though the school building has since been destroyed, a portion of Wythe Street on which the school was located has been renamed for the school.

Arrest at Queen Street Library

The second event that affected Alfred Street members was also related to education and pertained to the libraries for Negro youth. The city of Alexandria offered no library facilities for Negroes at that time. Even though the Alfred Street Lending Library of over 1,600 volumes partially filled the needs for Negro youth, many persons felt that the city-operated library should serve Negroes also. The city of Alexandria had opened the Alexandria Free Library on Queen Street for white residents in 1937. Although it was maintained with city funds, Negroes could not use it.

In August 1939, Samuel Wilbert Tucker (1913–1990), not a member of Alfred Street, organized a protest that became one of the first sit-in demonstrations some two decades before the famous lunch counter sit-ins that began in Greensboro, North Carolina. After several attempts to argue his case for a true public library, Tucker organized this protest in August 1939.[16] He instructed five African Americans—Otto Tucker, Edward Gaddis, Morris Murray, William Evans, and Clarence Strange—to go into the reading room of the Queen Street Library and refuse to leave. Tucker also gave instructions to the men to be respectably dressed and peacefully uncooperative. The five were arrested, charged, and soon released. A judge never ruled on the case as Tucker had wanted; rather, the charges were simply dropped. However, as a result of the case, the city soon built the small Robinson Library for Negroes on Wythe Street in 1940. Today, that small library is part of the Alexandria Black History Resource Center.

Life During the Early 1940s

The decade of the 1940s began with nineteen dollars and twenty-five cents in the treasury at Alfred Street. During the week of January 7–14, the church held a special week of services in which each department gave a program on an assigned night. Over twenty dollars were raised during the week-long service. Then, on February 25, the church held its annual Negro Night in celebration of Negro History Month. The Senior Choir performed its annual program for the church, singing music by Negro composers, in a concert entitled *A Night with Negro Composers*.

To raise additional funds, the church hosted other music productions as well. In April the church hosted a traveling production of *Uncle Joe* by a visiting troupe, and on June 27, 1940, the Tuskegee Jubilee Singers were in recital at the church, performing a production entitled *Songs of the South*. Over one hundred tickets were printed, though exact attendance is not known. That effort raised eight dollars. Total revenue for the entire second quarter of 1940 was about $625.

The second quarter was usually the best quarter financially, as the June rally was held in this quarter. Total receipts for the entire year still rarely exceeded $2,000. For comparison, annual income and expenditures for the second quarter (April–June) for the five-year period 1936–1940 were as follows:

Second Quarter Financial Status

YEAR	JUNE RALLY	TOTAL INCOME	EXPENDITURES
1936	$148	$498	$449
1937	95	689	689
1938	186	619	581
1939	—	—	—
1940	427	798	783

Over the summer of 1940, the pastor had his usual vacation and, in the fall, Reverend Adkins celebrated his 20th anniversary as pastor on August 20. Thirty dollars and forty cents were raised on that occasion. That year the Fall Rally netted only forty-seven dollars, evidence of the worsening depression. A total of $1,900 was raised for the entire year, and the church ended with a balance of fourteen dollars and forty-seven cents in the treasury. Yet, in spite of the financial difficulties, activities of the church continued. Women's Day, Negro Night, Homecoming, and the annual rallies gave the congregation a respite from the day-to-day cares of living during the depression.

Coulter Willis, Baritone

During these years, the Senior Choir continued to function with about twenty to twenty-five voices. The size of the choir was constrained by the seating arrangement in the choir loft, which was fairly small and had individual seats similar to those used in movie theaters. This limited the ability to squeeze additional persons on a row. Walter Butler and Coulter Willis were two prominent baritones in the choir. Other members included Robert Owens, Aldrich Adkins, Terris Hollinger, Pearl Willis, Eleanor Thaxson-Winston, and Cora Green—Jacqueline-Henry Green's mother. The choir primarily sang anthems. Only one service was held on most Sundays at 11:00 a.m. The offering was collected after the sermon, and the entire service was generally completed by 12:45 p.m. In the afternoon at 4:00 p.m., the Baptist Young People's Union (BYPU), the forerunner of the Baptist Training Union (BTU), held its meetings.

The Sunday School program at the church was well attended. It started about 9:30 a.m. and lasted until the 11:00 a.m. service began. The Sunday School had a band or orchestra that played during devotions and on other occasions. Most classes were held in the main sanctuary, with each class using one or two pews in each corner. Either Sister Benjie Burke or Sister Coultamae Willis-Wilson was the designated pianist for the Sunday school and they played when the orchestra did not lead devotions.

Generally, everyone sat in the same seat at Sunday service even though seats were not specifically assigned. One could tell with a quick glance who was present and who was absent. There were two sets of pews—about fifteen to twenty on the left side of the church and a comparable number on the right. Welton Quander's family sat about four pews from the rear on the right side, while Roberta Quander's family sat about halfway to the front on the left side near the center aisle. Terris Hollinger sat on the right side near the back, while the Hollie Burke family sat on the right side about halfway to the front. Mrs. Fannie Wair (Richard and Ralph's mother) sat near the center aisle on the right side, about four pews from the front. Sister Benjie Burke, the clerk, sat on the left side of the church, near the center aisle, about five pews from the front.[17]

Even the deacons sat in the same seat each Sunday. For the deacons, there were five chairs across the front by the pulpit, facing the congregation. Deacon Sherman Majors sat in the first chair on the right, while Deacon Wair sat in the second chair from the right. Deacons Sam Turner and George H. Turner (brothers) sat in the chairs on the left side while Deacon William Dickerson sat in the center. When Deacon Burruss joined the board later, his chair was also placed along the center.

As in prior years, occasionally an unpleasantness arose over conduct among the deacons. One of the deacons was once brought before the church for selling alcohol, a practice strictly forbidden by Baptists. His situation was complicated, however, by the fact that selling alcohol was part of his second job as a bartender at the Elks Lodge. The prohibition in the church's rules against selling alcohol was intended to restrict the sale of *illicit* alcohol, and made no reference to alcohol sold as part of one's job. Nevertheless, the situation created quite a stir within the congregation, but it does not appear he was ever expelled for the activity.

World War II Begins

In the midst of the financial difficulties that the church was experiencing due to the depression, yet another distraction loomed on the horizon—another world war. After World War I, most Americans concluded that participating in international affairs had been a mistake. They sought peace through isolation and throughout the 1930s most Americans advocated a policy of disarmament and non-intervention. In support of this policy, the U.S. Congress passed the Neutrality Act of 1935, asserting its neutrality during a conflict between Italy and Ethiopia. When Germany invaded Poland in 1939, touching off World War II, President Roosevelt called Congress into special session to revise the Neutrality Act to reassert the country's neutrality in the war. However, the revised act did allow the countries on both sides to purchase weapons from the United States on a cash-and-carry basis.[18]

Ultimately, efforts to remain neutral failed with the bombing of Pearl Harbor, and on December 8, 1941, Congress declared war against Japan with only one dissenting vote. Three days later, Germany and Italy declared war against the United States and Congress voted unanimously to reciprocate. The United States was now in another war in which over 15 million men and women would serve in the armed forces before its conclusion.

The war affected the lives of Negroes and whites alike. As the war approached, the mood of the Negroes was one of bitterness and brooding, emotions left over from World War I. Negroes had fought for human rights in Europe in World War I, and then were denied these same rights upon their return to the United States of America. Also, leading up to Pearl Harbor, Negroes faced two serious problems at home. First, they were denied participation in the enormous national defense industry, which offered skilled, high-paying jobs. The president of North American Aviation even said ". . . Regardless of their training as aircraft workers, we will not employ Negroes in the North American plants. It is against company policy."[19]

The second major problem was that Negroes faced discrimination even if they joined the military to support the war effort. Despite a standing army of approximately 230,000, only 4,450 were Negroes in 1940. Most of these were in labor-intensive quartermaster or truck and transportation units that remained totally segregated in housing, training, and combat. To add insult to injury, even the American Red Cross announced in 1941 that it would not accept the blood of Negro donors for blood banks for wounded soldiers.[20]

Yet, during the war, many Negroes were called and served gallantly. Some of the more notable ones include Dorie Miller, who was awarded the Navy Cross for heroism during the initial attack on Pearl Harbor. Benjamin O. Davis, Sr., became the nation's first black general officer during the war, and Chappie James and Benjamin O. Davis, Jr., demonstrated the abilities of Negroes as aviators as members of the Tuskegee Airmen, the country's first all-black fighter unit.

In addition to these prominent Negroes, men from Alfred Street were also called to serve. The pastor's three sons, Robert, Rutherford, and Aldrich Adkins, were called and served. Rutherford became an aviator as a member of the famed Tuskegee Airmen. Additionally, William Willis, Welton Quander, Emmet Quander, Harry and "Tip" Burke, Lorenza Funn, Ernest and Vernon Carroll, and Arthur Wilson also served. Most of these men were inducted into the U.S. Army as few opportunities existed in the other services. Within the Army most Negroes served in quartermaster or trucking units. Many of them experienced their induction and initial physical exams at Virginia Union in Richmond, before heading off to Basic Training at Camp Lejeune, North Carolina, or New Orleans, Louisiana.

The largest call-up for members from Alfred Street occurred in the summer of 1943. Following church service one Sunday in July of that year, Reverend Adkins called all the young men about to enter service together for prayer, and told them ". . . everything will be alright. . . ." Most of these young men were nineteen or twenty years old and would spend the next three years in Europe, not returning home even once until the war was over.

Life at Alfred Street in the Midst of the War

While the war's toll on human life was indescribable, the war did have the positive effect of ending the depression and by 1942 things were looking up financially at Alfred Street. Jobs were again plentiful and could almost be had by simply walking up to a factory and saying: "I want to work." In Alexandria, many of the members of Alfred Street got new jobs at the two torpedo plants that had been opened on Franklin Street and at the foot of King Street. Many of these new jobs were in menial labor, but jobs and paychecks were now plentiful.

With the increases in family income came a gradual increase in offerings at Alfred

Street. For the six-month period of January to June 1942, income totaled $1,321, including $471 for the June rally, $605 from envelopes, $10 from baskets, $27 from Negro Night celebrating Negro History, and $56 for Easter Offering. Women's Day was still held on the fourth Sunday in April, and the women raised $22 in special offerings in addition to the regular offering. A year later, in 1943, for the first six months, Alfred Street raised $2,005, and funds would continue to pour in at Homecoming and in the Fall Rally. Conditions were beginning to improve with collections almost double the income of the previous two or three years.

During this prosperous period, the church purchased a new set of hardwood pews. Vernon Carroll was chairman of the Committee on Pews for the church, and individual persons were invited to purchase a pew. The short pews could be bought for thirty dollars, while the long ones cost sixty dollars each. Sister Gladys Quander-Tancil remembered, as a young adult, purchasing a short one, while her parents purchased a long one.

During most of the war, Alfred Street had five to seven deacons, many of whom had been serving for five to ten years. Deacon Warren McKenzie Wair was the chairman during this time. He had been a deacon since 1933, and was the father of twin sons Richard and Ralph Wair, who were serving in Europe in the war. The Wair twins would later follow their father as deacons. Other deacons included William Dickerson, Robert Owens, Charles Burruss, and John Strange.

Deacon Dickerson was a widower who lived near the church on Duke Street. Robert Owens lived on Columbus Street, and was the youngest of the deacons. Charles Burruss had children in the church, one of which is a current member, Sister Reba Barnes-Burruss. And John Strange, the eldest of the deacons, was a member of the Fraternal Order of Masons as well. This group of deacons would continue to serve the church through the war and would do so for most of the next twenty-five years.

Additional activities were now also available for the youth. A chapter of the Baptist Training Union (BTU) was organized at Alfred Street in April 1945 and, in June, Ms. LaVerne Herbert obtained thirteen dollars from the church for a BTU social. The BTU collected dues totaling about one to three dollars at each of their weekly Saturday meetings. A Men's Club had also been formed and had twenty-two dollars in its treasury. Total receipts from all sources for 1945 were $2,744.

As the war progressed, more than 7,500 blacks became officers in the armed forces. Combat units were finally opened to Negroes, and by 1945 slightly more than ten percent of the 259,173 black troops belonged to combat units.[21] Most however, had continued to serve in labor-intensive units such as Transportation and Re-Supply.

During the war, in addition to the large number of people in uniform, civilian employment also rose, particularly among women and minorities. One of the results of the labor shortage was that women and Negroes made significant social and economic progress during this period. Although the armed forces had continued to practice segregation, as did the Red Cross blood banks, President Roosevelt, under pressure from Negroes, had earlier signed an executive order prohibiting racial discrimination in job training programs and employment among defense contractors. As the war progressed, nearly two million Negroes were at work in the defense industry.

The year 1945 would prove to be a pivotal one in the nation's history, for after four years of conflict, the spring and summer of 1945 witnessed a series of events that brought a change in the nation and the world. On April 12, America's president, Franklin D. Roosevelt, died suddenly in Georgia of a cerebral hemorrhage, and was succeeded by the vice president, Harry S. Truman. There was a national outpouring of grief, especially among Negroes, over the loss of their beloved president.

In the following months, the German armed forces collapsed in Europe, and on May 4 all German forces surrendered. In the Pacific, the invasion of Iwo Jima and Okinawa in early 1945 brought Japan under a state of siege. During the summer, before an invasion could take place, the United States dropped an atomic bomb on Hiroshima and Nagasaki and hostilities in the Pacific ended. On September 2, 1945, on a battleship in Tokyo harbor, Japan surrendered and World War II ended.

The war was now over. Things would begin to improve at Alfred Street Baptist Church.

Post-War Activities at Alfred Street

After the war, things began to return to normal at Alfred Street. The young men who returned to the church following the war noted that at the church and all through the community there existed a festive atmosphere and a sense of joviality and excitement. This excitement lasted for nearly two years after the war when the last of Alfred Street's young men returned home.

Welton Quander During World War II

When the war ended, there were still over four million soldiers in Europe, and the military adopted a point system to determine who came home first. Points were accumulated for length of time in Europe, time spent in actual combat, type of unit, etc., and those with the most points came home right away. Those with lower points continued to stay, accumulating additional points until it was time for them to return. For example, Welton Quander came home in the summer of 1946, almost one year after the end of the hostilities. Even a year later, returning soldiers were treated like heroes and given parades and other salutes.

Upon returning home, the soldiers found that not much had changed at Alfred Street. The size of the congregation was still about 200 persons. Services were still conducted in much the same manner. Giving through tithes and offerings were slightly up, as was attendance from additional people who had moved to Alexandria during the war in search of new jobs. Expenses at the church were about the same, including the cost for both wood and coal. A cord of wood cost eighteen dollars in January 1946, and three tons of coal cost twenty-five dollars. Soft coal (bituminous) was cheaper than hard coal

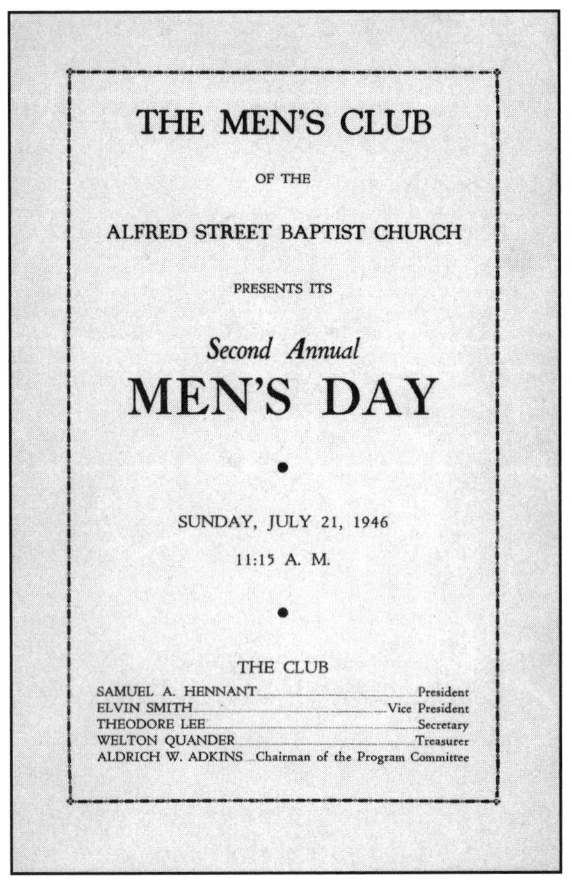

THE MEN'S CLUB

OF THE

ALFRED STREET BAPTIST CHURCH

PRESENTS ITS

Second Annual

MEN'S DAY

SUNDAY, JULY 21, 1946

11:15 A. M.

THE CLUB

SAMUEL A. HENNANT .... President
ELVIN SMITH .... Vice President
THEODORE LEE .... Secretary
WELTON QUANDER .... Treasurer
ALDRICH W. ADKINS ... Chairman of the Program Committee

Men's Day Program

(anthracite), and was used most frequently by the church. However, soft coal was hard to set afire, because it was brittle and became like a powder in handling. Sister Louise Tyler, the sexton, would set newspapers afire in her home across the street and bring them to the church to light the coals.

Women's Day was held as usual on May 5, the first Sunday, while the June rally was held on the third Sunday of June. In July 1946, the church held its second annual Men's Day. Brother Samuel A. Hennant was then the president of the Men's Club.

By 1947, the economic situation following the war had improved even more and the June rally raised eight hundred thirty-nine dollars and twenty cents—twice the amount raised in the previous year. Clubs were still encouraged to raise money and contribute to the church. The Men's Club donated seventy-two dollars and twenty-nine cents and the Shriners contributed fifty-one dollars and eighteen cents. The church contributed $100 to Virginia Union in February 1947, up from just over three dollars during the midst of the depression.

The young soldiers now returning from the war were gradually assimilated back into the congregation. Upon returning, Brother Welton Quander, who had served in Europe, was selected to be a church trustee. At just twenty-seven years of age, he was the youngest trustee recorded up to that time. He was also very active in the Men's Club that continued to raise funds on their special day in June or July of each year.

The church held a week-long Anniversary Rally in October 1948, raising four hundred thirty-five dollars. Sister Martha Miller was Chair of the Anniversary Planning Committee, and was assisted by Deacon Warren Wair who was now Chair of the Board of Deacons and Brother Richard H. Poole, Chair of the Board of Trustees. The anniversary committee consisted of ten other persons that included Deacon Elvin Smith, Sister Mattie Brooks, and Sister Mattie Adkins. This anniversary celebration was touted as the church's 115th anniversary, and represented yet another change in the assumed start date for the church. The celebration in 1948 assumed 1833 as a start date for the church twelve years later than the date used for the anniversary in 1934, when 1821 was the assumed date. This was also different from the original date, 1858, used for anniversary purposes during the 1920s. Over the next twenty-five years, the date on which church anniversaries were based would change several times, sometimes making the church older and sometimes making it younger.

The week-long anniversary celebration featured the Senior Choir performing at the

Sunday service, and with guest choirs and ministers for the remainder of the week. Each night a different auxiliary was in charge of services. On Monday night, the Deacons and the Men's Club were in charge, while the trustees were in charge on Tuesday when Reverend N.S. Harrave and his choir from Ebenezer Baptist Church in Alexandria served. Throughout the week there were nightly services, culminating in an anniversary sermon by Dr. J.A. Brinkley of Richmond on the following Sunday, and a reception on Monday night with the Ministers' Alliance and All Pastors Fellowship, two local ministerial affiliations, in charge.

Reverend Adkins was now being paid $900 per year, and the church had total expenses of about $2,900. By now the church had purchased new pews, installed central heating plants in both the sanctuary and the parsonage, installed new art glass windows in the sanctuary, and upgraded the electrical system from the older type with open wiring running along the walls on insulators, to a newer system with hidden wiring.

During this era, Reverend Adkins bought two lots south of the church, one of which he bought with his own funds to hold it for the church. The first was purchased in 1942, and the latter one in 1948. His purchase of one of the lots caused a great deal of controversy with the trustees and some of the members. They felt that he should not have bought the property without their agreement. During the dispute, he told the trustees that he would preach and teach, and let them attend to the financial and property matters of the church.

1833 to 1948

One Hundred - Fifteenth Anniversary of Alfred Street Baptist Church

SUNDAY, OCTOBER 17, 1948
to
MONDAY, OCTOBER 25, 1948

REV. A. W. ADKINS, *Pastor*

DEACON WARREN WAIR, *Chairman Deacon Board*
MR. R. H. POOLE, *Chairman Trustee Board*

MRS. MARTHA MILLER, *Chairman Committee on Planning*

115th Church Anniversary

The later purchase in 1948 was of the old Tombstone Company that was situated on the south side of the church. This land had a two-room building that was used sporadically for classrooms. The property cost $10,000 and was paid for in four years. Purchasing and paying for property was evidence that life was now good at Alfred Street Baptist Church.

The 19th-Century Saints

During the era spanning the depression and World War II, many of the old saints who had been born or had joined Alfred Street before the turn of the century were now entering that all-sufficient rest. Reverend Adkins performed most of these homegoing services, and was frequently called upon to leave his position as a teacher at Parker-Gray High School to render comfort to a family or to preach a funeral. For his schoolwork, he maintained a notebook of lesson plans for Latin, English, and social studies. And when called at school and notified of a death, he would frequently just turn the page in his notebook, and write a eulogy for the recently deceased in his school notebook there at his school desk. Most eulogies began with the quote: "Have not all past human beings parted; and must not all the present, one day part?"

The total number of members who departed during the period 1925–1950 and whose families he was required to leave school to console is not known with certainty. However, the following table lists many of the leaders of the church (e.g., deacons. trustees, choir members) in the order of their passing. Many of these members had lived through Reconstruction, the arrival of a new century, the depression, World War I, and now World War II. They had been baptized or married by former pastors, Reverend Samuel Madden or Reverend Alexander Truatt, and would now join their beloved pastors in Bethel Cemetery, just five short blocks from the church.

In October 1934, the church donated a floral design for Deacon Jerry Barrett. He had been Chairman of the Board of Deacons before Deacon Walter Butler, and passed on October 9. He was buried on October 13, 1934. Other persons listed were Reverend Edward Parker Dixon, Jr., son of Deacon Dixon, and one of the backbones of the church. Reverend Dixon passed in early June 1941, and the church purchased a wreath for the June 9 homegoing. At the time of his death, he lived in New Jersey, but his body was returned to Alexandria for a funeral at his home church and for interment with his family. Deacon Robert Quander, the father of Roberta Quander, was funeralized in 1942. Sister Susan Madden, the daughter-in-law of former pastor Reverend Samuel Madden, passed in February 1944, and her husband Samuel, the son of Reverend Madden, passed in November of the same year.

Deceased Members

Name	Sunrise	Sunset
Deacon Henry F. Burke	1873	1933
Deacon Jerry Barrett	—	1934
Helen Carrol	1898	1936
Mary F. Brooks	1854	1937
John Johnston	1865	1937
Mary Turner	1883	1940
Joseph B. Quander	1884	1940
Sarah Burke-Dent	1902	1940
Reverend Edward P. Dixon	1891	1941
Richard Hollinger	1891	1941
Deacon William Turner	1862	1942
Deacon Robert H. Quander	1879	1942
Susan Pinn Madden	1868	1944
Samuel W. Madden	1869	1944
Deacon Samuel Turner	1881	1944
Mary Jackson	1882	1944

In addition to these leaders of the church, others who passed during this period included Sister Eliza Bell Coleman, November 30, 1943; Sister Costella Horn, April 1, 1935; and Brother Fredrick H. Rich, May 6, 1935. In November 1935, the church buried Sister Wilhemina Burke and received a donation of $200 from the last will and testament of her estate. Ten dollars of that amount was donated to the Alexandria Hospital Building Fund as a memorial to her.

On March 31, 1936, Brother Walter Butler was buried. He had been Chair of Deacons and Chair of Trustees. Both the deacons and the trustees provided special tributes and the church purchased a special wreath. In April 1937, Sister Annie Gordon passed. A set of pulpit chairs was donated by Dr. Burke, her employer, as a memorial to her. Her estate also donated $171 to the church. Sister Louise Tyler, the sexton, passed during this era and was replaced by her son, Carlton Tyler, a current member of Alfred Street. He was seventeen at the time, and served as a sexton for a couple of years until someone else could be found.

Randolf Thompson, son of Joseph and Fannie Thompson, died at his home at 515 Pitt Street on June 9, 1938. He had been born in Alexandria on January 15, 1877, and had two brothers, Henry and Samuel Thompson. At the age of twenty-five he married Mary Hamlet of Lynchburg with whom he had three children, Rosier, Remelle, and Clayton. He joined Alfred Street around 1924.

On November 26, 1939, homegoing services were held for Joseph Decatur Lewis, who passed suddenly on Wednesday, November 22. "J.D.," as he was called, was born in Alexandria in 1889. He loved music and was an accomplished pianist who taught many young people to play the piano. Also, he accompanied many choirs in Arlington, his hometown, and in Washington, D.C. He left a widow, Mrs. Ilah Lewis, and three sisters, Mary Montague, Maud Beander, and Julia Campbell.

On April 29, 1941, Brother William Hansborough was funeralized. He had served as Secretary of the Deacon Board shortly after joining because of his sound judgment and valuable influence. He was still serving in that capacity when he was called home. At that time, Deacon George H. Turner was Chair of Deacons, and W.M. Wair became Acting Secretary.

In June 1947, Mary Hamlet Thompson, daughter of Anthony and Amanda Hamlet, died in Alexandria Hospital. She had been born in Appomattox County around 1875, but soon moved to Lynchburg. She initially joined Court Street Baptist Church in

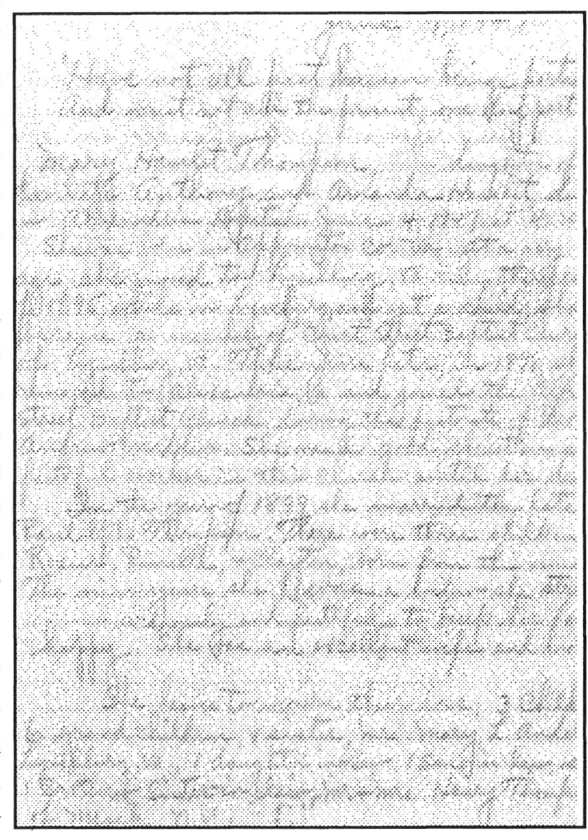

Eulogy for Mary Thompson

Lynchburg, and later moved to Alexandria and joined Alfred Street Baptist Church in 1895 during Reverend Samuel Madden's pastorate. In 1899, she married Randolf Thompson, who preceded her in death by nine years.

Sister Thompson's funeral was held at Alfred Street on June 7, 1947, with Reverend Adkins officiating. At her funeral, he began her eulogy with the quote that was used at most funerals at which he officiated: "Have not all past human beings parted; and must not all the present, one day part?"

Chapter Eight

1950–1970: Civil Rights and Vietnam

. . . The sufferings of this present time are not worthy to be compared with the glory which shall be revealed in you. (Romans 8)

On a national level, the period between 1950 and 1970 was characterized by a period of normalcy followed by periods of extreme turmoil created by the Civil Rights Movement and the war in Vietnam. Issues of race would dominate the national agenda for the first time since Reconstruction, but would compete with the war for national attention. Alfred Street Baptist Church would lose its beloved pastor of over forty years and would gain another one not yet forty years old. Under the new leader, the foundations would be laid at Alfred Street for great growth in membership and expansions of the facilities later in the century.

The Early 1950s

Following the end of World War II and the return to normalcy, the United States entered a period of peace and prosperity. The housing market in the suburbs expanded with the returning soldiers. The defense industry quickly converted to producing consumer goods. All this activity created millions of new jobs and the Serviceman's Readjustment Act, known as the G.I. Bill of Rights, helped ease military personnel back into civilian life and sent thousands of them off to college.

President Truman's last years in office were, however, marred by charges that he was lax about communists. The excessive fear of communism led to what was later called the McCarthy Hearings in 1950, during which Senator Joseph R. McCarthy invoked the communist scare which led to the Cold War that would last for the next forty to fifty years.

As the Cold War was gaining a foothold in the American psyche, a real war broke out on June 25, 1950, when a powerful invading force from North Korea swept south into the Republic of Korea (South Korea). Within days, President Truman resolved to defend South Korea and the nation entered yet another war in which the country would sustain some 142,000 casualties.[1] By the time of the Armistice in 1953, General of the Army Dwight D. Eisenhower, an immensely popular war hero in World War II, had become the new U.S. president. His first term was characterized by more good times of the mid-

1950s.

While President Eisenhower's first term is remembered for peace and tranquility, several landmark events occurred during the second term that related to Negroes. Race became a central national concern for the first time since the Reconstruction era. It was during the mid-1950s that civil rights actions first began taking place in the South. In the summer of 1955 in Money, Mississippi, fourteen-year-old Emmett Till of Chicago was lynched while visiting relatives. Occasional lynchings had continued since Reconstruction, but this lynching created a national uproar because of its brutality and his young age. Later that same year, a seamstress named Rosa Parks refused to give up her seat on a segregated bus in Montgomery, Alabama. Then, a twenty-six-year-old minister, Reverend Martin Luther King, Jr., led a boycott of segregated buses in Montgomery that gave rise to the nonviolent Civil Rights Movement.

While black Americans were engaged in civil rights issues, neither the president nor the U.S. Congress took any proactive steps until the segregationist governor of Arkansas blocked integration of a high school in Little Rock, Arkansas. To enforce the Supreme Court's order for integration, President Eisenhower sent federal troops to Arkansas and the U.S. Congress was prompted to pass the first civil rights law in eighty-two years. Their vote on the Civil Rights Act was the first serious effort made to protect Negro voters in the South.

Even so, civil rights activities in Alexandria and at Alfred Street Baptist Church were relatively quiet in the 1950s. There were no reported bus boycotts, even though the buses were segregated. Persons returning to Virginia from Washington, D.C., would have to move to the back of the bus in the colored section at the first bus stop in Virginia near the Pentagon. There were no major demonstrations at the department stores even though they prohibited Negroes from eating at the lunch counter at Woolworth's on King Street. Women were prohibited from trying on clothes in major department stores, as they were in most southern cities. But this was the ". . . way it was . . ." in the South, and so the local Negro population in Alexandria endured.

The city of Alexandria was still relatively small at the beginning of the 1950s, starting at the Potomac River and continuing west along Duke Street and ending near Quaker Lane. The areas today referred to as the *West End* in the vicinity of Cameron Station and Landmark Shopping Center were still out in the rural areas. These areas were annexed to the city in 1952, essentially doubling the size of Alexandria. The Negro population was 7,622 in 1950 and was roughly ten to twelve percent of the total population. In 1950, the average annual income for Negroes was $1,916 compared to $4,642 for whites.[2]

Over on Washington Street, the First Baptist Church of Alexandria, with which Alfred Street had been conjoined until 1850, was prospering. Though their sanctuary held only 600 persons, membership now stood at 2,300, with over 380 persons joining during some years. The Sunday School boasted a membership of over 1,700. The church would soon celebrate its 150th anniversary at which President Dwight D. Eisenhower was guest speaker.[3] The explosive growth would lead to the church moving from the relatively cramped quarters on Washington Street to a new facility on King Street. After moving, a small number of members would remain downtown at the old site and form another Baptist church—the Downtown Baptist Church.[4]

At Alfred Street Baptist Church, Reverend Adkins was in his thirtieth year as pastor. Membership hovered around 250 to 300, though attendance at Sunday services rarely exceeded 150 persons. Alfred Street began the 1950s with a balance in the bank of $748 as a carry-over from 1949. The church raised $464 in offerings in January and $216 in February. During March, the church held the first of several $2 rallies up from the Dollar Rallies of the depression. During this rally, the church raised $218. The church had recently purchased a new set of pews and the old ones were sold to Mt. Jezreel Baptist Church for $200. The church still kept separate checking and savings accounts and $2,000 was moved from savings to checking to pay Southern Desk Company for the new pews.

Also, the church calendar remained unchanged from the past decade. There was the June rally, Men's Day in June, Women's Day in July, and Homecoming, as usual, in October. Jacqueline Henry (Jackie Henry-Green after marriage) held a musical recital in August that raised sixty-one dollars. By year's end the church had raised $6,268 from all sources and expended $4,680. The church would continue collecting between five to six thousand dollars during most of the 1950s. Major monthly expenses included $100 to the pastor, $15 to the organist, and $25 to the sexton. Fuel costs averaged $40–50 a month. The pastor took his usual vacation and, in addition to being paid, was given an extra month's salary of $100 as a gift. Things were looking up.

1950

HOME COMING

AT THE

Alfred Street Baptist Church

FEATURING AS GUESTS

The Pastor, Choir & Congregation

OF

Shiloh Baptist Church

PHILADELPHIA, PA.

REV. A. W. ADKINS, PASTOR

Program for Homecoming in 1950

While the pastor was on vacation that year, Reverend Henry C. Brooks preached and was paid ten dollars each Sunday. Also, while the regular choir was on vacation, Miss Mary Etta Robinson acted as organist and Brother Leo Brooks, who later became one of the deacons at Alfred Street, acted as choirmaster. The church now had new church stationery that showed the church's new phone number, Overlook 3–2222, the same as today, forty-five years later. The church address was then listed as 307 South Alfred Street, and Sister Thelma Wair was the new clerk.

In August 1950, the church sent fifty dollars to the Lott Carey Convention along with a delegate, and twenty-five dollars to the NOVA Baptist Association. This was the first reference of a contribution to Lott Carey Convention in many years. During the depression and for many years thereafter, Alfred Street had curtailed much of its convention activities. But the good times of the 1950s permitted the church to resume involvement in the conventions.

The annual homecoming which had become a tradition at Alfred Street featured a special guest in 1950—Rev. W.R.H. Powell, D.D. He had served as pastor of Alfred Street during the period 1914–1918 in the midst of World War I. He, along with the choir of the Shiloh Baptist Church in Philadelphia, PA, returned to Alexandria to conduct the morning worship service. A special program was held at 3:00 p.m. at which the pastor, Reverend Adkins, spoke.

In 1951, affairs and finances at Alfred Street were continuing to improve. The June rally raised $1,275, over three times as much as the prior year. In this year, too, each auxiliary was asked to collect two hundred dollars. At that time, the church had nine auxiliaries that contributed to the rally in the following manner:

Auxiliary	**Amount**
Deacons	$250
Trustee	106
Usher Board	106
No. 1 Working Club	106
Sunday School	41
Optimist Club	200
Missionary Circle	170
Men's Club	35
Choir Club	207
Personal Contributions	
Reverend Adkins	35
Miss Georgia Lane	10
Mrs. Delia Slaughter	50
Mr. Carlton Tyler	3
TOTAL	**$1,275**

At this time, the church had five deacons who were quite elderly. The chair at that time was still Deacon Warren M. Wair. He had been ordained back in 1933, and had been chair for almost twenty years. The Board of Deacons also included John Strange, a member of the Fraternal Order of Masons, who would live to be 101 years old; Gilbert Dickerson, a widower who lived on Duke Street; Robert Owens, who lived on Columbus Street and was very active with the Men's Club; and Charles Burruss, who was responsible for starting the tape ministry. Deacon Burruss would tape the Sunday service on his personal tape recorder and then visit the homes of the sick and shut-in so they could hear the sermons. As most private homes were not equipped with a playback capability, he would carry his tape recorder with him to provide this capability.

At the start of the 1950s, Brother John H. Jackson was still the organist, and Miss Benjie V. Burke was the sexton. But, in June, both Brother Jackson and Sister Burke stepped down. Mrs. Coultamae Willis-Wilson became organist, and Sister Joyce Whitmore became the new sexton. Brother John Jackson resigned his position as organist due to age and declining health. When he played, however, members knew without seeing that he was at the keyboard, for he had a special touch that no one else possessed. Brother Jackson was funeralized at the church on January 31, 1952, after 30 years of service.

By the mid-1950s many of the other members who were born before the turn of the century were beginning to pass on to their final rewards. For each funeral, Reverend

Adkins would prepare a statement for the clerk to read expressing sympathy on behalf of the church. When Deacon Robert E. Owens, a strong member of the Men's Club, passed, Brother Richard Wair, Secretary of the Men's Club, provided a testimonial on behalf of the Men's Club at his funeral. There had been times when the Men's Club faced near certain dissolution due to lack of interest, but Brother Owens had pulled it together. He was sorely missed within the Men's Department.

On March 26, 1952, Sister Martha Miller was buried. She was superintendent of the Sunday school for many years, and is remembered for her love of little children.

On March 24, 1953, Emma Lena Watson was funeralized after passing at the Central State Hospital in Petersburg, Virginia. She came to Alexandria as a young woman and later met Thomas Watson, a law student. After a long courtship, they married and enjoyed a successful marriage until his death in December 1934. She seemed to lose interest in living afterwards and finally joined him in death.

Deacon Board of the Mid-1950s

On March 21, 1954, the church buried Clarence Henry Wair, the son of Richard and Hattie Wair, who passed at Freedman's Hospital (now Howard University) after an extended illness. He was born in Alexandria in May 1908, and was called *Snatches* in his youth. As there were no high schools in Alexandria when he was a young man, he attended Armstrong High School in Washington, D.C. He studied auto mechanics there and later attended Hampton University.

On June 22, 1954, a funeral was held for Deacon Sherman Majors. Shortly after his election to the position of deacon, he was elected as treasurer of the Deacon Board and held the position until his death.

Mary A. Poole Dishman died at her sister's home in Washington, D.C., on July 15, 1954. This followed an illness of more than twenty years. She was born in Stafford County, Virginia, the daughter of Willis and Mary Poole. Her mother died at a young age and Mary became mother to her sisters and brothers, the youngest of whom was only three years old when her mother died. Her siblings were Mrs. Carrie Poole Edwards, Henry H. Poole, and Richard Poole (who served as Superintendent of the Sunday School at Alfred Street during this era).

In August 1954, Sister Elizabeth Dorsey passed. She was particularly active in the Sunday School until her death and delivered literature to children who could not get to Sunday School. Even in her advanced years, she could always be found at her place in church every Sunday morning.

By 1954, Reverend Adkins had conducted funerals at Alfred Street for almost thirty-five years. He continued including the quote that ". . . all men must part . . ." in all his eulogies.

Activities at Alfred Street: 1955–1960

Reverend Adkins had retired from teaching in 1954, but continued as pastor at Alfred Street. During the late 1950s, the church calendar continued as in prior years and in October 1956 the church celebrated its 150th anniversary. The ten-day celebration (October 21–31) featured a series of nightly services, each sponsored by a different church auxiliary. As this was considered the 150th year of existence, the church was now using the start date of 1806, based on the founding of the Colored Baptist Society. This was a third change in the start date and different from the start date of 1852 that was used for the first anniversary celebration in 1912.

For the celebration, Deacon Warren W. Wair served as General Chairman of the Planning Committee, with Sister Evelyn Johnson as Chair of the Anniversary Program, and Miss Benjie V. Burke responsible for the souvenir book. For the anniversary, Sister Marie T. Boyd, the church historian, published a brief history of the church that was included in the souvenir book.[5]

At this time, Reverend Adkins had been at Alfred Street for more than thirty-five years and had established a favorable reputation within the community. He was thus able to secure the interest of the entire community to support the anniversary. The ten-night celebration began on Sunday, October 21, and ended with a banquet on Wednesday, October 30. Reverend J.B. Henderson, D.D., of Bank Street Baptist Church in Norfolk, Virginia, delivered the anniversary sermon on Sunday. There was music and preaching each subsequent night, with one night set aside for Alfred Street Baptist Church families and another set aside especially for visiting churches. On the Tuesday night prior to the closing banquet on Wednesday, the church performed a dramatic rendition of the church's

150th Anniversary Banquet

history, based on material prepared by the church historian, Sister Marie T. Boyd.

By the time of the 150th anniversary, the nine auxiliaries included three Missionary Circles (Esther, Dorcas, and Joint); and three Usher auxiliaries, including Junior Ushers and Missionary Ushers. All the ushers were still men, as was most of the leadership of the church. The ladies and youth who served in a similar capacity were referred to as the usher auxiliaries. The church also had a Finance Committee, a Ways and Means Committee, and a Records Committee, in addition to the Senior Choir, Sunday School, Men's Club, Optimist Club, and the Number One Willing Workers' Club.

The church had five deacons with Warren Wair serving as chair, and five trustees with Brother Wesley Whitmore serving as chair. The Senior Choir then numbered twenty-two persons with nine sopranos, five altos, two tenors, and six basses. Sister Elnora Winston directed the choir, with Coultamae Willis-Wilson as organist. The church had now divided the Junior Choir that had been started back in the 1940s into two groups—the teenagers and the younger children. Miss Jacqueline Henry directed the teenage group, and also served as their organist. Mrs. Marrietta O'Neal directed the younger group and served as their organist.

In early 1956, Alfred Street also decided to acquire some additional property for future needs while the property was available. After much debate, the lot and building adjacent to the church was purchased for $9,000. The Board of Trustees signed the Deed of Trust on January 20, 1956, and one year later on January 10, 1957, the loan was paid off. The church was again free of debt and an iron fence was installed to enclose the new site, the sanctuary, and entire church property.

Other changes were taking place at Alfred Street, including a change in the superintendent of the Sunday School. For twenty-five years, Brother Richard Poole, who worked at the old Arnold's Funeral Home, had been the superintendent, beginning in 1931. He resigned in 1956, but would remain active at Alfred Street for another 30 years. Brother Milton Turner (1956–1958) and then Joseph Burless (1958–1962) followed him as superintendents.

Board of Trustees, 1956

There were also changes in the music department with the organization by Sister Ardelia Hunter of a fourth choir, the Young and Adult Choir. Prior to this, the Senior Choir had been the only adult choir. The Young and Adult Choir was organized in 1959 for the purpose of providing more gospel songs and for utilizing more of the musical talent of the church.

Gospel hymns, as a new type of religious music, had been around since the mid-1920s. This music had emerged out of the northern part of the country and represented a northern counterpart to Negro spirituals that emerged from the south. Many of the songs expressed a joy of living and a deep religious faith. However, for many years, the songs had not been embraced by some mainline churches in part because of their pedigree and their emotionalism.[6] But now, 30 years after its birth, gospel music had finally arrived at Alfred Street. Mrs. Marrietta O'Neal was asked to play and direct this new group. During the early years, she provided her services free of charge.

The following persons were present at the first organizational meeting of the Young and Adult Choir:

Marrietta O'Neal	Mattie Funn Hopkins
Ruth Johnson	Jean Morris
Mae Randall	Mildred Harper
Janet Griffin	Billy Hopkins
Donald Owens	Ardelia Hunter

Ardelia Hunter, Founder of the Young and Adult Choir

Initially, the group was named the Adult Choir. Considering the interest of the youth, Sister Griffin suggested the name be changed to Young and Adult Choir. The group unanimously accepted. On the first Sunday of May 1959, the choir, now consisting of ten members, was introduced to the congregation. They were assigned to serve the first and third Sundays, which they would continue for the next fifty years. Sister O'Neal would serve as director for the first eight years of the choir's existence.

During this period, the church continued its affiliations in local and state conventions. It maintained membership in several organizations and contributed to them financially, but appears to only have attended the meetings of the local Northern Virginia Baptist Association (NVBA) regularly. As reported in the NVBA minutes, membership in 1957 was up to 322 persons and in 1959 membership was 352 persons. Mrs. Marie T. Boyd was clerk and submitted church statistics to the convention.

Membership statistics show slow growth during most of the 1950s, but as in every other era, older members continued to depart for that all-sufficient rest. On June 13, 1957, the church held the funeral for Sister Maud Lewis Beander, who died en route to Alexandria Hospital after a long illness. She was born in Alexandria on December 16, 1886. Before joining Alfred Street, she attended Sunday School at Ebenezer Baptist Church with her mother.

On July 25, 1957, the church held a funeral for Clinton Ray Wair, who died in Alexandria Hospital following a long illness. He, too, was born and reared in Alexandria and attended the old Snowden School for Boys, and later attended Howard University. He had great penmanship and was frequently called upon to do calligraphy. Because of his excellent penmanship he was assigned a position assisting in keeping the church records.

In September 1957, a funeral was held for Brother Henry C. Brooks. He was espe-

Henry C. Brooks

cially interested in the church school and prayer services and he had led prayer service about three weeks before his death. Whenever no one else could be found, he was always available to fill the gap of leading prayer services. He was also extremely conscientious about picking up other members and bringing them to church. He seldom came to church without an extra passenger.

Sister Cora Willis passed at Freedman's Hospital on December 15, 1957, and though she never officially joined Alfred Street, she was a part of the church family. Her home church was the First Baptist Church of Montgomery, West Virginia, and she never changed her membership. But she spent the last twenty years of her life in Alexandria and adopted Alfred Street Baptist Church.

On Friday, July 9, 1959, Mrs. Mary Rich Clisby, the widow of Reverend Robert L. Clisby, passed at the Piedmont Sanitarium in Burkeville, Virginia. She was returned to Alexandria for the homegoing at her home church. She had attended the old Hallowell School for Girls in Alexandria, and later the Virginia State Normal Teachers Training School in Ettrick, Virginia. She taught for several years in the schools at Lincolnia, Virginia, in the days when the classrooms only contained first through eighth grades. One of her prized pupils was Reverend Milton Sheppard. She was also active with Lyles Crouch School, the Parent-Teacher Association, and the Missionary Circle at Alfred Street. Her missionary zeal continued even after she was hospitalized. She offered inspiration to many patients at the sanitarium in Burkeville where she spent her final days.

Local School Integration Struggles

Even as affairs at Alfred Street were continuing under a sense of normalcy, the nation was about to experience a second wave of major national civil rights uprisings. A youth from Alfred Street would become involved in one of the major struggles of the civil rights era.

Since Reconstruction, only small civil rights advances had been made in the nation in general, and in Alexandria in particular. However, during the seventy to eighty years since Reconstruction, racial issues had simmered in the background, held at bay by the infamous separate but equal doctrine that emerged from the *Plessy v. Ferguson* case ruled on by the Supreme Court.

However, in the mid-1950s, the Supreme Court overturned *Plessy v. Ferguson*, and ruled that segregated schools were unconstitutional in a case known as *Brown v. Board of Education.* The controversial decision received some acceptance in the north but provoked intense resistance in the South. For example, in Washington, D.C., some schools were integrated the next summer, including Stuart Junior High where the student body grew to about twenty-five percent Negro by the next summer, and to eighty percent Negro two or three years later, as whites fled into the suburbs in droves.[7]

In the southern part of the country, however, things were different. Virginia was among the states that resisted the Supreme Court decision and took the leadership in what became known as Massive Resistance, a frontal assault to circumvent the *Brown v. Board of Education* case. Virginia governor Stanley used numerous legal means to maintain segregated schools in Virginia, and Prince Edwards County, the scene of the famous Nat Turner's Rebellion in 1831, was at the lead in the resistance movement. For four years, Virginia resisted the mandate of the Supreme Court, passing a near unanimous vote for a joint resolution proposing interposition or nullification of the U.S. Constitution ". . . to resist this illegal encroachment upon our sovereign powers . . . and to maintain racially separated public schools. . . ."[8] Virginia closed many public schools and authorized payment of tuition grants to private academies to educate the state's white youth.

It would be five years before a federal court and the Virginia Supreme Court of Appeals tore the heart out of Virginia's Massive Resistance legislation, declaring the school-closing law and the law authorizing payment of tuition grants unconstitutional. Shortly thereafter, the schools in Northern Virginia, to include Fairfax County and Alexandria, integrated their public schools.

Prior to this change in the law, Negroes still attended segregated schools in Alexandria and Fairfax County. In Fairfax County, all black elementary students attended school at Luther Jackson School near Tyson's Corner just off of U.S. Route 50. Students were bused to this single school from the Mount Vernon and Hybla Valley areas through Franconia and other neighborhoods.

In 1958, the county legislators decided to build a new white elementary school in the Hybla Valley area. To obtain property for the school site, the county took over property owned by the Quander families of Alfred Street along Quander Road. One of the ironies of the time was that Negro children could not attend the new school even though it was built on land owned by a Negro family. A young lady from Alfred Street would help to change all of that.

In 1958, Barbara Jackson's (Barbara J. McDowell) father sued Fairfax County to have his daughter admitted to this white school.[9] Barbara Jackson, at the time, was an Alfred Street youth in sixth grade. This new school on land owned by the Quanders was only about one block from her home, and she was commuting about fifteen miles to attend Luther Jackson School. The lawsuit went back and forth for several months, but finally, in the fall of 1960, Barbara Jackson was admitted to Bryant Intermediate School, becoming one of the first Negro students to integrate the secondary schools of Fairfax County.

Actually, the first schools to integrate in Virginia and indeed in the entire South were only ten miles away in Arlington, Virginia. There, on February 2, 1959, Stratford Junior High School (now H.B. Woodlawn) became the first breach in the South's massive resistance defense.[10] The elementary schools (William Ramsey) and high schools (Hammond) in Alexandria would also begin integrating in 1959, but would not completely integrate for another eleven years, an event made famous in the movie *Remember the Titans*, starring the black actor Denzel Washington.

The Early 1960s at Alfred Street

With civil rights issues looming in the background, Alfred Street continued its primary mission of religious service. In the fall of 1960, Alfred Street Baptist Church celebrated the 40th anniversary of Reverend Adkins' tenure as pastor during the period September 26, 1960, to October 2, 1960. This was a grand and glorious occasion with Dr. J.M. Ellison, Chancellor of Virginia Union University, delivering the anniversary sermon on Sunday morning to close out a week of celebration.

Reverend Adkins' 40th Anniversary Celebration

The Sunday School was reorganized in 1962. All members were grouped according to age from nursery to adult. In this way each class became an outgrowth of the prior one. Prior to this, classes were selected according to one's individual preference. Brother Charles Henry Wilson, the new superintendent, replaced Joseph Burless who had served for four years. The Sunday School also had a vibrant Vacation Bible School that had been in place since the early 1930s and drew children from across the city, including many who did not belong to Alfred Street. The Sunday School was perhaps the strongest arm of the church with its own Records Committee, Program Committee, Auditing Committee, and Treasurer. Each church auxiliary still maintained its own treasury, as a centralized treasury was still four or five years away.

In October 1962, the church held its last quarterly meeting for the year. It still met in January, April, July and October. The church congregation was aging and the needs of the seniors were increasing. The pastor proposed that the church set aside a special fund of $1,000 to be used to aid the senior members. The church agreed.

After having purchased the lot adjacent to the church in 1956, by the early 1960s the church was beginning to make plans to renovate the church and add an educational wing. Education—both religious and secular—had always been of great interest to Reverend Adkins, and finally the time had come to add an educational wing to Alfred Street Baptist Church.

The trustees reported that progress was being made in preparing for the new building addition, to include setting up a meeting with an architect. Welton Quander and Wesley Whitmore, then Chair of the Board of Trustees, were in charge of the building program. The expected cost of construction was $77,000.

ANDREW WARREN ADKINS MEMORIAL

Alfred Street Baptist Church

313 South Alfred Street • Alexandria, Virginia

Proposed Adkins Educational Wing

In the fall of 1962, one of the elder deacons, Brother Warren McKenzie Wair passed. He had served Alfred Street Baptist Church for thirty-three years. He had been Chair of the Deacon Board for many years. Mrs. Thelma Wair asked permission to organize a Heart Fund Drive dedicated to Deacon Wair, a drive that continued at Alfred Street into the next century. Collections for the Heart Fund were taken on a Sunday in September of each year.

With the passing of Deacon Warren Wair, there was now a vacancy on the Deacon Board. At the January 1963 meeting, his twin sons, Ralph and Richard Wair, were both nominated and approved as new deacons. At the April 10 meeting, three more deacons, William Willis, Joseph Burless, and Henry Wilson, were nominated and accepted. On the fourth Sunday of July 1963, William Willis, Joseph Burless, Richard Wair, Ralph Wair and Charles Henry Wilson, most in their mid-thirties, were ordained as deacons. This was a radical departure from prior experience as, historically, Alfred Street had added only one new deacon at a time, and most had been fairly senior in age at the time of their ordination. The addition of five young deacons increased the number to nine and was expected to strengthen the Deacon Board.

After functioning for almost a year without a chair, at the October meeting a decision was made to fill the position of Chair of the Board of Deacons. One of the younger deacons was nominated, but some of the older deacons objected to having a young person with limited experience as chair. However, after much debate, Brother William Willis was selected.

Beloved Pastor Passes

Reverend Adkins' proposed building expansion project that consumed so much of the church's attention during the summer of 1962 and 1963 did not come to fruition. Death intervened to alter the congregation's plans. On Thursday evening, November 14, 1963, immediately after he and his wife arrived home from prayer service, Reverend Andrew Warren Adkins was called home. In fact, he never left his automobile, but expired there in front of the church parsonage at 816 Queen Street.

Reverend Adkins' death was unexpected and was seen as a major tragedy throughout the Negro community in Alexandria. He was liked and respected—an honorable man of great culture, intellect and human dignity who was proudly acclaimed as the Dean of Preachers. The impact of his death within the city was so profound that even some forty years after the event, many persons still recall exactly what they were doing when they first heard of his passing.

During this period, it was still common practice for families to have the remains of the deceased returned to their home to lie in state until the funeral. And so it was with Reverend Adkins. The body was brought back to the parsonage on Queen Street for friends and family to pay their respects during a wake prior to the funeral.

When the casket was first brought back to the parsonage, the mortician ran into a technical problem. There was insufficient room to maneuver the casket into the house because doors in the entryway and the anteroom on the front of the house were too small. To solve the problem, the windows on the front porch were removed so that the coffin could be placed inside the living room of the home. On the day of the funeral, the windows were again removed so that the casket could be taken out.[11]

Dr. A. W. Adkins Dies; Pastor in Alexandria

Funeral services were held yesterday for the Rev. Dr. Andrew W. Adkins, 79, at the Alfred Street Baptist Church in Alexandria, where he was pastor for more than 40 years.

Mr. Adkins died Thursday after a heart attack at his home, 816 Queen street, Alexandria.

A native of Charles City, Va., he received both his bachelor of arts and doctor of divinity degrees from the Virginia Union University at Richmond, where he received an honorary degree in 1961.

He became pastor of the Alexandria church in 1920 and served there until his death. In 1920 he began teaching at the Parker-Gray Elementary School, now the Charles Houston School. The next year he

REV. A. W. ADKINS

Obituary for Reverend Adkins

The funeral was held at the church on Sunday, November 17, three days after he passed. The body was taken from the parsonage to the church where it lay in state from noon until the funeral at 3:00 p.m. No 11:00 a.m. church service was held that Sunday as this was a day of city-wide mourning. Reverend Dr. J.M. Ellison, Chancellor of Virginia Union, Reverend Adkins' alma mater, provided the eulogy and was the officiating minister. Music was provided by an octet from the university and the Alfred Street Baptist Church Senior Choir. Attendance at the funeral was quite large and

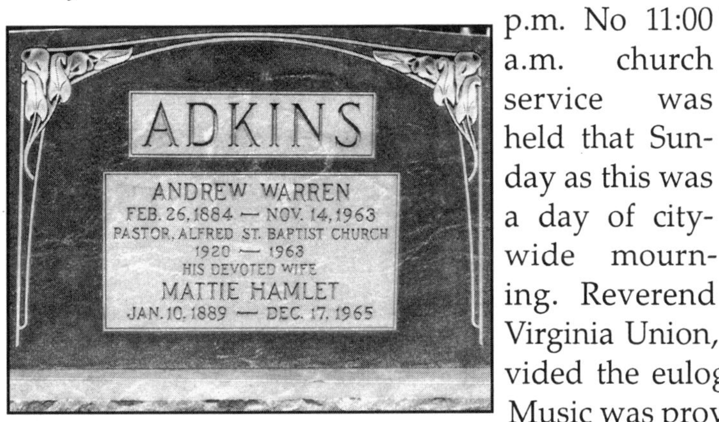

Headstones of Reverend and Mrs. Adkins

reflected his esteem within the community.

Following the funeral, Reverend Adkins was interred in Bethel Cemetery, just five short blocks from the church. There he was buried near two of his predecessors at Alfred Street Baptist Church, Reverend Samuel Madden (1896) and Reverend Alexander Truatt (1916). The church agreed to pay sixty dollars or one-half the cost of the headstone.[12] Shortly after his death, his wife, Sister Mattie Adkins, left Alexandria to live with their children in Tennessee. She passed there in 1965, but was returned to Alexandria for homegoing services at Alfred Street and was buried next to her husband at Bethel Cemetery.

The William Willis Years: 1963–1964

A few weeks following the loss of Reverend Adkins, the nation suffered an even more dramatic loss. Just two weeks later in November 1963, President John F. Kennedy was assassinated in Dallas, Texas, an event that shook the nation and the world. Just as black persons in Alexandria remembered where they were when they learned of the death of Reverend Adkins, so would most Americans remember where they were when they learned that President Kennedy had been shot. Both events left indelible scars on the psyches of their respective constituencies.

Deacon William Willis

Following Reverend Adkins' death, the church was without a pastor for thirteen months. During this period, Deacon William Willis, the young Chair of the Board of Deacons, still in his first year on the job, together with the other officers and dedicated members, made satisfactory progress in holding the church together. In the Baptist church, in contrast to some other denominations, the chain of command for leadership of the church goes from the pastor to the Board of Deacons' chair. So, the young William Willis, who had been ordained only in the prior year, took charge of the church.

At the January 1964 quarterly meeting, the first one held without a pastor, business continued as usual. Officers for the year were maintained, except Brother Richard Poole resigned as treasurer, and Mrs. Corrine Pouncy was elected to replace him. A salary of fifteen dollars was set for visiting ministers during the pastoral hiatus, top pay at that time. Plans for the new building proceeded. A new deacon, Deacon Wilbert Harris, was added to the board of deacons. He had previously been a deacon in Danville, Virginia, for fourteen years, before joining Alfred Street Baptist Church.

Until that time, the Sunday School had maintained a separate budget from the church, and was in many ways a separate entity. Efforts had been underway to bring it more in line with other activities of the church. To bring it and all the auxiliaries together, a decision was made at the January meeting that all clubs be united under a single treasury, and Deacon Willis oversaw the implementation of this initiative. Also, the church decided to name the building fund for the proposed new wing the "Annual

Adkins Memorial Fund." Also, Sister Ardelia Hunter was selected as Chair of the Young People's Committee, as she had expressed interest several times. She also requested and received funds to give gifts and other recognition to the 1964 graduates. Ten dollars each was given to that year's two high school graduates, Donald Owens and Craig Taylor, from the Sunday School.

Over the summer, the church continued to get bids on the proposed education wing. In July, the church received four bids in the $120,000–140,000 range, well above the $70,000 that was expected. Because of the large disparity, the church attempted to get loans from several banks, but was turned down.

During this same time, the church was considering converting the parsonage at 816 Queen Street into apartments. It had been empty now for several months following Reverend Adkins' death, and a decision was made to divide the parsonage into two apartments and rent them out. The upstairs had five bedrooms which, based on contractor estimates, could be turned into a complete apartment at a cost of $4,435 in about eight weeks. The intent was that the lower half, which was also being remodeled, could still be used as a parsonage even though the pastor would now have only one of the floors of the building.

During this thirteen-month period, worship services continued in the same manner as they had when Reverend Adkins lived. Several new members were added to the church roster—some by baptism, others by Christian experience or letter. Expenses were met as usual. The annual rally was held and netted more than $1,000 to meet obligations of the church and add to the Building Fund. Sister Roberta Quander volunteered to be Women's Day chair for a service to be held on November 1, 1964.

As the business portion of church operations was proceeding, the biggest open issue was selecting a new pastor. There were two key committees formed to assist with the pastoral transition, the Pulpit Group and the Pulpit Committee. The Pulpit Group was comprised of church officers and members who met with Deacon William Willis to ensure that the pulpit was filled with a minister every Sunday for thirteen months. In addition to Sunday services, there were funerals, weddings, Women's Day, anniversaries, and other special occasions that required a minister. Throughout the period, however, there was always a minister to speak or officiate at all the ceremonies.

Deacon Willis recalls that during the year, the job of governing the church was somewhat difficult, and that filling the pulpit every Sunday required some effort. But finding a minister each Sunday, which could have been a challenge, was not as difficult as had been assumed. Instead, the difficult part was *sorting* among the several possible candidates who wanted to preach during a given service.

Then, as now, Alfred Street had established something of a reputation within Virginia and the nation due to its church program and history of strong leadership. So, serving as pastor at Alfred Street was viewed as an elevated position among black Baptist preachers. Thus, on many Sundays there were four or five visiting ministers who wanted to preach, hoping for an opportunity to leave a favorable impression on the congregation, and perhaps be selected as the next pastor. Many excellent sermons were witnessed, and many of the ministers were called back more than once to serve. Many of these ministers who preached are today pastors of other large local congregations.

As the Pulpit Group went about the business of ensuring that the pulpit was adequately occupied, there was also a Pulpit Committee whose sole function was that of search committee. This committee consisted of Richard Poole, Vernon Carroll, Robert Adkins, Theodore Lee, Wesley Whitmore, Thelma Wair, Mazie Bowden, Nellie Quander, Laura McPhail, and Ardelia Hunter. Brother Vernon Carroll was the chair. The Pulpit Committee received a report from the Clerk, Mr. Theodore Lee, on the status of the church for purposes of describing the congregation to potential applicants. He reported in a letter of June 9, 1964, that the church had 196 financial members, though there were 293 on the rolls. Additionally, the Sunday School had sixty-eight pupils and collected about ten dollars each Sunday.[13]

In conversations with the committee members, they have indicated that even though it was thirteen months before a replacement was found, this was not entirely due to difficulty in sorting through the many candidates who came to preach. In previous turnovers, the church had found a new pastor in five to six months. However, in this case, the former pastor, Reverend Adkins, had been a very revered individual within Alexandria. Many members felt a respectable period of mourning was appropriate before installing someone else in his most revered position.

1211 Gibbon Street
Alexandria, Virginia
June 25, 1964

Rev. John O. Peterson
6021 North Dakota Avenue, N. W.
Washington, D. C.

Dear Rev. Peterson:

After a pastorate of nearly forty four (44) years in the Alfred Street Baptist Church of Alexandria, Virginia, the Reverend Andrew W. Adkins died in November of 1963. A Pulpit Committee has been formed to seek and recommend a successor; it is in this connection that I am writing you.

The Alfred Street Baptist Church had its beginning with the purchase of land in 1818. We have a membership of approximately three hundred (300), however, we have about two hundred (200) financially participating members. There is an average Sunday attendance of one hundred forty five (145) members. Last year we received about twelve thousand dollars ($12,000) in income and our expenditures were about nine thousand dollars ($9,000). We have an active church school of about sixty eight (68) members. We have living quarters available for a minister and we would hope to be able to reach an agreeable salary. We are in the planning stages of a new education building. Naturally, since our church cooperates with the National Baptist Convention, The Northern Virginia Baptist Convention, National and State Allied Bodies, we are interested only in a pastor who can participate in these denominational relationships.

Since your last visit to our church, your name has been suggested as one who might give us outstanding leadership. Without any commitment, either on your part or that of our church, we should like to know whether you would be in a position to consider pastoral service with us should our later contacts and conferences lead to a mutual interest? It goes without saying, that should you have any possible interest in our church, we shall see that added details are supplied to you regarding our total situation. In the meantime, we shall be most happy to answer any question you might raise. You may contact me at the above address or by telephone at 548-1526. You may also get in touch with the secretary of the Committee, Mrs. Nellie Quander, 309 Dawn Drive, Alexandria, Virginia, or telephone SO. 56865.

Sincerely,

Vernon Carroll

Vernon Carroll, Chairman
Pulpit Committee

Offer Letter to Reverend John Peterson

Many candidates were screened and letters of interest were sent in July 1964 to four ministers, including Reverend Frank Tucker, Reverend Donald Walker, Reverend Henry Gregory, and Reverend John O. Peterson. The selection process being followed included a provision that only a single name would be recommended to the congregation for vote. If acceptable to a majority, that person would be named pastor. If not, the committee would resume the search until another single name could be agreed upon. That single name would again be submitted to a vote by the church until a majority agreed.

At a special call meeting on September 9, 1964, the key item on the agenda was the election of a new pastor. Ballots were passed out to the 110 persons present. The criterion was that sixty percent majority would be required for election. On the first balloting, Reverend John Otis Peterson received eighty-nine for and twenty-two against, or seventy-eight percent. John Otis Peterson, then thirty-one years old, was named the new pastor of the Alfred Street Baptist Church.

After selecting the new pastor, the Pulpit Committee was disbanded with a vote of thanks and appreciation for all of their efforts and accomplishment. The church also extended gratitude to Deacon Willis and his family, wife Emma, and children Eric, Robert, and Carol for their sacrifices during the thirteen months that he led the flock.

At the next regular meeting, the church minutes noted that Reverend John O. Peterson accepted the invitation to be pastor, and that he would submit his resignation to his present church in October 1964, with an effective date of December 27, 1964. The terms of the contract for the new pastor included $300 per month for salary and a one-month paid vacation.

A New Pastor Arrives

During the thirteen months that the pulpit was empty, John O. Peterson had been one of the frequent visitors to Alfred Street, and had been called upon several times to preach. At that time, he was pastor at the First Baptist Church of Louisa, Virginia, where he had been pastor for nine years, dating back to January 1955.

John Peterson was born in Horse Head, Virginia, in Northumberland County in the Northern Neck region of the state. This is a rural area, with an economy based on farming and fishing. Few industries existed in that region of the state then or even today. As a child, John Peterson attended his father's church in Heathsville. There he taught Sunday School, becoming a teacher at age twelve and the Sunday School superintendent at age sixteen. He attended the public schools in the area and graduated from the Julius Rosenwald High School in 1951 as class valedictorian. The school he attended was one of thousands of Rosenwald schools, primarily in the South, that had been founded by Julius Rosenwald, the president of Sears, Roebuck and Company. Mr. Rosenwald was a Chicago philanthropist who started a fund to contribute to the building of schools for Negroes, and between 1917 and his death in 1932 over 4,900 Rosenwald schools were built in fifteen states.

Following graduation from high school, John O. Peterson entered Virginia Union in Richmond to pursue a degree in mathematics and science. During his third year of undergraduate studies, he was required to leave school for a year to return to Horse Head and tend the farm. His father had passed, and he returned home to plant and harvest the tomato crops to support his mother and sister. It was during this period that he felt the call to the ministry, and was ordained at his home church, First Baptist Church of Heathsville, on September 11, 1953, at the age of 19 years.

He returned to school in the fall of 1954 and met a young lady, Joyce Keemer of Washington, D.C., in one of his science classes who would later become his wife. As a minister and college student, he spent the weekdays studying and the weekends preaching. In January 1955, while still a student, he was elected pastor of the First Baptist Church of Louisa and he served there until he came to Alfred Street.

In June 1956 he graduated from Virginia Union with a degree in mathematics and science, and started a career as a high school science teacher in Warwick, Virginia. In December 1956, John O. Peterson and Joyce Keemer were married at the Metropolitan Methodist Church in Washington, D.C. They soon began teaching in the high schools of Northern Virginia and spent essentially all of their teaching careers in that area. John O. Peterson received the call from Alfred Street in September 1964 and accepted the offer as pastor on October 4, 1964.

Before leaving the First Baptist Church of Louisa, however, there was a minor issue with his resignation. Of course, the church there loved their young pastor and some members had become a little disturbed earlier in the summer when Reverend Peterson was tendered an offer from the Third Baptist Church, also of Alexandria. He declined that offer, but some members were disturbed that he had even considered leaving. So, when he accepted the Alfred Street offer, there were some hurt feelings, but the church accepted the resignation, and he left the church in good financial shape and on friendly terms.

Installation Services

for

Reverend John O. Peterson

at the

ALFRED STREET BAPTIST CHURCH

313 South Alfred Street

Alexandria, Virginia

SUNDAY, FEBRUARY 7, 1965

Installation Program for Reverend John O. Peterson

Before coming to Alfred Street Baptist Church, Reverend Peterson had established a cordial relationship with the former pastor, Reverend Adkins. Reverend Adkins met and got to know John O. Peterson after learning that he was fond of and a student of Thomas Henderson, Dean of Students at Virginia Union. Reverend Adkins had invited Reverend Peterson to preach for him several times after 1958, including baptizing for Reverend Adkins once when he was not well. At some point following that baptism in 1962, Reverend Adkins asked Reverend Peterson if he would accept an invitation to be his assistant at Alfred Street. Reverend Peterson did not want to give up the pastorate of one church to become assistant minister at another, so he admits to avoiding discussion of such a change after that conversation.

A few months before Reverend Adkins died, he called Reverend Peterson and asked if he could borrow some published materials in which they were both interested. Reverend Peterson carried the documents to the parsonage, gave them to Reverend Adkins on the porch, and left without engaging in much conversation. Dr. Adkins did not get the opportunity to return the books, for his funeral was held that following

Sunday. And soon, Reverend Peterson, only thirty-one years old, would replace this extraordinary man, so dearly loved by the members of Alfred Street Baptist Church and the community of Alexandria.

Reverend Peterson's first official business meeting as new pastor and moderator of Alfred Street was on January 6, 1965. Several items of note were discussed at this first meeting between the new pastor and the congregation. First, Deacon Willis recommended the establishment of a Deaconess Board. There had been such a board under Reverend Madden in the 1880 time frame, and for a period of time Sister Catherine McQuay Butler was one of two deaconesses who served. Now, eighty-five years later, a new group of women were recommended and approved by the church as deaconesses. They were Mrs. Laura McPhail, Mrs. Mazie Bowden, Mrs. Ruth Dade, Mrs. Juanita Wilson, and Mrs. Ulysses Jackson, with Mrs. McPhail selected as chair. A deaconess board would remain part of the Alfred Street family of ministries for most of the next forty years, before being dissolved again.

A full slate of activities for the year was also discussed at this first meeting. Previously, Christmas morning service had been at 5:00 a.m. A change was made in the yearly schedule to an 11:00 a.m. service so that all of the Alfred Street family could attend. Also, the new pastor appointed a Building Committee to work with the trustees to study ways to use the current building and integrate it into the new addition that was being proposed. That committee consisted of Miss Ardelia Hunter, Mr. Vernon Carroll, Mrs. Mattie Brooks, and Mr. Richard Poole.

Though he was elected in October 1964, installation services for Reverend John O. Peterson were not held until Sunday, February 7, 1965, approximately four months after he was elected.[14] His installation as pastor was a daylong celebration. The speaker for the 11:00 a.m. service was Dr. E.D. McCreary, Jr., Professor of Philosophy and Religion at Virginia Union University in Richmond. During the 3:30 p.m. installation service, Dr. John M. Ellison, Chancellor of Virginia Union, spoke.

The entire day was filled with excitement and wonderment. Reverend Peterson was presented as a candidate by his uncle, Reverend Captain S. Peterson, while the welcome for the installation service was extended by the Honorable Frank E. Mann, Mayor, City of Alexandria. Following the installation, a reception and banquet followed immediately in the lower auditorium of the church. The installation banquet cost $143.80.

The Early Peterson Years

At the time that the new pastor arrived, the nation was in turmoil over two competing interests, the Civil Rights Movement and the war in Vietnam. The Civil Rights Movement had started about ten years earlier and was now in full swing. Much of the activity was taking place in the Deep South: North Carolina, Alabama, Mississippi, Georgia, and Louisiana. However, even as protests and sit-ins and bombings were taking place in the South, the North witnessed a series of troubling riots tied to civil unrest as well. In 1964, a major riot broke out in Harlem, New York, and destroyed many blocks of property. In 1965, the Watts area of Los Angeles was burned. In the summer of 1966, Chicago burned, while the next summer Newark, New Jersey, and Detroit, Michigan, burned. Each summer during the period between 1964 and 1967, there was at least one major riot to cause countless dollars of destruction.

In addition to civil rights issues, as Reverend Peterson was getting his footing in the new church, simmering in the background was a war in a far-off land that consumed the attention of the nation. The Vietnam War, which began in the mid-1960s and covered most of the next eight years, was a very controversial war, splitting the nation, universities, churches and even households. This was a civil war in which North Vietnam sought to unify the country as a communist regime, while South Vietnam sought to stop the communist offensive and remain a democracy. The issue for the average American, however, was less political and more a question of whether we should continue the war, or cut our losses and withdraw support for the Vietnamese. By April 1965, there were 35,000 U.S. troops in Vietnam, and by war's end, there were over 540,000 troops there.[15] Nearly everyone had a relative, a classmate, a friend, or an acquaintance serving there.

As more soldiers went to Vietnam and more and more were killed, opposition mounted among U.S. citizens. Protests were staged daily, particularly on college campuses and near the Pentagon in northern Virginia. President Johnson's economic program called the Great Society suffered. It was largely halted to pay for an unpopular war. Blacks were particularly affected by these cutbacks, and black leaders who had initially supported the popular democratic president turned on him and began protesting his programs. But a series of new civil rights laws were passed, and riots, protests, and boycotts related to race issues began to subside.

With the war and civil rights attracting national attention, Reverend Peterson was settling into his role of pastor of this small, historic church in Alexandria, Virginia. The conversion of the parsonage into two apartments was now complete, and rental was set at $125 per unit per month. The new pastor chose not to accept the offer to reside there, but chose instead to live in Washington, D.C., on North Dakota Avenue, Northwest. So, after having served as the residence for Alfred Street Baptist Church pastors for almost fifty years, the parsonage was now just another set of rental units.

By now, the new pastor was recommending that the church begin participating in additional convention affiliations. He enrolled the church in the Hampton Minister's Conference, which met in June 1965 in Hampton, Virginia; and in the Baptist World Alliance, which met in Miami, Florida, in June 1965. The church continued its affiliation with the Virginia Baptist General Association that met in Richmond in June, and with the Northern Virginia Baptist Association. The church also continued its membership in the Lott Carey Baptist Foreign Mission Convention. Soon the church was accepted into the American Baptist Convention, bringing the total number of convention affiliations to six.[16]

The construction project involving the main sanctuary and the education wing of the church still consumed a considerable amount of the congregation's time and energy. Mr. Marion S. Davis was then Chair of the Planning Committee. At that time, the membership in the Sunday School was seventy-two persons, consisting of seven classes from Beginner through adult. The Annex would provide additional Sunday School class rooms, an assembly room, a snack and lounge area, and a nursery for preschool age children.

Much of the discussion centered on whether the old building housing the main sanctuary would be remodeled as part of the new expansion. By now the old sanctuary was in need of a new ceiling, and steel beams were needed as support under the floor of the main auditorium. The building inspector indicated that while the walls were in good condition, the overall structure needed lots of work. The debate continued and at times became quite contentious over whether to remodel the old building or build an entirely new one. The estimate for remodeling was approximately $143,000, while the cost for a new building was set at $195,000. At the July 2, 1965, quarterly meeting, by a vote of thirty-nine for and six against, the church officials voted to proceed with plans to build a new building.

Activities During 1966–1970

During the first few years of his ministry, Reverend Peterson initiated several new reforms and ministries. Some had existed prior to his arrival and had become inactive, while other initiatives were truly new. The church began advertising worship services in the *Alexandria Gazette,* the local newspaper. Services during the summer switched from 11 to 10 a.m. according to newspaper accounts. Also, the young people of the church who had maintained a series of loose affiliations were soon organized into a Youth Department. Under the direction of Miss Jacqueline Neal, the youth requested that they become a full-fledged auxiliary of the church. The church had maintained some form of youth ministry since 1932 when Mrs. Adkins first formed the Junior Church. Miss Neal agreed to serve this resurrected ministry, and she would serve as Youth Director for two years until January 1967. The newly formed Youth Department's first activity was a Halloween party at the church.

Other musical groups were also coming into existence. Prior to 1964, the Singing Deacons were the only male singers serving at Alfred Street. They sang on special occasions such as evening services or Deacon's Day. In 1964, Claude Green became the director and Jacqueline Henry-Green, his wife, was the accompanist. During this period the group continued to hone their singing skills and techniques. In 1964, the group changed its name to the Male Ensemble. The newly named group began singing at special services at the church and throughout the community. In 1965, the name changed again to the Men's Chorus. Sister Ellen McCord became the group's director and accompanist in 1968. She devoted many years of service developing the men into a chancel choir.

Also in 1965, the Alfred Street family was introduced to the Alfred Street Choral Society, a new musical ensemble. The society began as part of a presentation of a Lenten cantata on Palm Sunday in 1965. At that time, the society consisted of the combined choirs of the church, Young and Adult, Senior, and the Men's Chorus, and was called the Combined Choirs of Alfred Street. As choirs from other churches were invited to join, the name was changed to Choral Society.

There had been a Youth Choir in the 1950s, but its membership and viability fluctuated as the number of children in the church diminished in the early 1960s. And so a new teenaged choir called the Little Acorns was started in August 1967. Their first director was Mrs. Willie Mae Wormley. Other choirs were also revamping their leadership. Mr.

Joseph Lucas, who had led the Young and Adult Choir for several years, resigned and was replaced by Sister Ellen McCord, who also directed the Men's Chorus.

In January 1966, a need was identified for four more deaconesses as the church and these ministries grew. Mrs. Mattie Brooks, Mrs. Anna Lee, Mrs. Sarah McMillian, Mrs. Alberta Willis, and Mrs. Pearl Willis (honorary) were named. The nine deaconesses assisted the pastor and deacons in visiting the sick and shut-in, prepared the elements for Communion, and were in charge of preparations for baptism.

Deaconess Mattie Brooks

As the church continued to grow, a need was identified to get a better accounting of the actual membership. Mr. Theodore Lee, the church clerk, circulated a complete member list to update the membership of the church, which ultimately showed a total membership of 293 persons. Alexandria remained the hometown of most of the members, as the move of blacks to the suburbs was still several years off. Of the membership, only three families lived in Maryland: Richard and Mary Wair, LaVern and Frances Lee, and Wesley and Geraldine Whitmore. About forty persons lived in Washington, D.C., mostly the children of former Alexandrians who had moved to the city for better jobs, schools, and a better way of life. These members included William and Emma Willis, the entire Charles Henry Wilson family, and members of the Leon Ferguson family.

In 1966, Reverend Peterson instituted Membership Groups at Alfred Street. Membership Groups, sometimes called "Tribes" or "Cells" in some other churches, were an attempt to organize the entire membership in small groups that worked together for fellowship and mission efforts. Each group initially consisted of 20–25 persons and had a deacon assigned as a Lay Leader. The Lay Leader was responsible for mentoring the membership group. That individual kept track of attendance, sickness, death, graduations, births, weddings and other activities of members of the group. The Membership Group elected officers and met five or six times a year to conduct its business. Some groups would plan special worship services, while others completed mission projects within the community.

Initially the church members were divided into six Membership Groups. Their primary goal was to make everyone feel a part of the church, and also to relieve the pastor of some of the visiting and daily involvement with personal affairs that consume so much of a pastor's time. Groups became a permanent fixture at Alfred Street and as the congregation grew the number of Membership Groups (Discipleship Groups) would increase to thirty.

William Willis, who had been Chair of the Board of Deacons at Reverend Peterson's arrival, traveled frequently with his work with one of the government's intelligence agencies. At the October 1966 meeting, Richard Wair replaced him as Chair and Wilbert Harris became Vice Chair of the Board of Deacons. In January 1967, two new deacons, Mr. James Neal and Mr. Theodore Lee, were elected. On Sunday, April 6, 1967, Brothers

Neal and Lee were ordained as deacons, with Reverend Joseph E. Penn, pastor of Third Baptist Church delivering the ordination sermon. They were the first new deacons ordained during Reverend Peterson's pastorate.

Brother Theodore Lee began attending Alfred Street as an infant and was baptized in 1922. He had served as an usher, trustee, church clerk, and sexton. His family had been a part of Alfred Street Baptist Church since the Reconstruction period.

Brother Neal was a native of Reidsville, North Carolina, and had originally joined a church in Winston-Salem, North Carolina in 1932. After several career moves where he united in different churches, he moved to Alexandria, Virginia, in 1963 and joined Alfred Street that year. He was president of the Men's Department and the Senior Choir, and he taught Sunday School.

By now, Brother Whitmore was Chair of the Board of Trustees. Two new trustees, Mr. Ernest Carroll and Mrs. Mariam Bracey, were nominated to replace outgoing members, Mr. Julian Dove and Mr. Leon Ferguson, whose terms had expired. However, after a heated debate, the church chose to keep Mr. Dove, and named Mr. Carroll to the other position, so Sister Mariam Bracey's name was dropped.

At the same time that new activities were starting under the new pastor, many of the old saints who had joined when Reverends Truatt and Powell served as pastors were now going to that final reward. Like Reverend Truatt, Reverend Peterson had entered the ministry with somewhat of a fear of death and funerals. But after several incidents among the congregation at the church in Louisa involving visits to isolated farmhouses, he had overcome these fears by the time he arrived at Alfred Street.

Like Reverend Adkins before him, Reverend Peterson was teaching full-time and serving as pastor part-time. So, when there was a death or funeral, he would sometimes be called from the classroom to comfort the family or prepare a eulogy. However, most funerals were still held on Sunday when most members of the families involved were off from work.

At a church meeting in 1967, Reverend Peterson spoke of a plan being considered by the Northern Virginia Morticians Association and Northern Virginia clergy to abolish all Sunday funerals, and to offer funerals at night. Funerals on Sundays were more expensive than other days, in part because cemetery workers were given overtime pay. Moreover, Sunday funerals created conflicts for other events already on the church calendar. However, Sunday funerals would continue for a while, but ultimately the church would cease funerals on Sundays.

One of the early saints Reverend Peterson eulogized was Sister Emma Corbin Osborne, who passed on April 14, 1967. She held the distinction of being the oldest known female member of Alfred Street Baptist Church, having lived to be 100 years and 5 months. She was born on October 28, 1866, shortly after the close of the Civil War.

Also passing in 1967 was Sister Anna Jackson. She was followed in 1968 by Regina Harris, Levi F. Jackson, Elizabeth Quander, and Grayce Quander. Deacon Theodore Lee, who had been the church clerk, passed in March 1968. The last minutes with his name were recorded in October 1967; however, he remained the official clerk until his death on March 26, 1968. In the interim, minutes were taken by Brother James Neal and, at the July meeting following Deacon Lee's death, it was announced that a memorial gift in his name would be used to purchase new Bibles.

The Building Campaign Begins in Earnest

Plans for a new building were first considered during the summer of 1962 when Reverend Adkins was pastor. Prior to Reverend Peterson's call to the church as pastor, the trustees prepared plans for an education building to be added onto the back of the church and extending southward. By 1966, however, little had been done. Construction had not begun because the application for a loan to build was denied. After studying the project, Reverend Peterson recommended that the church study other options because the value of the requested loan was more than the value of the new addition and the old building. Reverend Peterson concluded, along with the bank, that this was not in the best interest of the church. So the plans for that addition were scratched.

Reverend Peterson later recommended that the church consider rebuilding on its current lot or relocating to a new site. The church building was in terrible disrepair. The tin roof was loose and wobbled under any wind; all windows were loose; some of the floor boards had holes large enough to see in the basement; the pool leaked very badly; the two- to three-inch plastered ceiling had two cracks that went from wall to wall (one over the pulpit); bricks had been painted red on the outside but the paint had peeled badly; mortar between the bricks had eroded; the basement ceiling was not high enough for occupancy, although rooms for prayer meetings, choir, and trustees, makeshift office rooms, and toilets were in the basement. The church studied many options including buying an old church building in the 200 block of South Patrick Street and relocating to another site. After much debate among the congregation, the conclusion was to either rebuild or refurbish the building at the present location.

In 1966, the building campaign activity became more intense. Deacon Wilbert Harris was appointed Chair of a Planning and Survey Committee and at the January 1966 meeting, permission was granted for the church to purchase the land in the rear of the church on which to build an addition at a not-to-exceed cost of $35,000. This amount was in addition to the lot purchased, when Reverend Adkins was pastor, on the south side of the building. The church began buying additional individual homes along Patrick Street for $4,550 each in early 1966.

At a special call meeting on February 21, 1966, various subcommittees of the Planning and Survey Committee made initial reports and recommendations. Committees recommended that the choir loft of the new structure hold thirty-five people and that the new sanctuary provide for new kitchens and bathrooms. Costs to tear down the old building remained a big issue. On June 9, the church held another special call meeting to settle on an architect and selected Mr. Robert Nash, AIA.

Robert Nash was initially directed to prepare a set of drawings for a new building that included an education annex. But before anything of significance was planned, the city of Alexandria threatened to padlock the building. The rafters in the ceiling and roof had separated and come apart by as much as two and one-half inches, creating a very serious situation. Mr. Nash and his associates had cast iron braces fabricated to secure the joists. The bulged walls and braced beams remained in place for several years.

As the church wrestled with issues of keeping the old building in operation and designing a new one, a series of events occurred that set the church on a different path. In the mid-1960s, the city of Alexandria was selected as an *All-American City*, bringing a bit of prestige to the small town of approximately 15,000 people. The *Dip* area, also called the Bottoms, surrounding Alfred Street Baptist Church, was an economically depressed area, and was one of the first sights travelers saw when approaching the city from the south on U.S. Route 1, still a major north-south route along the eastern seaboard of the United States. In parallel, urban renewal had become the new phenomenon sweeping the country and was wiping out numerous slums and old black neighborhoods similar to the ones that surrounded Alfred Street Baptist Church.

Upon surveying the neighborhood with its blighted conditions, Mr. Nash recommended that Alfred Street seek the cooperation of the city of Alexandria in renewing the area to provide decent housing for the local residents. The city had already declared a sixteen-square-block area south of Duke Street as a depressed area in need of urban renewal. The city was favorable to Mr. Nash's proposal and the Dip Urban Renewal Project was born. The local citizens organized into the Alexandria Neighborhood Citizens Improvement Association (ANCIA) that met in the basement of the old church every Monday night to plan the urban renewal project.

Alfred Street had been designated as a liaison between the community and the authorities for revitalizing the area known as the Dip. The community was broken down into blocks, with an individual representing each block. A council, the Community Advisory Council, was formed to formulate plans and ensure that all concerns were addressed. Reverend Peterson, Trustee Welton Quander, and Deacon Wilbert Harris were the key working leadership members of the committees that met with the neighbors. Brother Quander was selected as Vice Chair of the Advisory Committee and Mr. Henry Burke, the Chair of the Board of Trustees, was the ANCIA Treasurer.

While the construction consumed most of the energy of the church, other decisions had to be made as well. At the first quarterly church meeting of 1969, Reverend Peterson proposed several recommendations. His first recommendation was to reorganize the Building Committee. A committee of some sort had now existed since early 1962 when the idea of a new building first surfaced. After being on the job for six years now, Reverend Peterson recommended increasing the seven-person committee to sixteen persons and that several younger members replace the older members listed as committee members—two of whom had already passed. Thus, the church began that year with a new building committee.

Reverend Peterson further recommended that Dr. James S. Burton become a part of the Alfred Street Baptist Church Board of Deacons. Dr. Burton had previously been ordained at the Belle View Baptist Church in Fairfax County. He joined Alfred Street in mid-1968, and Reverend Peterson recommended that he be installed as a deacon on the night of annual installation of officers.

The minutes of this first meeting in 1969 suggest that some small amount of discord existed among some of the various auxiliaries. Reverend Peterson admonished them to ". . . work together toward breaking down the old walls of prejudice, strife, envy and disunity that are rampant in our church and work toward strengthening the bonds of

Christian love. . . ." One of the issues causing strife was the compensation for the musicians in the Department of Music, an issue that had also plagued Reverend Adkins in the 1920s. The Director of the Choral Society was being paid $300 a year, which some members felt was too much. Reverend Peterson expressed the opinion that this was the wrong time to cut back, and recommended that the current compensation stand.

The Missionary Circle continued as a strong organization. It had been in existence now for over 75 years. It included among its members the church's First Lady, Mrs. Joyce Peterson, who was at that time among the youngest in the group.

Missionary Circle in 1969

By now Sister Ellen McCord had become director of the Young and Adult Choir, replacing Sister Marrietta O'Neal, their original director, and Mr. Joseph Lucas who served briefly. Sister Jackie Henry-Green continued with the Senior Choir, a position she had held since 1966, and would be joined the next year by Sister McCord as accompanist.

Another choir for small children was formed in 1969, reinstating a choir that had started earlier in 1955 and had then been discontinued. The new children's choir made its first appearance in a Lenten cantata on March 12, 1969, and consisted of twenty-one members. Dr. James Burton, who was a new deacon at Alfred Street, led the new children's choir. This was the third choir formed or reconstituted under Reverend Peterson, and brought the number of church choirs to five.

The King Assassination and Its Aftermath

As Alfred Street Baptist Church wrestled with issues of construction and urban renewal in the late 1960s, the nation was still struggling with the civil rights issues. The early 1960s had ushered in the Great Society programs of President Lyndon Baines Johnson, the most important of which was the Civil Rights Act of 1964. That Act provided the machinery to secure equal access to accommodations, to prevent discrimination in employment by federal contractors, and to cut off funds to segregated school districts.

Despite these gains, many blacks remained dissatisfied with the slow progress. The nonviolent Civil Rights Movement being led by Dr. King was challenged by younger black power advocates, and race riots broke out in many of the nation's large cities. Four summer riots left whole neighborhoods ruined and their residents more distressed than ever. During the summer of 1968, Reverend King planned a Poor People's Campaign in Washington, D.C., to address some of the problems and to highlight the plight of the poor. The Negro ministers of Alexandria, through their secretary Reverend Peterson, requested a meeting with Dr. King to better understand their possible involvement.

However, in March of 1968, Dr. King gave his famous *I've Been to the Mountain Top* sermon in Memphis, Tennessee, and he was assassinated the next day. The entire country was impacted, with riots occurring in many areas. There was severe rioting in nearby Washington, D.C., and Prince George's County in Maryland. Baltimore burned as did Philadelphia. Burning occurred in Richmond, Atlanta, Augusta, in cities of the Northeast, and on the West Coast.

Little damage occurred in Alexandria, Virginia, however. Newspaper accounts of the days and weeks following the assassination show few or no outbreaks of violence. In fact, the mayor and police chief are quoted in the local paper as saying ". . . our citizens were well-behaved." During this period when outrage and violence ruled the day in most black communities, crime actually went down in Alexandria compared to previous weeks.[17] Reverend Peterson and some of the local clergy were called to meet with the civil authorities, but calm prevailed throughout most of the city. Sporadic violence was reported in the city and county, with the most severe violence occurring at Mount Vernon High School where $500 worth of furniture was damaged.[18]

THE BAPTIST MINISTERS CONFERENCE
of The City of Alexandria, Virginia
HEADQUARTERS
909 Queen Street
Alexandria, Virginia

Rev. A. A. Booker
President

Rev. John O. Peterson
Secretary - Treasurer

December 27, 1967

The Reverend Doctor Martin Luther King, Junior
President - Southern Christian Leadership Conference
Alanta, Georgia

Dear Doctor King:

We have learned via the national news media that there is planned by your organization a "March on Washington" to begin sometime in April of 1968. We are sure that we do not have the facts as to the specifics of this demonstration. We have also learned that the Baptist Ministers Conference of Washington, D.C. and Vicinity has requested to meet with you to discuss this matter. We also desire to confer with you on this subject. Therefore we request that you notify us as to when you plan to be in Washington so that we may meet with you at the same time.

We pray that this matter may be resolved as quickly as possible.

Many warm and personal regards are extended to you, your family and the Conference for the coming New Year.

Yours in brotherly love,

Rev. A.A. Booker, President

Rev. John O. Peterson,
Secretary - Treasurer

Letter to Dr. King from Alexandria's Ministers

Nationwide, over 61,000 troops were mobilized to occupy troubled cities, even though fires and looting were beginning to subside over the weekends. Alexandria and Alfred Street Baptist Church had not been very active in civil rights efforts to this point and little outrage was evident in media accounts of activities in the city regarding Dr. King's assassination. The *Alexandria Gazette* reported on April 9, 1968, that calm still prevailed in the local area, following a day of violence nationwide. While the schools in the city and county maintained the usual schedule, the Retail Merchants Association in Alexandria asked all stores to remain closed for the day on the following Tuesday, the day of Dr. King's funeral.[19]

Following Dr. King's funeral, the Poor People's Campaign that he had planned arrived on schedule in Washington, D.C., in the spring of 1968. When the Poor Peoples' Campaign passed through Alexandria, members of the Alfred Street Baptist Church were asked to help with food and housing. As the mule train moved through the area, members of Alfred Street helped in various ways, and were thanked publicly at a church meeting held in July 1968.

In the wake of the assassination, there were various religious and civic actions to address some of the causes Dr. King had promoted. For example, on the religious front, appeals were made by religious groups to raise funds to support various poverty causes that Dr. King had espoused. The American Baptist Convention, of which Alfred Street was a member congregation, started a Martin Luther King Memorial Fund to provide services to local communities. However, at the July 1968 church meeting, Alfred Street members felt that the church should not contribute. They argued that the church was already responding to needs in the community such as those advocated by the Poor People's Campaign. So no contributions were sent.

On the civic front, in the wake of Dr. King's death, cities and states looked for new ways to honor his legacy. The most frequently selected tribute was renaming a street after him. In Washington, D.C., the old Nichols Avenue, running through southeast Washington, was renamed Martin Luther King, Jr. Avenue. The old George Palmer Highway in Prince George's County, Maryland, was also renamed. Streets were likewise renamed in Baltimore, Maryland; Philadelphia, Pennsylvania; Greensboro, North Carolina; Atlanta, Georgia; and Tallahassee, Florida. Even small towns in the American Southwest in Arizona and New Mexico renamed streets in his honor, particularly small towns near military bases where there was a strong black presence. Travelers throughout the country looking for the black sections of towns could generally find them by following the freeway to a Martin Luther King Drive or Street.

Interestingly, there was no street renamed Martin Luther King Drive in Alexandria; nor in Arlington, Falls Church, Fairfax, Burke, Centerville, Reston, Lorton, or Annandale. In all of Northern Virginia, there were no streets renamed for Dr. King.[20] Thus, as the national flurry of activity was ongoing to honor this slain civil rights pioneer elsewhere, these sentiments appear to have skipped over all of Northern Virginia.

Martin Luther King, Jr. Avenue in Washington, D.C.

Chapter Nine

1970–1990: A Suburban Church

. . . This life of mortal breath is but a suburb of the life Elysian . . .
(Headstone of Reverend S. Madden)

The civil rights era that began to ebb around the 1970s left several legacies at Alfred Street Baptist Church. Members who had been "Colored" or "Negro" for over 150 years were now "black"—*Black and Proud!* Positions of leadership at Alfred Street that had been closed to women would open and would create a great controversy. Growth in membership would require the construction of a new sanctuary that in turn generated even more growth. The church was transformed from a local urban congregation to a congregation of suburban commuters.

Alfred Street During the Period 1970–1975

Richard M. Nixon was serving as president when this period began. He had been elected in the fall of 1968 and inherited the civil unrest and the war in Vietnam that still plagued the nation. He soon began bringing more and more of the troops home under a doctrine in which the Vietnamese would take more and more responsibility for the fighting in Vietnam. In the spring of 1972, while preparing for reelection to a second term as president, a scandal surfaced when five men who supported his reelection campaign broke into the Democratic National Headquarters in Washington, D.C. The break-in occurred in the Watergate Hotel and this incident, which led to impeachment hearings and Nixon's resignation two years later, became known simply as Watergate.

Gerald Ford, the vice president, replaced Richard Nixon. President Ford's principal concern was the economy, which had begun to show signs of weakness as prices rose more than ten percent in 1974 and unemployment exceeded nine percent. This combination of a recession and inflation called stagflation was to exist for the remainder of his brief term in office.

As the 1970s began, Reverend Peterson was beginning his sixth year as pastor at Alfred Street Baptist Church. Following a practice that he started in 1960 as pastor at Lively Hope Baptist Church in Louisa, Virginia, he gave his annual report of the state of the church at the first quarterly meeting on January 4, 1970. In that report, he related that membership was beginning to decline slightly from previous years. Total membership at this time was 355 active communicants who were divided into six membership groups, each with a deacon as Lay Leader. However, on a typical Sunday the number of persons attending worship service totaled approximately 175 persons. On major events such as Easter Sunday, attendance might reach 315. On other Sundays when people were traveling or on vacation, attendance sometimes reached a low of eighty-three persons, as it did on the June 22, 1969.

Another item in the annual report showed that the church budget hovered around $17,000. The church was still saving for a building fund, and from the time of Reverend Peterson's arrival in 1964 to 1969, the amount in financial reserve for a new building had grown from $12,000 to $70,000.

According to his report, the auxiliaries were operating smoothly. The three boards, deacons, deaconesses, and trustees, had been active and had responded positively to each request brought before them by the pastor. The Young and Adult Choir had traveled over 1,200 miles outside of Alexandria and conducted twenty-six performances during 1969. They sometimes performed as many as three times on a given Sunday. Membership Group Number 6 and the Optimist Club had taken on the difficult assignment of feeding the needy at the beginning of the year.

The Church at Worship, circa 1970

In the Pastor's Annual Report, Reverend Peterson recognized Deacon Charles J. Burruss as an ". . . uncalled and unsung assistant pastor . . ." for his work in visiting the sick and the down-hearted. Especially noteworthy was the tape ministry he had started at Alfred Street. Deacon Burruss recorded church services on a portable tape recorder that was placed on the pulpit. Then he carried the taped sermons to the homes of the sick to play on his own recorder, as most homes did not own one.

Beginning in 1970, for the first time, the church hired a part-time church secretary. Miss Jacqueline Neal, the daughter of Deacon James Neal of Reidsville, North Carolina, accepted the position to assist with the large amount of paperwork and other secretarial activity within the church office. Reverend Peterson remained a part-time pastor, and he still taught full-time at a middle school in Arlington. Sister Remell T. Lomax was now church clerk, and Sister Corrine E. Pouncy was treasurer. Brother Charles Butler, who lived across the street at 310 South Alfred Street, was the sexton. The church maintained office hours daily from 4:00 p.m. until 8:00 p.m. after the pastor got off from his full-time job as a science teacher.

By 1970, the church was affiliated with ten associations that included memberships in the local Northern Virginia Baptist Association, the State Baptist General Convention of Virginia, the National American Baptist Convention, and the Council of Churches United. Additionally, there were youth organizations (Baptist Training Union), a vibrant Sunday School, and various activities for women who were kept busy attending conventions.

During this period, Reverend Peterson also remained active with associations outside of the sanctuary. During the previous year, he had attended nineteen association meetings or conventions away from the church. He was then president of the Baptist Minister's Conference of the City of Alexandria, and held positions in the Northern Virginia Baptist Association, the Baptist General Convention at the state level, and the American Baptist Convention at the national level.

Shortly after Reverend Peterson's arrival, the church had also increased its involvement in local religious associations. The church had been a member of the Northern Virginia Baptist Association, an affiliation of black churches in neighboring counties, since 1910. But seeing a need for even more local involvement, Reverend Peterson became involved with the Alexandria Baptist Minister's Conference of Baptist Churches in the city. The group held city-wide revivals and joint Easter sunrise services, as well as other functions to unite the Baptist churches of the city. Joint worship services among member churches of the conference were a frequent occurrence.

The Minister's Conference also served as a clearing-house for civic matters in the city such as school board issues or civil rights issues. For example, prior to Dr. Martin Luther King's Poor People's Campaign in 1968, the Conference had written to him to see how they might become involved. Reverend Peterson was treasurer from 1970 to 1972, and later became president. His involvement, and that of the church, with this group and with the Northern Virginia Baptist Association were severed some ten years later over an incident in which these bodies withdrew the hand of fellowship from Alfred Street Baptist Church.

On November 21, 1970, the church celebrated its 167th anniversary. As discussed previously, the start date had changed several times, resulting in conflicting church anniversary dates. The 1970 observance was the first to recognize 1803 as the start date versus 1852, 1833, 1821, or 1806 that had served as start dates for previous anniversaries. As late as 1968, the assumed start date was 1806, as the church celebrated its 162nd anniversary that year.

For the 1970 anniversary, a special dinner was held at 3:00 p.m. on Anniversary Sunday at the First Citizens National Bank in Alexandria. A special play entitled *Forgive Us Our Chicken Coops*, directed by Sister Joyce Peterson, was presented by the recently formed Drama Ministry. The affair netted over $1,000 for the Church Building Program.

Sister Mattie Brooks, though now elderly and on a cane, continued to shepherd Usher Board Number One. She was responsible for attracting more people to attend Sunday afternoon or evening services than any other person or auxiliary. Usher Board Number One also held the distinction of being the only auxiliary to make and keep its yearly pledge to the Building Fund. The members had pledged and submitted $500 yearly, or more than $2,500 during the first five years of Reverend Peterson's tenure.

On December 6, 1970, Deacon Charles Henry Wilson of Alfred Street delivered his trial sermon. He had been ordained as a deacon in 1963 by Reverend Adkins, and was the first minister to be ordained during the pastorate of Reverend Peterson. He spoke from Mark 5:25–28 on a sermon entitled *Only Believe*, and was granted a license by the church. The church, at this time, had only a pastor and no assistants. So, soon after ordination, Minister Charles Henry Wilson began assisting with pulpit responsibilities.

The installation of officers for 1971 was held on the second Sunday in January at 6:00 p.m., as was the custom. Reverend Austin A. Booker, accompanied by his choir and congregation from Ebenezer Baptist Church in Alexandria, delivered the installation sermon as he had done for several years. The installation service included an audiovisual presentation by Harry and Costella Burke, in which each officer's responsibility was flashed on a screen along with a picture of the club or auxiliary for which the officer was responsible. By now, the list of auxiliaries and clubs had grown to twenty-three and included four choirs (Little Acorns, Senior Choir, Young and Adult Choir, and the Men's Choir), six membership groups, the Optimist Club, two usher boards, and the Sunday School, which remained perhaps the strongest auxiliary.[1] Deacon Wilbert Harris served as superintendent of the Sunday School. The Youth Department was also growing with Sister Reba Burruss, daughter of Deacon Charles Burruss, as president.

As part of the installation of new officers, the church recognized persons who had previously served on the major boards. The church could identify thirty-eight persons who had previously served as trustees going back to 1834. In addition to one woman (Mrs. Thelma Wair), other trustees had included a physician (Dr. Albert Johnson), and two persons who were ministers while also serving as trustees—Reverend Edward Dixon and Reverend W.A. Price. The church identified forty-nine persons who had served as deacons, and they included George L. Seaton (a former Virginia state legislator), Dr. Albert Johnson, Dr. James Burton, Reverend Dixon, and Reverend Price. A total of eleven persons had also served on both the Board of Deacons and Board of Trustees at some point during their stay at Alfred Street.

The Young and Adult Choir, 1971

Prior to 1971, the church had ten deacons, seven deaconesses, and six trustees. Thelma Wair remained the only female trustee. In March 1971, five more deaconesses were added,

The Deaconess Board

including Maggie Butler, Mary Wair, Louise Harris, Emma Willis, and Barbara Keller.[2] Sister Alberta Willis remained as chair of the group. The Deacon Board that consisted of ten men included William Willis as chair and Richard Wair as vice chair. Deacon John Strange was senior in terms of years of service and age and was approaching his 92nd birthday. Five members of the group had been ordained in 1963, and the others came later as older ones passed on.

Brother Charles H. Butler was ordained as a new deacon on May 31, 1971, joining the ten men who then served. Brother Butler was a native of Emanuel County, Georgia, and had moved to Alexandria in 1949. He and his wife Maggie initially became "watch-care" members of Alfred Street, while maintaining their membership at a church in Metter, Georgia. They remained watch-care members at Alfred Street for twenty years until they joined as regular members in 1969. Maggie Love-Butler was consecrated a deaconess at Alfred Street in March 1971.

The Butler family lived near the church and its members were of immeasurable assistance to the pastor. During this period, Reverend Peterson continued to teach full-time at a local middle school and pastor part-time at Alfred Street. Because of that, an occasional issue would arise while he was not available. Reverend Peterson left a spare set of keys with Brother Charlie Butler and his family who lived nearby. There were numerous times during the year when a member of the Butler family, either Charlie, Sister Maggie Butler, or the teenage daughter Claudette, would open the church to locate a record, return a phone call, or just let someone else enter the building to take care of an issue. The pastor acknowledged and thanked the Butler family in his annual report.

During these years, the choirs of the church continued to grow and develop. In 1972, two men, Elwood Lewis and Harvey Tunstall, Jr., took over direction of the Men's Chorus from Sister Ellen McCord who had directed them since 1964. The Men's Chorus continued to develop to the point where it was given a regular slot in the performance rotation at regular services. They were assigned the fifth Sunday worship services, of which there are generally four in the calendar year. As an encouragement for younger men to join, the name was soon changed from the Men's Chorus to the Male Chorus.

In the fall of 1973, the Deacon Board held its first off-site retreat at New Windsor,

Maryland. Richard Wair had replaced William Willis as Chair of Deacons. Later that year, on October 28, 1973, Brothers Walter Payne, Welton Quander, and Lenzy Robertson were ordained as new deacons. Pastors and deacons from twenty churches were invited to attend and to sit in Council to consider *setting the candidates apart* for the work of the diaconate.

Brother Payne, from Charlottesville, Virginia, and a chemist by profession, had moved to Alexandria in 1966. He immediately joined Alfred Street, where he taught Sunday School with his wife, and he was on the Budget Committee and the Percentage Giving Campaign.

Brother Quander was a native Alexandrian and a member of a family that had then belonged to Alfred Street for almost 150 years. He had been baptized at Alfred Street in 1936, and had been a member of the Board of Trustees for over twenty-five years, having served as chair and vice chair. He had also been president of the Men's Chorus since its inception. He was a career employee at the National Archives where he developed a keen interest in preserving the church's records.

At this time, membership at Alfred Street Baptist Church was approximately 450 persons, with most members living in Alexandria near the church. A majority of the members lived within the zip code 22314, in which the church is located, or in the zip code 22306, in the vicinity of Quander Road or Beacon Mall south of the city along the U.S. Route 1 corridor. There were about thirty persons listed with Washington, D.C., addresses, including the pastor, who lived at 6021 North Dakota Avenue, Northwest.[3] Most of the other members living in the District of Columbia were former Alexandrians who moved to the city for jobs or a better lifestyle.

Only four families were listed with Maryland addresses: the LaVern Lee, Richard Wair, and the George Wilson families lived in the Landover area; and the Walter Payne family lived in Suitland, Maryland. Most of these families were former Alexandrians who had moved to Maryland. There were no listings for persons from Falls Church, Fairfax, Annandale or other suburban areas of Northern Virginia. The migration to the Virginia suburbs was still over a decade away.

Membership at Alfred Street continued to grow during the early 1970s. By now the Youth Department was fully functional. Youth activities included Youth Fellowship Programs, Leadership Training, Evangelism Programs, Christian Education Week, Children's Day and Sunday School outings. Vacation Bible School was also being strengthened. The following table shows growth in the church membership (active and inactive persons) and the Sunday School during the 1970–1975 time frame, and for 1965, Reverend Peterson's first full-year, for comparison.

Year	Membership	New Members	Sunday School
1965	324	41	72
1970	327	18	105
1971	353	21	110
1972	365	32	125
1973	433	73	130
1974	481	48	140
1975	494	13	154

The Missionary Society, previously called the Mite Society until late into Reverend Truatt's pastorate, offered major activities for the women of the church. Because of distance and lack of transportation, the members on the south side of Alexandria near Alfred Street and members on the north side (closer to the present-day Braddock Road Metro Station) formed two missionary circles: Esther Circle and Dorcas Circle. Sister Ida Jackson was chair of the Esther Circle, on the south side, while Sister Mattie Adkins was president of the Dorcas Circle, on the north side. Meetings were held in the homes of members who belonged to each group. After a few years, the two groups disbanded and reunited as a single body, and have remained a unified body ever since. During the period 1969–1975, Ruth Dade served as president of the missionaries. Then, as now, few men participated in missionary activities.

To support their activities, the missionaries held various fund-raising projects. Their projects included bazaars, baby contests, rummage sales, bake sales, and dinners, which were sold in large numbers. However, in the early 1970s, fund-raising activities were discontinued. Instead, for many years the fifth Sunday was set aside as Missionary Sunday so that members of the church could make monthly, sacrificial contributions to mission efforts. After Reverend Peterson started the Tithing and Enlistment Program, members made larger pledges and money for missions was budgeted through the general church treasury.

The Optimist Club was also still functioning in the early 1970s. It was named for an international service club, and had begun at Alfred Street in 1949 under Reverend Adkins with Mrs. Lorraine Funn-Atkins as its first president. Its mission of welcoming new people, encouraging young members and, in general, ". . . remaining optimistic . . ." had continued, and it now included about twenty-five members. Mrs. Lorraine Funn-Atkins was still their president in 1974.

During the early 1970s, the building program campaign that began in 1962 under Reverend Adkins continued in the background of church activity. Progress was tied to the Dip Urban Renewal Project that took several years to formulate and plan due to numerous studies and federal regulations. The Dip Urban Renewal Project sought to revitalize approximately a twenty-block area that surrounded the church and extended from Duke Street southward to Jefferson Street, and from Washington Street on the east to North Henry Street on the west. Alfred Street Baptist Church had been considering several options for a church structure, including remodeling the old church at a cost of approximately $250,000; remodeling and adding an education wing to the old church at a total cost of approximately $400,000; or demolishing the present old structure and building a complete new combination church with education wing for approximately $500,000.[4] The church was also considering possible sites for the sanctuary including staying on Alfred Street or moving to a site at the corner of Wilkes Street and U.S. Route 1 in Alexandria.

Finally, in 1974, after twelve years of considering options for a new building, construction efforts took on a new sense of urgency and Reverend Peterson appointed a ninety-nine-member Survey and Planning Committee to research various options for a new sanctuary. After a year of research and planning, the committee became the Building Committee, and the church selected the architectural firm of Vosbeck, Vosbeck,

Killenger and Ringinger (VVKR) to design a new edifice. Deacon Wilbert Harris, who was originally from Danville, Virginia, was selected as Chair of the Building Committee.

1975–1980: Pastor's Illness

By 1975, Reverend Peterson had been pastor for more than ten years. Members of the church decided to honor him with a tenth anniversary celebration during the third week of January in 1975. Planning meetings for the celebration began in August 1974 with Mary and Richard Wair as co-chairs.

The congregation was still essentially a local congregation, with most members living within a short distance from the church in Alexandria. There were now about fifteen families commuting from Maryland. These families in Maryland included those of Ozetta Boseman, Dottie Cobbs, Fred and Faye Gunn, Betty Harmon, James and Pat Johnson, Cherlyn and Jewel Kilpatrick, Arvid Lee, Helen McCoy, Ellen McCord, Laura and Walter Moore, Mary and Walter Payne, Russell and Poinsettia Peterson, and Mary and Richard Wair, Chairman of the Board of Deacons.

By 1977, Reverend Peterson had been at Alfred Street for thirteen years, and was leaving his imprint in activities at the church and within the community. He continued with his duties as pastor to the congregation of 450 members, and to teach full-time now at the Stratford Junior High School in Arlington, the first school in Virginia to integrate following the state's Massive Resistance campaign. He was also active in local and state religious associations, including the Baptist Minister's Conference of Alexandria, of which he had earlier been president. He participated in the Northern Virginia Baptist Association, of which he had been third vice president from 1969 to 1973. He was also active in the Baptist General Convention of Virginia, of which he would later become president.

However, the heavy load of activities took its toll. On November 7, 1977, Reverend Peterson suffered a heart attack at the age of forty-four years. The heart attack left him homebound for several months. During that time, Richard Wair, the Chair of the Board of Deacons, ran the affairs of the church.

The illness presented Reverend Peterson a difficult choice. His doctor felt that he was carrying too heavy a workload, and recommended that he give up one of his two full-time jobs, teaching or preaching. The choice was complicated by the fact that he had been teaching now for over twenty-two years, and was progressing well in that career. It also paid more than the relatively small church, which consumed so much of his time. Moreover, he had a family of a wife and two school-aged children ages eleven and twelve. The two full-time jobs permitted him to care for his family in the way many characterized as the American Dream. So there was motivation to continue with both.

But health concerns required that he give up one job. Though he found teaching gratifying, preaching was his first love, and was also his calling. So, in early 1978, Reverend Peterson exited the classroom, where he taught mathematics, chemistry, and physical sciences, for good and took to the pulpit as his sole full-time job.

With all his energies now focused on Alfred Street, a new vitality was infused in the church. Activities involving a new building took on new urgency, and Russell Peterson, a cousin of Reverend Peterson's, became Chair of the Building Funds Campaign Committee. At this time the church conducted visits to members' homes as part of its Percentage Giving Campaign, and the Building Committee piggybacked its visits with this effort. Calvin Harris was Chair of Home Visitations for the Building Fund. Home visits were generally conducted in November.

During the year 1978, Alfred Street membership grew by fifty-six to a total of 555 persons, though seven members passed away that year. In spite of growing at a sustained pace, Alfred Street was not the largest black Baptist church in Alexandria, or in the Northern Virginia area, as it would become by the end of the century. In Alexandria, Ebenezer Baptist (894) and Mt. Jezreel (861) were black Baptist churches with larger memberships than Alfred Street. Mt. Olive (956) and Mount Zion (685), in Arlington, were larger churches. Additionally, in Fairfax County, Mount Pleasant (682) and Bethlehem Baptist (586) in Gum Springs were also larger than Alfred Street. Most other black churches in the Northern Virginia area were then two- or three-hundred-member congregations.[5]

Alfred Street had always maintained several affiliations with other religious bodies, going all the way back to the late 1850s, and Reverend Peterson continued this tradition. During 1979, Reverend Peterson was elected president of the Baptist General Convention of Virginia and would serve until 1982. Locally, the Northern Virginia Baptist Association to which Alfred Street belonged boasted 123 ordained ministers and seventeen licentiates. Approximately 109 churches were then members of the association along with Alfred Street. They ranged from the close-in ones in Alexandria and Arlington, to remote ones in Culpepper, Loudon, Fauquier, and Prince William Counties. Additionally, a small number (eight) of churches from the District of Columbia were members. Reverend Peterson served as Chair of the Constitution Revision Committee, while his uncle, Reverend Captain S. Peterson, served as Chair of the Executive Board.

Women in Leadership Positions

Alfred Street, like most churches of that era had a congregation that was predominately female and, like most churches, positions of leadership were held primarily by men. The pastor was male and all the deacons were male. The ushers were initially all male until around 1965 when the female usher auxiliary was given full status as ushers. Trustees had also been all male until Sister Thelma Wair was selected as a trustee in the early 1970s.

Thus, while some women were beginning to be accepted at Alfred Street and at other churches in administrative or nonbiblical leadership positions within the church, most persons felt that the position of deacons and ministers—the two biblically based positions—were different. Few black churches in the country had women in these positions, and even fewer black Baptist churches, particularly in the conservative South, were receptive to women preachers or deacons.

On October 28, 1979, Alfred Street ordained its first woman deacon, Sister Mary Williams Wair. The ordination caused quite a local stir that was highlighted daily in newspaper and television media reports. She was not the first woman in the state of

Virginia to be ordained, nor was she the first black Baptist woman to be ordained. In fact, Dr. Paul Nichols, Dean of Virginia Union's School of Theology, had earlier ordained several women deacons at Good Shepherd Baptist in Richmond where he served as pastor; so had Dr. Edward D. McCreary, Chair of the Humanities Department at Virginia Union University and pastor of Mount Carmel Baptist Church in Richmond. However, this was a new phenomenon for the areas outside of Richmond, and particularly in the Northern Virginia area.

Sister Mary Wair had been a deaconess at Alfred Street for eight years. She grew up in Wilson, North Carolina, but moved to Washington, D.C., as a child and joined the Turner Memorial Methodist Church. After studying at West Virginia State University and the University of Maryland, she joined Alfred Street—her husband Richard Wair's church. Richard's father had been Chair of the Board of Deacons at Alfred Street from 1934 until his death, and now Richard was serving as vice chair when his wife, Mary, was ordained as deacon.

Mary Wair joined Alfred Street in 1963, prior to the arrival of Reverend Peterson, and served with the Missionaries and the Pastor's Aide, and she sang on two choirs. She had been elected to the Board of Deaconesses in 1971, and had served as chair of that board since 1975. After her ordination, Deacon Mary Wair received mixed receptions as she traveled the country as a deacon. Some churches welcomed her as a fresh sign of progress. Others shunned her and refused to seat her, even when traveling with the pastor and choir. The poor receptions were not limited to the conservative Baptist churches of the South, but spilled over even to larger more progressive churches in New York.

As a new deacon, Mary Wair joined the board with several deacons who had been there to experience the transition from the Adkins to the Peterson administration. Brother James Neal, who had been ordained in 1976, was still a deacon. Brother Lenzy Robertson had transferred as a deacon from Beulah Baptist Church, while Robert Butler had been ordained in 1971. Sister Mary Wair was thus joining a board of ten male deacons, including the five relatively young deacons who had been ordained as a group in 1963.

As a result of this controversial ordination, Reverend Peterson was expelled from the Baptist Ministers Conference of Alexandria of which he had been president just ten years prior. The conference ". . . withdrew the Right-Hand-of-Fellowship," a practice among Baptists dating from the earliest years of Alfred Street's existence. This caused a great deal of controversy in Northern Virginia and Washington, D.C., which brought attention to the church and, in turn, caused an explosion in attendance. In fact, on one Sunday after the ordination, the long unused balcony was so crowded it drooped onto the swinging doors on the main level which

Pastor Ordains Woman, Is Ousted at Baptist Meetin

By Ed Briggs
Times-Dispatch Religion Writer

The Rev. John O. Peterson, president of the 300,000-member Baptist General Convention of Virginia, has, like many of his pastor friends, advocated bringing women into the mainstream of black Baptist congregational life.

And because he took a step in that direction last week by ordaining a woman deacon in his Alexandria church, he was thrown out of the Baptist Ministers' Conference of Alexandria.

The action came Monday after Mr. Peterson had ordained Mary William Wair in his Alexandria congregation, Alfred

Spokesmen for the Alexandria ministerial association could not be reached for comment.

The shunning of Mr. Peterson by local Baptist pastors took by surprise several women's ordination advocates here.

Has Received Word

Dr. Paul Nichols, dean of Virginia Union University's School of Theology, where one woman is in the ministerial program, said he had not received word of the ouster, referred to in Baptist jargon as "withdrawal of the hand of fellowship."

Nevertheless, Dr. Nichols, who as pastor of Good Shepherd Baptist Church here has ordained several women deacons, again voiced his support for

Mr. Powell and Dr. Edwa D. McCreary Jr., chairman the humanities department VUU and a pastor of Mount C mel Baptist Church Richmond, have ordain women deacons in th churches.

Dr. McCreary was a ma voice in raising gospel libe tion themes to get the state c vention to change its stand 1975.

And Dr. McCreary has bee help to those pastors, includ Mr. Peterson, who wanted to dain women, yet needed to c vince their congregations it proper.

Reverend Peterson Ordains Women Deacons

became support braces for the balcony.

Following the ordination of Mary Wair as a deacon in 1979, and its associated discord among churches in the Association, in 1980 Reverend Peterson ordained a woman minister—Sister Doris Ashton. In so doing, she became the first African American female Baptist to be ordained to the Christian ministry in the state of Virginia.

Deacon Mary Wair and Reverend Doris Ashton

By the end of 1979, the size of the Deaconess Board had also increased. There were now 12 deaconesses, who had begun holding annual retreats off-site. The list now included Mazie Bowden, Maggie Butler, Ruth Dade, Edith Elliott, Louise Harris, Ulysses Jackson, Barbara Keller, Anna Lee, Sarah McMillian, Laura McPhail, Mattie Owens, and Emma Cook Willis.

By 1979, the number of children at the church had increased significantly since Reverend Peterson's arrival, and several new initiatives were instituted. Sister Carolyn Rowe assisted with restarting a new children's nursery. The Children's Choir had been reconstituted with Harriet Westbrook Smith as director. At that time, there were still only enough children for a single children's choir for all age groups up to teenagers. There might have been ten or twelve children who formed this choir, with ages ranging from three to twelve. The split into two children's choirs (i.e., Children's Choir and Junior Gospel Inspirers) would come some years later when there were enough children to divide them.

Among the members of the 1979 Children's Choir were James and Patricia Johnson's girls (Deidre and Tanya); Booker T. and Mamie Woodard's son Brian Todd; Russell and Poinsettia Peterson's daughter Rhonya; Garland Tanks' two sons; and Carolyn Rowe's two daughters, Anitra and Tamara Denise Rowe. Tamara was also one of the child ushers.

1980–1985: A New Sanctuary and the Great Divide

In 1980, the former governor of California, Ronald Reagan, defeated incumbent President Jimmy Carter for the presidency of the country. He took office with a pledge to reverse the trend toward big government and to rejuvenate the economy by implementing supply-side economics. In the short term, his economic policies succeeded. However, revenues did not increase as predicted, resulting in a staggering growth in the budget deficit. Even so, he would remain as president for the next eight years.

Reverend Peterson had now been at Alfred Street for sixteen years, and by October 1980 the membership stood at 504 persons.

Construction of the new church was intimately tied to the urban renewal project that was taking place in the Dip area of Alexandria. As part of the urban renewal process, the church had transferred the title to all of its property to the city of Alexandria, and then repurchased it. According to Deed Book 963, City of Alexandria, Page 385, September 14, 1979, a bargain and sale deed transferred the property from the Alexandria Redevelopment Housing Authority (ARHA) to the trustees of Alfred Street Baptist Church. At the time these trustees were Harry S. Burke (Chair), Welton A. Quander,

Roger C. Anderson, Lenzy M. Robertson, Carlton A. Funn, Sr., Julian M. Dove, and Thelma R. Wair. The deed shows that the property had been sold to ARHA on January 5, 1979, for $99,000. The deed describes the property as being ". . . all of Lot 600 as shown on a plot of re-subdivision of Lot 500 and Lot 501 . . . and part of other Lots. . . ."[6]

In the planning for the new church, the city of Alexandria offered Alfred Street Baptist Church several areas of the Dip area on which to build a new church. The selected site was the one-half block of Alfred Street, north of and including the site of the old building constructed circa 1883. Also, in planning for the displacement of local residents and new housing for them near the church, Alfred Street decided to wait until new homes were built in the area before building a new edifice. The planning and approvals from the federal Housing and Urban Development Department for the new homes took ten years. The building of new homes adjacent to the church finally began in 1978.

The U.S. Department of Housing and Urban Development, the ARHA, and Alfred Street Baptist Church agreed on the land purchased for the edifice in 1978. Although ARHA had some reservations about allowing the church to have the prime location in the entire Dip area, it granted Alfred Street the one-half block beginning at the southwest corner of Alfred and Duke Streets. Some members of ARHA did not think the church had enough money to pay for both the land and a structure that was estimated to cost about $1.3 million. However, Alfred Street paid cash for the land and began searching for a $700,000 construction loan to get the project started. Interest rates had skyrocketed to eighteen and twenty-one percent and construction loans were hard to get. Trustee Welton A. Quander and Reverend Peterson traveled to New York City; Hartford, Connecticut; and Richmond and Norfolk, Virginia, trying to secure a loan, to no avail.

New Church Under Construction

Reverend Peterson went to Richmond a second time to discuss this matter with a college friend, Mr. Hanley, the president of Consolidated National Bank. Mr. Hanley indicated he would have given the church a loan if it had not been almost one hundred miles from the bank in Richmond. Instead, he suggested a different way of marketing the application. The loan application was redone and Trustee Harry Burke, Chairman of the Trustees, presented the new proposal to the First Federal and Loan Association of Alexandria while the deaconesses led a prayer meeting at the church. The loan was approved that day.[7]

Construction began in late 1979, with a groundbreaking ceremony on September 22.[8] The construction was planned for three phases: Phase I construction was for the main building, offices and sanctuary; Phase II consisted of completion of the kitchen and lower level; and Phase III provided for an extension of the front thirty-four feet toward Alfred Street. Initial estimates to completion were one year, but construction was delayed several times. The longest delay, for several months, occurred when construction was halted during a dispute between the architect and the builder. The dispute was over who was responsible for an error in the design when it was discovered that the arched wood beams that held up the roof were short by several inches. After a protracted legal negotiation, an agreement was reached, and construction continued as scheduled.

While the conflict with the builder and architect was finally settled, the battle was not over. The battleground moved from outside the church to within the congregation. The internal disagreement centered on what to do with the old church.

One of the stipulations of the construction permit was that the church must provide adequate parking. To provide for parking, the church had planned to tear down the old church at 313 South Alfred Street and construct a parking lot that would accommodate twenty-one cars. Some members viewed this as a progressive move, as parking was necessary to move forward with completion of the church construction project. The side for demolition included Reverend Peterson and most of the newer members of the congregation, many of whom had been there less than five years.

Opposing the "progressives" was a group of "preservationists" who felt it criminal to tear down the old church, the sole remaining positive influence in the area of the city called the Dip area. The preservationists felt it should be preserved and made into a museum. On the side for preservation were a loose coalition of concerned neighbors, local history buffs, and a handful of the church's 500-person congregation. Members of the church for preservation tended to be persons who had been there thirty, forty, or even fifty years.

The Washington Star / Ken He

The Rev. John O. Peterson, pastor of the Alfred Street Baptist Church, stands in front of his rapidly rising ne church. At left is the old church, center of a controversy over whether it should be torn down.

Alexandria History Buffs Battle Plan By Blacks to Demolish Own Church

Media Coverage of Dispute Over Old Church

Daily, as the walls of the new sanctuary went up, the walls of the old sanctuary stared back, waiting to be torn down under a demolition contract that had already been signed. A series of heated hearings between the progressives and the preservationists, both within the church and at the Alexandria City Hall, were held over what to do with the old building. The preservationists retained Robert L. Montague III as their lawyer. He sought to have the building listed on the State Registry of Historic Landmarks, a move that would have essentially halted the tear-down option. He was supported by some of the city historians who argued that the building was over one hundred years old and, as such, was subject to city ordinances that such old buildings could not be disturbed.

Earlier in 1975, the city of Alexandria had passed an ordinance ruling that the city's Board of Architectural Review must approve all demolition permits for buildings over one hundred years old. In order to circumvent the provisions of the new ordinance, the church that had previously boasted that the old church building was 120 years old (based on an 1855 article in the *Alexandria Gazette*) hired Theodore L. Pryor, a restoration architect, to disprove their own claim. When his data showed an 1880s date as the likely date the old church was built or last modified, the progressives now changed their argument. Upon discovering that the building was over one hundred years old, their tact and arguments shifted to ". . . the history of the church lives in the people; not in the building. . . ."

The Board of Architectural Review initially declined jurisdiction in the case. Hearing upon hearing was held as the animosity increased. Articles concerning the dispute appeared in the local media almost daily. Sister Lorraine Funn-Atkins, a leader among the preservationists, is quoted in the *Washington Star* newspaper (May 21, 1980) as saying, ". . . It's ridiculous to tear down a lovely old church for twenty-one parking spaces. . . ." Reverend Peterson is quoted in the same article as saying, ". . . This is Alexandria and there seems to be some type of holiness about old things. Keeping the old church will be economically disastrous for us. . . ." And so it went.

Throughout most of 1980 as construction continued, the debate also continued. In November 1980, a public hearing was held at Alexandria City Hall. Members of the Alfred Street Baptist Church congregation, pros and cons, testified. The following individuals presented arguments in favor of or against demolition of the old church.[9]

Individuals Providing Testimony on Old Church

FAVORING DEMOLITION	AGAINST DEMOLITION
Reverend J.O. Peterson	Carlton Funn
Richard Wair	Harry Burke
Florine Grayson	Roger Anderson
James Lewis (Attorney)	Lorraine Atkins
Elbert Ransom	Jennifer Moses (Dance Troupe)
Frank Heard	Robert DeForrest
Mrs. Jackson	Annie Rose
Thomas Howell	Nancy Payne
James Garrett	Gladys Tancil
Garland Tanks	Bruce Adkins
Harriet Westbrook	Robert Adkins
Rogers Davis	Robert Montague (Attorney)
Walter Moore	
Faye Gunn	

The arguments presented at the hearing were similar to those playing out in the press. The preservationists felt it criminal to tear down an old church to build parking spaces. The progressives felt that it was inappropriate for an old building to stand in the way of progress. They argued that while history was important, the church's history was resident in the people, not in the walls of the old building.

Ultimately, the dispute ended in a stalemate of sorts, with both sides winning and both sides losing. The city of Alexandria ruled that the structure was over one hundred years old and therefore could not be torn down. Thus, the preservationists won. However, as there were no funds to build a museum, it was a hollow victory. The progressives also won as the city issued a waiver on parking requirements, permitting construction to continue. Occupancy of the new building was thus approved and the old church would sit empty and boarded up for most of the next decade.

The disagreement over the old church versus parking lot was perhaps the most volatile and divisive issue during Reverend Peterson's pastorate. Even a quarter century later, some resentment and hurt feelings would still exist among some of the members. And, as with the major disagreement raised over the choir director during Reverend Adkins' pastorate during the 1920s, several members left the congregation during this dispute. The most visible member who departed at this time was the Chair of the Building Campaign, Deacon Wilbert Harris.

The Great March-In

After almost twenty years of waiting, as far back as when a building fund was first established under Reverend Adkins in 1962, the congregation finally marched in to their new home on February 1, 1981! For the march-in, the congregation assembled in the old church and, after prayer, the choir and entire congregation marched the twenty yards from the old church to the new one. Multiple choirs filled the choir stand. Following the march-in, the church held *40 Nights of Dedication*, with a new speaker each night, as each room (e.g., kitchen) or major furnishing (e.g., pews) was dedicated. The dedication finally ended on March 25.

Many of the speakers during the forty nights were close friends of the pastor and included Dr. Grady Powell; Reverend T. Wright Morris; Reverend Robert E. King, who had been ordained at Alfred Street; Reverend Lawrence Davies of Shiloh Baptist in Fredericksburg, Virginia; Reverend Cessar L. Scott; Reverend Windell Somerville; and the pastor's uncle, Reverend Captain S. Peterson, pastor of a church in Midland, Virginia.[10]

When the congregation marched into the new sanctuary, the building could be occupied, but it was not finished. The baptismal pool above the choir loft was operational, as were offices for the pastor and staff to the rear of the sanctuary on the main floor. The choir loft looked much as it does today. New pews were in place, and a beautiful elevated pulpit rostrum with bench chairs occupied the pulpit area. However, several areas were still not completed. The organ was a loaner that would be used for several years. The area of the church above the choir loft where the organ pipes were to be installed later was covered with a burlap-like material, which would remain in place for several years.

The main sanctuary contained about fifteen long pews on each side of a center aisle with total seating to accommodate about five hundred persons.[11] There was no balcony. There was an audio control room in the rear of the sanctuary on the main level for recording the sermons and music. On the lower level, there was a kitchen and large mul-

The New Sanctuary at March-In

tipurpose room for meetings and banquets. This multipurpose room also contained a stage to be used for plays and dramatic performances. Sunday School classes also met in the lower level in this large room, and portable dividers were placed between the various classes. There were two or three small classrooms along the back wall adjacent to Patrick Street, the more frequently used and larger of which was called the Television (TV) Room. This room was used for Bible study, prayer meetings and other small meetings. It took its name from the numerous old TVs that were placed there for viewing events as parents waited for children who participated in youth activities.

Choir rehearsals were held in the main sanctuary. On Sunday mornings, the choirs formed in the lower level multipurpose room for brief rehearsals prior to the start of services. The pastor and deacons would meet first in the pastor's study and then join the choir in the multipurpose room for prayer before moving with them to the sanctuary. Sister Jackie Green still directed the Senior Choir, which performed on the second and fourth Sundays. In January 1981, Sister Joyce Garrett of Maryland, who had been directing the Gospel Inspirers, became director of the Young and Adult Choir, replacing Sister Ellen McCord who had served for six years after an earlier stint as director in 1968.

Phase I construction of the main level had been completed at a cost of $934,000. Phase II was to be completed in two years, but was completed by September 1981 through the labors of Deacon Welton Quander, then Chair of the Board of Trustees, the late Trustee Julian Dove, Brother Dennis William, and Reverend Peterson. Phase II consisted of completing the kitchen and laying tiles on the floor of the lower level, which was used for Sunday School. Phase III was planned to begin five years later, around 1986, to extend the front of the sanctuary thirty-four feet toward Alfred Street. This would increase the seating capacity to approximately 700 persons, but was never executed as originally planned.

By the time of the completion of construction and the march-in, the Dip Area Urban Renewal Project was progressing, and new residents were beginning to move into the revitalized homes near the church. Most of the old residents who had previously owned homes, and had moved out during revitalization, never moved back as they were unable to afford their revitalized neighborhood. In fact, the only revitalized home repurchased by a black family was one across the street from the church purchased by Deacon

Charles Butler. Thus, one of the unintended consequences of the revitalization effort to save the Dip Area was that it transformed home ownership in the area surrounding Alfred Street Baptist Church from predominantly black to predominantly white. Only one home in the entire block was now black-owned.

The Maryland Commuters

. . . He humbled you, causing you to hunger and then feeding you with manna from heaven. . . .

Following the march-in in February 1981, the church set about improving worship in many areas. The increased attendance resulting from the new attractive edifice permitted the church to go through a series of infrastructure developments. The deacons, deaconesses, and trustees went on several retreats for training. A new Singles Ministry had recently been instituted. The music department was upgraded when Jacqueline Henry-Green became director of the Senior Choir; Ellen McCord began playing for the Senior Choir; and Harriet Westbrook (Smith) was directing the Children's Choir. With this excellent music department, attendance continued to slowly increase.

However, there was one very troublesome aspect of the church's program. Membership still hovered around 500 and the trustees were concerned that revenues from a congregation of this size would be insufficient to cover the large mortgage.[12] Various proposals were considered for increasing membership and revenues, including perhaps recruiting new members through door-to-door home visitations as some other denominations had done. But, as the trustees wondered, something happened at Alfred Street Baptist Church that paralleled an Old Testament situation when the children of Israel hungered for food when lost in the desert. As God fed them with manna from heaven, so it was that manna fell on Alfred Street Baptist Church from Maryland.

In 1981, the number of families from Maryland within the congregation still numbered less than twenty. Records indicate that the first family from Alfred Street to move to Maryland was that of Richard and Mary Wair in the 1960s. Subsequent to their move, some of the older families from Alexandria who were already members of the church moved to the northern Maryland suburbs. Few people from the southern part of Prince George's County, in Oxon Hill, or Fort Washington attended Alfred Street even though these areas lay just across the Potomac River. The Woodrow Wilson Bridge and the Beltway, which had been completed now for over fifteen years, connected these areas to Alexandria. However, persons from the southern part of Maryland, especially Oxon Hill and Fort Washington, soon began to join Alfred Street Baptist Church in numbers the trustees could have never imagined.

Following the Civil Rights Act of 1964, with its provisions on nondiscrimination in employment and accommodations, federal jobs in the Washington, D.C., area that had previously been closed to minorities opened. The opening of jobs created a mass exodus of educated blacks from the South to Washington, D.C., to get the proverbial ". . . good government job. . . ." Young, educated blacks flocked to Washington from Tuskegee Institute, Spelman College, Bennett College, Southern University, North Carolina A&T

State University, Hampton University, Fisk University, and Alabama A&M.

As the suburbs were still somewhat hostile to black residents, many moved into the Southeast area of the District of Columbia. Southeast was undergoing a renaissance in the late 1960s and early 1970s as new garden apartments sprang up overnight. The large number of young college graduates who moved into the new garden apartments of this area created a situation where, for a short period, Southeast D.C. contained perhaps one of the largest concentrations of educated black people in America.

By the early 1970s they were also beginning to marry and move into southern Maryland in Prince George's County. The movement of these professionals represented the first time in U.S. history that a majority black population replaced a majority white population and both the education and income levels increased. Upon arriving in Prince George's County, the blacks initially integrated the local churches, as they had integrated the neighborhoods.

With time, the black Prince Georgians discovered subtle differences in worship practices that left them unfulfilled. The white churches held spaghetti dinners, while the blacks were accustomed to fried chicken. The blacks were accustomed to gospel music, while the white church choirs sang anthems. Worship services were exactly one-hour at the white churches, whereas blacks were accustomed to two or three-hour services. Other subtle differences left the blacks longing for a church of the type they remembered from back home in the South.

Sister Helen McCoy was the first of these new immigrants from Fort Washington to cross the Woodrow Wilson Bridge to join Alfred Street Baptist Church in 1972. James and Pat Johnson, the Walter Moore family, Carolyn Rowe and her daughters, the Mary and Walter Payne family, Booker and Mamie Woodard, and the Russell and Poinsetta Peterson families followed. Many of these early pioneers either worked together or lived in close proximity to each other. Henry and Priscilla Thompson soon joined; and then James and Joyce Garrett and Tom and Vernell Howell came to Alfred Street also. Within a few years, hundreds more would come until the Marylanders would become the largest growth segment of the congregation. They continued to come at such a rate that by the end of the decade, the largest concentration of members at Alfred Street was located in zip code 20744, Fort Washington, Maryland, with more families living there than any comparable area of Virginia.

The arrival of such large numbers of Marylanders solved the immediate issue of new members and financial contributions that had concerned the trustees. Over time, this group of Marylanders would stay and would move into most major leadership positions within Alfred Street. In the coming years, there was a period when Marylanders from Fort Washington simultaneously held both the position of Chairman of the Board of Deacons and Chairman of the Board of Trustees.

Soon, new members throughout Northern Virginia joined the new members from Maryland. The move to the suburbs was on. Addresses of members from Northern Virginia included Annandale, Reston, Sterling, Springfield, and Oakton. By now, even the pastor had moved from Washington, D.C., to a home in Alexandria at 902 North Howard Street near the new Alexandria Hospital.

By the fall of 1982, when a new church directory was printed, membership had grown from 500 to 850 in two years. It grew by another ninety-eight members, including twenty more from Maryland, between November 1982 and March 1983 when an updated directory was released. A total of 235 members listed Maryland as an address, with the Fort Washington and Oxon Hill areas dominating. Overall, Marylanders had grown from four families in 1973 to 235 members in one decade.[13]

Pastor's Home in Alexandria

The increase in membership represented a significant milestone. After having reached more than 700 persons in 1880 during Reconstruction, Alfred Street membership had fallen during the latter part of the 19th century and the early part of the 20th century. Membership reached a low of 183 persons in the midst of the depression and hovered in the 250- to 350-person range since then. Now, 100 years after the 700-person peak under Reverend Samuel Madden during Reconstruction, the church again attained a membership equal to the one that existed when the church hosted the meeting of the American Baptist Missionary Convention in the 1880s.

New Deacons and Other Officials

The move to the new sanctuary, coupled with its excellent music department, soon expanded Alfred Street's reputation locally, and the congregation continued to grow. By 1982, this growth necessitated two additional ministers on staff, Reverend Albert Blue and Reverend Doris P. Ashton. The Deacon Board now consisted of twelve persons, with Deacon Oliver Hutchinson having recently joined. Brother Hutchinson had transferred from Shiloh Baptist on Duke Street in Alexandria. He was ordained there in 1980, but transferred to Alfred Street in 1981. Deacon Willie Lazenby had also recently transferred from a local church. There were still only six trustees, with Attorney Garland Tanks, a transplant from Maryland, having joined the board. There were now fifteen deaconesses, with Sister Emma Willis as chair.

In 1983, the Alfred Street Baptist Church ordained ten new deacons at once to fulfill lay leader responsibilities for ten new groups that were formed to keep up with population growth. This was the largest group of deacons that had ever been ordained at once. Indeed, as late as the early 1960s, there had been only five deacons, total.

The ten new deacons ordained in 1983 were a diverse group. Two (James and Patricia Johnson) were husband and wife. Sister Johnson joined Sister Mary Wair as the second female deacon. Six of the ten new deacons hailed from Fort Washington, Maryland, con-

The New Deacon Board

sistent with the large numbers of Marylanders joining Alfred Street. The new Maryland deacons included Rogers Davis, an attorney; James Garrett, an engineer; Thomas Howell, a retired military officer; Garland Tanks, another attorney; and James and Patricia Johnson. New deacons from Virginia included Isaiah P. Morrison, III, a dentist; David Rollins, a building engineer; Frank Heard, a retired military officer; and Francis Crawford, also a retired military officer.

On Anniversary Sunday in 1981, the church also honored members who had attended Alfred Street for more than fifty years. Persons so honored included:

NAME	YEAR JOINED	YEARS AT ALFRED STREET
Ulysses Jackson	1911	71
Ruth Dade	1917	65
Callie Early	1917	65
Joyce Henry	1919	63
Nellie Evans	1921	61
Marion Harris	1921	61
Nellie Hargrove	1921	61
Evelyn Williams	1921	61
Esther Neal	1921	61
Lillian Tyler	1921	61
Louis Jackson, Sr.	1923	59
Richard Poole	1924	58
Amelia Weaver	1931	51
Mary Jackson	1931	51
Eunice Lewis	1930	51
Edith Reaves	1930	51
Juanita Stanton	1931	51
Gladys Tancil	1931	51

The oldest living member was Mrs. Ulysses Jackson. She had joined when Reverend Truatt was pastor and was the only person from that era. She was consecrated a Deaconess in 1965 as part of the first group of Deaconesses in Reverend Peterson's administration.

More Parking Woes and New 8 a.m. Service

The early 1980s were indeed exciting times at Alfred Street! Very shortly after moving into the new church, the sanctuary would be packed every Sunday. Members grew accustomed to rushing into the sanctuary early just to get a seat. The *Alfred Street Squeeze,* in which persons removed their coats and Bibles from the pews and slid over as close as possible to their neighbor to make more room for seating, became a common practice. Soon, red padded folding chairs were donated to the church, and each Sunday these chairs would be placed along the center aisle to accommodate parishioners as soon as the choirs marched in. A similar set of folding chairs ringed the sanctuary along the outer walls for other late arrivals.

The move to the new church was not without its problems, however. In addition to problems of seating in the sanctuary, the large influx of new members created more cars and the resurrection of parking problems that had haunted the church since 1980. Except this time the dissension was no longer among members within the church, but between the church and its neighbors.

Alfred Street parking wars approach truce

Olde Towne West, baptist church dispute no longer a 'near riot'

By DAVID SCHUMACHER
Gazette Staff Writer

A parking dispute between residents of an apartment complex and a neighboring church was quiet Sunday.

It was a marked contrast to the previous week when attempts to tow the supposedly improperly parked cars of Alfred Street Baptist Church members from the Olde Towne West Apartments' lot resulted in much fist waving and threats.

Church members used their cars to block the parking lot and eventually the police were called to try and put a lid on what tenants called a "near riot."

The minister claims the church is entitled to use a portion of the Olde Towne West Apartments parking lot, a claim disputed by tenants of the complex.

Nobody denies last week's altercation and it seems that all parties want to settle the dispute quietly. Lawyers for the church met Friday with apartment management to try to work out their differences.

This Sunday a church member was stationed at the entrance to direct worshippers to park elsewhere and the towing firm was told by the apartment management to stand by for now.

But come next Sunday, tow trucks will be back on the scene to haul away any improperly parked cars from the tenant's lot.

The dispute has resulted in a lot of name-calling and some tenants

Parking Woes at Alfred Street

Because of the shortage of parking, worshippers frequently took the closest place they could find to park. In many cases, this meant taking spots adjacent to the church at the new townhouses in Olde Towne West apartments which had been constructed as part of the Dip Renewal. By 1983, according to the *Alexandria Gazette,* a near riot broke out one Sunday in the parking lot when neighbors began calling tow trucks to tow away cars illegally parked there. After several cars were towed, church members left in the midst of the church service and used their cars to block the tow truck drivers. The residents had asked members several times not to park there, but members had continued to do so. A stalemate ensued for many years, with the church finally conceding and erecting signs advising worshippers not to park at the Olde Towne West apartments.

Attendance soon reached a point where there was a need to explore the possibility of a second morning service. On most Sundays, there was an overflow crowd at the 11:00 a.m. service that soon began watching the service on a TV monitor set up on the lower level. There still continued to be evening services at 6:00 p.m. led primarily by the church auxiliaries who held musicals and dramas, or invited visiting speakers. But the church leadership saw the need for an alternative to the morning services where there was *regular* preaching.

In December 1982, a Feasibility Study Committee appointed by Reverend Peterson to explore the issue presented a report. The committee, chaired by Brother James F. Garrett, had explored several formats at other churches and considered various issues among groups at Alfred Street, especially those who would be affected by an additional service (such as deacons, ushers, and trustees who must serve each Sunday). According to the report, the idea of a second morning service was feasible, but the most significant obstacle to another service was the need for an additional choir. Each existing choir already had a full performance schedule. At a church meeting in 1983, Alfred Street adopted the recommendation to start a second morning service and the next year the format was realized.

Starting a new choir was the first order of business in getting the new morning service started. A similar choir had been formed earlier in January 1984 as part of the New Members Classes. That choir consisting entirely of new members was directed by Sister Alma Upshaw and was formed for a one-time appearance at an 11:00 a.m. service. However, they sang so well that Reverend Peterson asked them to remain in place. Many of these new members would form the nucleus of the new choir for the early morning service.

Twenty-eight persons responded to a call to join the new choir that rehearsed on Monday nights. The Early Morning Choir, as it was then called, performed for the first time on the first Sunday in April 1984 under Harvey Tunstall and Samuel Wilkins, co-directors. At that initial performance, no robes had been ordered as the concept was to be on a trial basis for three or four months, with a planned follow-up reevaluation. So, for that first performance, the choir wore white tops (shirts or blouses) and black bottoms (pants or skirts). Brother Raymond Wilson was the only male who sang that morning, so there were not a lot of pants.

The 8 a.m. service concept proved a success, and the church approved the purchase of robes for them in the summer of 1984. In August of 1984 the Cross of Triumph was selected as the emblem for the new choir and, concurrently, the named was changed from Early Morning Choir to the Voices of Triumph (VOT). The choir and format of having two Sunday morning services proved a success, and the church has continued with two morning services since 1984.[14]

Other Ministries and Activities

In 1984, the church released an updated directory of all members. Membership now stood at 1,100. In four short years, the membership had doubled from five hundred to over a thousand. The massive influx of Marylanders continued as their ranks had swollen to two hundred fifty persons—mostly from Fort Washington. This was almost one-fourth the entire membership, and was almost equal to the size of the entire congregation when Reverend Peterson arrived in 1964.[15]

Reverend Albert Blue was now an assistant to the pastor, though several other ministers attended regularly. Other ministers who assisted with pulpit activities included Reverend Doris Ashton, Reverend Robert King, and three recent licentiates, Reverend Faye Gunn, Brother John Christopher Tabler, and Brother Elbert Ransom, Jr. Reverend Gunn had delivered her trial sermon on December 12, 1982, during a 3:00 p.m. service at which the Senior Choir sang.

The Board of Deacons now consisted of twenty-one persons and included two women. There were six trustees, including three deacons (Welton Quander, James

Garrett, and Garland Tanks). Sister Evangeline Robinson had replaced Sister Thelma Wair as the lone female trustee. The Deaconess Board consisted of twenty active women and three deaconesses emeriti who were now senior in years. The deaconesses and deacons were each assigned to a membership group and they performed additional tasks for baptism and Communion preparations.

Members of the Alfred Street Baptist Church are presenting a live Nativity scene. From left are Jeanene Harris, George Turner, Peggy Young, Raym Young, Gail Turner, A Young, Cherlyn Harris and F Gunn.

Alfred Street's Live Nativity Scene

During the early 1980s, Alfred Street initiated a live nativity scene at the church each Christmas as a gift to the community. On the night of the Christmas cantata, the cast (e.g., Mary, Joseph, shepherds, Baby Jesus) would proceed from the church to the outside stable located adjacent to the street near the front of the church. The live nativity scene would continue nightly for the two weeks leading to Christmas Eve. Some years 40–50 persons would rotate through the various cast positions. The concept was initiated by Deacon Thomas Howell and his wife Vernell Howell, who had observed live nativity scenes in Europe while in the military. After several years, leadership for manning the nativity scene was taken over by Deacon David Rollins and his wife Gwen Rollins.

Following on the heels of the new early morning choir, a new handbell choir began to offer music in 1985. The choir began as a temporary choir to perform at the church's annual Christmas cantata under the direction of Dr. Elwood Lewis. Subsequently, a temporary choir was formed and trained. Because the response was so positive, Sister Joyce Peterson, affectionately known as the founder, convinced the pastor and several church officials to create a permanent handbell choir. The choir became a permanent organization of the church and officially became part of the Music Department in 1990. The choir was originally composed of three octaves or thirty-seven bells. Later, it grew to four octaves or forty-eight bells. Reverend Elbert Ransom was the first permanent director, and was followed in a couple of years by Mr. Gregory Winstead and later by Mr. Keith Perkins.

Within the Male Chorus, new directors had also arrived. Sister Alma Upshaw became director and accompanist of the Male Chorus in 1984. She joined Elwood Lewis, who had been directing the choir since 1972 along with Harvey Tunstall. Sister Joyce Garrett continued as director of the Young and Adult Choir that sang on the first and third Sundays. She was soon joined by Ralph Herndon as pianist. In March 1985, Mark Prioleau, a recent college graduate from Washington, D.C., began directing the Gospel Inspirers. Mark belonged to Shiloh Baptist Church in Washington, D.C., where he also conducted their Male Chorus. Also, in March 1985, Sister Doris Hall joined the music

Music Ministry circa 1985

department as pianist/director for the Voices of Triumph and replaced Brother Wilkins.

In January 1985, two new trustees joined the four incumbents—Ardelia Hunter and Russell Peterson were added with Welton Quander remaining as chair, and Vernon Carroll as vice chair. The trustees usually met on the fourth Tuesday of each month, but in 1985, they changed their meeting to the third week.

A Youth Department of some type had existed at Alfred Street since 1932, with Reverend Adkins. It went by several titles including the Junior Church, and at varying times had varying levels of support and participation. In the late 1960s Deacon Richard Wair and his wife Sister Mary Wair were Youth Directors. In the 1970s, Brother Walter and Sister Laura Moore directed the youth for a short period. They were followed by Deacon Oliver Hutchinson and his wife Blanche Hutchinson. By 1986, the Youth Department had grown into a major enterprise at Alfred Street under the direction of Sister Vernell Howell and her husband, Deacon Thomas Howell. Fueled by the growth associated with the new building and new ministries, the Youth Department grew as well.

The calendar for youth activities included several functions that the youth looked forward to years in advance. There was an annual trip to Eagle Eyrie, a religious retreat near Charlottesville where Baptist youth from all over the state of Virginia attended. Alfred Street Baptist Church youth were frequently named president of the State Youth Division. Youth elected to the position of president included Rosalyn McAllister-Brock and Darrell Howell. Additionally, Alfred Street youth were frequently winners of first and second place in a Speaker's Bureau competition that was held each year. At the church, the youth also engaged in an annual black-tie dinner that permitted them to dress up for the first time in formal attire. On Youth Sunday, held in March, young people conducted the morning services and selected youth

Junior Youth Choirs in 1986

delivered the Sunday message. During the summer, youth would attend an out-of-state work camp where they had an opportunity to help the elderly by repairing and painting homes.

While the teenagers of the Youth Department dominated youth activities, younger children eight to twelve years of age also had opportunities to serve. A Junior Youth Department, headed by Sisters Debbie Easter and Margaret Wiggins (affectionately called Aunt Deb and Ms. Mew), was also very active and attracted thirty to forty children. Additional youth choirs were also started for youth. The Children's Choir was composed of children ages three to six, while the Junior Gospel Inspirers was for children ages seven to fourteen. During this period, the director of these groups was Sister Doris Winstead. Anitra Rowe and Kendra McCoy served as accompanists for the young choirs.

As an additional outlet for youth, the church sponsored Boy and Girl Scout troops. The Girl Scouts were started at Alfred Street in 1983 by Sister Betty Everett. Sister Everett was soon joined by Patricia Wallace, Gwen Rollins, Gwen Brown and Bonita Brown as troop leaders. After a few years, Sister Wallace became coordinator for all the troops, and eventually the Girl Scout troops boasted over one hundred girls at all levels from five to eighteen years of age. The troops won numerous local and state awards and provided assistance during two U.S. presidential inaugurations.

Growth Requires New Sanctuary

The growth in membership was creating new financial opportunities as well as worship opportunities. By 1985, the proposed budget for the year was approximately $300,000. Income through tithes and offerings for March 1985 was $46,000, for May $34,000 and for June $62,000. With these financial resources, the church agreed to purchase a new ebony piano at $14,400 and a new organ between $55,000 and $60,000 to replace the loaner. In May 1985, the church also purchased a fifteen-passenger Dodge van at a cost of $17,704.

During this period, Alfred Street annually held a special service in February on the first Sunday of each year to celebrate the 1981 march-in to the new building. In 1986, Licentiate Robert Easter was the speaker, and a special memorial was held for the Challenger astronauts who had recently been killed.

While activities were prospering at the new church at 301 South Alfred Street, right next door at 313 South Alfred Street, the old church sat abandoned and boarded up. The church had considered razing the old structure on several occasions; however, razing the structure was a complicated issue. For example, in August 1982 the Board of Architectural Review in Alexandria had denied the church an application for a permit to raze the old church because of its historical significance.

Since the church could not obtain a permit directly to raze the old structure, the church sought to sell the property in 1983 through a realtor as a remedy. But even a sale of the old building was complicated. The city's laws on historical properties permitted the church to be torn down if it was advertised for sale, but not sold within one year. As part of an agreement, the city's Housing Authority even agreed to demolish the building with city funds, if the congregation could not find a willing buyer within a year. Neither the city nor the church really anticipated a real sale. Nevertheless, the property was offered for sale to meet the conditions of the law.

One of the bidders to buy the old church was the city of Alexandria itself. In March 1983, the city offered to buy the old church for $205,000, including the 96x80 feet-wide lot on which it stood. However, as this was less than the church felt it was worth, Alfred Street refused the offer. Subsequently, there was a legal disagreement between the church and the realtor over a payment of a fee of $12,000 for listing the property and finding a buyer. This disagreement was settled, but ultimately the old church was not sold, and remained empty and boarded up for several more years.

By 1986, the congregation had outgrown the new sanctuary after only six years of service. The congregation had grown from 500 to almost 1,800 members and the sanctuary seated only about 500, so there was always an overflow. Each Sunday, even with the two morning services, red padded chairs for latecomers continued in use and Reverend Peterson frequently asked the congregation to do the Alfred Street Squeeze to use all available space on the pews. Additionally, a large screen television placed in the lower level for latecomers was still in use. On special occasions such as Easter, the entire narthex would be outfitted with folding chairs. Rushing to the sanctuary in time to get a seat continued to be a way of life at Alfred Street Baptist Church.

In November 1986, the church submitted yet another proposal to the city to convert the old church into a Black History Museum. The proposal recommended converting the structure into three floors of space that would house a museum, classrooms, library, and conference rooms. The proposed cost of $845,650, which included funds for the first year of operations, was to be shared by the church and the city. Alfred Street requested a grant of $487,200 from the city of Alexandria and the church would provide the remainder. The museum proposal sat in limbo for several years, and before it could be acted upon, a final proposal was offered to integrate the old church into the new expanded church about to be constructed.

After several years of considering raze options and sale options and museum options for handling the old church and simultaneously enlarging the new church as prescribed in the original Phase III planning, the church finally took action in February 1986. That year, Reverend Peterson appointed a 199-member Expansion, Parking and Renovation Study Committee. Trustee Ronald Johnson and Deaconess Grace Albritton served as co-chairs of the planning phase. Committees were assigned to look at the possibility of building a nursery, a choir room, a kitchen, a bell tower, more office space, boardroom, etc. The committees soon found that the original Phase III plans approved in 1980 needed to be expanded as the needs were now far greater than they had been at the original planning stage.

The projected requirements necessitated a complete new design. The trustees again retained the architectural firm of Robert J. Nash, FAIA and Associates in August 1988 to present a complete new design for the sanctuary. The initial design for an enlarged edifice that the firm proposed integrated the old and new church into a single structure. The church approved the design at a special call meeting in January 1990. A redesign phase was then conducted, and by December 1990 it was completed as well. Soon the church obtained all city approvals for expanding the sanctuary, except the building permit. Not long after, a second construction project within a decade was underway at Alfred Street.

Anniversaries for Pastor and Church

Even as issues associated with construction consumed most of the energy of the church leadership, the church continued to grow and hold major events. By the late 1980s the congregation was approaching almost 2,000 persons in total membership. The combined attendance for the two morning services was approximately 1,100 persons, with numerous persons joining each Sunday. For example, on November 28, 1988, twenty-five new persons were given the right hand of fellowship. During this time, twenty to twenty-five new members joining per month was not uncommon.

In 1988, the church celebrated its 185th anniversary on November 13. During this period, on each yearly anniversary, the church honored one of the former pastors, and in 1988, Reverend Alexander Truatt was honored. He had served as pastor at Alfred Street Baptist Church from 1897 to 1913. The living members of his family were invited to attend the service and participate in the unveiling of his portrait, which now hangs in the Hall of Pastors. Members of his family who were present included his granddaughter, Mrs. Marie Madden Ford, and his great-grandson, Professor Ossie S. Williams. At the 11:00 a.m. service, Dr. Charles Adams of Hartford Memorial Baptist in Detroit was the speaker. At 6:00 p.m., a special musical program was presented, directed by Sister Joyce Garrett.

During this period, the church again honored 50-year members. New members in this group included Jacqueline Green, Carlton Tyler, Juanita Stanton, Roberta Quander and William Willis.

In addition to honoring individuals, seventeen families were also honored as having been members for more than one hundred years. These families included the Burkes, Lees, Wairs, Willises, Burlesses, and Quanders. Among the families honored, the Quander family was perhaps the largest and best known, being one of the oldest (1684) documented black families in America. They initially settled in Maryland, but soon began migrating and subsequently settling in various areas, including the area just south of Alexandria.

Golden (50-Year) Honorees

The Quanders had been members of Alfred Street since 1830, when Mariah Quander became a member.

In 1986, the church held a twenty-second anniversary celebration for Reverend Peterson at the Hilton Hotel in Springfield, Virginia. The affair, on a Sunday afternoon after service, featured skits by some of the church's youth and a roast by some of Reverend Peterson's relatives. The Pastor's Aide Society planned the celebration, with Sister Zelma Lockley as banquet chair. Reverend Peterson was presented a portrait as a gift from the Young and Adult Choir.[16]

By 1989 the church decided to hold a much larger function to honor Reverend Peterson and celebrate his twenty-five years of service to the Alfred Street family. Sister Queen Gladden was chair of the twenty-fifth anniversary celebration and banquet that was held at a hotel near Tyson's Corner. The banquet speaker for this anniversary was Dr. Benjamin L. Hooks, then Executive Director of the National Association for the Advancement of Colored People (NAACP). The formal banquet on a Saturday night featured tributes from various church auxiliaries and a brief video of some of Reverend Peterson's accomplishments.

In a statement of accomplishments during Reverend Peterson's tenure, the anniversary program states that the church had grown from 200 to 2,000 members in the past twenty-five years; from two choirs to seven; from eight male deacons to twenty-five men and women; and finances had increased from an operating budget of $12,000 to $1 million in 1989. The first phase of construction of a new sanctuary had been completed at a cost of $1.25 million, and plans for an expansion were underway.[17]

The Single and Single Again Ministry

During the late 1980s, one of the strongest organizations in the church was the Single and Single Again (SSA) Ministry. Several presidents and other officers led the group, but its core leadership resided with Deaconess Grace T. Joseph and Brother Wallace King. The group held numerous fellowship activities and off-site retreats. But they were best known for their giving. For many years, the Singles were among the largest group of tithers in the church.

The Old Saints

As new buildings were being built and planned, and as the church membership grew during the 1980s, the old saints continued to pass on to that final reward. Many of those who passed away had been born in the early 1900s. They remembered a world without automobiles, electric lights, or radio. From church minutes, the number of persons who passed away each year during this decade follows:

YEAR	NO. OF MEMORIAL SERVICES
1980	5
1981	7
1982	8
1983	6
1984	6
1985	9
1986	4
1987	12
1988	5
1989	6
1990	4

During the decade 1980–1990, approximately seventy members are known to have passed on to that final reward. Members who passed included Sister Lillian Poole in February 1980. Her husband, Richard Poole, Jr., former chair of the Board of Trustees and superintendent of the Sunday School, preceded her in death two years earlier. They had been married in 1924.

Deacon John Strange passed in August 1981 at the age of 101. To date, he is the oldest member, male or female, to be funeralized at Alfred Street Baptist Church. He joined Alfred Street in 1917 and was a member for sixty-four years. He lived just up the street from the church at 807 Duke Street. He was buried next to his brother in Bethel Cemetery almost one hundred years after his younger brother Jacklyn passed away in April 1890.[18]

Sister Willie Mae Wormley passed in September 1982. She had been instrumental in forming the Little Acorns that became the present-day Gospel Inspirers. She joined Alfred Street in 1926. In December 1982, Deaconess Ruth Dade was funeralized at the age of 80. She had joined Alfred Street during Reverend W.H.R. Powell's pastorate and had served on the choir, the Missionary Board, and the Deaconess Board. She was a frequent delegate to the Lott Carey Baptist Foreign Mission Convention.

Deacon Strange

Brother Lucius Kennibrew, the father of Sister Harriett Perkins, who sang in the Young and Adult Choir, passed in January 1983. He was ordained and had transferred his membership to Alfred Street where he expressed a desire to serve as a deacon. His wish was granted, and he served briefly before sickness curtailed his activities.

Sister Lorraine Funn Atkins passed in February 1985. She had been one of the preservationists and a staunch opponent of the destruction of the old church during the debates of the early 1980s. She was a founding member of the Society for the Preservation of Black Heritage in Alexandria, a non–church affiliated society formed specifically to preserve the old church and the history of black Americans in Alexandria.

Deacon Lenzy Robinson passed in May 1986. He had been ordained at Beulah Baptist on Washington Street, but joined Alfred Street in 1980. In 1989, Brother Julian Dove, who had served as a trustee at Alfred Street, passed in September.

Over time, funeral practices at Alfred Street changed somewhat. During the early part of the century, most funerals were on Saturday or Sunday when members of the family were not working. By the 1980s, most funerals were held during midweek, and the time of the service had shifted from mid-afternoon (e.g., 2 p.m.) to late morning, with 11:00 a.m. becoming the preferred hour. Viewings and wakes that had generally been held in the home (e.g., for Reverend Adkins) were now held at the church the night prior to the funeral or the next morning just prior to the ceremony. Further, whereas most burials for members during the earlier periods were at Bethel Cemetery near the church, with the surburbanization of the congregation, burials were now also held in Woodbridge, in Reston, in Laurel, Maryland, and at other suburban sites.

During much of Reverend Adkins' administration, a common factor in most funerals was the use in the eulogy of the quotation, "Have not all human beings parted? And must not all the present one day part?" Under Reverend Peterson, the common factor was a song, Hymn #542, *When We All Get to Heaven.* This became the closing musical selection at most funerals. Its words are:

When we all get to heaven
What a day of rejoicing that will be
When we all see Jesus.
We'll sing and shout the victory.

Chapter Ten

1990–2003: Approaching the Bicentennial

. . . I once was young; but now I'm old . . . (Psalm 37:25)

As the church approached two hundred years of service, membership continued to grow at the beginning of the 1990s, requiring yet another expansion of the church facility. Following this construction, however, the rate of growth would slow and the size of the congregation would decrease somewhat as other churches began to compete with Alfred Street. The church would pay off the mortgage for the new building within a few years, and would approve a constitution—a new set of rules similar to the ones that governed the early Baptists in 1803. Preparations would begin for the bicentennial celebration.

The Setting

The small town of Alexandria with approximately 4,970 people in 1800 at the start of this volume had now grown to over 111,000 people by the 1990 census. It had grown from about 500 free Negroes and a comparable number of slaves in the 1800 census to over 24,000 African-Americans in 1990, now all *free*. Negroes who had initially been limited to living in the Bottoms and Hayti neighborhoods near Alfred and Royal Streets now lived freely as African-Americans throughout Alexandria. The city limits that initially covered only a sixty-acre tract adjacent to the river now extended over five miles from the Potomac River on the East to beyond I-395 on the west end, and from the Beltway (I-95) in the south to Crystal City (on the north) in the vicinity of Reagan National Airport.

Across the Potomac River in Washington, D.C., the 1990s began with President George H.W. Bush in the White House. He had served as vice president under the extremely popular president Ronald Reagan, but would serve only one term as president. The major crisis of his administration occurred when the country of Iraq invaded Kuwait in August 1990 and a short war ensued that was referred to as Desert Storm. This short and relatively inexpensive war was popular within the United States while it lasted, but stimulated a recession that when coupled with mounting federal deficits diminished President Bush's approval rating. William Jefferson Clinton, a Democrat from Arkansas and infinitely popular within the African-American community, replaced him as president two years later.

However, the big political news within the black community in Virginia was occurring not at the federal level but at the state level. On January 13, 1990, a milestone was achieved when Virginia's sixty-fifth governor, Lawrence Douglas Wilder, was sworn in as the first elected African-American governor in U.S. history. What made the event all the more meaningful was that he was elected in Virginia, a state that was the former capital of the Confederacy, the home of Massive Resistance, and had once denied him admission to its all-white schools.

Governor Wilder had entered politics in 1969 as a state senator in Virginia, the first black since Reconstruction. During his five terms in that position, he chaired committees on transportation, rehabilitation and social services; privileges and elections; the Virginia Advisory Legislative Council; and the Democratic Steering Committee. He also served a four-year term as lieutenant governor in Virginia, beginning in 1986.

Governor Wilder was an alumnus of Virginia Union University in Richmond, where Reverend Peterson, pastor of Alfred Street Baptist Church, had also attended. During his campaign for governor, Wilder visited Alfred Street on several occasions, as did numerous other politicians. By the 1990s, Alfred Street had become an influential congregation with a large African-American vote that created numerous opportunities to participate in the political arena. For example, the Male Chorus from Alfred Street was invited to perform in Governor Wilder's inauguration ceremonies in Richmond.

The Women Deacons and the Preachers of Alfred Street

By the 1990s, Reverend Peterson was serving in his twenty-sixth year as pastor of Alfred Street, and his level of activities had increased with additional responsibilities. Alfred Street was now a member of several conventions and Reverend Peterson kept a busy travel schedule outside of the church attending these conventions. During 1990, his calendar indicates he attended more than ten sessions at the various conventions. Additionally, there were outside meetings with the Alexandria School Board, the Chief of Police, the City Manager, the Urban League, and at the White House.

Activities within the church also kept him busy. One of his busiest days was on July 21, 1990, when he performed four weddings at the church. Beginning at 10:30 a.m., he officiated at the wedding of Denise Turner and James E. Green. At 1:00 p.m., he performed the wedding ceremony for Mona Ross, and at 3:00 p.m. the wedding for Susan Washington. At 5:00 p.m., he was back before the altar officiating at the ceremony of Rosita Menuet and Victor Basier. As far as records uncovered to date, this set a one-day record for weddings at Alfred Street Baptist Church.

All of the choirs continued to grow and prosper. The Gospel Inspirers, or the Teenage Choir as it was sometimes called, had now grown to almost 40 members. Mark Prioleau, their director, was now in his fifth year.

Gospel Inspirers circa 1990

In addition to conventions, weddings, choirs and other in-house church activities, ordinations of women dominated activities at the church during these years. The church had always taken a lead in providing opportunities for women, and in the early 1990s several new advances were made. With the tremendous growth and the need for more deacons, and the demonstrated spiritual leadership of women, Alfred Street again set a precedent by ordaining several women at once.

In 1991, the church ordained nine women at one time to join the two women deacons then serving on the Board of Deacons. All of the nine women had previously been deaconesses, having been consecrated at various times from 1971 to 1988. Shown below is the then existing Deaconess Board from which the new deacons were selected.

Deaconesses Become Deacons

Those ordained included Grace Albritton, Ellen Anderson, Helen Crawford, Bessie Johnson, Betty Jones, Grace Joseph, Barbara Keller, Alvina Scott and Eva Simmons. Sister Crawford was joining her husband on the board, Deacon Francis Crawford, who had been ordained in 1983. Sister Keller was the longer-termed member among the group, having joined Alfred Street in 1963 before Reverend Peterson became pastor. Sister Alvina Scott, in contrast, had only recently joined Alfred Street after transferring from Second Baptist Church in Falls Church, Virginia.

By now, the idea of women deacons was gaining some acceptance. Even though this was an especially proud moment for Alfred Street, the event created little media attention outside of the church.

More women were also being introduced to the Christian ministry as preachers. Sister Kim L. Coleman and Sister Minnie D. Davis were both granted licenses to preach by the church in June 1989. Sister Ruth D. Harvey was also granted a license to preach by Alfred Street Baptist Church. She had transferred from the Garden of Gethsemane Baptist Church in Los Angeles, California, where she had been granted a license to preach in 1986. These three women joined Reverend Doris Ashton and Reverend Faye Gunn who were ordained earlier. There were now five female ministers at Alfred Street.[1]

Alfred Street at Worship—1990

Young men from Alfred Street were also entering the ministry during this period. Brother James Ashton joined his wife, Reverend Doris Ashton, as a minister in 1984. Doris Ashton was one of the first women to be ordained to the Christian ministry in Virginia in 1980. Earlier, Brother Robert Easter had been ordained, and on November 3, 1989, Brother Samuel Nixon gave his trial sermon before returning to Harvard Divinity School for a degree in theology. The new ministers preached to a packed audience on those opportunities when they were permitted to occupy the pulpit.

There Arose a Murmuring

In those days when the number of disciples was increasing, there arose a murmuring among the Grecian Jews against the Hebraic Jews. (Acts 6:1)

In 1992, as the congregation was increasing in size and requiring new deacons and more ministers, a murmuring arose within the congregation at Alfred Street. Members felt left out of the planning and execution process and began voicing their displeasure in the fall of 1992. They were primarily concerned with the issues of church rules and regulations, and the extent to which some decisions appeared to be arbitrary. There was also concern that the congregation was not being adequately informed of ongoing church activities and, as such, could not make informed decisions at business meetings. Some members of the congregation wanted to know: "What were the rules?" This was not a new concern at Alfred Street, as rules had been the focus of church meetings for most of its first 125 years of existence.

In addition to the rules and regulations for the conduct of church business and the rules and regulations for informing the congregation, the third issue that incited the murmuring was the budget. Members felt left out of the budget process. By 1992, the church's budget was over $1 million a year. For example, annual revenue for 1991 was $1.2 million. Similarly, for 1992, the income was $1.2 million and for 1993, a total of $1.4 million was budgeted.

MEMBERSHIP GROUP #17

Membership Group #17 met on December [illegible], 1992. The group woul like to communicate with other membership groups to determin whether they have similar concerns and questions as those raise in our December meeting. In order to facilitate that objective the following concerns and questions are presented for discussio and resolution.

CONCERNS

The quality of sermons is lacking and has been identified as a reason some members are leaving Alfred Street.

The leadership of the Church may not be meeting the needs of the people due to poor information flow.

The request for prayer over only those who stood and had submitted their annual giving pledge cards during Sunday services was not appropriate.

The impact on the Church if Rev. Peterson were incapacitated since he has many of the procedures and information about Church affairs in his head rather than documented.

QUESTIONS

How can membership groups receive more information about the business affairs of the Church on a continual basis? For example, who is available to discuss with the group the cause of the present construction delay and the Church's position on assigning minority contractors?

Active members of the Church would like more information about the Church budget? For example, the recent budget meeting was not well publicized. How can members learn more about the present process? How can the process be changed?

How are Deacons and Trustees selected? Is there a document available that describes the functions, selection criteria etc. for these positions?

Does the Church have written policies that state how decisions are made and lists responsibilities?

What is the basis used to assign projects to membership groups? How should a group communicate its concerns such as project continuity, and proper lead time?

Minutes of Group #17 Meetings

The murmuring was first articulated within Membership Group #17, of which Deacon Charles Monterio was Lay Leader. Minutes from one of their meetings expressed concern with ". . . being kept in the dark . . . and wondering where all the offering money goes." They also expressed concern about how deacons and trustees were selected.

Deacon Monterio first took these concerns to the Board of Deacons. Within that group, an ad hoc committee soon determined that there were rules in existence covering many areas of church operation, but no one know precisely what they were. Rules formulated and documented around the turn of the century (1890–1900) had been long forgotten, and many of those formulated one at a time over the years had been discarded. After a series of meetings, some of which were quite contentious and some of which were held off-site, the deacons and trustees brought before the church a proposal to formulate a committee to develop a constitution for the church.

Thus, at the June 1, 1993, mid-year church meeting, a Policy and Procedures Committee was established to ". . . prepare, revise, update, and supplement all existing policies and procedures." The motion for such a committee was made by Deacon Richard Wair, the Chair of the Board of Deacons. The same motion also requested formulating a Budget Process Committee to more closely reflect budgeting desires of the church. After much disagreement and concern from the pastor and some members of the church's Legal Committee that the church was getting away from theological perspectives, the congregation voted to form both committees, each to be chaired initially by Senior Deacon William Willis until each group elected their own officers.

Each committee was to have elected representatives from the congregation, plus appointees by the pastor, trustees, and deacons. Eventually, the Policy and Procedures Committee became the Constitution and By-Laws Committee. Fifteen persons, including six elected from the floor, plus nine appointees served on the committee. They included Leo A. Brooks, Archie E. Williams Jr., George Sykes Jr., Grace I. Albritton, Ralph B. Everett, Daniel R. Gill, Frank S. Heard, James W. Johnson, Walter Moore, Isaiah P. Morrison III, Joyce K. Peterson, Welton A. Quander Sr., James L. Scott, Alton S. Wallace, and William M. Willis. Deacon Leo Brooks, a retired military officer, was elected as chair at their first meeting.

The committee met over a period of approximately eighteen months before bringing a document before the congregation for consideration. As these meetings occurred during the period when the church was being remodeled and classroom space was scarce, many of the meetings were held off-site at the Tyler House on Columbus Street, a private home that had been inherited by the church from the estate of the late Sister Lillian Tyler, who purchased the home working as a charwoman.

The constitutional committee agonized over numerous issues such as the composition of various boards, and the terms of service of certain officials. One of the most agonizing questions confronting the committee was what to do about the deaconesses. Alfred Street, like most Baptist churches of the era, had both a Board of Deacons and a Board of Deaconesses. The church now had eleven female deacons, including one who had been serving now for over twelve years. At issue was whether to consolidate the boards, or continue with two separate ones.

After considering various options and relying on Alfred Street's interpretation of the scriptures, the committee, in concert with the pastor, agreed to disband the Deaconess Board and have a single joint board of male and female deacons. All deaconesses were not to be automatically transferred to the joint board; however, those selected would be ordained as deacons. This action would lead to an even greater increase in the number of female deacons in the coming years.

Another issue that required special crafting was procedures for removing an individual (e.g., pastor or deacon) from office. Within Baptist churches, removal of pastors has historically been one of the most difficult acts, resulting in many split congregations. The Constitutional and By-Laws Committee developed procedures that required a series of steps that involved adequate notification of the intent to remove an individual from office.

THE CONSTITUTION AND BY-LAWS
OF THE
ALFRED STREET BAPTIST CHURCH
ALEXANDRIA, VIRGINIA

Adopted by the membership of Alfred Street Baptist Church at a Church meeting on November 22, [illegible] to become effective January [illegible].

Richard M. Wair
Chairman, Board of Deacon

Ralph E. Everett
Chairman, Board of Trustees

John O. Peterson
Pastor

Constitution of the Alfred Street Baptist Church

As the Constitution and By-Laws Committee was completing its work, the Budget Process Committee proposed several new actions. The Budget Process Committee consisted of Helen McCoy, Leroy Miles, Charles Monterio, Joseph Nickens, Alfred Roscoe, Jr., Henry Thompson, Deacon Betty Jones, Deacon Richard Wair, Ardelia Hunter, Ronald Johnson, Evengeline Robinson, Mary Touchstone, Wallace King, Barbara Latham, and Harriet Smith. The new process they proposed established an elected Budget Committee composed of laypersons who were charged with developing an independent annual church budget. The budget was to reflect the congregation's wishes, but with the pastor's recommendations as input also. In the past, the congregation had exercised limited input, as the pastor's proposed budget had essentially become *the* budget.

The final drafts of both committee reports were presented to the church at a special call meeting on November 22, 1994, and became effective January 1, 1996, after a one-year transition period. Both the constitution and the new budget process were ratified, and Alfred Street reentered an era of rules similar to those of a century ago.[2]

Construction of a New Temple

Who is left among you that saw this house in her first glory? And how do you see it now?
Haggai 2:3

As the new constitution and budget processes were being developed, the activity most visible to members of the congregation was the construction of an expanded building complex. After several years of considering raze, sale, and museum options for handling the old church and enlarging the new church, Reverend Peterson had taken action in 1986 with the appointment of a 199-member Planning Committee to review plans for Phase III.

To meet projected requirements, it was soon realized that the original Phase III plans were now inadequate, and a complete new design was necessary. The trustees retained the architectural firm of Robert J. Nash, FAIA and Associates again and they proposed a design for an enlarged edifice that would integrate the old and new church into a single structure. By December 1990, the church had obtained all city approvals, except the building permit. Soon that permit was in hand and the church met in a special session to authorize construction to begin. Trustee Ronald Johnson was Chair of the Building Program and worked closely with the builder and banks to complete the planning phase.

The new building was to consist of an expanded sanctuary that would increase the area from 16,000 square feet up to 30,000 square feet, and increase seating from 650 up to 1,200 persons. Also, a balcony would be added that would contain a communications control room and a cry room for infants. Additional office space for the pastor and office staff, to include a boardroom, was to be provided in the rear of the church. A connector building with classrooms would unite the old and new churches. The old church would be remodeled and converted into three floors of classrooms, with a choir room for music rehearsals on the second floor, and the basement would contain a new kitchen and a small chapel. So, after being vacant and boarded for twelve years, the old church would get a new lease on life, and partially satisfy the desires of the preservationists who had fought to save it in 1980.

The estimated cost of the remodeling was $5 million. The financial arrangement with the bank called for the church to raise approximately $1 million before construction began, and to finance the remaining $4 million. Deacon Frank Heard led an eighteen-month churchwide building campaign to raise the first $1 million.

Following a groundbreaking ceremony on a Saturday in February, actual construc-

Groundbreaking Ceremony

tion began in 1992. In addition to the congregation, both city and state officials attended the groundbreaking ceremony. Trustee Ronald Johnson, then Chair of the Building Program, turned the first spade of dirt along with the pastor and the Alexandria City Manager. At the time, the construction was estimated to take eighteen months during which services would continue to be held in the main sanctuary. Many of the auxiliary meetings were moved offsite to the Tyler House, the church property on Columbus Street.

Though construction time was originally estimated at eighteen months, completion actually required nearly twenty-four months. The march-in date slipped two to three months every six months. The march-in finally occurred on February 6, 1994, and the formal dedication followed.

The Renovated Church—1994

For the march-in ceremony, the church held a single morning service (10 a.m.), and an afternoon (3 p.m.) service, instead of the usual 8 and 11 a.m. services, as was the custom. Between services, the congregation was fed "dinner on the grounds," a tradition that dates back to the earliest years of church history. Reverend David Forbes, pastor of Christian Faith Baptist Church in Raleigh, North Carolina, and a close personal friend of Reverend Peterson, spoke at both services from the Old Testament book of Haggai, describing a situation where the children of Israel were considering a new temple after their return from exile.[3] His text was:

"Who is left among you saw this house in her first glory, and how do you see it now? . . . The glory of this later house shall be greater than the former; and in this place will I give peace, saith the Lord of hosts. . . ."

Following the march-in, forty nights of dedication of special rooms such as the board-room, the sacristy for Communion elements, the choir rooms, and the new classrooms followed as it was done in 1981 when the church held its first march-in. Each week an additional part of the edifice would be dedicated, with local churches participating in the dedication services.

More Deacons, Trustees, and Officials

Following the march-in and dedication of the new temple, life returned to normal at Alfred Street Baptist Church, but with a new excitement now that the church could boast one of the more beautiful sanctuaries in Alexandria. New ministries were started. Choirs resumed holding special anniversaries, and Christmas pageants were planned again.

An expanded slate of officers assumed new leadership positions. The constitution adopted in late 1994 made provisions for nine trustees versus the six who had previously served. The new slate included the incumbents, plus three additional ones. Those selected included Henry Thompson, Helen McCoy, and Marla Hawkins. Beginning in the early 1970s, the church had always had at least one female on the Board of Trustees, beginning with Thelma Wair, who was followed by Evangeline Robinson, Ardelia Hunter, and Zenobia Anderson. The new board now contained three females, Zenobia Anderson, Helen McKoy, and Marla Hawkins. Zenobia Anderson would later become the first female to chair the Board of Trustees.

Additionally, growth in membership necessitated the need for new deacons. One or two new deacons had been added each year in the 1990–1995 time frame. But, by 1995, additional growth required even more deacons. In 1995, seven deacons were added, including four more women. This brought the total number of women deacons to fifteen and included the large group of women ordained in 1991. All the female deacons had previously been deaconesses. The newly ordained deacons included Lucille Day, Karen DeSandies, Vernell Howell, Elizabeth Middough, and three men—Earl Stafford, Dave Evans, and George Sykes. The total number of deacons was now forty. They served as lay leaders for thirty membership groups, plus various other ministries.

Sister Lucille Day was the older member among the group of women deacons, having joined Alfred Street in 1946 during Reverend Adkins' pastorate. Most of the others had joined during the period of explosive growth that began during the 1978–1982 time frame. Karen DeSandies, a speech pathologist, had joined Alfred Street in 1978. Sister Vernell Howell had been director of the Youth Ministry for many years after joining in 1979, while Elizabeth Middough and George Sykes had been ushers since joining in 1984.

In addition to the elected positions, the pastor appointed individuals to several positions. One of the more coveted positions, at least among the women, was Chair of Women's Day. Women's Day had always been one of the most anticipated events in the church calendar year at Alfred Street and was usually held in October. During the depression years of the 1930s, Women's Day and every special day was basically a fund-raiser, and the focus was on which auxiliary could raise the most money on their special day. In those early years Women's Day was a fairly simple event with a newly appointed women's choir, and the selection of a prominent woman speaker. Generally, these speakers were laypersons, as the idea of women preachers had not taken hold in the early years. There may or may not have been refreshments after the service, depending upon the wishes of the chairperson for the event. Women's Day continued in this manner through the 1970s and the 1980s, though the fund-raising aspect was dropped shortly after Reverend Peterson arrived.

By the mid-1990s, Women's Day began to take off in different directions. No one remembers how the tradition got started, but being selected chairperson of Women's Day at Alfred Street was like being selected homecoming queen. At the end of the service in one year, the pastor would appoint the chair for the following year. And all the women would be eager to see who was going to be selected.

In 1993, Sister Paula Blunt was selected Chair of Women's Day. Sister Blunt extended the Women's Day celebration from just Sunday activities to include a banquet on Saturday. The next year, Sister Patricia Wallace was selected and she extended it even further to include a series of religious workshops and midnight Communion on Friday night. In selecting the facilitators for the various workshops, Sister Wallace selected pastors mostly from the AME denomination[4] as Baptists particularly in southern areas were still a bit slow to open up some areas of the ministry to women. Therefore, few Baptist women pastors were available to handle the workshops.

In 1994, the Saturday luncheon speaker was Congresswoman Eva Clayton of North Carolina, who was introduced by Congresswoman Cardiss Collins, an Alfred Street Baptist Church member at the time. The Sunday preachers were listed in *Ebony* magazine as some of the best in America: Reverend Vashti McKenzie of Baltimore and Reverend Cecelia Williams-Bryant of Dallas.

In subsequent years, the Women's Day celebration continued to grow in size and scope. It soon went from a two-day affair to three days with off-site retreats. By the end of the century it had become a year-long event with activities scattered throughout the church calendar year. Other chairs of the event during these later years included Deacon Eva Simmons, Blanche Hutchinson, Reverend Dr. Faye Gunn, Minister Marla Hawkins, Sister Marva Evans, Sister Linda Prioleau, Sister Jean Morris, and Sister Beverly Ferguson. Still later, Women's Day gave rise to a Women's Ministry, with Sister Janet Green as the first to lead the new ministry.[5]

Pastor's Absence and Recognition

In the summer and fall of 1996, things were going well at Alfred Street Baptist Church and with Reverend Peterson's ministry. He was now in his thirty-second year as pastor. In mid-November, he was planning an overseas trip on church business with his wife, Joyce Peterson. On the evening of November 11, after making final preparations, he retired for the evening, but observed a burning sensation in his chest during the night.

He was rushed to the local hospital and advised that he had suffered a stroke.

He immediately issued a written statement to ensure that lines of authority were clear and that the church continued to function properly. As in prior periods when the pastor was unavailable, the Chair of the Board of Deacons was next in the chain of command.

Deacon James Johnson, Chair of the Board of Deacons, assumed the responsibility for ensuring that the church would run smoothly. As it turned out, Reverend Peterson was absent from the pulpit for about four months until Easter Sunday of 1997. During his absence the pulpit was occupied with speakers from around the country and frequently from among the ministers on staff, including Reverend Dr. Faye Gunn, Reverend Robert Easter, and Reverend Dr. Elbert Ransom.

On recovering from his illness, the pastor returned to the pulpit. Then, during the fall of 1997, the church elected to honor the pastor with a special celebration for his thirty-three years of service. This was unusual, as Alfred Street Baptist Church does not have a history of frequent pastor anniversary Sundays as some churches do. In fact, whereas some churches celebrate annually, Alfred Street had honored the pastor fewer than five times in the past thirty years, the most recent celebration having been Reverend Peterson's twenty-fifth anniversary almost ten years earlier in 1989. Before that, he had been given a celebration at his tenth anniversary and at his twenty-second anniversary in 1986, which was held at the Hilton Hotel in Springfield, Virginia, on a Sunday evening.

For his thirty-third anniversary, however, the church decided to do

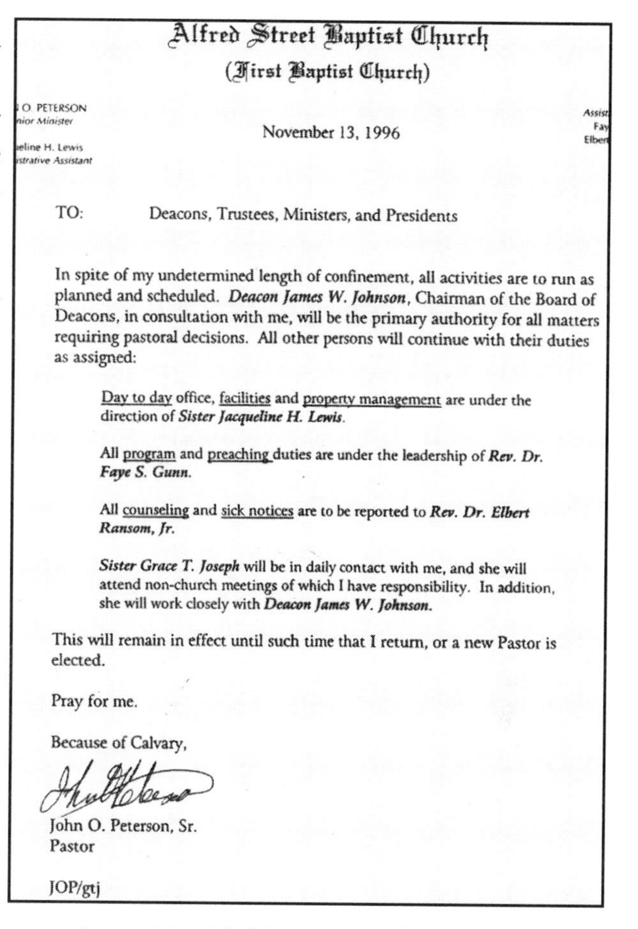

Alfred Street Baptist Church
(First Baptist Church)

O. PETERSON
nior Minister

eline H. Lewis
strative Assistant

November 13, 1996

TO: Deacons, Trustees, Ministers, and Presidents

In spite of my undetermined length of confinement, all activities are to run as planned and scheduled. ***Deacon James W. Johnson***, Chairman of the Board of Deacons, in consultation with me, will be the primary authority for all matters requiring pastoral decisions. All other persons will continue with their duties as assigned:

Day to day office, facilities and property management are under the direction of ***Sister Jacqueline H. Lewis***.

All program and preaching duties are under the leadership of ***Rev. Dr. Faye S. Gunn***.

All counseling and sick notices are to be reported to ***Rev. Dr. Elbert Ransom, Jr.***

Sister Grace T. Joseph will be in daily contact with me, and she will attend non-church meetings of which I have responsibility. In addition, she will work closely with ***Deacon James W. Johnson***.

This will remain in effect until such time that I return, or a new Pastor is elected.

Pray for me.

Because of Calvary,

John O. Peterson, Sr.
Pastor

JOP/gtj

Letter Establishing Lines of Authority

Pastor's 33rd Anniversary Banquet

something more formal and selected Sister Patricia Wallace to plan a celebration. Reverend Peterson's thirty-third anniversary celebration was held on the weekend of October 4–5, 1997, and included a black tie gala in Crystal City, Virginia, on Saturday night. Three services were held on Sunday. In addition to the usual 8 and 11 a.m. services, activities that day included a *This Is Your Life*–type presentation at 4 p.m. on Sunday with videos and testimonials by old friends.

The planning for all the events associated with the anniversary went smoothly, but some portions of the congregation were unresponsive to various appeals. Reservations for the banquet were particularly troubling as over 400 spaces were reserved. At the last minute sufficient tickets were distributed and both the banquet on Saturday night and a testimonial on Sunday evening were well received by the pastor and congregation.

Close personal friends in the ministry provided testimonials at the banquet: Reverend Clinton Washington of the Progressive Baptist Convention; Reverend Lawrence Davies of Shiloh Baptist Church in Fredericksburg; Reverend Dr. T. Wright Morris of Shiloh Baptist in Heathsville, Virginia; Reverend E. D. McCreary, former pastor of Mt. Carmel Baptist in Richmond; and Reverend Dr. Andrew Jack White of Zion Baptist in Petersburg, Virginia. Testimonials for the *This is Your Life* segment were given by Rosalyn McAllister-Brock, a young adult that Reverend Peterson had helped as a youth; Reverend Robert Easter, a young minister whom he had ordained; Mrs. Drusillia Clark, a fellow teacher who taught with him at Hoffman Boston High School in Arlington, Virginia; and other members of his family and the church.

In honoring Reverend Peterson's service to the church and the world's Christian community, attention was brought to his various positions at the local, state, national, and international levels.[6] Those positions included President of the Baptist Ministers Conference in Alexandria; Third Vice President of the Northern Virginia Baptist Association; Chaplain of the Alexandria Police Department and Alexandria Hospital; President of the Virginia Baptist General Convention; First Vice President of the Lott Carey Baptist Foreign Mission Convention; and Vice President of the Baptist World Alliance. In education, he had served on the Alexandria School Board and on the Board of Trustees at his alma mater, Virginia Union University, which would later grant him an honorary Doctorate of Humane Letters for his worldwide efforts.

Within Alfred Street Reverend Peterson's accomplishments were many: he increased the size of the congregation from around 300 when he came to almost 2,500 persons (more than three times its size in 1880 with Reverend Madden when the congregation had reached its previous peak). The growing congregation had created the need for two major construction projects in 1981 and 1994, expanding the church complex to its present size. The operating budget had grown from about $12,000 in 1964 to $1.6 million in 1997. Reverend Peterson was instrumental in ordaining the first women deacons and preachers in Northern Virginia and had continued to support women in these positions by ordaining a total of six women ministers and fifteen women deacons.[7]

Other Aspects of Life at Alfred Street: 1995–2000

During the period 1995–2000 at Alfred Street Baptist Church, all of the nearly thirty ministries continued to function and grow. The church continued to have one of the stronger music departments in the area and it continued to draw new members and visitors to the church for special music festivals such as the Easter cantata, the Christmas music festival, and the annual choir anniversaries. The Male Chorus remained under the direction of Sister Harriett Westbrook and Sister Alma Upshaw. The Voices of Triumph that sang primarily at the 8 a.m. services experienced several directors during this time, including Doris Hall and Keith Perkins. Both of the children's choirs remained under the direction of Sister Doris Winstead. The Senior Choir remained under the direction of Jacqueline Henry-Green, now in her 30th year, while the Young and Adult Choir was headed by Sister Joyce Garrett.

Sister Garrett later relinquished leadership of the Young and Adult Choir to focus on choral groups at the high school and college level. Mr. Mark Prioleau replaced her and would soon direct two choirs, including the Gospel Inspirers. In 1994 and 1995, the Gospel Inspirers, under his direction, participated in the Quaker Oats Company Youth Choir Competition, a regional musical competition among youth choirs. For two years in a row, Alfred Street's youth were awarded second place.

The growing membership at Alfred Street contributed to a strong financial program. At the March 1996 meeting, the Budget Committee reported a yearly budget of $1.79 million. At that time, the church owned three properties that were free of debt—the parsonage at 816 Queen Street, and two houses that were donated to the church: Mrs. Mazie Bowden donated the house at 226 West Street and Mrs. Lillian Tyler donated the Tyler House on Columbus Street. The total church assets at that time were approximately $9.1 million, mostly in buildings. The Alfred Street sanctuary complex was listed as an $8.9 million property value, and the Queen Street parsonage at $490,000. The pipe organ in the sanctuary was valued at $157,000.

In 1996, the church also approved a plan to eliminate the mortgage left from the construction of the new sanctuary that was completed in 1994. When completed, the new structure had cost $5.2 million, of which $3.7 million was mortgaged. The church was paying approximately $40,000 on that mortgage monthly. A new program called the Mortgage Elimination Program called for retiring the mortgage by the end of the century, at midnight on December 31, 1999. The pastor appointed Deacon James Garrett as chair of the program to retire the mortgage, approximately $3.5 million, within three years.

The mortgage retirement program began in the spring of 1997 and involved twice-yearly rallies on Mortgage Elimination Sunday in June and November of each year.[8] At most rallies, between $60,000 and $80,000 would be raised. Additionally, some members contributed each Sunday in special envelopes, and the trustees, then chaired by Ronald Johnson, increased monthly payments by an additional $15,000 from the general offering. The church also passed a resolution that any budget surplus from the prior year's expenses would be added to the mortgage. Some years this amounted to over $750,000. In total, some years almost $1 million was paid to the mortgage in addition to the usual expenditures collected in giving in tithes and offerings.

Also, at the December meeting, Sister Irma Davis stepped down as church clerk after twelve years, and Brother Larry Simmons, a local undertaker, was selected as a new trustee. During this time, the church clerk still read announcements at morning services, and several of the church's youth wanted to grow up to be clerks after watching Sister Davis for all of those years.

A special committee to name rooms of the church after current and past pastors was formed at the request of Sister Mildred Harper.[9] Mrs. Harper, a long-time member of Alfred Street, was active during the era when the new building plans were initially being formulated under Reverend Adkins in 1962. Since the original plan had been to name the planned annex after him, she felt it important to name some part of the new structure for Reverend Adkins. A committee chaired by Deacon Bessie Johnson was appointed to review legacies of all the pastors and existing areas of the church and select appropriate areas to name for them.

Name Plate Honoring Pastor

During a ceremony in December 1998, the Trustee Room was named for Reverend William Evans, a trustee who signed the deed for the original lease of the site on Alfred Street in 1818. The Sunday School office was named for Reverend Sampson White. The choir room in the old church was named for Reverend Samuel Madden, whose likeness adorns a beautiful stained glass window placed in his honor in 1897. The nursery on the lower level was named for Reverend Truatt, while the parsonage was named for Reverend W.H. Powell, its architect and a principal builder of the building. The chapel in the lower level of the old church was named for Reverend Adkins. He had held prayer services there as his last act at Alfred Street before passing in 1963. The recently renovated library in the rear of the sanctuary was named for Reverend Peterson.[10] Though these efforts to honor the pastors had been initiated by Sister Mildred Harper, she passed shortly before the dedications took place.

Reverend Gunn, Reverend Moses and Reverend Hawkins

Other items emerging from the March 4, 1997, church meeting included the beginning of two new Sunday School classes, *Mothers with Babies,* taught by Jewelette Peterson-McDaniel, and *High School and Above,* taught by Deacon Earl Stafford and Brother McDaniel. Alfred Street also agreed it would help the Northern Virginia Urban League and other churches raise $1 million to purchase the old *Slave Pen* on Duke Street that had been used for commerce in trading slaves during the early 1820s–1850s. The building would become the Northern Virginia Urban League's new headquarters.

At the June quarterly meeting in 1997, the church voted to permit Sister Beverly Moses to give a trial sermon immediately after the 11 a.m. service on July 20. Her initial sermon was entitled "It Is Good To Be Here." Sister Moses was joining a sisterhood of several other women at Alfred Street, including Reverend Faye Gunn who had been ordained in 1982, and Minister Mary Murphy, who had been granted a license to preach the previous year. They would soon be joined in the pulpit by Reverend Marla Hawkins, who was ordained at Alfred Street some years later.

Beverly Moses was an Alexandria resident who has been active in evangelism, while Mary Murphy had been a member of the Young and Adult Choir for more than ten years. Sister Murphy was a staunch supporter of the Commission on Evangelism and the Jail and Prison Ministry.

The church also continued with its practice of ordaining women deacons. Soon Sister Patricia Wallace was ordained a deacon, joining sixteen other females in the diaconate sisterhood. All female deacons prior to her ordination had previously served as deaconesses, many of whom were transferred to the Board of Deacons when the two boards were joined. Sister Wallace was the first female layperson, not previously a deaconess, who was ordained to the Board of Deacons.

By 1997, the church constitution had been in effect for two years, and the church was meeting according to the required schedule. Meetings were to be held quarterly in March, June, September, and December. However, as attendance was poor (100 persons were required for a quorum), particularly at the March and September meetings, the number of meetings was subsequently changed to just twice yearly, effective in 1998. At a meeting on March 10, 1998, amendments were made to the constitution to formally effect this change.

The church remained active in conventions, sending representatives to each of them. In 1998, the Baptist General Convention of Virginia met in Richmond; the Lott Carey met in the District of Columbia; the National Baptist Convention USA met in Denver; and the Progressive Baptist Convention met in Buffalo. Several persons from the Department of Missions, headed by Sister Rosette Graham, attended these meetings. For meetings of the Baptist World Alliance, Reverend Peterson and Reverend Emmett Dunn were the primary attendees.

On the weekend of May 30–31, 1998, the Alfred Street family honored Reverend Faye Savage Gunn for her ten years of service to the church as an assistant minister. The weekend celebration was chaired by Deacon Bessie Johnson and included a black-tie banquet on Saturday afternoon at the Officer's Club at Andrews Air Force Base. A special worship service was held in Reverend Gunn's honor on that Sunday where the guest speaker was Reverend Minnie Davis, a fellow "Sister in Christ" who is also a product of Alfred Street.

During this time, Alfred Street passed several musical milestones. For much of its history, there were disagreements at Alfred Street regarding the use of various musical instruments in the worship services. During the 1910s and 1920s, there were debates about the use of the mandolin and the violin. During much of the 1980s and 1990s, the instrument most debated was the drum. Reverend Peterson had a practice of not allowing drums during worship service, in part because he felt that most drummers played much too loudly. On select occasions such as choir anniversaries, the timpani were permitted; however, the snare and bass drum sets used by many gospel groups were generally not allowed. On many occasions, an auxiliary of the church would invite a visiting choir to perform at Alfred Street that would arrive with drums. After they were ready to perform, there would be quiet negotiations behind the scene to get the drums removed from the sanctuary. This frequently caused anxious moments for the church's musicians and some embarrassment for the auxiliary that had extended the invitation.

In the late 1990s the opinion on the use of various types of musical instruments finally changed. A new gospel version of Handel's *Messiah* featuring African-American artists was released and Sister Joyce Garrett decided to have the Young and Adult Choir perform the *Hallelujah Chorus* from that album for Christmas. Brother Stuart Bowers, who played the bass guitar, approached the choir director about playing with the choir. He was permitted to perform that Sunday and the guitar was well accepted by the congregation. Soon, he was playing regularly with the Young and Adult Choir and later with all the choirs.

After the bass guitar was accepted in worship services, the rules concerning drums also became more relaxed. Soon, Mr. Lester Saucers began playing the snare drums annually at choir anniversaries. With the increased frequency of their use and general acceptance within the religious community, Alfred Street finally relented on the drums. And as the century approached its end, Alfred Street officially added two new positions for musicians, bass player and percussionist, to its music department.

A Commuter Congregation

During this period, the church continued to experience sustained growth in membership, just as had occurred following the initial construction in 1981. By 1995, membership was approximately 2,200, and it grew to a maximum of approximately 2,800 in 1997 before leveling off or declining slightly toward the end of the century.[11] Persons still continued to join at a rate of about 150 persons per year. However, about 200 were leaving for other churches, so there was a net loss of about fifty members a year. Membership finally stabilized at about 2,600 persons.[12]

Some of the new members were new arrivals to Northern Virginia who moved there as the Virginia suburbs became more accepting of African Americans. Many new church members also continued to come from Maryland, though the number of new Maryland arrivals had been reduced from the rapid growth years in the mid-1980s. During the intervening years, several black mega churches that boasted memberships of five, ten, or even fifteen thousand members had opened in Prince George's County. Now, instead of African Americans crossing the Woodrow Wilson Bridge from Maryland to attend Alfred Street and other close-in churches in Virginia, they were leaving Virginia to attend the close-in mega churches in Fort Washington, Oxon Hill, and Temple Hills areas of

Maryland.

Alfred Street had long ceased being a local church as it had been at the beginning of the century when most members walked to its services. It was now a commuter church of suburban congregants. The advent of the automobile and the opening up of the suburbs to African Americans resulted in most worshippers driving over ten miles to attend services. Some came to worship each Sunday from as far south as Fredericksburg, Virginia, and others from as far north as Owings Mill, Maryland, north of Baltimore. However, most Alfred Street members were clustered in several neighborhoods within the close-in suburbs. The ten most popular zip codes where members lived around the end of the century are listed below. The values shown are the number of households that may include a single individual or a family of four or five persons.[13]

Zip Code	Area	Major Landmark	No. of Households
20744	Ft. Washington	Indian Head Hwy.	160
22304	Alexandria	Landmark Mall	97
22309	Alexandria	Mount Vernon	91
22315	Alexandria	Kingstowne	76
22306	Alexandria	Beacon Mall	75
22310	Franconia	Hayfield HS	65
22314	Alexandria	Alfred Street	59
22305	Alexandria	Arlandria	59
22079	Lorton	Old Reformatory	46
22153	Springfield	Springfield Mall	36

Fort Washington, Maryland, became the most populous zip code at Alfred Street in the early 1980s and remained so for most of the 1990s. Further, though the number of new persons from that region who joined each year had declined, fully one-third of all new persons who joined Alfred Street in 1999 came from Fort Washington and the close-in suburbs of southern Maryland.

Even though most members now lived in the suburbs, Alfred Street was still a church of country folks, most of whom had migrated to the Washington, D.C., area from the Deep South. The backgrounds and birthplaces of the deacons provide insight into the hometowns of the congregation in general. Of the forty deacons, only two hailed from New England, with seven others coming from the Mid-Atlantic States. The remaining thirty-one deacons hailed from the South, with fifteen of them hailing from Virginia and eight from North Carolina, many coming from rural areas.[14]

The congregation and Board of Deacons were thus composed primarily of a diverse group of country folk from the Deep South who now lived in the suburbs. Thirty percent of the deacons lived in the Maryland suburbs and almost forty percent of the Board of Deacons were now female. A third of the trustees were also now female.

Among the groups least represented in the congregation were local residents from neighborhoods very close to Alfred Street Baptist Church. Within the black neighborhoods of the city of Alexandria, there were many who had labeled Alfred Street as "snobbish" or "too bougie" (bourgeois) to meet their needs. As a result, many local residents hesitated to join.

The divide within the black community embodied in the term "bourgeois" had existed in Alexandria since the founding of Alfred Street. In the early days of the 1800s, the divide among Negroes had been slave vs. free, or field-hand vs. house-servant. Two hundred years later, that divide still existed. And from its very beginning, Alfred Street had always been viewed by many as remaining on the "bourgeois" side of that great divide.

In the early 1800s, Alfred Street had been built in a neighborhood of free blacks at a time when slavery was the order of the day. Among the church leaders there had been some of the more prominent blacks in Alexandria such as Reverend Samuel Madden, a commissioned officer during the Civil War—a rank held by fewer than one hundred black soldiers. A housing project called the "Berg" had been named for him. George L. Seaton, perhaps the most accomplished black man in Alexandria during Reconstruction, had been a deacon at Alfred Street and had served in the Virginia Legislature. Reverend Adkins, a leading educator in the city, was pastor at Alfred Street for 43 years, and was one of the city's most beloved residents. A housing development had also been named for him. And the current pastor, Reverend Peterson, had served on the School Board and been instrumental in redeveloping the Dip area of the city.

These individuals and their civic contributions added to the image of Alfred Street as a "bougie" church two hundred years later. In the minds of many of Alexandria's black community, Alfred Street was a church for the middle class, and this resulted in many local persons feeling uncomfortable attending services. Its music program and its restrained worship style (compared to some of the more evangelical Baptist churches) and the economic status of its membership contributed to this perception. As a result, many local Alexandria residents chose to join other churches. Alfred Street would labor under this perception for another decade, but would increase efforts to change this image during its bicentennial year.

Political Visitors

In October 2000, Alfred Street Baptist Church parishioners witnessed a first, a visit by a sitting U.S. president. On Sunday, October 29, President William Jefferson Clinton visited Alfred Street at the 8:00 a.m. worship service. The Gospel Inspirers sang and the service received wide coverage in the press. President Clinton visited Alfred Street and several other churches that weekend in a *Get Out the Vote* drive for the upcoming presidental election.[15] He was especially popular with African Americans, even during his impeachment hearings, and was warmly received by them wherever he went.

President Clinton was not the first political figure to visit Alfred Street Baptist Church, however. As Alfred Street was the largest African-American congregation in Northern Virginia, many politicians considered it a *must stop* in their appeals to black voters. The church had been visited previously by numerous mayoral and congressional candidates in Northern Virginia for many years. When Governor Lawrence Douglas Wilder, the first black governor in U.S. history, was campaigning, he had also visited Alfred Street Baptist Church.

The president sings with Pastor John Peterson, center, Assistant Pastor Edward Jackson and the choir at Alfred Street Baptist Church.

President Clinton Visits Alfred Street

In addition to political visits, many other political personalities visited on other occasions. The various mayors of the city attended Alfred Street Baptist Church numerous times. Some of them visited during Reverend Peterson's installation and more recently during the groundbreaking and march-in ceremonies. Governor Mark Warner and most mayoral and city council candidates visited. Additionally, Mayor Marion Barry of the District of Columbia visited to attend the funeral of Brother John Touchstone, who had served as his Director of Public Works in an earlier administration. General Colin Powell visited Alfred Street to attend a funeral. Numerous members of congress visited as speakers, and Congresswoman Cardiss Collins of Michigan was a member of the church and of the senior choir for many years during the 1990s.

2000—and Beyond

As the church witnessed the end of the 1990s, Alfred Street continued to grow and prosper. On Sunday, July 23, 2000, Reverend J.O. Peterson announced to the Alfred Street congregation that the Lott Carey Baptist Foreign Mission Convention was responding to the HIV/AIDS crisis. The Lott Carey Convention had committed to a substantial faith-based response to the pandemic that was ravishing the African continent. HIV/AIDS had become a leading cause of death in Africa, wiping out decades of progress on Africa's development fronts, with over eighty percent of all AIDS deaths worldwide occurring in sub-Saharan Africa. Alfred Street committed to support this initiative with a $75,000 grant to the Lott Carey Foreign Mission Baptist Convention to help fund the initial development phase. Alfred Street also provided leadership to the initiative through the services of Reverend Samuel Nixon, Jr., the newly appointed Project Director for the Lott Carey AIDS Initiative.

Habitant for Humanity House

Alfred Street had a long relationship with the Lott Carey Convention, going back to initial membership in 1901. Reverend Peterson had recently become president of the Lott Carey Convention, after having served as vice president for several years. The announcement of Alfred Street's support for AIDS was made at the Lott Carey Annual Session in Norfolk in August by Trustee Ronald Johnson, Chair of Alfred Street's Trustees Ministry, who presented the check to the Lott Carey Convention. Alfred Street's initial contribution was matched by an additional $75,000 in offerings and pledges that evening by other delegates at the annual session.

The contribution to the Lott Carey Convention was part of the church's proposed budget for 2001 of over $2.6 million or a thirty-two percent increase over the year 2000 contribution. The church's total contribution to missions that year totaled $300,000, and included $44,000 for AIDS and $45,000 for the Pastor's Initiative to attempt to get the other conventions to which Alfred Street belonged to work together on missions projects.[16]

To extend its mission outreach that was focused primarily on efforts at the national and local levels, Alfred Street teamed with the Old Presbyterian Meeting House, another local church, to build a home under the auspices of Habitat for Humanity. Deacon David Rollins headed Alfred Street's contribution to the effort.

Work on the new home at 702 North Patrick Street began in October 2000 and was completed the next summer. The home was similar in size and design to others constructed by Habitat for Humanity throughout the local area. The home would be owned and occupied by a family from the East African nation of Eritrea. The family had to perform 300 to 500 hours of sweat equity in the actual construction of their new home. A dedication service was held for the completed Habitat for Humanity house built by Alfred Street members in partnership with members of the Old Presbyterian Meeting House of Alexandria, a congregation dating back to 1795.[17]

At the December 2000 annual meeting, more deacons and ministers were added to Alfred Street's rolls. Brother Alphonso Hall, who was ordained previously at the Braddock Baptist Church in Falls Church, was recommended as an active Alfred Street deacon. His wife, Sister Lottie Hall, who also transferred to Alfred Street, was installed as a deacon the next year. Two new ministers also began assisting with ministerial activities: Chaplain Wally Vaughn, assigned to the U.S. Air Force, began teaching Bible study and occasionally preaching from the pulpit, as did Reverend Jerry Jones, a recent transfer to Alfred Street from another church in Washington, D.C. Reverend Emmett Dunn (Baptist World Alliance), Reverend Tyrone Pitts (Progressive Baptist Convention) and Reverend Emanuel Goatley (Lott Carey Convention) were now also members of Alfred Street Baptist Church and they preached when their schedules permitted.

In addition to Sunday School and Vacation Bible School, the church initiated other new outlets for children. When Reverend Peterson first came to Alfred Street in 1964, there were only a small number of children in the entire congregation. This was a reflection of a congregation that was primarily beyond the period of child-bearing.

By the year 2000, all that had changed, as babies had become a growth industry at Alfred Street. There were frequent baby dedications, generally held on the third Sunday during the 11 a.m. worship service. To accommodate the large number of babies, the church instituted a Moms with Babies Sunday School class in which over ten babies enrolled. The nursery, located on the lower level, had grown to such an extent that membership groups were tasked to man the facility and assist the overtaxed caregivers. Also, in the balcony opposite the control room there was a cry room for those mothers who wanted to enjoy the service with their children. The room was outfitted with padded rocking chairs and was glass-enclosed to shield the congregation from the occasional outbursts.

The number of babies at Alfred Street was a reflection of other changes in the congregation. Most of the babies were the offspring of young adults who were now pouring into the congregation. By 2000, there were more than 600 young adults, persons aged twenty-two to thirty-five, in the congregation.

Church Burns $3.5 Million Mortgage

On Anniversary Sunday in 2001, the Alfred Street congregation burned the mortgage on the current sanctuary.[18] The mortgage burning was the culmination of a four-and-a-half-year, churchwide Mortgage Elimination Campaign that sought to leave the church debt-free to do greater works. The campaign began in May 1997, with the goal of retiring a $3.5 million mortgage on New Years Eve, December 31, 1999. When that original goal was not met, the church extended the campaign and successfully completed all payments in September 2001.

The Mortgage Burning ceremony was conducted on November 11, 2001. That year, Anniversary and Trustee Sundays were combined. The worship service began at 10:45 a.m.

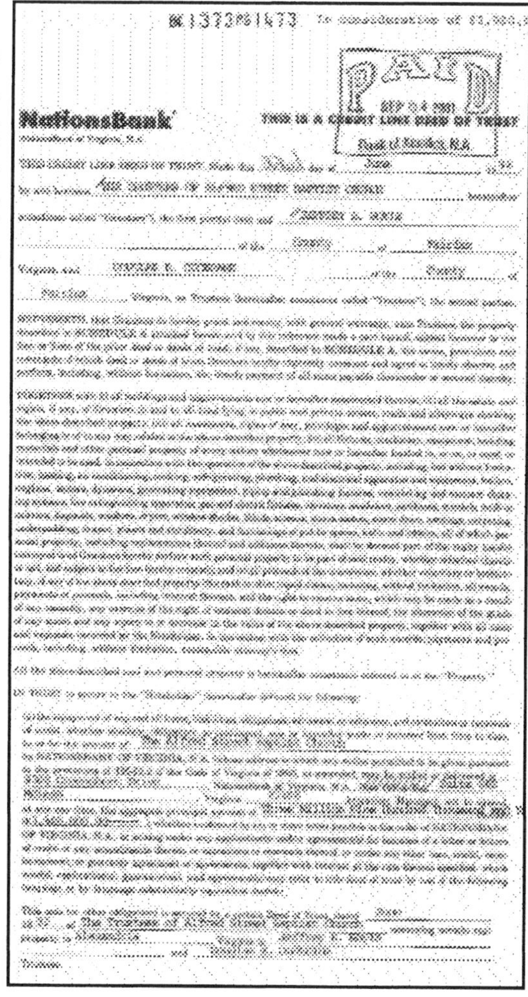
PAID

NationsBank

Copy of Mortgage

with an outdoor ceremony to re-lay the old cornerstone in the rear of the church near the entrance adjacent to the back elevators. The old cornerstone had originally been laid on the front portico of the original structure that was built in 1980. When the new construction began to extend the sanctuary and balcony in the early 1990s, the old cornerstone was removed and stored for several years. After completing the new structure in the spring of 1994, a new cornerstone was laid on the front portico. The old one was placed in the rear, but in a part of the original building.

After the re-laying of the cornerstone, the congregation moved inside for the Anniversary Sunday service. At that service, each attendee was given a laminated copy of the mortgage. Current and former trustees who were officers at the time the loan was first secured in 1992 burned a facsimile of the mortgage.

In the fall of 2001, Alfred Street again celebrated homecoming, after a forty-year hiatus. Homecomings had been popular in the 1940s, when old members who had moved away would return in the late summer for a weekend of preaching and eating. Alfred Street had celebrated its first homecoming in 1926, and had continued to do so for many years. But they had been discontinued by the time of the Reverend Peterson's arrival in 1964. The homecoming celebrated in 2001 was thus touted by the organizers as the ". . . *first* in the history of the church," as many of the congregation were relatively new arrivals and were unaware of the old traditions of the church.

Reverend Edward Jackson chaired the 2001 homecoming and was assisted by members of the YAM ministry.[19] Only one Sunday morning service was held, followed by "dinner on the grounds," an old tradition among rural Baptist churches. And as in years gone by, all the former members who had left the area were invited to return home. Following service, a catered meal was served to worshippers in a large tent set up in the parking lot adjacent to the church. Those who attended enjoyed the service and the meal that followed.

However, Reverend Peterson elected to discontinue the homecomings after this one attempt, in part due to attendance and cost. Because the congregation at Alfred Street is fairly transient—as is most of the Washington area—numerous former members have moved away. Most people who left in recent years were never at the church long enough to develop a real strong attachment as they had to the old churches back home. Thus, relatively few of the former members returned. Additionally, the cost of the event was fairly substantial because of the catered meal and the cost of a full-color membership directory that was distributed to all members. Homecomings were dropped from the yearly church calendar again.

The Bertha Mack House

On Tuesday, December 4, 2001, the Alfred Street family held its annual church meeting as required by the church constitution. Now that the mortgage had been paid, key issues discussed at the 2001 annual meeting included a decision by the church to acquire the old Bertha Mack property on North Henry Street, to be converted into a mission project. Mrs. Bertha Mack is a long-term member who vacated the property when she became ill. A committee explored possible uses for the site after the existing house was to be remodeled or torn down, and proposed that the house be used as a home for troubled girls. A decision was also made to initiate a mission project in Hayti to assist with replacing roofs on twelve churches damaged in recent storms. Additionally, the church decided to explore the possibility of creating an Alfred Street Foundation, separate from the church. A foundation development committee would present a recommendation to the church at the June meeting.

At the December meeting, the church also passed a church budget of $2.6 million, which included funds for the purchase of a new church van, a new piano, upgrades to the sound system, and repairs to the sanctuary. Church meetings had changed considerably since the earlier part of the century when such meetings were primarily occasions to check up on the conduct of members. Over time, personal conduct had become less of an issue, and the meetings took on the air of a business event, with reports by key committees, the election of new officers, passing yearly budgets, and announcing major new initiatives.

The New Ministries

With the mortgage paid off, the focus of activity at Alfred Street turned to ministry and missions. Many new ministries were created and many older ones were revitalized. The list of ministries grew to over forty as shown in this list:

Board of Christian Education
Boarder Babies and Family Services
Children's Church
Deacons
Drama
Evangelism
Family Bereavement
Fitness
Girl Scouts
Health and Wellness
Helping Hands for Caregivers
AIDS/HIV
Jail and Prison
Junior Youth
Lawyers Committee
Library
Liturgical Dance
Married Couples
Media
Men's Department
Missions
Music
Newsletter
Nursery
Pastor's Aide
Recovery
Scholarship
See the Gospel (Signing)
Senior Fellowship
Shepherding
Single and Single Again
Sister Church
Sports/Athletics
Sunday School
Tape Visitation
Trustees
Tutorial
Ushers
Volunteer
Wedding Coordination
Women's Department
Young Adult

The Music Ministry continued as perhaps the most visible organization within the congregation. After several years of debate and interviews for a Minister of Music, Alfred Street Baptist Church instead hired two music coordinators, a position initially held jointly by Sister Theron Johnson and Brother Mark Prioleau. The Music Ministry now consisted of seven choirs, each performing a slightly different form of music ranging from gospel to high anthems. There were now three choirs targeted at youth, plus a Bell Choir that provided additional musical opportunities for all ages.

Liturgical Dance Ministry

A new Recovery Ministry, headed by Sister Dorothy Clark, was formed for recovering addicts and persons requiring assistance with organizing life skills. The Alfred Street Recovery Center, established in November 2000, has as its primary goal helping those who are lost spiritually, mentally, and physically and who are affected by alcohol, drugs, or other social ills and dysfunctional behaviors. This new ministry is similar to a successful program in Baltimore where veterans who have been substance abusers are provided training and new life skills, but more importantly are provided a spiritual foundation.

The AIDS/HIV Ministry

A new AIDS/HIV ministry, headed by Sister Rosalind Hoover, was formed to heighten awareness of the global pandemic caused by AIDS. A new signing ministry called See the Gospel was formed under the direction of Deacon Karen DeSandies. Members of this ministry sign for hearing-impaired members during services.

Under the leadership of Deacons William Willis and Dave Rollins, the church began supporting the Carpenter Shelter in its homeless program.[20] Each night during the winter months when there is an overflow of persons at the shelter, ten to fifteen men stay at Alfred Street Baptist Church on the lower level. Each night a different Membership Group is responsible for providing meals and two male chaperones to stay over with the homeless men.

The newly formed Library Ministry reported cataloguing over 650 new books, and provides a variety of resources to support religious studies. Ten volunteer librarians man the desk during Sunday and weekday hours, with Dr. Curtis Howard serving as the church librarian. The new library is housed in the recently renovated J.O. Peterson Library just off the main sanctuary, and continues a tradition of library service dating back to the 1,600 volume lending library of the 1920s.

The Men's Department increased its membership and level of activities. This department had been in existence since just before World War II, but had experienced ebbs and flows in its effectiveness. Under the leadership of Monty Richards and Deacon Earl Stafford, this department experienced a new vitality as the ministry expanded its outreach services.

The Alfred Street Newsletter, edited by Sister Cynthia Casey, was being published quarterly with Brenda Lambert, Joyce Putman and Deborah Crawford as principal writers. The Alfred Street Newsletter was begun in the summer of 1982 and was now over twenty years old. There had been some breaks in publication as editors left the area.

Alfred Street also began to improve its education program by introducing two major annual education weekends. The Board of Christian Education holds several functions annually, but two major ones each year are the Family Weekend, which is generally held in early February or June, and the Christian Education Institute. The Christian Education Institute is held in late July and offers a week of courses that provide insight into daily living for disciples.

The Sunday School continued to prosper with Deacon Charles Monterio serving as its superintendent. Vacation Bible School, also under the auspices of the Board of Christian Education and the Sunday School, averaged about 250 persons nightly during the summer period. In addition to Vacation Bible School, led by Sister Mary Brown, one of the more successful educational activities of the church was the Tutorial Program. Each year the program supplies fifty-five to sixty tutors for an equal number of students. Reverend Faye Gunn served as the original director of the very successful Tutorial Program and Sister Margaret Wiggins recently replaced her in that position.

The Health and Wellness ministry, which began in 1994 under Dr. Kenneth DeSandies, continued to hold aerobic classes and annual health fairs in September of each year. This ministry was concerned with overall health issues of the congregation, but was particularly concerned that diets rich in fats and lack of exercise were resulting in members of the congregation passing at relatively young ages.

There were now ministries for all ages of the congregation. There was an expanded ministry for Junior Youth for children eight through twelve, headed by Sister Velma Perkins, and one for older persons called the Seniors' Fellowship Ministry, headed by

Sister Isabelle Smith. The Seniors' Fellowship Ministry met weekly for midweek religious services and also served as an outreach and social opportunity for seniors. Birthdays were celebrated each quarter, sometimes during luncheon cruises. A new Liturgical Dance Ministry had been formed under the direction of Mrs. Donna Upshaw-Wright for women—young and old.

There was now also a ministry for young adults started by Deacons Vernell and Thomas Howell. Over 110 young adults attended a kick-off meeting in early January 2000 to form the new Young Adult Ministry (YAM). The Howells recruited Melanie Garrett, Jessica Stafford, and Tonya Johnson to assist in initiating this effort. The YAM mission is to provide young adults a focused ministry and enable them to apply the principles of Christian living to their everyday lives. Participation was high from its initial kick-off and attendance continues to be strong through its first year.

The Youth Ministry, which caters to teenagers, was turned over to Darrell and Sharnelle Howell, the son and daughter-in-law of Deacons Tom and Vernell Howell, who have been directors since 1983. One year, ten members of Alfred Street's Youth Ministry traveled to Kinston, North Carolina, to participate in an annual youth work camp. The young people, along with approximately 300 others, repaired eighty-four houses that had been damaged by Hurricane Floyd. Also in 2002, three other young people (Jennifer Westbrook, Yanique Moore and John Howard) and Deacon Vernell Howell attended a spiritual work camp in Jamaica, West Indies, for seven days. These international work camps were sponsored by Lott Carey Foreign Missionary Convention, of which Alfred Street is a member. Another of the activities that the Youth Ministry and the congregation looked forward to each year was the Martin Luther King, Jr., ceremony in February. Each year, the youth depicted a different aspect of the Civil Rights era in drama in order to expose the youth to the struggles required to obtain human rights.

The activities the youth were now conducting had been part of the church calendar since the early 1980s. Many of the youth who had participated in these same activities fifteen years prior had now finished college and were returning to Alfred Street as adults in new capacities. Youth from the late 1980s and early 1990s that had returned included Melanie Garrett, Jessica Stafford, and Tonya Johnson who had teamed to assist in starting the Young Adult Ministry (YAM). Keisha DeSandies now sang in the Senior Choir and Charnika Harrell now sang with the Young and Adult Choir. Many other former youth had gone off to law school: Truth Smith, Anne Young, Aisha Johnson, Christopher Cox, Charles Monterio, Jr., and Jason Everett. Other youth from the late 1980s had studied in fields related to medicine: Kimberly Perkins, Tiy Smith, Jennifer Wallace, Kimberly Wallace, and Krystal Archer. Chrystal was married at the church in the summer of 2002, as several of the other former youth had been.

The Old Saints

As these youth and former youth were beginning new careers, a constant at Alfred Street Baptist Church in each of the decades since its founding has been the funeralizing of the old saints. The church had been burying its older members since at least 1814 when Nelson Healy, Nelly (Mason's), Rose Grant, and Phebe Hall were laid to rest most likely in the old Penny Hill Cemetery, first opened in 1796.

Beginning in the early 1990s, in addition to individual funerals, each year during the month of May, the church honored all persons from the congregation who passed during the previous year in a special ceremony. The number of persons honored each year has increased significantly since the arrival of Reverend Peterson. In late 1960, there were perhaps three or four persons a year. By 1998, there were ten persons honored and seventeen in 1999. The number of persons passing began to increase gradually as the baby boomer generation entered the window of vulnerability. In 2001, ten persons were honored during a special service on Sunday, May 27, 2001. In 2002, another ten persons were honored on May 26. Those honored during these years are listed below.[21]

Persons Honored at Annual Memorial Services

NAME	SUNRISE	SUNSET
Mr. Gillie Jones	—	17 February 2000
Mrs. Margaret Jones	—	11 April 2000
Mrs. Olivia Priscilla James	21 December 1954	22 July 2000
Mrs. Rose Rozetta Mitchell Morris	24 March 1922	30 July 2000
Mrs. Ruby May Butler	28 August 1932	1 August 2000
Mr. Clarence Luther Anderson	6 October 1918	4 September 2000
Mr. Ralph Montgomery Wair	9 April 1931	30 September 2000
Mrs. Arnell Burnett Jones	7 September 1941	24 October 2000
Mr. Alfred Forrest Jackson	28 June 1918	20 November 2000
Master Joseph William Jordan	10 December 1986	6 December 2000
Mr. Alfred Reginald Catlin	18 December 1939	7 January 2001
Mrs. Grace Helena Banks Brooks	20 October 1931	6 February 2001
Mrs. Edith P. Miller	2 September 1923	May 2001
Mr. Carlton R. Willis	17 July 1930	23 June 2001
Mr. Carroll E. Brittan, Jr.	2 February 1940	17 July 2001
Mr. Leo White	3 October 1932	31 July 2001
Mrs. Ada L. Mason-Acker	20 June 1941	11 September 2001
Mrs. Audrey B. Turner	28 October 1927	29 October 2001
Mr. Oliver T. Willis, Sr.	4 July 1910	2 November 2001
Ms. Myra M. Lars	11 March 1941	5 December 2001

Ada Mason-Acker

Among the memorial honorees, perhaps the death that was most unexpected, most untimely, most unexplainable, was that of Sister Ada Mason-Acker. She was killed at the Pentagon during the events of September 11, 2001. On that day, terrorists used loaded airplanes to attack the Twin Towers of the World Trade Center of New York and the Pentagon near Washington, D.C., killing more than 3,000 persons, including 124 at the Pentagon. Ada was the mother of college-aged children and a government employee. She was killed while at work.

Each of the other deaths also seemed untimely. Sister Audrey

Turner, who passed in October 2001, was looking forward with great anticipation to the wedding of her son, who had recently become engaged. But her illness forced the wedding date to be moved up several weeks and was held at her bedside so that she might witness it. Brother Oliver T. Willis, listed near the bottom of the chart, at the age of ninety-one years old, was the oldest male member of this congregation at the time. Several of the deacons had planned to take him Communion over the weekend, but he passed suddenly and their mission was never fulfilled.

Gladys Tancil

In April 2002, Sister DeNita Houston, who was only nineteen years old and a month shy of her twentieth birthday, joined those listed. In June 2002, Brother Harvey Tunstall passed. He had been instrumental in starting the Early Morning Choir, later called the Voices of Triumph, in 1983 and had directed that choir for ten years.

In November 2002, Sister Gladys Quander-Tancil passed at age eighty-one years. Gladys had a great interest in history and in addition to having been one of the preservationists who fought to save the old church in 1980, she assisted with preparing this book on the history of Alfred Street Baptist Church. Gladys had also been the first African-American tour guide at Mount Vernon. She was a direct descendant of Sukey Bay and her daughter Nancy Carter Quander, who were slaves at the Mount Vernon farms when George Washington was still at the estate.[22]

She and the others listed joined a continuing chain of saints who had labored at Alfred Street since 1803 and gone to that great reward. Funeral services for these individuals were generally still held at 11:00 a.m. on a weekday at the church. And at the end of each such ceremony, the congregation continued singing Hymn 542, *When We All Get to Heaven.*

The Bicentennial Approaches

Persons from Alfred Street had now been joining, singing, ushering, and going to that final reward for almost 200 years. Reverend Peterson had long dreamed of a special observance to celebrate these years of worship. He began making those wishes known as early as 1997, when he appointed Deacon Patricia Wallace as chair of a bicentennial celebration following her chairing of his Thirty-Third Pastor's Anniversary. Reverend Peterson also appointed a Core Committee that included Deacon Wallace and Deacons Patricia Johnson, Thomas Howell and Alton Wallace.

The Core Committee solicited volunteers and soon selected several other persons to begin planning. However, most of the early activity consisted of observing similar ceremonies at other local churches. For example, Christ Church, where George Washington and Robert E. Lee had worshipped six blocks from Alfred Street, celebrated their 225th anniversary in 1998 and some committee members attended. Bute Street Baptist Church in Norfolk also celebrated a bicentennial in 2000 and materials were obtained from their celebration for ideas.

The Core Committee considered various formats for the celebration with perhaps the most important issue being the duration of the celebration. Some other churches that were celebrating bicentennials settled for a single weekend of activities. For example, First Baptist Church of Washington, D.C., which had been founded in 1802 by Reverend Jeremiah Moore who was also instrumental in the formation of the early Baptist congregations in Alexandria, elected to have a single weekend of activity in the summer of 2002. Presidents Jimmy Carter and Harry S. Truman had attended there during their terms as president.[23] Other churches such as Bute Street Baptist Church in Norfolk chose an 18-month-long celebration. First Baptist Church of Alexandria, which with Alfred Street Baptist Church constituted the first Baptist assembly in the city of Alexandria, was planning five months of activity, starting at a very low level in January and culminating with a special concert in May 2003 during a weekend of festive activities.

The Core Committee, in concert with Reverend Peterson, settled on a hybrid celebration—not an entire year, yet more than a single weekend of activities. They planned a celebration of about eleven months, culminating with a series of activities during the church's anniversary weekend in November 2003. Plans for the celebration were presented at the mid-year church meeting in 2002.[24]

The long-lead item in the celebration planned for Alfred Street Baptist Church was historical research, and Reverend Peterson appointed Deacon Alton Wallace, the church historian, to chair that effort. This committee was also tasked to write a historical book. The committee, consisting of Carolyn Rowe, Gladys Q. Tancil (deceased), Thomas Howell, Katherine Cain, Joyce Peterson, Reverend Sam Nixon, Reverend Beverly Moses, Guinevere Jones, Margarette Peterson, Wanda Gill, and Sue Briggs, began their efforts in earnest in the summer of 2001. Soon afterwards, the Core Committee developed a theme for the bicentennial celebration. The theme was taken from King David's life and reads: *Two Hundred Years, Yet Not Forsaken.* The passage is from Psalm 37:25, which says: "I have been young, and now am old; yet have I not seen the righteous forsaken, nor his seed begging bread."

Later, a bicentennial logo was developed by Sister Andrea Sargent-Futrell. The logo brought together the old and new aspects of Alfred Street Baptist Church. The logo was a picture of the oldest known representation of the old church and the modern cross that is located in the new sanctuary above the baptismal pool. The seven stars in the sky represent seven pastors called by God to bring light and leadership to the church through those 200 years.[25]

The Bicentennial Logo

As the bicentennial approached, the church held its annual Watch Night Service on New Year's Eve, which included the ordination of a new deacon—Deacon Herbert Harvell. The speaker for the Watch Night Service was Reverend Lawrence Davies of Shiloh Baptist Church in Fredericksburg, Virginia, who has been delivering the Watch Night message at Alfred Street since Reverend Peterson arrived in 1964.

Ordination of Deacon Herb Harvell

At five minutes after midnight, immediately following the annual Watch Night Service, the bicentennial celebration began on January 1, 2003, with a statement by Deacon Patricia Wallace. A Bicentennial Breakfast in the lower level followed the service. The bicentennial year had arrived!

On the following Sunday, January 5, 2003, the church held its annual Installation of Officers at a special 3:00 p.m. service. The guest speaker for the installation was Reverend Dr. John C. Compton from First Baptist Church of Alexandria, and music was provided by the choir from Downtown Baptist Church on Washington Street in Alexandria. Their pastor, Reverend Dale Seley, was also in attendance. Alfred Street Baptist Church, along with these two congregations, had comprised the assembly that in 1803 established the Alexandria Baptist Society, the first Baptist congregation in the city. And so, just as they had in early April of 1803, members of Alfred Street Baptist Church joined again with First Baptist Church and Downtown Baptist Church in worship.

The year-long bicentennial celebration proceeded much as planned. On the first Sunday of January and the third Sunday of each subsequent month, short reenactments of the church's history were presented. These short reenactments were called *Bicentennial Moments.* Each reenactment presented a brief look at blocks of twenty years of history.

An Evangelistic Program formed the cornerstone of the celebration, with the goal of bringing 200 souls to Christ in 2003. This effort involved all members of Alfred Street, whether young or old. In February, a Bicentennial Quilt Project began with participation of all of the ministries and membership groups. This project produced a quilt that depicted the church's history on artistic squares.

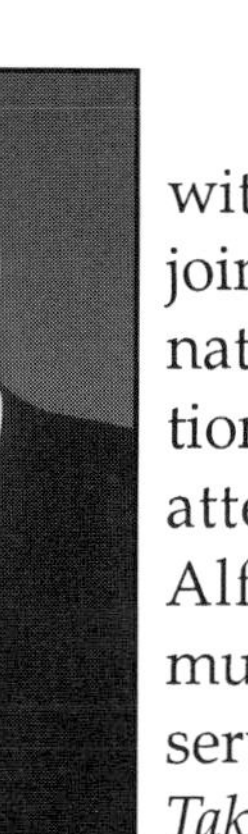

Current Pastors of the Early Baptist Churches

In May, Alfred Street joined with First Baptist Church for a joint worship service that culminated their bicentennial celebration. First Baptist reciprocated by attending a joint worship at Alfred Street in June. Communion was held during each service. In June, the first of three *Taking It to the Streets* campaigns commenced as part of the Evangelistic Program to take the evangelism message to local neighborhoods. Other campaigns were held in August and October. In July, historical tours were held every weekend to tour the old landmarks of the church that included Alfred Street Baptist Church and 25 other sites that are a part of its history. In September, the church held a *Down By the Riverside* worship service with an afternoon of worship, food, and fellowship to experience what it must have been like to worship on the Potomac River banks in the early years.

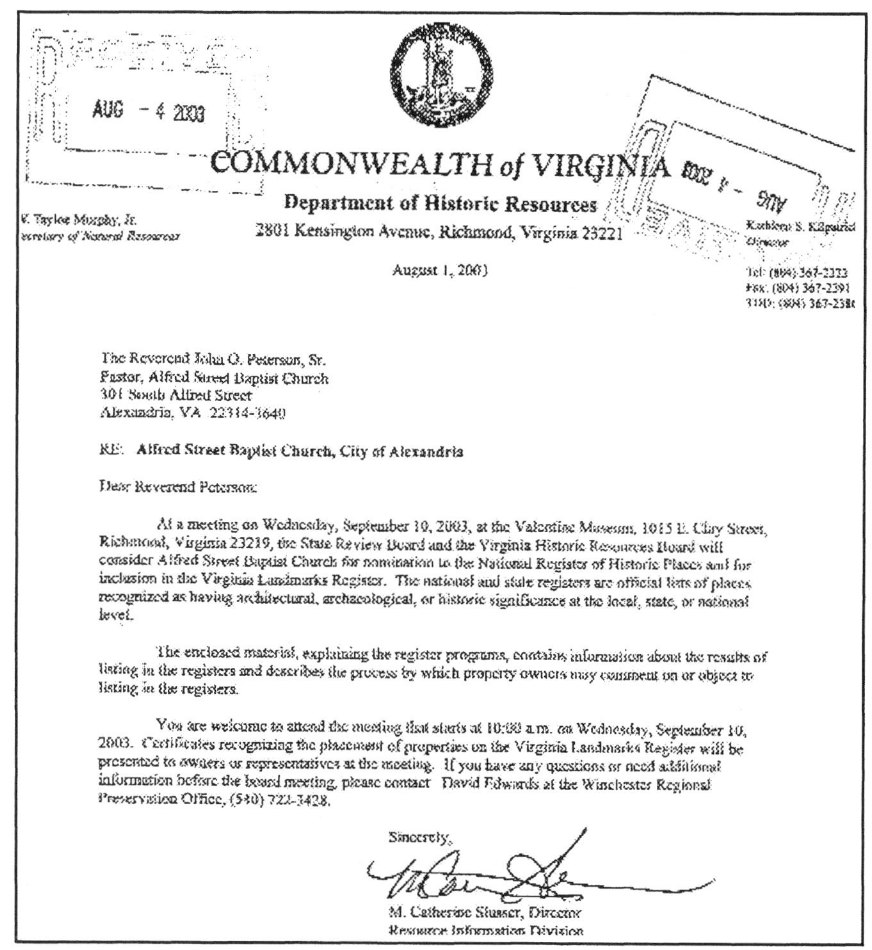

AUG - 4 2003

COMMONWEALTH *of* VIRGINIA

Department of Historic Resources

2801 Kensington Avenue, Richmond, Virginia 23221

W. Tayloe Murphy, Jr.
Secretary of Natural Resources

Kathleen S. Kilpatrick
Director

Tel: (804) 367-2323
Fax: (804) 367-2391
TDD: (804) 367-2386

August 1, 2003

The Reverend John O. Peterson, Sr.
Pastor, Alfred Street Baptist Church
301 South Alfred Street
Alexandria, VA 22314-3640

RE: **Alfred Street Baptist Church, City of Alexandria**

Dear Reverend Peterson:

At a meeting on Wednesday, September 10, 2003, at the Valentine Museum, 1015 E. Clay Street, Richmond, Virginia 23219, the State Review Board and the Virginia Historic Resources Board will consider Alfred Street Baptist Church for nomination to the National Register of Historic Places and for inclusion in the Virginia Landmarks Register. The national and state registers are official lists of places recognized as having architectural, archaeological, or historic significance at the local, state, or national level.

The enclosed material, explaining the register programs, contains information about the results of listing in the registers and describes the process by which property owners may comment on or object to listing in the registers.

You are welcome to attend the meeting that starts at 10:00 a.m. on Wednesday, September 10, 2003. Certificates recognizing the placement of properties on the Virginia Landmarks Register will be presented to owners or representatives at the meeting. If you have any questions or need additional information before the board meeting, please contact David Edwards at the Winchester Regional Preservation Office, (540) 722-3428.

Sincerely,

M. Catherine Slusser, Director
Resource Information Division

Nomination to the National Register of Historic Places

In November, Alfred Street culminated this celebration with several activities that included a prayer breakfast, honoring those members who had been members of this church for fifty or more years or whose families had been in this church for one hundred years or more. An historic marker was dedicated on the grounds near the front of the church to designate Alfred Street Baptist Church a historic site.

This initial recognition by the state of Virginia was the first step in obtaining national recognition of the historical significance of the church. In August of 2003, Alfred Street had been nominated by the state for inclusion on the National Register of Historic Places, the nation's official list of cultural resources worthy of preservation. The nomination review process for national recognition had not been completed by the end of the bicentennial celebration.

In the final weeks of the bicentennial, three of the most anticipated events of the year were held. The Music Department performed a musical extravaganza at the Hylton Chapel, and a bicentennial dinner was held at the Hyatt Regency in Crystal City. The church's history book entitled *I Once Was Young,* researched and written by members of the congregation, was dedicated and distributed to the congregation on Anniversary Sunday as the terminating bicentennial event.

The history just described and that now being written under the current pastor, Reverend John O. Peterson, is but a prologue of the great things that lie ahead for the Alfred Street Baptist Church.

Pastor John O. Peterson

THE END.

****

Epilogue

. . . We've come this far by faith; leaning on the Lord. . . .

The two hundred years just described in the history of the Alfred Street Baptist Church have been characterized by a series of challenges, as well as by a series of contrasts and conflicts. Yet, throughout these two hundred years, the church has survived and prospered.

The church evolved from a small group of twelve white worshippers who were joined in May 1803 by the first black member. For almost fifty years, Alfred Street Baptist Church was conjoined with this white group before they dissolved into two separate Baptist congregations. These two congregations began worshipping at a time when Baptists—neither white nor colored—were considered a substantial religion on a par with their more liturgical counterparts. Yet in 2003, each church has a congregation of approximately 2,500 members, and they are now among the largest churches of any denomination in the city of Alexandria.

Throughout its two-hundred-year history, Alfred Street Baptist Church has witnessed conflict and turmoil. It survived the Civil War with the confiscation and desecration of the church facility. The church saw its membership grow to more than 700 persons during Reconstruction, and then watched it decline to about 180 members during the years of the depression. A full 105 years would pass between its early peak in membership in 1880 and when the church would return to that size in 1985.

The pastors and officials of Alfred Street Baptist Church were not spared challenges either. In the middle of the 19th century, the church chose as its pastor a man who was so well loved that more than 2,000 people attended his funeral, even before the advent of the automobile. That pastor was followed by one to whom the Board of Deacons eventually gave a vote of "no confidence" with the simple proclamation ". . . Your usefulness is at an end."

Contrasts and conflicts also occurred within the congregation. In the early years, membership was taken very seriously. Potential congregants were required to publicly profess their conversion and be voted into membership by the existing congregation. By the time of the church's bicentennial, persons need only ". . . present themselves to a church official. . . ." at anytime during the worship week to become members. In the early years, discussions of sins and personal deportment consumed a large portion of the church's activities. By the 21st century, conflicts over sins were replaced by dissensions among the members over the use of drums, mandolins and other instruments for worship, over parking lots, and over scarce parking spaces in the neighborhoods.

Yet, throughout all these conflicts and contrasts, the church survived. But, not only has it survived, the church has thrived in His service. Alfred Street Baptist Church now has an annual budget of over $3.2 million and more than 40 ministries that provide services to the nation and the world. This growth contrasts with the period during the depression when, on four successive nights of a revival, less than $1 was collected in the general offering. Also, as late as the 1900s, the church was still baptizing new members in the Potomac River near the foot of the Wilson Bridge. In its bicentennial year, baptisms are held indoors in a church complex valued at over $8 million. These two hundred years have surely witnessed constantly changing times.

King David of the Old Testament experienced a similar life of challenges. He, too, survived and flourished. During his lifetime he experienced poverty and wealth, wars and famine, adultery, incest and fratricide. But, through both his youth with its mischief, and later through his agedness with its wisdom, God's faithfulness sustained him.

Through years of turbulence, Alfred Street Baptist Church has also been sustained by God's divine providence. And now that the church has completed two centuries of worship, it, too, can testify as King David did in the 37th Psalm:

I have been young,
And now I'm old.
Yet have I not seen the righteous forsaken,
Nor his seed begging bread.

The Alfred Street Baptist Church congregation looks forward to a third century of toil in His service and, as we move forward, may the grace of our Lord Jesus Christ be with you and with us.

Amen.

Bicentennial Core Committee

Bicentennial Reflections

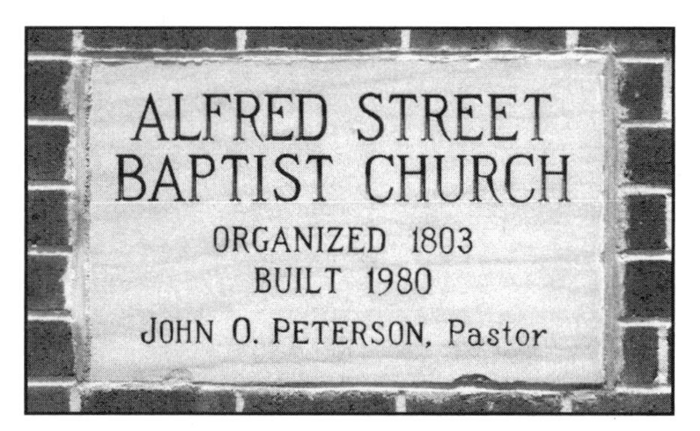

1980 Cornerstone

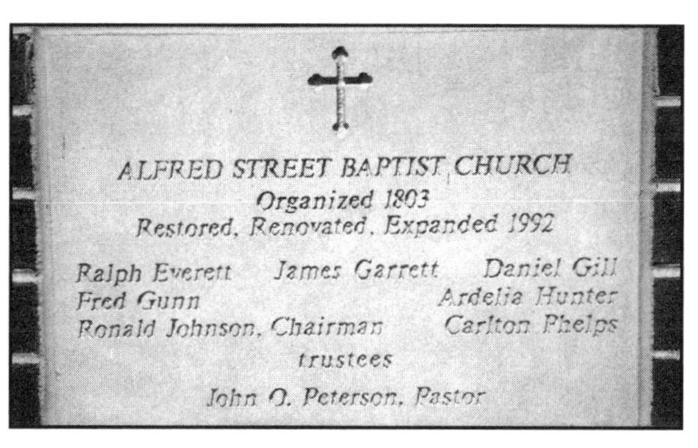

1992 Cornerstone

Bicentennial Breakfast

Downtown Baptist at ASBC

ASBC at First Baptist

Baptist Ministers

HBCU College Fair

ASBC's Gift to Urban League

YAM Choir and Dancers

ASBC Step Team

Women's Day Choir

Women's Day Committee

Men's Day Choir

Father-Son Banquet

Vacation Bible School

Youth Sunday

Ordination of Rev. Hawkins

Adia Blackmon's Trial Sermon

YAAC Reunion Choir

Senior Choir

Children's Church

Sunday School in the Park

Tour Guides

Bethel Cemetery

Charge to Evangelism

Mission to Haiti

Clothes for Mission Project

"Down by the Riverside" Worship

Bicentennial Quilt

Breakfast Honoring 100-Year Families

Musical Extravaganza at Hylton Chapel

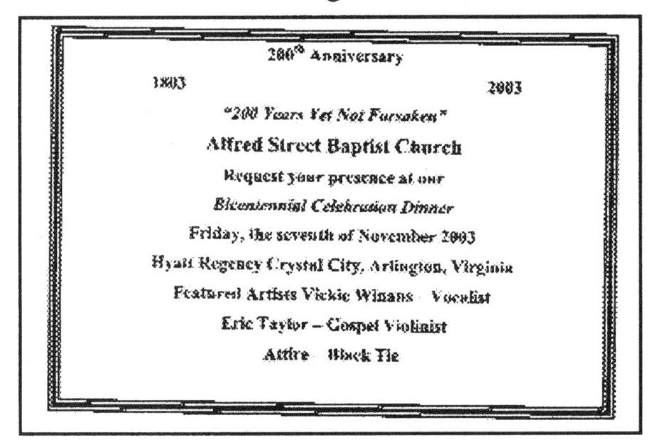

200th Anniversary

1803 2003

"200 Years Yet Not Forsaken"

Alfred Street Baptist Church

Request your presence at our

Bicentennial Celebration Dinner

Friday, the seventh of November 2003

Hyatt Regency Crystal City, Arlington, Virginia

Featured Artists Vickie Winans – Vocalist

Eric Taylor – Gospel Violinist

Attire – Black Tie

Bicentennial Dinner

Appendix A

Timeline of Key Historical Dates

1800–1820

- 1776 American independence from Great Britain
- 1791 Freedom of Religion added to the Bill of Rights.
- 1801 Thomas Jefferson becomes 3rd U.S. president.
- 1803 Louisiana Purchase from France doubles size of U.S. territories.
- 1803 Baptists in Alexandria separate from the Back Lick Baptist Church on Little River Turnpike, forming the ***Alexandria Baptist Society***. (April)
- 1803 Susan Black (or Black Susan) is baptized as first colored member of Alexandria Baptist Society (May).
- 1806 Colored members form ***Colored Baptist Society*** as conjoined church with Alexandria Baptist Society.
- 1810 First Negro minister (Charles) permitted to preach to colored members.
- 1815 Slaves from Mount Vernon join Colored Baptist Society.
- 1818 Members of Colored Baptist Society rent property on Alfred Street at current site. Church has worshipped on same site since 1818.
- 1819 Alexandria Baptist Society (white) granted privilege to Negroes to open their meeting house for worship on Sundays at 313 South Alfred Street.
- 1820 Negroes continue to worship separately and as part of conjoined Alexandria Baptist Society (white).

1820–1840

- 1820 Missouri Compromise admitted slave and free states into Union.
- 1820s Rev. William Evans first assumed leadership/pastoral role of Colored Baptist Society.
- 1830 Nat Turner's Rebellion in South Hampton County, Virginia
- 1831 Near complete shutdown of independent assembly privileges for colored Baptists and Methodists in Alexandria due to above rebellion.
- 1831 Rev. William Evans of Colored Baptist Society and 45 others sign petition from free Negroes to the Mayor asserting that Negroes in Alexandria will not revolt against whites, as did Nat Turner.
- 1830s Mr. Nuthall of Washington, D.C., and other Negroes operate school for free

blacks at Colored Baptist Society meeting house on Alfred Street.

- 1839 Famous Amistad case in which blacks mutinied to take over slave ship.
- 1840 Congress passes Gag Resolution stipulating it will no longer even consider proposals related to slavery issue.

1840–1860

- 1842 Members of Colored Baptist Society purchase site at Alfred Street after 18 years of leasing (September 1).
- 1850 Colored Baptist Society granted complete independence from conjoined Alexandria Baptist Church (white); adopts Alexandria Baptist's Constitution.
- 1850 Membership of newly independent colored assembly numbers 83 persons.
- 1853 Colored Baptist Society seeks membership in Maryland Baptist Union Association, a predominantly white organization.
- 1855 Colored Baptist Society erects new brick church at 313 South Alfred Street site. Church now has 200 members and changes name to First African Baptist Church.
- 1855? Senior Choir formed as first organized choral group.
- 1856 First African Baptist Church accepted into Potomac Baptist Association of Northern Virginia, an organization of white and black churches.
- 1857 Church pays off mortgage on new building in two years. Also pays $250 (total) to various interim preachers. Still no pastor.
- 1859 Rev. William Evans attends American Baptist Mission Convention in New York on behalf of First African Baptist Church. He meets Rev. Sampson White and Minister Samuel Madden—both of whom will pastor at Alfred Street later in the century.
- 1859 Rev. Sampson White arrives as first *bona fide* Negro pastor at First African Baptist Church.
- 1860 Abraham Lincoln elected as Republican president—an event that will eventually lead to war.

1860–1880

- 1861 Abraham Lincoln inaugurated president of the United States (March).
- 1861 Civil War begins in April. First African Baptist Church taken over by Union Soldiers and used as a hospital and recruiting station.
- 1861 Worship services went underground for colored and white churches.
- 1863 Emancipation Proclamation frees slaves in states in rebellion.
- 1863 Rev. Madden receives commission from Executive Mansion (White House) as Union chaplain; arrives as new pastor at First African Baptist Church, replacing Rev. Sampson White.
- 1865 The Civil War ends; slaves freed under 13th Amendment. First African

Baptist Church hosts American Baptist Mission Convention for its 25th anniversary.

- 1870s Reconstruction period begins following war. Numerous black colleges founded.
- 1872 First African Baptist Church ordains Rev. Dr. Harvey Johnson who became a prominent Baptist preacher in Baltimore. Deacons begin taking up Poor Saints offering.
- 1877 Mr. George L. Seaton, a deacon from First African Baptist, serves in the Virginia State Legislature. Earlier, he built two schools for Negroes and founded YMCA in city.
- 1870s Name of church changed from First African to First Colored Baptist Church.
- 1880 Arrival of Jim Crow laws and Black Codes.

1880–1900

- 1880 Membership at Alfred Street reaches a high of almost 700 members.
- 1880 Church organizes Number One Willing Workers' Club to raise funds for construction project.
- 1880s Church begins expansion program on sanctuary in preparation for hosting American Baptist Mission Convention.
- 1883/4 Church hosts convention of American Baptist Mission Society.
- 1880s Rev. Madden establishes Board of Deaconesses, with Catherine McQuay Butler as one of two women who served.
- 1880s Founding of the Mite Society, forerunner of current Department of Missions.
- 1884 Membership declined from high of 700 persons in 1880 to 400 due to the enforcement of rules/by-laws.
- 1888(?) Church changed name from First Colored Baptist Church to Alfred Street Baptist Church to avoid confusion with First Baptist Church (white).
- 1890 Church remodeled.
- 1894 Dr. Albert Johnson, among first Negro doctors in Alexandria, joins Alfred Street Baptist Church; later becomes a deacon.
- 1896 Rev. Madden passes after 33 years as pastor; Rev. Alexander Truatt called as new pastor.
- 1898 Alfred Street Baptist Church joins Northern Virginia Baptist Association—a local organization of colored Baptist churches.

1900–1920

- 1900 Rev. Truatt in fourth year as Pastor of Alfred Street.
- 1900 Church baptism site moved to Battery Rodgers near Wilson Bridge.
- 1900 Dedication of stained glass window of Rev. Madden in choir room.

- 1901 Alfred Street joins Lott Carey Baptist Foreign Mission Convention.
- 1906 Federal government settles claim over use of church as hospital in Civil War.
- 1907 First permanent ushers (men) appointed at church.
- 1910 Church hosts annual meeting of Northern Virginia Baptist Association.
- 1911 New set of rules/by-laws approved for Christian living.
- 1912 First Church Anniversary held as fund-raiser for winter fuel. Anniversary assumed a start date for church of 1852.
- 1913 Rev. Truatt resigns as pastor after 17 years.
- 1913/4 Rev. George O. Dixon serves as Supply Pastor during interim.
- 1914 Rev. W.H.R. Powell arrives as new pastor.
- 1915 Church joins Virginia Baptist State Convention, a statewide association of black churches.
- 1915 Federal government finally pays Alfred Street $900 for use in Civil War.
- 1915 Rev. Powell weds Miss Oscelletta Davies of Lynchburg, Virginia.
- 1916 Former pastor, Rev. Alexander Truatt, passes.
- 1917 Country enters World War I.
- 1917 Rev. Powell builds parsonage and moves his family in at 816 Queen Street.
- 1917 Alfred Street opens lending library of 1,600 volumes in church to serve colored community of Alexandria.
- 1918 Entire Powell family quarantined in parsonage during Spanish Flu epidemic that killed over 550,000 persons nationwide—ten times more than killed in the war.
- 1919 World War I ends.
- 1920 Rev. Powell departs as pastor after five years at age of 34.

1920–1940

- 1920 Rev. Andrew Warren Adkins arrives as new pastor.
- 1921 Rev. Adkins begins teaching first high school classes at Parker-Gray School; previously no high school classes for Negroes in the city.
- 1926 New church organ dedicated in special ceremony.
- 1926 First reported church Homecoming ceremony in fall of the year.
- 1928 Rev. George O. Dixon passes, Supply Pastor during 1913/14.
- 1929 Great Depression begins with big drop in stock market.
- 1932 Size of church membership reaches low of 185 members—down from 700 in the 1880s.
- 1932 Junior Church, predecessor to current Youth Department, formed by Mrs. Adkins.
- 1933 Pastor's Aide formed by Mrs. Martha Miller, first president.
- 1934 First reported Women's Day; was also a $1 Rally to raise funds.
- 1934 Church celebrated 113th anniversary; assumed start date of 1821.
- 1934 Junior Choir (predecessor to Gospel Inspirers) served during summer months when Senior Choir was on vacation.

- 1935 Church celebrates Rev. Adkins' 15th anniversary, and Re-Opening Ceremony following construction project that closed church.
- 1936 Parker-Gray High School, where high school classes initially taught by Rev. Adkins, finally accredited and graduated its first high school class.

1940–1960

- 1940 Rev. Adkins celebrates 20th anniversary.
- 1941 World War II begins after bombing of Pearl Harbor.
- 1945 Baptist Training Union (BTU) organized at Alfred Street.
- 1945 Men's Club organized—predecessor to current Men's Department.
- 1945 World War II ends; soldiers begin returning to Alfred Street.
- 1948 Church celebrated 115th anniversary, with assumed start date of 1833.
- 1948 Church purchases lot adjacent to church on old tombstone lot for $10,000; pays off in four years.
- 1950 Church celebrates Rev. Adkins' 30th anniversary.
- 1956 Church celebrates 150th Anniversary with 1806 assumed start date.
- 1959 Young and Adult Choir of ten members organized by Ardelia Hunter.
- 1959 Barbara Jackson (McDowell), an Alfred Street youth, becomes part of lawsuit to integrate area schools, ending Virginia's Massive Resistance school segregation campaign.
- 1960 Church celebrates Rev. Adkins' 40th anniversary as pastor.

1960–1980

- 1962 Church begins plans for new education wing to be called Andrew W. Adkins Educational Annex on lot adjacent to church.
- 1963 Rev. Adkins passes after 43 years as pastor; Deacon William Willis serves as church administrator for 14 months.
- 1964 Male Ensemble organized—predecessor to Male Chorus.
- 1964 Rev. John O. Peterson elected new pastor in September; installed in February 1965.
- 1965 Deaconesses reinstituted after 70-year hiatus. Six women consecrated in first group.
- 1965 Church joins Baptist World Alliance.
- 1966 Membership Groups instituted to reorganize congregation. Average church attendance on Sunday around 105 persons.
- 1966 Rev. Peterson appoints Planning and Survey Committee to explore building options for new church. Purchases lot at rear of church.
- 1976 Junior Choir resurrected as Little Acorns; precursor to Gospel Inspirers.
- 1968 Dr. Martin Luther King assassinated; little violence in Alexandria.
- 1970 Church celebrated 167th anniversary; first use of 1803 as start date.
- 1970 Church budget now at $17,000; up from $12,000 at Rev. Peterson's arrival.

- 1977 Pastor suffers heart attack; stops teaching in public schools and assumes preaching as sole profession.
- 1979 Rev. Peterson ordains Deaconess Mary Wair as first female deacon at Alfred Street; church expelled from local associations.
- 1980 Construction begins on new church after 18-year wait.
- 1980 Major internal disagreement within congregation over whether or not to tear down the old church.

1980–2003

- 1980 Church membership numbers 504 congregants.
- 1981 March-in ceremony to new church, followed by 40 nights of dedication.
- 1983 Major influx of Maryland residents; ten new deacons ordained to keep up with growth.
- 1984 New 8 a.m. Sunday service started.
- 1985 Church budget of $300,000; membership up to 1,200 persons.
- 1986 Growth requires larger sanctuary; pastor appoints Expansion, Parking and Renovation Committee.
- 1986 Church honors pastor with 22nd anniversary celebration.
- 1989 Church honors pastor with 25th anniversary celebration.
- 1991 Rev. Peterson ordains nine female deacons from among deaconesses.
- 1992 Church begins construction to enlarge church complex.
- 1993 Church establishes Policy and Procedures and Budget Process Committees to revise existing church policies.
- 1994 Church approves new Constitution and Budget Process to provide additional administrative controls.
- 1994 March-in ceremony to expanded church complex; 40 nights of dedication follow.
- 1996 First new set of church officers (e.g., trustees) installed under new constitution. Church budget at $1.8 million.
- 1997 Pastor suffers a stroke; absent from pulpit for four months.
- 1997 Church celebrates Rev. Peterson's 33rd anniversary.
- 1997 Mortgage Elimination Program started to pay off mortgage on new sanctuary complex.
- 2000 President William J. Clinton attends 8 a.m. worship service.
- 2001 Many new ministries started (e.g., YAM, AIDS); now 40 ministries total.
- 2001 Church celebrates Homecoming after 40-year hiatus.
- 2001 Church burns mortgage during 198th church anniversary celebration.
- 2003 Bicentennial (1803–2003) celebration begins on January 1, 2003.

Appendix B

Key Historical Church Officials

(NOTE: Dates are when individual was *installed,* or *first reference* found in minutes)

Pastors

Name	Years/Period
William Evans *(Leader)*	1820s–1859
Sampson White	1859–1863
Samuel L. Madden	1863–1896
Alexander Truatt	1896–1913
George O. Dixon *(Supply Pastor)*	1913–1914
W.H.R. Powell	1914–1920
Andrew Warren Adkins	1920–1964
John O. Peterson	1964–present

Ministers Licensed By Church

Name	Year
Charles Thomas	1810
Jesse Henderson	1815
William Evans	1820s
...	...
Harvey Johnson	1872
Wilson Gordon	1873
Lawrence Laws	1873
A.A. Lott	1880s
George O. Dixon	1899
Henry Tyler	1901
J.A. Hickerson	1903
Albert Price	1903
J.T. Diamond	1903
John Chase	1912
Rev. W.A. Price	1913
Wilbur Brown	1928
W.T. Henry	1934
....	...
Charles H. Wilson	1970
Robert E. King	1979
Elbert Ransom, Jr.	1980
Albert F. Blue	1980
Doris W. Ashton	1980
Faye S. Gunn	1982
James P. Ashton	1984
Robert L. Easter	1985
Ruth Harvey	1986
Kim Coleman	1989
Minnie D. Davis	1989
Samuel Nixon	1989
Carl H. Hall	1996
Kevin Norton	1996
Edward Jackson	1996
Mary Murphy	1996
Beverly Moses	1997
Marla C. Hawkins	2001
Adia Blackmon	2003

Deacons

Name	Year
...	...
Pompey Jackson	...
George L. Seaton	1878
J. Webster	1885
Albert Johnson, M.D.	1895
Rev. George O. Dixon	1899
John R. Smith	1899
Griffin Brooks	
Beverly Diggs	
Robert Palmer	...
Wellington Thomas	
Emanuel Webster	...
Daniel Corbin	...
William Scroggins	1901
Phillip Johnson	1901
Brother Range	1901
Edward O. Dixon, Sr.	1901
Major Johnson	1901
Luke Raines	1901
James Johnson	1901
Henry C. Boyd	1908
Robert Burke, Sr.	1908
George Carroll	1908
Marshall Carroll	1908
Brother Legrange	1908
Rev. W.A. Price	1912
Stephen Blue	1914
Robert Palmer	1914
Jerry Barrett	1926
Walter A. Butler	1930
Robert F. Quander	1930
Henry F. Burke	1930
Warren M. Wair	1933
John Cole	1935
William Russell	1935
George Hurbert Turner	1935
Milton Grossner	1935
Milton Franklin	1935
William Hansborough	1935

Name	Year
Hezekiah Goffney	1940
Sherman Majors	1940
Samuel Turner	1940
William Turner	1940
Charles C. Burruss, Sr.	1940
William C. Dickerson	1940
Robert Owens, Sr.	1942
John E. Strange	1942
Fred H. Rich	1948
Elvin E. Smith	1948
Ralph M. Wair	1963
Richard M. Wair	1963
William Willis	1963
Joseph Burless	1963
Charles Henry Wilson	1963
Wilbert P. Harris	1964
James T. Neal	1967
Theodore Lee	1967
Dr. James S. Burton	1968
Charles Butler	1971
Robert Butler	1973
Walter Payne	1973
Welton A. Quander	1973
Lenzy Robertson	1973
Mary W. Wair	1979
Oliver Hutchinson	1981
Willie Lazenby	1981
James W. Johnson	1983
Patricia Johnson	1983
Rogers Davis	1983
James F. Garrett	1983
Thomas H. Howell	1983
Garland Tanks	1983
Isaiah P. Morrison	1983
Frank Heard	1983
David Rollins	1983
Francis E. Crawford	1983
Moses Erkins	1984
Leo A. Brooks	1985

Deacons

Name	Year	Name	Year
James E. Gladden	1985	Gilbert Mays	1995
Robert Cosby	1986	Lucille P. Day	1996
Alton S. Wallace	1988	Karen Y. DeSandies	1996
James L. Scott	1988	Dave Evans	1996
Lionel A. Martin	1990	Vernell P. Howell	1996
Charles J. Monterio	1990	Elizabeth C. Middough	1996
Grace I. Albritton	1991	Earl W. Stafford	1996
Ellen Anderson	1991	George Sykes	1996
Helen F. Crawford	1991	Winston H. Gaskins, Jr.	1997
Bessie W. Johnson	1991	Earl Brown	1997
Alfred Jones	1991	Robert L. Bogan	1997
Betty J. Jones	1991	Patricia L. Wallace	1999
Grace T. Joseph	1991	Lawrence Clark	1999
Barbara P. Keller	1991	Johnnie Brown	1999
Alvina G. Scott	1991	Willard Jasper	1999
Eva R. Simmons	1991	Alphonso L. Hall	2000
Wally King	1991	Lottie B. Hall	2001
S. Levi Pearson	1992	Herbert Harvell	2002
Charlie Amos	1995	Gilbert A. Knowles	2003

Deaconesses

Name	Year	Name	Year
...	...	Barbara Keller	1971
Catherine McQuay Butler	1890s	Katherine Lazenby	1972
...	...	Edith Elliot	1972
Laura McPhail	1964	Margaret Neal	
Mazie Bouden	1964	Edith Miller	
Ruth Dade	1964	Patricia Buster	1981
Juanita Wilson	1964	Doris Tanks	1981
Ulysses Jackson	1964	Annette Thomas	1981
Mattie Owens	1966	Edith Reeves	1981
Anna Lee	1966	Jacqueline Henry-Green	1983
Sarah McMillan	1966	Gloria Gibson	1983
Alberta Willis	1966	Julia Woodward	1983
Pearl Willis (Honorary)	1966	Emma Waller	1983
Maggie Butler	1971	Lucille Day	1983
Mary Wair	1971	Elizabeth Ampey	1983
Louise Harris	1971	Grace Joseph	1983
Emma Willis	1971	Ellen Anderson	1983

Deaconesses

Name	Year	Name	Year
Helen Crawford	1983	Eva Simmons	1988
Elizabeth Middough	1984	Alvina Scott	1988
Bessie Johnson	1986	Karen DeSandies	1988
Mercedes Morrison	1986	Vernell Howell	1988
June Monterio	1986	Amanda Stafford	1990
Betty Jones	1986	Grace Albritton	1990
Margaret Young	1986		

(NOTE: Position terminated in 1996 under new Constitution.)

Trustees

Name	Year	Name	Year
Jesse Henderson	1818	George Turner	1926
Evans William	1818	Fred H. Rich	1926
Daniel Taylor	1818	Walter Butler	1926
William Evans	1820s	Jerry Barrett	1926
Beverly Yates	1845	Rev. W.A. Price	1926
William Weaver	1845	Wilbur Brown	1931
James Webster	1845	Samuel Turner	1932
...	...	Milton Franklin	1935
James Ross	1899	Milton Grossner	1935
Rev. Edward P. Dixon	1901	Marion Butler	1948
Robert Gains	1905	Coulter Willis	1948
W.A. Price	1905	John Strange	1948
Stephen M. Pritchett	1905	Rosier Thompson	1948
Beverly Diggs	1905	Henry Brooks	1948
James Ross	1905	Marion Thomas	1948
Emanuel J. Webster	1905	Theodore Lee	1948
James Buchner	1905	Richard P. Poole, Sr.	1945
Henry Brooks	...	Welton A. Quander	1947
Robert Palmer	1905	Wesley B. Whitmore	1950
Peter Price		Julian Dove	1960
Walter Stanton		Leon Ferguson	1960
Roland Williams		Roland Williams	1960
William Waugh		Ernest Carroll	1967
William K. Lee	1907	Harry S. Burke	1967
Robert Burke	1908	Carlton A. Funn	1968
Robert Palmer	1914	Thelma Wair	1970
William Stanard	1926	Roger C. Anderson	1978

Trustees

Name	Year	Name	Year
Lenzy M. Robinson	1978	Zenobia Gardner-Anderson	1992
Julian Dove	1978	Fred Gunn	1994
Garland Tanks	1981	Marla C. Hawkins	1994
James F. Garrett	1984	Helen T. McCoy	1996
Evangeline N. Robinson	1984	Henry Thompson, Sr.	1996
Russell Peterson	1985	Joseph Nickens, Sr.	1996
Ardelia M. Hunter	1985	James L. McNeil	1997
Ralph Everett	1986	Clinton L. Evans	1997
Ronald C. Johnson	1986	Larry L. Simmons	1998
Carlton Phelps, Sr.	1988	Wilburt L. Jenkins	2002
Alfred L. Barrett	1988		
Daniel R. Gill	1992		

Treasurers

Name	Year	Name	Year
Robert Burke	1904	Corinne Pouncy	1964
James Johnson		Roberta H. Quander	1978
Samuel Turner	1932	Evangeline N. Robinson	2000
Richard Poole	1945	Roberta H. Quander	2002

Clerks

Name	Year	Name	Year
H.B. Diggs	1895	Roger Thompson	1940
James M. Buchner	1899	Vernon Carrol	1950
Edward O. Dixon	1902	Thelma Wair	1952
Jesse J. Madden	1904	Hester Willis	1954
F.H. Rich	1911	Marie T. Boyd	1956
J.A. Wooten	1913	Theodore Lee	1963
Richard Hollinger	1925	Jacqueline Neal	1968
Hattie F. Parker	1926	Remell T. Lomax	1970
Thelrecia B. Dean		Elwell Lewis	1978
George P. Douglas		Gloria J. Gibson	1980
James C. Tancil		Irma R. Davis	1984
Warren M. Wair		Blanche Hutchinson	1996
Robert N. Whiting		Renee L. DeSandies	1998
William Weaver		Mattie E. Bynum	2002

Sextons

Name	Year	Name	Year
Martha Parker	1890	Benjie Burke	1940
Louise Tyler	1932	Joyce Whitmore	1950
Carlton H. Tyler	1937	Charles Butler	1970

(NOTE: Was elective church position until circa 1975, when janitors assumed functions)

Sunday School Superintendents

Name	Year	Name	Year
G.W. Simms	1873	Charles Henry Wilson	1962
Claude Lane		Wilbert Harris	1970
Attorney J. Edmond Hill		Robert Butler	1975
Henry C. Boyd	1896	James Johnson	1980
Rev. George O. Dixon	1899	Paulette Gray	1988
W.A. Price	1900	George Sykes	1992
Martha Miller	1925	Charles Monterio	1994
Richard Poole	1931	Winston Gaskins	1997
Milton Turner	1956	Charles Monterio	1999
Joseph Burless	1958		

Senior Choir Directors

Name	Year	Name	Year
Rev. Jacquelyn Strange	1860s	Aldrich W. Adkins	1950
James Buckner	1905	Coultaemae Willis-Wilson	1953
Henry Buckner		Benjie Burke	
Edgar J. Johnson		Elinor Winston	
Richard Brooks	1915	Jacqueline Henry-Green	1966
Walter Butler	1925	Joyce Garrett	2000
Coulter Willis			

Teenage Choir/Little Acorns

Name	Year	Name	Year
Unknown	1934	Edwin Sanders	
....	...	Eleanor Major	
Jacqueline Henry-Green	1956	Mildred Harper	
...	...	Mary and Richard Wair	1970
Willie Mae Wormley	1967	Ellen McCord	
Doris Ashton		Harriett Westbrook	1976
Barbara Austin		Joyce Garrett	1979
Margaret Brown		Edward Vinson	
Richard Payne		Mark Prioleau	1985

Young and Adult Choir

Name	Year	Name	Year
Marrietta O'Neal	1956	Ellen McCord	1974
Joseph Lucas	1965	Joyce Garrett	1981
Ellen McCord	1968	Mark Prioleau	1997
Harriett Westbrook	1972		

Children's Choir/Junior Gospel Inspirers/King's Kids

Name	Year	Name	Year
Marietta O'Neal	1956	Harriett Westbrook-Smith	1979
...	...	...	...
Dr. James Burton	1970	Doris B. Winstead	1985
...	...	Gilbreta Ashton-Jones	2000

Men's Choir/Male Chorus

Name	Year	Name	Year
Claude Green	1964	Harvey Tunstall	1972
Ellen McCord	1968	Alma O. Upshaw	1984
Elwood Lewis	1972	Harriett Westbrook-Smith	1989

Voices of Triumph (VOT)

Name	Year	Name	Year
Harvey Tunstall	1984	Eugene Harper	1990
Samuel Wilkins	1984	Keith A. Perkins	1995
Doris Hall	1985	Theron E. Johnson	1998

Handbell Choir

Name	Year	Name	Year
Elbert Ransom	1989	Keith Perkins	1998
Keith Perkins	1990	Gregory Winstead	2001
Gregory Winstead	1991	Harriett Westbrook-Smith	2003

Appendix C

Officers of the Alfred Street Baptist Church

(Taken from Church's Installation Program)

–2003–

Rev. John O. Peterson, Senior Pastor
Rev. Faye S. Gunn, Assistant to the Pastor
Rev. Edward Jackson, Special Assistant

Office Staff

Jacqueline H. Lewis
Brenda E. Farrare
Rosette T. Graham
Opoku Boamah
Sybil R. Marshall
Tamara L. Smith
Raymond M. Bell
Garry High
Suzanne J. Hailstalk

Ministry of Deacons

James W. Johnson, Chairman
Isaiah P. Morrison, Vice Chairman
William M. Willis, Senior Deacon

Grace I. Albritton
Robert L. Bogan
Leo A. Brooks
Johnnie Brown
Lawrence Clark
Francis E. Crawford
Helen F. Crawford
Karen Y. DeSandies
James F. Garrett
Winston H. Gaskins, Jr.
James E. Gladden
Alphonso L. Hall
Lottie B. Hall
Thomas H. Howell
Vernell P. Howell
Willard Jasper
Bessie W. Johnson
Patricia Johnson
Betty J. Jones
Grace T. Joseph
Barbara P. Keller
Gilbert Knowles
Lionel A. Martin
Elizabeth C. Middough
Charles J. Monterio
S. Levi Pearson
Charles Perkins
Welton A. Quander
James L. Scott
Eva R. Simmons
Earl W. Stafford
George Sykes
Mary W. Wair
Richard M. Wair
Alton S. Wallace
Patricia L. Wallace

Ministry of Trustees

Clinton Evans, Chairman

Zenobia Garner-Anderson
Joseph E. Nickens
Helen T. McCoy

Wilburt Jenkins
Larry L. Simmons
Henry Thompson, Sr.

Ronald C. Johnson, Vice Chairman
Marla C. Hawkins

Treasurer
Roberta Quander

Financial Secretary
Evangeline N. Robinson

Assistant Financial Secretary
Patricia Lawrence

Clerk
Mattie Bynum

1st Assistant Clerk
Sandria Scott

2nd Assistant Clerk
Edda Carter

Nominating Committee
Deloris Baskfield
Patricia Buster
Jeanine Grain
Phyllis W. Holloway
Virgil Lewis
Clarence Miller
Al Phillips
Al Stokes
Ethel Underwood

Budget Committee
Karen L. Croom (Chair)
Helen Catlin
Tanya J. Green
Jacqueline S. Henderson
Wilbert Jenkins
Robin G. McCoy
Nancy Myrick
Lebaron K. Reid
Beverly Hatton
Thomas Langhorne
Robert Bogan
Eva Simmons
Willard Jasper
Zenobia Gardner-Anderson
Henry Thompson

Personnel Committee
Rita J. Womack (Chair)
James Johnson
Isaiah Morrison
Clinton Evans
Ronald Johnson
Otis Langford
Deidre Stokes Miles
Zenobia Gardner-Anderson

Records Committee
Lamanthia Barfield-Roberts
Raynard Bolding
Ardelia Hunter
Youner McLeod
Manie Woodard

Discipleship Group #2

President	Sandra Barrett
Vice President	Queen Carroll
Secretary	Sue Briggs

Discipleship Group #3

President	Walter Howard
Vice President	Bettie L. Applewhite
Secretary	Michael Jackson
Treasurer	Thomas O. Langhorne Jr.
Chaplain	Allison Hendrix
Reporters	Walter Howard; Bettie L. Applewhite

Discipleship Group #4

President	Mark Morris
Vice President	Aretha Cunningham
Secretary	Sandra Ford

Discipleship Group #5

President	Norman Moore
Vice President	Jim Carter
Secretary	Peggy Drain
Missions Coord.	Marentha Moore
Activities Coord.	Edda Carter

Discipleship Group #6

President	Phyllis W. Holloway
Vice President	Kelly Clarke
Secretary	Frances Williams
Assistant Sec.	Wendell Chesson
Chaplain	John Williams

Discipleship Group #7

President	Mary Armstrong
Vice President	Dean Boseman
Secretary	Marva Evans
Benevolent Treas.	Morine Blake

Discipleship Group #8

President	Regina Howard
Vice President	Verna Payne
Secretary	Alexis Howard
Treasurer	Beth Howard

Discipleship Group #9

President	Dolton Nicholas
Vice President	Charles Slade
Secretary	Ray Wilson
Treasurer	Kenneth Knight

Discipleship Group #10

President	Michael Tucker
Vice President	Hal Walls
Secretary	Lorraine Ward
Treasurer	Larry Sherrod

Discipleship Group #11

President	Barbara McDowell
Vice President	Susan Hailstalk
Secretary	Beverly Ferguson
Chaplain	David Toliver

Discipleship Group #12

President	Phyllis Coleman
Vice President	Kenneth DeSandies
Secretary	Jacqualine Stewart
Treasurer	Patricia Smith

Discipleship Group #13

President	Iva Richey
Secretary	Anita Richmond
Treasurer	Erika Richey-Jackson
Missions Coord.	Jackie Skinner
Bereavement	Walter Washington

Discipleship Group #14

President	Alvah T. Beander
Vice President	Cherie Halyard
Secretary	Debbie Crawford
Treasurer	Shirley Jackson
Chaplain	Joseph Blunt

Discipleship Group #15

President	Rose Free
Vice President	Rosetta Jeter
Secretary	Anita Lockett
Assistant Sec.	Mamie Woodard

Discipleship Group #16

President	Erroll Moore
Vice President	Angela Moore
Secretary	Janice Kendall

Discipleship Group #17

President	Leroy Miles
Vice President	Lewis Heffner
Secretary	Wendy Williams

Discipleship Group #18

President	Jacqueline P. Lewis
Vice President	Lillian Coleman
Secretary	Teresa Johnson

Discipleship Group #19

President	Olwin Burke
Vice President	Larry Poole
Chaplain	Sherman White, Sr.

Discipleship Group #20

President	Moses C. Brooks
Vice President	Walter C. Kelly Jr.
Secretary	Myrtis Gant
Treasurer	Pamela Shavers
Hospitality Comm.	Fairfax Davis
Membership	Linda Scott
Remembrance	Patricia Buster
Chaplain	Isabelle Smith

Discipleship Group #21

President	Jeffrey Owens
Vice President	Selwyn Cox
Secretary	Rosalind Brooks
Hospitality	Shirley McQueen
Chaplain	Lawrence Clarke

Discipleship Group #23

President	Philip Lacy
Vice President	David Todd Myrick
Secretary	Betty Brown
Treasurer	Maria Farmer
Chaplain	Leslie Roberts

Discipleship Group #24

President	Bernard Poindexter
Vice President	Lillie Langley-Glover
Secretary	Eunice W. Chege
Treasurer	Jacqueline S. Henderson
Chaplain	Kevin Price

Discipleship Group #25

President	Jackie M. Taylor
Vice President	Reda Broadnax
Secretary/Treas.	Debra Lilley
Hospitality Chair	Evelyn Graham
Chaplain	Janet Gardner

Discipleship Group #26

President	James Berry
Vice President	Walt Winston
Secretary	Rebecca Knight
Chaplain	Rita Womack

Discipleship Group #27

President	Alice P. Mosely
Vice President	Dale Gray
Secretary	Anginette Jordan
Treasurer	Barbara Cox
Program Chair	Mary King
Hospitality Chair	Trudy William

Discipleship Group #28

President	Quanda Finch
Vice President	Ronald Pompey
Chaplain	Eva Barker

Discipleship Group #29

President	Ron Simmons
Vice President	Sandra Leftwich

Discipleship Group #30

President	Charles William
Vice President	Tara Melvin
Secretary	Barbara Sanders
Chaplain	Charles Sanders

HIV/AIDS Ministry

President	Roslyn Hoover

Men's Ministry

President	Monte Richards
Vice President	Mike Laidlaw
Vice President	Bill Haymon
Vice President	Terrill Garrison
Secretary	Dennis Dunston
Assistant Secretary	James Ross
Chaplain	Charles Davis
Assistant Chaplain	Ed Smith

Missions Ministry

President	Amanda Stafford
Vice President	Katherine Washington
Secretary	Catherine Jan Jones
Treasurer	Morine Blake
Chaplain	Georgianna Covington

Drama Ministry

Co-President	Jean Davis
Co-President	Louise Harrell
Vice President	Ardith Collins
Secretary	Stacey Davis
Treasurer	Ethel Underwood
Chaplain	Rev. Samuel Nixon
Public Relations	Catherine Jan Jones
Public Relations	Reba Barnes

Guest Transportation

President	John Watson

Health Wellness Ministry

Director	Dr. Kenneth DeSandies
Secretary	Linda Woods

Helping Hands for Caregivers Ministry

President	Lavinia Cohen
Vice President	Suzanne Hailstalk
Secretaries	Cynthia Jackson, Karen Croom
Chapel	Dea. Welton Quander
Publicity Chair	Mary Brown

Junior Youth Ministry

President	Brandi Doswell
Vice President	Malcolm Montgomery
2nd Vice President	Alexandria Collins
Secretary	Jaleesa McCallum
Chaplain	Raven Bobing
Co-Chaplain	Kevin Price

Pastor's Aid Ministry

President	Sandra Leftwich
Vice President	Barbara McDowell
Secretary	Youner McLeod
Assistant Secretary	Janice Harrison
Treasurer	Barbara Cox
Chaplain	Catherine Jan Jones
Benevolent Comm.	Regina Howard

Senior Youth Ministry

President	
Chaplain	Mia Richards

Shepherding Ministry

President	Tracy Bunch

Young Adult Ministry

Co-President	Heidi Jackson
Co-President	Melanie Garrett
Secretary	Jennifer Lewis
Treasurer	Ron Pompey
Historian	Stacey Davis

Gospel Inspirers

President	Ashlee Ealy
Vice President	Maria Strong
Secretary	Brittany Bolden
Chaplain	Lauren Haymon
Librarian	Javai Evans
Historian	Lauren Burke

Handbell Choir

Director	Harriet Smith
President	Grace Joseph
Vice President	Brenda Lambert
Secretary	Sanita Walker-Resper
Treasurer	Henry Thompson Sr.
Chaplain	Barbara Driggins
Librarian	Aretha Cummingham
Publicity	Joyce Peterson

Male Chorus

President	Leslie Roberts
Vice President	Lloyd Scott
Secretary	George Walton
Treasurer	Lamont Bessick
Chaplain	Charlie Williams

Senior Choir

President	Jane Cotton
Vice President	Bobby Gentry
Secretary	Marantha Moore
Assistant Secretary	Emma Brittan
Treasurer	Amanda Stafford
Chaplain	Grace Albritton
Ombudsman	William Brown

Voices of Triumph

President	Dianne Williams
Vice President	Carol Womack
Secretary	Catherine Vaughn
Assistant Secretary	Carolyn Haymon
Chaplain	Deacon Willard Jasper

Young & Adult Choir

President	Eileen Wilson
Vice President	Jean Morris
Secretary	Sandria Scott
Treasurer	Claudette Smith
Chaplain	James Carter

Junior Ushers Ministry

President	Briana Haymon
Secretary	Lauren Haymon
Chaplain	Blake Bynum

Men Ushers Ministry

President	Edward Thomas
1st Vice President	Joseph Nickens
Secretary	Ardith Collins
Treasurer	David Miller
Activity Chair	Clarence Miller
Chaplain	George Sykes

Women Ushers Ministry

President	Loretta Thompson
Vice President	Joyce L. Johnson
Secretary	Verna Payne
Assistant Secretary	Rachel Gregory
Treasurer	Jacqueline Henderson
Assistant Treas.	Sandra Carrington
Chaplain	Rethon Sykes
Program Coord.	Barbara McDowell

Year 2003 Appointed Positions

Bicentennial Committee
Deacon Patricia Wallace, Chairperson
Deacon Alton Wallace, Co-chairperson
Deacon Patricia Johnson, Secretary
Deacon Thomas Howell, Chaplain

Board of Christian Education Ministry
Deacon Francis Crawford, Chairperson

Boarder Babies & Family Services Ministry
Deacon Johnny Brown, Layleader

Children's Church Ministry
Deacon Mary W. Wair, Director

Church Attorney
Kenneth O. Bynum, Esquire

Decorating Committee
Amanda Stafford, Chairperson
Deacon Vernell Howell,
1st Co-chairperson
Deacon Grace Albritton,
2nd Co-chairperson
Deacon Thomas Howell,
3rd Co-chairperson
Beverly Ferguson,
4th Co-chairperson

Drama Ministry
Jean Davis, Director

Family Bereavement Ministry
Emma C. Willis, Coordinator

Fitness Ministry
Brenda Lambert

Girl Scouts
Kim Winston, Scout Leader

Health-Wellness Ministry
Dr. Kenneth DeSandies, Director

Helping Hands for Care Providers Ministry
Joyce K. Peterson, Director

Historian
Deacon Alton Wallace

HIV/AIDS Ministry
Barbranda Walls, Director

Hospitality Committee
Rev. Marla Hawkins, Chairperson

Jail & Prison Ministry
Rev. Edward Jackson, Director

Junior Youth Ministry
Patrick and Lisa Xantus, Directors

Lawyers Committee Ministry
Attorney Ludwig Gaines, Director

Liturgical Dance Ministry
Donna U. Wright, Director

Married Couples Ministry
Deacon Charles Perkins, Director

Media Ministry
Walter Wright, Director

Men's Ministry
Deacon Earl Stafford, Director

Ministry of Deacons
Deacon James W. Johnson, Chairman

Ministry of Evangelism
Deacon Patricia Johnson, Director

Ministry of Missions
Rosette T. Graham, Director

Ministry of Trustees
Clinton L. Evans, Chairman

Music Ministry
Theron Johnson, Coordinator
Mark Prioleau, Coordinator

Newsletter Ministry
Cynthia Casey, Editor

Scholarship Committee Ministry
Deacon Bessie Johnson, Chairperson
Joyce Peterson, Vice Chairperson
Deacon Vernell Howell
Mary Payne
Angela Graham

See the Gospel Ministry
Deacon Karen DeSandies, Director

Senior Fellowship Ministry
Cynthia Gibbs, Director

Senior Youth Ministry
Darryl and Sharnell Howell, Directors

Single and Single Again Ministry
Cynthia Gibbs, Director

Sister Church Committee
Wendell Chesson
Rosette T. Graham
Jacqueline H. Lewis
Gilbretta Ashton-Jones
Deacon Grace Joseph

Sports/Athletics Ministry
Ronald Randolph, Director

Sunday School Ministry
Deacon Charles Monterio, Superintendent

Tape Visitation Ministry
Emma Waller, Director

Transportation Ministry
Men's Ministry

Tutorial Ministry
Rev. Faye S. Gunn, Director

Volunteer Ministry
Jacqueline H. Lewis, Coordinator

Wedding Coordination Ministry
Harriet W. Smith, Director

Women's Ministry
Janet Green, Director

Young Adult Ministry
Tom and Vernell Howell, Advisors

Appendix D

Bicentennial Committees

(* denotes Chairperson)

CORE COMMITTEE

Alton S. Wallace
Patricia M. Wallace*
Patricia M. Johnson
Thomas H. Howell

HISTORICAL RESEARCH COMMITTEE

Rebecca S. Briggs
Katherine E. Cain
Wanda E. Gill
Thomas H. Howell
Guinevere S. Jones
Rev. Beverly A. Moses
Joyce K. Peterson
Margarette Peterson
Rev. Samuel Nixon, Jr.
Carolyn C. Rowe
Gladys Q. Tancil (deceased)
Alton S. Wallace*

EVANGELISM COMMITTEE

Rev. Marla C. Hawkins*
Patricia M. Johnson
Patricia L. Wallace
Kathryn H. Weaver
Rita Womack

BICENTENNIAL BLOOD DRIVE (APRIL)

Dr. Kenneth DeSandies*

JOINT ASBC-FIRST BAPTIST CHURCH WORSHIP SERVICE (MAY)

Theron Johnson*

"TAKING IT TO THE STREETS" EVANGELISM—THE YOUTH (JUNE)

Christian Carnival/Sunday School in the Park/Concert

Gilbretta Ashton-Jones
Charles Monterio*
Charles Perkins
Donna Wright
Lisa Xantus
Patrick Xantus

HAITI MISSIONS PROJECT (JUNE)

Rosette Graham
Walter Kelly
Isaiah P. Morrison III
David Rollins
Earl Stafford, Sr.*

HISTORICAL TOURS (JULY)

Eleanor Ashley Carlton
Lavern Coleman
Curtis O. Howard
Jean Morris
Joyce E. Putman
Roberta H. Quander
Barbara Sanders*
Edward (Chuck)Thomas
Alton S. Wallace
Wendy Williams

"TAKING IT TO THE STREETS" EVANGELISM—THE COMMUNITY (AUG.)
"I AM MY BROTHER'S KEEPER" (Clothing/School Supplies/Health Services)

Kimonia Alfred
Stella Armstrong
Melodye Berry
Helen Caitlin
Juanita Davis
Keisha DeSandies
Rose Free*
Beverly Ferguson
Rosette Graham
Gladys Hamilton
Patricia Johnson
Patricia Jones
Carolyn Knowles
Jennifer Lewis
Marva Lofton
Sybil Marshall
June Monterio
Marentha Moore
Joyce Putman
Angela Richards
Amanda Stafford*
Katherine Washington
William Willis

"DOWN BY THE RIVERSIDE" WORSHIP SERVICE (SEPTEMBER)

Grace Albritton
Maggie Butler
Sandra Carrington*
Lavinia Cohen-Hopkins
Barbara Cox*
Florence Foster
Lula Gaskins
Mattie F. Hopkins
Regina Howard
Ardelia Hunter
Sandra Leftwich*
Ellen McCord
Jean Morris
Juanita Stanton
Margaret Wiggins
Emma Willis

BICENTENNIAL QUILT (OCTOBER)

Morine Blake
Olwin Burke
Phyllis Coleman
Shirley Downes
Barbara McDowell
Lynda Prioleau*
Gwen Rollins
Jacqueline Simms

HISTORICAL DISPLAYS (OCTOBER)

Grace Albritton
Beverly A. Ferguson
Amanda L. Stafford
Patricia M. Wallace*

"TAKING IT TO THE STREETS"—YOUNG ADULTS (OCTOBER)

Skating Party

Vernell Howell*
Stephanie Patterson*

PRAYER BREAKFAST—50-YEAR MEMBERS/100-YEAR FAMILIES (NOV.)

Nora Bell
Raynora Bell-Riley
Morine Blake
Georgianna Covington
Beverly Ferguson
Barbara Keller*
Shirley Nell
Augustine Green-Smith
Dannie Smith
James Taylor
Katherine Washington

MUSICAL CELEBRATION COMMITTEE (NOVEMBER)

Jean Davis
M. Joyce Garrett*
Louise Harrell
Theron E. Johnson
Steven Key
Mark Prioleau*
Virginia Raye
Alma O. Upshaw*
Donna Wright

HISTORICAL MARKER (NOVEMBER)

Thomas H. Howell*
Alton S. Wallace

BICENTENNIAL PRAYER SERVICE (NOVEMBER)

Reverend Faye S. Gunn*
Reverend Edward Y. Jackson*
Reverend John O. Peterson

BICENTENNIAL CELEBRATION DINNER (NOVEMBER)

Melodye W. Berry
Robert Bogan
Mattie Bynum
Barbara Cox
Irma P. Davis*
Gwendolyn Everrett*
Alfred Finch
Darryl Jasper
Calvin Kearney
Michael Maness
Youner McLeod
June Monterio*
Katrina Moss
Theodore Nell
Joyce Putnam
Margarette Peterson
Herbert Richardson
Maxine Sharpe
Anthony Zanfordino

ANNIVERSARY SUNDAY WORSHIP (NOVEMBER)

Mary Armstrong
Gloria Gibson
Tanya Green
Barbara Jackson
Patricia M. Johnson*

BICENTENNIAL TIME CAPSULE (NOVEMBER)

Evelyn Graham
Wilma Jenkins*
Catherine (Jan) Jones
Judith Turrentine

PUBLICITY COMMITTEE

Lorraine Carter
Helen Caitlin
Karen Croom
Rosette Graham
Carolyn Haymon
Jacqueline H. Lewis
Todd Myrick*
Patricia Traynor
Barbaranda Walls
Wendy Williams

BICENTENNIAL LOGO & BANNER DESIGNS

Andrea Sargent Futrell

PHOTOGRAPHY, VIDEOGRAPHY & PRODUCTION

Gary Carter
John Graham
Rosette Graham*
Henry Thompson

DISCIPLES SERVING AT ASBC FOR FIFTY (50) OR MORE YEARS

Name	No. of Years
Juanita Stanton	72
Jacqueline Henry-Green	67
Carlton Tyler	67
Welton Quander	67
William Willis	67
Ora E. Butler	66
Roberta H. Quander	65
Charles H. Quander	65
Florida Quander Ford	63
Eleanor Harris Major	62
Louis Jackson, Jr.	62
Bertha Mack	62
Mattie Funn Hopkins	61
Richard M. Wair, Sr.	61
Ardelia Hunter	58
Lucille P. Day	57
Arnita Briggs	57
Calvin Jackson	57
Robert Burke	55
Jean Morris	55
Ernest Carroll	55
Charlton Funn	55
Morine Blake	54
Emma C. Willis	53
Nellie Brooks Quander	51
Joseph Burless	50
Lovell Lee	50
Terris Mountain	50
Eva Thomas	50

FAMILIES THAT HAVE BEEN AT ASBC FOR 100 OR MORE YEARS

Oldest Traced Disciple	Current Disciple
Mary Francis Brooks	Leo Brooks
James Webster	Harry Burke
James Butler	Milton Turner, Jr.
Mary Diggs	Vernon Carroll
Lucy Lee	Lovell Lee
Eliza Pritchett Willis	William Willis
Mariah Quander	Roberta/Welton Quander
Susan Carter	Richard Wair
Lavinia Johnson/Ulysses Jackson	Sheila Jackson
Rev. William Bolo	Ora Butler
Lelia Thomas	Eva Thomas
Charles/Cassie Whitmore	Gale Ogden Brooks

Appendix E

Notes

(Note: Selected published references that were major sources of information are listed by chapter. Other source materials including church bulletins, funeral obituaries, deeds, census records and loose church notes taken at meetings are available in the Alfred Street Baptist Church archives.)

Chapter 1

1. *Alexandria Gazette,* 19 July 2001, p. 20.

2. Holmes, David, L. Pamphlet 1972–17, *The Early Days of the Church in Virginia and of Christ Church,* prepared by Christ Church, Alexandria, VA. 1972.

3. *The Historic First Baptist Church Celebrating Two Hundred Years of Christ-Centered Ministries,* First Baptist Church, Norfolk, VA, Tapestry Press, Ltd. Acton, MA, 2000, p. 4.

4. Brooks, Walker Henderson, D.D. *The Silver Bluff Church: A History of Negro Baptist Churches in America.* Washington, D.C.: Press of RIL Pendleton, electronic version from University of North Carolina at Chapel Hill Library, 1910.

5. *The Beginning of Negro Baptists,* published 1911 by National Baptist Publishing Board, p. 154.

6. Semple, Robert B. *A History of the Rise and Progress of the Baptists in Virginia,* publisher unknown, 1810, pp. 335–336.

7. Jackson, Luther P. *Journal of Negro History,* Vol. 16, Issue 2 (April 1931), p. 187.

8. Maffy-Kipp, Laura. *Introduction to the Church in the Southern Black Community,* e-copy from University of North Carolina at Chapel Hill Library, May 2001.

9. *To Witness the Past: African American Archeology in Alexandria, Virginia,* Alexandria

Archeology Museum, 1993.

10. Deines, Ann. *The Slave Population in 1810 Alexandria, Virginia: A Preservation Plan for Historic Resources,* M.S. thesis: George Washington University, 1994.

11. Blomberg, Belinda. *Free Black Adaptive Responses to the Antebellum Urban Environment: 1790–1850.* Ph.D. thesis, American University, Washington, D.C. 1988.

12. Kaye, Ruth L. *Alexandria, A Composite History (Streets and Alleys of Old Alexandria),* edited by Elizabeth Hambleton and Marian Van Landingham.

13. Cromwell, John. *The First Negro Churches in D.C.,* University of North Carolina—Chapel Hill, 1846.

Chapter 2

1. Fasy, Jennifer and Ione, Jacquelyn. *After Prayer and Praise: The Record Book of the Alexandria Baptist Church: 1803–1816,* M.S. thesis, Utah State University, Logan, Utah, 1992.

2. *Thine Is the Power: The Story of the First Baptist Church, Alexandria, Virginia, 1803–1953.* First Baptist Church's 150th Anniversary Program.

3. Ibid.

4. Ibid.

5. Personal interview with Mr. Wilson Gaines, former historian of First Baptist Church, Alexandria, Virginia, 16 April 2002.

6. Semple, pp. 335–336.

7. Gaines, Wilson. *History of First Baptist Church, Alexandria, Virginia,* Church Archives, 1988.

8. Ibid.

9. Thine is the Power

10. *A Study of Historical Sites in the Metropolitan Washington Region Related to Afro-Americans, Part III,* Afro-American Institute for Historic Preservation and Community Development, August 1979, p. 87.

11. *Hush Harbor: A Sacred Secret: Annual Heritage Celebration at Slave Memorial— Mount Vernon,* Black Women United for Action, 23 January 2001.

12. Graham, Rev. A.A. *A Century of Development of Negro Baptist in Virginia,* Religious Herald, November 15, 1923, Lott Carey Baptist Foreign Missionary Convention, p. 21.

13. Howard, James. *History of Robert's Chapel,* Vertical Files, Alexandria Black History Resource Center, 1943, p.188.

14. Fasy and Ione. *After Prayer and Praise.*

15. Ibid.

16. Ibid.

17. *Washington Post,* Metro Section, August 2, 2002, p. B-7.

18. Lynch, Anna. *Compendium of Early African Americans in Alexandria, Virginia, Vol. II.* Alexandria, Virginia: Alexandria Archeology, 1993–1995.

19. Thompson, Mary. *Slave Worship Practices at Mount Vernon, "In the Hands of a Good Providence": The Practice of Religion at George Washington's Mount Vernon.* Mount Vernon Ladies' Association, August 8, 2001.

20. An Inventory of the Slaves at Arlington Belonging to the Estate of G.W.P. Custis. Recorded at Alexandria County Court, National Park Service, McLean, Virginia, September 1855.

21. Thompson, V. Mary, Research Specialist, Mount Vernon Ladies, Association, e-mails to Alton S. Wallace of December, 7, 2001 and March 5, 2002 on slaves at Mount Vernon and Arlington House.

22. Minutes of the Ketocton Baptist Association, 1800–1820, available at University of Richmond Baptist Library.

23. Fasy and Ione. *After Prayer and Praise,* p. 106.

24. Census, District of Columbia, Alexandria County: National Archives, MRR 5 M33, pp. 186, 209.

25. Special Report of the Commission on Education on the Condition and Improvement of Public Schools in D.C., Submitted to U.S. Senate, June 1868, published by Government Printing Office, 1871, p. 291.

26. Lynch, *Compendium of Early African Americans.*

27. Minute Book II of First Baptist Church, Microfiche at Queen Street Library, Alexandria, Virginia.

28. Alexandria County Deed Book N2, P. 73–74, Recorder of Deeds, 520 King Street, Alexandria, Virginia.

28. Zaborner, John. *Slaves for Rent,* Ph.D. thesis, University of Maine, 1977.

29. George Washington Slave List, 1977. Abstracted and indexed by Dorothy S. Provine. Bowie, Maryland: Heritage Books.

30. District of Columbia, Free Negro Registers 1821–1861, abstracted and indexed by Dorothy S. Provine. Bowie, Maryland: Heritage Books.

31. Alexandria County Deed Book I.2, p. 339. Alexandria Courthouse, 540 King Street.

32. Program and History Sketch, 125th Anniversary, First Baptist Church, Alexandria, Virginia. April 22, 1928, p. 20.

33. Miller, T. and Dinnee,Tim. *Discovering the Decades: The 1840s.* Series 14—March 1999, Alexandria Archeology.

Chapter 3

1. Minute Book I of First Baptist Church (January 1, 1819), Microfiche at Queen Street Library, Alexandria, Virginia.

2. Lynch, *Compendium of Early African Americans.*

3. Minute Book II of First Baptist Church.

4. Pippenger, Wesley E. *Tombstone Inscriptions of Alexandria, Volume I* (Penny Hill), published by Family Line Publications, Westminster, MD, 1993.

5. *A Remarkable Journey* (Booklet), Alexandria Convention and Visitors' Association, Alexandria, Virginia, 2001, p. 6.

6. Nat Turner's Rebellion at Web site www.historybuff.com/library/ref. Accessed June 2002.

7. Blomberg, *Free Black Adaptive Responses,* p. 331.

8. *A Study of Historical Sites in the Metropolitan Washington Region Related to Afro-Americans, Part III.*

9. Daniel, Harrison W. "Virginia Baptists in the Antebellum Era," *Journal of Negro History,* Volume 56, Issue 1, January 1971.

10. Lynch, *Compendium of Early African Americans.*

11. Minute Book IV of First Baptist Church (1850), Microfiche at Queen Street Library, Alexandria, Virginia.

12. Ibid.

13. Religious Herald, September 16, 1850, available at University of Richmond Baptist Library, Richmond, Virginia.

14. Howard, *History of Robert's Chapel,* p. 188.

15. Cromwell, *The First Negro Churches in D.C.,* p. 77.

16. Ibid.

17. Matthews, Peter. Alexandria (D.C.) Directory 1834, Occupational Listing, City of Alexandria, Alexandria Archeology, circa 1988.

Chapter 4

1. Miller, Michael T. *Discovering the Decades: The 1850s.* Series 15. Alexandria Archeology. April 1999.

2. *Alexandria Gazette,* February 12, 1858.

3. First Baptist Church Program and History Sketch, April 1928, Alexandria, Virginia.

4. Telephone discussion with Mary Ann Browlee, historian for Maryland Baptist Association, Columbia, Maryland, March 2002.

5. Minutes of the Potomac Baptist Association, 1856–1860, available at University of Richmond Baptist Library.

6. McPhail, Laura. "History of Alfred Street Baptist Church." Unpublished manuscript in Alfred Street Baptist Church Archives, Alexandria, Virginia, 1971, p. 3.

7. Minutes of the Potomac Baptist Association.

8. Ibid.

9. Religious Herald, March 29, 1860, available at University of Richmond Baptist Library, Richmond, Virginia.

10. Jordan, Rev. Lewis G. *Negro Baptist History, USA 1750–1930. Vol. II.* Sunday School Publishing Board, Nashville, Tennessee.

11. History of 19th Street Baptist Church, 19th Street Baptist Church 150th Anniversary, Washington, D.C., 1982, p. 54.

12. Miller, Michael T. *Discovering the Decades: The 1860s.* Series 16. Alexandria Archeology. June 1999.

13. Dols, Jonathan. "Military Occupation and Cultural Perceptions in Alexandria, Virginia: 1861–65." U.S. Military Academy, May 1990.

14. History of Shiloh Baptist Church, Alexandria, Virginia. Electronic version at www.Shiloh-bc.org/history.

15. *Ebony Magazine Pictorial History of Black America,* The Southwestern Company, Nashville, Tennessee, Vol. 1, 1971, p. 277.

16. Pippenger, Wesley E. Alexandria Virginia Death Records 1863–1868. (The Gladwin Record). Westminster, Maryland: Family Line Publications, 1995.

17. Madden, T.O., Jr. *We Were Always Free.* New York: W. W. Norton and Co., 1992, p. 28.

18. Alfred Street Baptist Church Anniversary Program, 1988, Alexandria, Virginia.

19. Records of the Court of Claims, Congressional Judiciary Case Files 1884–1943: Box 1317, Row 9, Stack Area 16E3, Alfred Street Baptist Church Trustees, National Archives, Washington, D.C., p. 4.

20. Madden. Record Group, p. 4, Letters Received by Commission Branch of the Adjutant General's Office 1863–1870. Congressional Jurisdiction Case Files of Court of Claims. Microfilm Publication #1064, year 1864. Roll #108. National Archives and Records Administration Washington, D.C. Row 9, Compartment 156–164.

21. McPhail, "History of Alfred Street Baptist Church," p. 3.

22. Madden letters.

23. Minutes of the Potomac Baptist Association, 1860, available at University of Richmond Baptist Library.

24. Cromwell, *The First Negro Churches in D.C.*

25. History of the Senior Choir, Choir Anniversary Concert, May 22, 1988. Alfred Street Baptist Church.

26. Jordan, *Negro Baptist History, USA,* p. 63.

27. Records of the Court of Claims.

28. *Black Baltimore 1870–1920* (Harvey Johnson). Maryland State Archives (www.Mdarchvives.state.md.us.msa), accessed June 2002.

29. 1860 U.S. Census, Alexandria, Virginia. National Archives, Washington, D.C. p. 197.

30. Johnson, R. L. *Integration of Schools in Alexandria,* M.S. thesis, Howard University, 1970.

31. *A Remarkable Journey,* p. 12.

32. "Historical Figures and Sites in Alexandria." Alexandria African American Heritage Park Booklet, Alexandria Black History Resource Center.

33. Special Report of the Commission on Education, p. 291.

34. *Washington Post,* Metro Section, July 6, 2002.

35. Jordan, *Negro Baptist History USA,* pp. 49–51.

Chapter 5

1. *Ebony Magazine Pictorial History of Black America, Vol. 2, The Exodus of 1879.* Nashville, Tennessee: The Southwestern Company, 1971, p. 55.

2. African American Pamphlets: Time Line of African American History, 1881–1900; Web site at http://memory.loc.gov/ammem/aap/timelin2.html, accessed on December 12, 2002.

3. Pippenger, *Tombstone Inscriptions of Alexandria.*

4. Claim filed by Alfred Street Church (Civil War), Records of the U.S. Court of Claims, Congressional Jurisdiction Case Files 1884–1943, Box #1317, HM 1441, Stack Area 16E, Row 9, Alfred Street Trustees, NARA, Washington, D.C.

5. Minutes of the Willing Workers Club, 1881–1884, Archives of Alfred Street Baptist Church, Alexandria, Virginia.

6. Minutes of the Virginia Baptist State Convention—1870s, available at University of Richmond Baptist Library, Richmond, Virginia.

7. Personal interview with Dr. Scott E. Casper, Department of History, University of Nevada, interview on January 8, 2003, Alexandria, Virginia.

8. Pippenger, Wesley. *Tombstone Inscriptions, Volume IV* (Bethel Cemetery), published by Family Line Publications, Westminster, Maryland, 1993.

9. McPhail, "History of Alfred Street Baptist Church," p. 23.

10. Anniversary Program—1988, Alfred Street Baptist Church, Alexandria, Virginia.

11. McKinney, Richard I. *Keeping the Faith: A History of the First Baptist Church of Charlottesville, 1863–1980.* Charlottesville, Virginia, First Baptist Church, 1981.

12. Trussell, Jacqueline. *The Convention Movement of the Black Baptist Church,* at www.blackandchristian.com/articles/academy/trussell1.shtml, accessed September 2002.

13. McKinney, *Keeping the Faith.*

14. History of the Senior Choir, 150th Anniversary Bulletin—1956. Alfred Street Baptist Church.

15. *A Study of Historical Sites in the Metropolitan Washington Region Related to Afro-Americans, Part III.*

16. Wallace, Alton S. *The Saints of Alfred Street*, Alfred Street Baptist Church, 1996.

Chapter 6

1. United States of America—A Chronology, Plessy vs. Ferguson: 1892. History Department of Northpart University (www.Campus.Northpart.edu/history), accessed May 2003.

2. *Ebony Magazine Pictorial History of Black America*, Vol. 2, pp. 93–96.

3. Ibid.

4. *Songs of Zion.* Nashville, Tennessee: Abingdon Press, 1981, p. 172.

5. Book of Minutes of Church Meetings (1891–1912), Alfred Street Baptist Church, Alexandria, Virginia.

6. *The Quanders United: Tricentennial Celebration, 1684–1984* (Souvenir Journal), June 24, 1984, Washington, D.C.

7. Personal interview with Mrs. Gladys Quander-Tancil, Fairfax County, Virginia. March 2001.

8. Records of the U.S. Court of Claims, Congressional Jurisdiction Case Files 1884–1943, Box #1317, HM 1441, Stack Area 16E, Row 9, Alfred Street Baptist Church Trustees, NARA, Washington, D.C.

9. Book of Minutes of Church Meeting (1898–1912), Alfred Street Baptist Church.

10. Ibid.

11. *The Black Bee* Newspaper, Revival by Rev. A. Truatt, Washington, D.C., 1913.

12. Minutes of Church Meeting (1914), Alfred Street Baptist Church.

13. McPhail, "History of Alfred Street Baptist Church."

14. Ibid.

15. *St. Mary's: 200 Years for Christ,* by St. Mary's Catholic Church, Alexandria, Virginia, printed by Thomson-Shore, Inc., 1995.

16. Personal interview with Ms. Roberta Quander, Fairfax County, Virginia, November 2002.

17. Loan Book of the Lending Library, 1920–1935, archives of Alfred Street Baptist Church.

Chapter 7

1. "History of the United States of America." *Encyclopedia Britannica*, Vol. 29, 15th Edition, 1989, p. 254.

2. Personal interview with Mr. Welton Quander, Fairfax County, Virginia. November 2002.

3. Personal interview with Ms. Roberta Quander.

4. Personal interview with Mrs. Hattie Gaskins, Alexandria, Virginia, May 2002.

5. Personal interview with Mr. Ellis Eubanks, Alexandria Virginia, 22 June 2002.

6. Personal interview with Mrs. Gladys Quander-Tancil, Fairfax County, Virginia, 10 July 2002.

7. Book of Minutes of Church Meetings (1925–1935), Alfred Street Baptist Church, Alexandria, Virginia.

8. *Ebony Magazine Pictorial History*, Vol. 2, p. 197.

9. *Songs of Zion*, p. 172.

10. Personal interview with Ms. Roberta Quander.

11. Personal interview with Mr. Welton Quander.

12. Telephone interview with Mr. Carlton Tyler, Washington, D.C., January 2003.

13. Book of Minutes of Church Meetings (1925–1935), Alfred Street Baptist Church.

14. Minutes of Church Meeting, Alfred Street Baptist Church, 1934, p. 103.

15. Telephone interview with Mr. Carlton Tyler.

16. A Remarkable Journey.

17. Personal interview with Mr. Welton Quander.

18. "History of the United States of America," *Encyclopedia Britannica*, p. 258.

19. *Ebony Magazine Pictorial History*, Vol. 2, p. 245.

20. Ibid.

21. Ibid., p. 250

22. *A Study of Historical Sites in the Metropolitan Washington Region Related to Afro-Americans, Part III.*

Chapter 8

1. "History of the United States of America," *Encyclopedia Britannica,* Vol. 29, p. 257.

2. 1950 Census of Population: Characteristics of the Population, Vol. II, Part 46, Virginia (U.S. Bureau of the Census, Washington, D.C.) GPO, 1952, pp. 46–130.

3. Thine is the Power.

4. Personal interview with Wilson Gaines.

5. 150th Anniversary of Alfred Street Baptist Church, Marie T. Boyd, Church Historian. Alexandria, Virginia, October 31, 1956.

6. *Songs of Zion,* p. 172.

7. *Washington Post,* Metro Section, August 2002, p. C-3.

8. Senate Joint Resolution No. 3, Minutes of the General Assembly of Virginia, February 1, 1956, pp. 462–64.

9. *Washington Post,* October 12, 1960, p. B-8.

10. *Washington Post,* Metro Section, May 12, 2001.

11. Personal interview with Mrs. Juanita Quander-Stanton, July 2002, Alexandria, Virginia.

12. Church Minutes of Alfred Street Baptist Church, April 1964.

13. Report of Pulpit Committee by Theodore Lee, Clerk of Alfred Street Baptist Church, June 9, 1964.

14. Installation Services of John O. Peterson, January 24–February 7, 1965, Alfred Street Baptist Church, Alexandria, Virginia.

15. "History of the United States of America," *Encyclopedia Britannica,* Vol. 29, p. 362.

16. Minutes of Business Meeting, June 7, 1965, Alfred Street Baptist Church, Alexandria.

17. *Alexandria Gazette,* April 5, 1968.

18. *Alexandria Gazette,* April 8, 1968.

19. *Alexandria Gazette,* April 9, 1968.

20. Northern Virginia Street Map, published by ADC, Alexandria, Virginia, 1988, pp. 9–10.

21. *Washington Post,* Metro Section, August 11, 2002.

Chapter 9

1. Bulletin for Installation Service, January 1971, Alfred Street Baptist Church.

2. Program of Consecration of Deaconesses, March 21, 1971, Alfred Street Baptist Church.

3. 1972 Church Directory, Alfred Street Baptist Church, Alexandria Virginia.

4. Church Minutes of Sale of Church Properties, 1974.

5. Minutes of the 102nd Session of the Northern Virginia Baptist Association, August 1979, Gainesville, Virginia.

6. Alexandria Deed Book 963, City of Alexandria, Register of Deeds, September 14, 1979, p. 385.

7. Notes from Joyce K. Peterson, First Lady of Alfred Street Baptist Church, 1979.

8. Ground-Breaking Ceremony Souvenir Journal, September 22, 1979, Alfred Street Baptist Church.

9. Vertical File on Alfred Street Baptist Church (Court Testimonies—1980), Alexandria Black History Resource Center.

10. Grand March-In Souvenir Program, Alfred Street Baptist Church, February 1981.

11. *The Baptist Herald,* April 1981. Published by the Baptist General Convention of Virginia. Virginia Union University, Richmond, Virginia, p. 5.

12. Personal interview with Mr. Welton Quander.

13. 1982 Church Directory, Alfred Street Baptist Church, Alexandria, Virginia.

14. Voices of Triumph 4th Anniversary Program, 1988, Alfred Street Baptist Church.

15. Membership Directory, June 10, 1984, Alfred Street Baptist Church.

16. Alfred Street Baptist Church Newsletter, Fall 1986, Volume 3, No. 3 (Pastor's Anniversary).

17. 25th Anniversary Program of Rev. John O. Peterson, 1989. Alfred Street Baptist Church.

18. John Strange's Funeral Obituary, Alfred Street Baptist Church, August 1981 (Church files).

Chapter 10

1. Certificates: "License to Preach," issued by Alfred Street Baptist Church (archives).

2. The Constitution and By-Laws of the Alfred Street Baptist Church, adopted November 22, 1994, Alexandria, Virginia.

3. Grand March-In Program Bulletin, Alfred Street Baptist Church, March 1994.

4. Woman's Day 1994—Souvenir Journal, Alfred Street Baptist Church, October 1994.

5. Alfred Street Baptist Church Newsletter, Vol. 13, Issue 1, Winter 2000, p. 4.

6. Wallace, Patricia L. "Rev. John O. Peterson, Sr.: 33 Years of Accomplishments to Alfred Street Baptist Church." Compiled for Anniversary Celebration, October 1997.

7. Ibid.

8. Minutes of Church Meeting (Mortgage Elimination), March 1997, Alfred Street Baptist Church, Alexandria, Virginia.

9. Minutes of Church Meeting (Adkins' Memorial), 1996, Alfred Street Baptist Church, Alexandria, Virginia.

10. Dedication Litany, Special Dedication Program, December 1997, Alfred Street

Baptist Church.

11. Alfred Street Baptist Church Membership Directory, 1994.

12. Alfred Street Baptist Church Membership Directory, 1997.

13. Alfred Street Baptist Church Newsletter, Vol. 10, Issue 3, Fall 1999, p. 3.

14. Wallace, Alton S. *History of the Deacon Board*. Alfred Street Baptist Church, Fall 1995.

15. Alfred Street Baptist Church Newsletter, Vol. 13, Issue 1, Winter 2000.

16. Alfred Street Baptist Church Newsletter, Vol. 12, Issue 3, Fall 2000, pp. 1, 9.

17. Alfred Street Baptist Church Newsletter, Vol. 13, Issue 2, Summer 2001.

18. Burning the Mortgage, Sunday Bulletin, 198th Church Anniversary, November 11, 2001.

19. Alfred Street Baptist Church Newsletter, Vol. 14, Issue 3, 3rd Quarter 2001, p. 1.

20. Alfred Street Baptist Church Newsletter, Vol. 12, No. 1, Spring 1998, p. 2.

21. Alfred Street Baptist Church Newsletter, Vol. 14, Issue 2, 2nd Quarter 2001, p. 4.

22. *Washington Post*, p. C-11, December 1, 2002.

23. *Washington Post*, "Bicentennial Celebration: Church of Presidents and the Oppressed," March 7, 2003, p. D-3.

24. Wallace, Patricia L. Report of Bicentennial Core Committee, Mid-Year Church Meeting. Alfred Street Baptist Church, June 2002.

25. Minutes of Church Meeting, Alfred Street Baptist Church, Alexandria, Virginia, March 1997.

26. Alfred Street Baptist Church Newsletter, Vol. 15, Issue 3, 2nd Quarter 2002, p. 12 (Bicentennial).

27. Minutes of Church Meeting, 1999, Alfred Street Baptist Church, Alexandria, Virginia.

Index